TEST ITEM FILE • ROSS L. FINK
Bradley University, Foster College of Business Administration

Operations Management

SIXTH EDITION

Principles of Operations Management

FOURTH EDITION

JAY HEIZER

BARRY RENDER

Prentice Hall

Upper Saddle River, New Jersey 07458

www.prenhall.com/heizer

Acquisitions Editor: *Tom Tucker*
Associate editor: *Jennifer Surich*
Project editor: *Theresa Festa*
Manufacturer: *Victor Graphics, Inc.*

Printed in the United States of America

10 9 8 7 6 5 4

ISBN 0-13-019596-0

Prentice-Hall International (UK) Limited,London
Prentice-Hall of Australia Pty. Limited, Sydney
Prentice-Hall Canada Inc., Toronto
Prentice-Hall Hispanoamericana, S.A., Mexico
Prentice-Hall of India Private Limited, New Delhi
Prentice-Hall of Japan, Inc., Tokyo
Pearson Education Asia Pte. Ltd., Singapore
Editora Prentice-Hall do Brasil, Ltda., Rio de Janeiro

Table of Contents

CHAPTER 1: OPERATIONS AND PRODUCTIVITY

TRUE/FALSE

1. Whirlpool's increases in productivity have enabled the firm to control prices and benefit its stockholders at the same time.
    True (Whirlpool, moderate)

2. Some types of technology are drivers for globalization of economic growth and world trade.
    True (Introduction, moderate)

3. Operations management refers to the creation of goods whereas production refers to the creation of services.
    False (What is operations management? moderate)

4. All organizations, including service organizations such as banks and educational institutions, have a production function.
    True (What is operations management? moderate)

5. Production is the creation of goods and services.
    True (What is operations management? easy)

6. W. Edwards Deming is known as the Father of Scientific Management.
    False (The heritage of operations management, easy)

7. Lillian Gilbreth is credited for the early popularization of interchangeable parts.
    False (The heritage of operations management, easy)

8. The person most responsible for initiating use of interchangeable parts in manufacturing was Whitney Houston.
    False (The heritage of operations management, easy)

9. The origins of the scientific management movement are generally credited to James Taylor.
    False (The heritage of operations management, easy)

10. Operations Management is the set of activities that create goods and services by transforming inputs into outputs.
    True (What is operations management? easy)

11. Operations Management only applies to the creation of tangible goods.
    False (What is operations management? easy)

12. An example of a "hidden" production function is money transfers at banks.
    True (What is operations management? moderate)

13. Operations Management has benefited from advances in other fields of study.
True (The heritage of operations management, easy)

14. In order to have a career in operations management, one must have a degree in statistics or quantitative methods.
False (The heritage of operations management, easy)

15. The operations manager performs the management activities of planning, organizing, staffing, leading, and controlling of the OM function.
True (What operations managers do, easy)

16. "Should we make or buy this item?" is within the Human Resources and Job Design critical decision area.
False (What operations managers do, easy)

17. Marketing is one of the three functions critical to an organization's survival.
True (Organizing to produce goods and services, easy)

18. Students wanting to pursue a career in operations management will find multi-disciplinary knowledge beneficial.
True (Where are the OM jobs? easy)

19. The quality of a product is more difficult to measure than that of a service.
False (Operations in the service sector, moderate)

20. Customer interaction is often high during the manufacturing process.
False (Operations in the service sector, moderate)

21. Productivity is the total value of all inputs to the transformation process divided by the total value of the outputs produced.
False (The productivity challenge, easy)

22. Measuring the impact of a capital acquisition on productivity is an example of multi-factor productivity.
False (The productivity challenge, moderate)

23. Productivity is more difficult to improve in the service sector for several reasons, including the fact that services are frequently individually processed.
True (Operations in the service sector, moderate)

24. Service activities **cannot** take place within good producing operations.
False (Operations in the service sector, moderate)

25. Services now constitute the largest economic sector in advanced societies.
True (Operations in the service sector, moderate)

26. A knowledge society is one that has migrated from work based on knowledge to one based on manual work.
False (The productivity challenge, easy)

MULTIPLE CHOICE

27. _____ has been the main driver to the globalization of business.
    a. The higher standards of living in the U.S. and Europe
    b. Technology
    c. The NAFTA trade agreement
    d. The increasing ethnic diversity within countries
    b (Introduction, easy)

28. Operations management is applicable
    a. mostly to the service sector
    b. mostly to the manufacturing sector
    c. to manufacturing and service sectors
    d. to services exclusively
    e. to the manufacturing sector exclusively
    c (What is operations management? moderate)

29. The person most responsible for popularizing interchangeable parts in manufacturing was
    a. Eli Whitney
    b. Frederick Winslow Taylor
    c. Henry Ford
    d. Whitney Houston
    e. Lillian Gilbreth
    a (The heritage of operations management, moderate)

30. The "Father of Scientific Management" is
    a. Lillian Gilbreth
    b. Frederick W. Taylor
    c. W. Edwards Deming
    d. Frank Gilbreth
    e. just a figure of speech, not a reference to a person
    b (The heritage of operations management, easy)

31. Walter Shewhart is listed among the important people of operations management because of his contributions to
    a. assembly line production
    b. measuring the productivity in the service sector
    c. statistical quality control
    d. Just-in-Time inventory methods
    e. all of the above
    c (The heritage of operations management, moderate)

32. Henry Ford is noted for his contributions to
    a. quality control
    b. assembly line operations
    c. scientific management
    d. time and motion studies
    e. standardization of parts
    b (The heritage of operations management, easy)

33. Taylor and Deming would have both agreed that
    a. Whirlpool's global strategy is a good one
    b. management must do more to improve the work environment and its processes so that quality can be improved
    c. Eli Whitney was an important contributor to statistical theory
    d. productivity is more important than quality
    e. the era of Operations Management will be succeeded by the era of scientific management
    b (The heritage of operations management, moderate)

34. Who among the following is associated with contributions to quality control in operations management?
    a. W. Edwards Deming
    b. Charles Babbage
    c. Alfred P. Sloan, Jr.
    d. Frank Gilbreth
    e. Henri Fayol
    a (The heritage of operations management, moderate)

35. Which of the following statements is **true**?
    a. The person most responsible for initiating use of interchangeable parts in manufacturing was Eli Whitney .
    b. The origins of management by exception are generally credited to Frederick W. Taylor.
    c. The person most responsible for initiating use of interchangeable parts in manufacturing was David Whitwam.
    d. The origins of the scientific management movement are generally credited to James Taylor.
    e. tTe person most responsible for initiating use of interchangeable parts in manufacturing was Henry Ford.
    a (The heritage of operations management, moderate)

36. The field of operations management is shaped by advances in which of the following fields?
    a. industrial engineering and management science
    b. biology and anatomy
    c. information sciences
    d. chemistry and physics
    e. all of the above
    e (The heritage of operations management, moderate)

37. The responsibilities of the operations manager include
    a. planning, organizing, staffing, procuring, and reviewing
    b. planning, organizing, staffing, leading, and controlling
    c. forecasting, designing, planning, organizing, and controlling
    d. forecasting, designing, operating, procuring, and reviewing
    e. designing and operating
    b (What do Operations Managers do? easy)

38. The five elements in the management process are
    a. plan, direct, update, lead, and supervise
    b. accounting/finance, marketing, operations, and management
    c. plan, lead, organize, manage, and control
    d. organize, plan, control, staff, and manage
    e. plan, organize, staff, lead, and control
    c (What do Operations Managers do? easy)

39. Which of the following is **not** an element of the management process?
    a. staffing
    b. planning
    c. controlling
    d. leading
    e. pricing
    e (What do Operations Managers do? easy)

40. All of the following decisions fall within the scope of operations management **except** for
    a. financial analysis
    b. design of products and processes
    c. location of facilities
    d. quality management
    e. facility maintenance
    a (What do Operations Managers do? easy)

41. An operations manager is **not** likely to be involved in
    a. the identification of customers' wants and needs
    b. the design of products and services to satisfy customers' wants and needs
    c. the quality of products and services to satisfy customers' wants and needs
    d. work scheduling to meet the due dates promised to customers
    e. forecasting sales
    a (What do Operations Managers do? easy)

42. Which of the following are the primary functions of **all** organizations?
    a. operations, marketing, and human resources
    b. marketing, human resources, and finance/accounting
    c. marketing, quality control, and operations
    d. marketing, operations, and finance/accounting
    e. research and development, finance/accounting, and purchasing
    d (Organizing to produce goods and services, moderate)

43. Which of the following would **not** be an operations function in a fast-food restaurant?
   a. making hamburgers and fries
   b. maintaining equipment
   c. designing the layout of the facility
   d. advertising and promotion
   e. purchasing ingredients
   d (Organizing to produce goods and services, moderate)

44. The three major functions of business organizations
   a. overlap
   b. are mutually exclusive
   c. exist independently of each other
   d. function independently of each other
   e. do not interface with each other
   a (Organizing to produce goods and services, moderate)

45. Budgeting, paying the bills, and collection of funds are activities associated with the
   a. management function
   b. control function
   c. finance/accounting function
   d. production/operations function
   e. transformation function
   c (Organizing to produce goods and services, moderate)

46. The marketing function's main concern is with
   a. producing goods or providing services
   b. generating the demand for the organization's products or services
   c. procuring materials, supplies, and equipment
   d. building and maintaining a positive image
   e. securing monetary resources
   b (Organizing to produce goods and services, moderate)

47. Among the new trends in operations management are
   a. global focus and just-in-time performance
   b. supply chain partnering and mass customization
   c. empowered employees and rapid product development
   d. all of the above are new trends in operations management
   e. none of the above
   d (Exciting new trends in Operations Management, moderate)

48. Which of the following is **not** a current trend in operations management?
   a. just-in-time performance
   b. global focus
   c. supply chain partnering
   d. mass customization
   e. all of the above are current trends
   (Exciting new trends in Operations Management, moderate)

49. Typical differences between goods and services do **not** include
    a. cost per unit
    b. uniformity of output
    c. timing of production and consumption
    d. customer interaction
    e. knowledge content
    a (Operations in the service sector, moderate)

50. Which is **not** true regarding differences between goods and services?
    a. Services are generally produced and consumed simultaneously, tangible goods are not.
    b. Services tend to be more knowledge-based than products.
    c. Products tend to have a more inconsistent product definition than services.
    d. Services tend to have higher customer interaction than goods.
    e. none of the above are true.
    c (Operations in the service sector, moderate)

51. Which of the following services is **not** unique, i.e., customized to a particular individual's needs?
    a. hairdressing
    b. elementary education
    c. legal services
    d. dental care
    e. computer consulting
    b (Operations in the service sector, moderate)

52. Which of the following is **not** a typical service attribute?
    a. intangible product
    b. often easy to automate
    c. customer interaction is high
    d. simultaneous production and consumption
    e. difficult to resell
    b (Operations in the service sector, moderate)

53. Which of the following is **not** a typical attribute of goods?
    a. output can be inventoried
    b. often easy to automate
    c. high customer interaction
    d. output can be resold
    e. production and consumption are separate
    c (Operations in the service sector, moderate)

54. Gibson Valves produces cast bronze valves on an assembly line. If 1600 valves are produced in an 8-hour shift, the productivity of the line is
    a. 1600 valves/hr
    b. 200 valves/hr
    c. 80 valves/hr
    d. 40 valves/hr
    e. 2 valves/hr
    b (The productivity challenge, easy)

55. Gibson Valves produces cast bronze valves on an assembly line, currently producing 1600 valves each 8-hour shift. If the productivity is increased by 10%, it would then be
   a. 1760 valves/hr
   b. 880 valves/hr
   c. 220 valves/hr
   d. 200 valves/hr
   e. 180 valves/hr
   c (The productivity challenge, moderate)

56. Gibson Valves produces cast bronze valves on an assembly line, currently producing 1600 valves each 8-hour shift. If the production is increased to 2400 valves each 8-hour shift, the productivity will increase by
   a. 50%
   b. 40%
   c. 25%
   d. 20%
   e. 10%
   a (The productivity challenge, moderate)

57. The Dulac Box plant produces 500 cypress packing boxes in two 10-hour shifts. What is the productivity of the plant?
   a. 5000 boxes/hr
   b. 50 boxes/hr
   c. 25 boxes/hr
   d. none of the above
   e. not enough data to determine
   c (The productivity challenge, moderate)

58. The Dulac Box plant produces 500 cypress packing boxes in two 10-hour shifts. The use of new technology has enabled them to increase productivity by 30%. Productivity is now approximately
   a. 32.5 boxes/hr
   b. 60 boxes/hr
   c. 65 boxes/hr
   d. 150 boxes/hr
   e. 300 boxes/hr
   a (The productivity challenge, moderate)

59. The Dulac Box plant produces 500 cypress packing boxes in two 10-hour shifts. Due to higher demand, they have decided to operate three 8-hour shifts instead. They are now able to produce 600 boxes per day. What has happened to production?
   a. it has increased by 50 sets/shift
   b. it has increased by 37.5 sets/hr
   c. it has increased by 20%
   d. it has decreased by 8.3%
   e. it has decreased by 9.1%
   c (The productivity challenge, moderate)

60. Productivity measurement is complicated by
    a. the competition's output
    b. the fact that precise units of measure are often unavailable
    c. stable quality
    d. the workforce size
    e. the type of equipment used
    b (The productivity challenge, moderate)

61. Current trends in operations management include all of the following **except**
    a. Just-in-Time performance
    b. rapid product development
    c. mass customization
    d. empowered employees
    e. all of the above are current trends
    e (Exciting new trends in Operations Management, moderate)

62. Which of the following is a current trend in manufacturing operations?
    a. supply chain partnering
    b. intermittent production
    c. scientific management
    d. ecologically sound manufacturing
    e. all of the above are current trends
    a (Exciting new trends in Operations Management, moderate

63. The service industry makes up approximately what percentage of all jobs in the United States?
    a. 20%
    b. 40%
    c. 66%
    d. 74%
    e. 90%
    d (Operations in the service sector, moderate)

64. The total of all outputs produced by the transformation process divided by the total of the inputs is
    a. utilization
    b. greater in manufacturing than in services
    c. defined only for manufacturing firms
    d. multi-factor productivity
    e. none of the above
    d (The productivity challenge, moderate)

65. Productivity can be improved by
    a. increasing inputs while holding outputs steady
    b. decreasing outputs while holding inputs steady
    c. increasing inputs and outputs in the same proportion
    d. decreasing inputs while holding outputs steady
    d (The productivity challenge, moderate)

66. Which of the following inputs has the greatest potential to increase productivity?
    a. labor
    b. management
    c. capital
    d. globalization
    e. none of the above
    b (The productivity challenge, moderate)

67. The largest contributor to productivity increases is _____, estimated to be responsible for
    _____ of the annual increase.
    a. Mr. Deming; one-half
    b. labor; two-thirds
    c. capital; 90%
    d. technology; over one-half
    e. management; one-half
    c (The productivity challenge, moderate)

68. Three commonly used productivity variables are
    a. quality, external elements, and precise units of measure
    b. technology, raw materials, and labor
    c. education, diet, and social overhead
    d. labor, capital, and management
    e. quality, efficiency, and low cost
    d (The productivity challenge, moderate)

69. The service sector has lower productivity improvement than the manufacturing sector because
    a. the service sector uses less skilled labor than manufacturing
    b. the quality of output is lower in services than manufacturing
    c. service sector productivity is hard to measure
    d. services usually are labor intensive
    e. none of the above
    d (The productivity challenge, moderate)

70. Productivity tends to be more difficult to improve in the service sector because the work is
    a. typically labor intensive
    b. frequently individually processed
    c. often an intellectual task performed by professionals
    d. often difficult to automate
    e. all of the above
    e (The productivity challenge, moderate)

71. Which of the following is **not** true when explaining why productivity tends to be lower in the
    service sector than in the manufacturing sector?
    a. Service operations are typically capital intensive.
    b. Services are typically labor intensive.
    c. Services are typically individually processed.
    d. Services are often an intellectual task performed by professionals.
    e. Services are difficult to automate.
    a (The productivity challenge, moderate)

FILL-IN-THE-BLANK

72. _____ is the set of activities that transforms inputs into goods and services.
    Operations management (What is Operations Management, easy)

73. _____ is the ability of the organization to be flexible enough to cater to the individual whims of consumers.
    Mass customization (Exciting new trends in Operations Management? moderate)

74. _____ is a long-term relationship that helps organizations deal with shorter product life cycles.
    Supply chain partnering (Exciting new trends in Operations Management, moderate)

75. _____ is the operations management trend that moves more decision making to the individual worker.
    Empowered employees (Exciting new trends in Operations Management, moderate)

76. _____ is the total of all outputs produced by the transformation process divided by the total of the inputs.
    Multi-factor productivity (The productivity challenge, easy)

77. Productivity is the ratio of _____ to _____. Using this relationship, productivity can be improved by _____ or _____.
    inputs, outputs; reducing inputs while holding outputs constant; increasing outputs while holding inputs constant. (The productivity challenge, moderate)

SHORT ANSWER

78. "A modern university can learn much about productivity gains from the Whirlpool example." Discuss, with attention to what the Whirlpool lessons are, and how they might apply to a modern university.
    Whirlpool has penetrated new markets, has reengineered organization and communication to speed processes. Universities, faced with slow growth in traditional markets, may use the Internet to penetrate new markets. (Whirlpool, moderate)

79. "A modern hospital can learn much about globalization from the Whirlpool example." Discuss, with attention to what the Whirlpool lessons are, and how they might apply to a modern hospital.
    Whirlpool connected suppliers, customers, and manufacturers. Hospitals can connect suppliers electronically; can obtain diagnoses and test results from distant sites. (Whirlpool, difficult)

80. Who are some of the people who have contributed to the philosophies and methods of operations management? Briefly describe a major contribution of each.
Pick from Babbage (division of labor), Deming (14 points; quality), Taylor (scientific management), Shewhart (statistical sampling, quality), Ford (assembly line), Gantt (best processes, charts), Gilbreth (best processes), Whitney (interchangeable parts), Erlang (queuing theory), Harris (EOQ), and Dantzig (linear programming). (The heritage of operations management, moderate)

81. List four disciplines whose contributions benefit Operations Management.
Industrial engineering, management science, physical sciences, and information sciences. (The heritage of operations management, moderate)

82. Operations managers should be well versed in what disciplines in order to make good decisions?
Management science, information sciences, and often one of the biological or physical sciences. (The heritage of operations management, moderate)

83. According to the textbook, why should you study OM?
To study how people organize themselves for productive enterprise; to know how goods and services are produced; to understand what operations managers do, and because OM is a costly part of an organization. (Why study Operations Management? moderate)

84. The Fisher Company example illustrates that Operations Management is an important lever for contribution and profit. Is it possible that marketing, not operations, could provide the greatest gain in contribution? Discuss.
The greatest gain can come from any of the three areas. But production cost exerts greater leverage than other options. Therefore, it is easier for cost reductions to have greater leverage than other options. (The heritage of operations management, moderate)

85. Name the ten decision areas for operations managers.
Quality management, service and product design, process and capacity design, location, layout design, human resources and job design, supply chain management, inventory, scheduling, and maintenance. (What Operations Manager do, moderate)

86. List the five elements of the management process.
Planning, organizing, staffing, leading, and controlling. (What Operations Manager do, moderate)

87. List the three primary functions of a business.
Marketing, production/operations, and finance/accounting. (Organizing to produce goods and services, easy)

88. Mass customization and rapid product development were identified as current trends in modern manufacturing operations. To what extent are these two trends complementary? Discuss possible links between these trends; provide brief examples.
Mass customization is the flexibility to produce in small batches, perhaps to individual measure, without sacrificing the low cost of assembly line work. Rapid development is a source of competitive advantage. Both rely on agility within the organization. (Exciting new trends in Operations Management, moderate)

89. How do services differ from goods? List five ways.

    Pick from the following: a service is usually tangible; it is often produced and consumed simultaneously; often unique; it involves high customer interaction; product definition is inconsistent; often knowledge-based, and frequently dispersed. (Operations in the service sector, moderate)

90. What are the measurement problems that occur when attempting to measure productivity?

    Quality may change, while the quantity of inputs and outputs remains the same; external elements may cause an increase or decrease in productivity for which the system may not be directly responsible; and precise units of measurement may be lacking. (The productivity challenge, moderate)

91. List the three productivity variables used in the text. What other variables are possible? Discuss, provide an example.

    The three common variables are labor, capital, and management. The text also uses "material" and "miscellaneous" in its examples. Any resource could be named as a productivity variable. (The productivity challenge, moderate)

92. List four keys to improved labor productivity.

    Basic education appropriate for an effective labor force, diet of the labor force, social overhead that makes labor available, and maintaining and expanding the skills of the labor force. (The productivity challenge, moderate)

93. State five reasons for the claim that service sector productivity is difficult to improve.

    Typically labor intensive, frequently individually processed, often an intellectual task performed by professionals, often difficult to mechanize and automate, and often difficult to evaluate for quality. (The productivity challenge, moderate)

94. Describe some of the actions taken by Taco Bell to increase productivity so that restaurants can serve "twice the volume with half the labor."

    Designed meals that were easy to prepare; actual cooking and food preparation done elsewhere; automation to save preparation time; reduced floor space; manager training to increase span of control. (The productivity challenge, difficult)

95. If the U.S. is a "knowledge society," as it has been described, how does this affect productivity measurement in the U.S., and affect the comparison of productivities between the U.S. and other countries?

    Productivity is harder to measure the more intellectual the task; a knowledge society implies that work is more intellectual, therefore harder to measure. As the U.S. is more a knowledge society than some other countries, its productivity would be harder to measure; it would be difficult to obtain comparable productivity calculations. (The productivity challenge, difficult)

PROBLEMS

96. Susan has a part-time "cottage industry" producing seasonal plywood yard ornaments for resale at local craft fairs and bazaars. She currently works a total of 4 hours per day to produce 10 ornaments.

a. What is her productivity?

b. She thinks that by redesigning the ornaments and switching from use of a wood glue to a hot-glue gun she can increase her total production to 20 ornaments per day. What is her new productivity?

c. What is her percentage increase in productivity?

a. 10 ornaments/4 hours = 2.5 ornaments/hour

b. 20 ornaments /4 hours = 5 ornaments/hour

c. Change in productivity = 2.5 ornaments/hour

   Percent change = 2.5/2.5 = 100% (The productivity challenge, moderate)

97. Mabel's Ceramics spent $3000 on a new kiln last year, in the belief that it would cut energy usage 25% over the old kiln. This kiln is an oven that turns "greenware" into finished pottery. Mabel is concerned that the new kiln requires extra labor hours for its operation. Mabel wants to check the energy savings of the new oven, and also to look over other measures of their productivity to see if the change really was beneficial. Mabel has the following data to work with:

	Last Year	This Year
Production (finished units)	4000	4000
Greenware (pounds)	5000	5000
Labor (hrs)	350	375
Capital ($)	15000	18000
Energy (kWh)	3000	2600

Were the modifications beneficial?

The energy modifications did not generate the expected savings; labor and capital productivity decreased. (The productivity challenge, moderate)

Resource	Last Year					This Year					Change	Pct. Change
Labor	4000	/	350	=	11.43	4000	/	375	=	10.67	-0.76	-6.7%
Capital	4000	/	15000	=	0.27	4000	/	18000	=	0.22	-0.04	-16.7%
Energy	4000	/	3000	=	1.33	4000	/	2600	=	1.54	0.21	15.4%

98. A firm cleans chemical tank cars in the Bay St. Louis area. With standard equipment, the firm typically cleaned 60 chemical tank cars per month. They utilized 10 gallons of solvent, and two employees worked 20 days per month, 6 hours a day. The company decided to switch to a larger cleaning machine. Last April, they cleaned 60 tank cars in only 15 days. They utilized 12 gallons of solvent, and the two employees worked 6 hours a day.
1. What was their productivity with the standard equipment?
2. What is their productivity with the larger machine?
3. What is the change in productivity?

Resource	Standard Equipment	Larger Machine	Percent Change
Solvent	$\dfrac{60}{10} = 6$	$\dfrac{60}{12} = 5$	$\dfrac{5-6}{6} = -16.67\%$
Labor	$\dfrac{60}{240} = 0.25$	$\dfrac{60}{180} = .33$	$\dfrac{.33 - .25}{.25} = 32\%$

(The productivity challenge, moderate)

99. Pierre grows mirlitons (that's Cajun for Chayote squash) in his 100 by 100 foot garden. He then sells the crop at the local farmers' market. Two summers ago, he was able to produce and sell 1200 pounds of mirlitons. Last summer, he tried a new fertilizer that promised a 20% increase in yield. He harvested 1350 pounds. Did the fertilizer live up to its promise?
Since the productivity gain was 12.5%, not 20%, the fertilizer was not as good as advertised. (The productivity challenge, moderate)

Two summers ago	Last summer	Change
1200 ÷ 10000 = .12 lbs/sq. ft	1350 ÷ 10000 = .135 lbs/sq. ft	(.135 - .12) ÷ .12 = 12.5%

100. A company has asked you to evaluate the firm's productivity by comparing this year's performance with last year's. The following data are available:

	Last Year	This Year
Output	10,500 units	12,100 units
Labor Hours	12,000	13,200
Utilities	$7,600	$8,250
Capital	$83,000	$88,000

Has the company improved its productivity during the past year?
Productivity improved in all three categories this year; utilities showed the greatest increase, and labor the least. (The productivity challenge, moderate)

Resource	Last Year				This Year				Change	Pct. Change
Labor	10500	/	12000	= 0.88	12100	/	13200	= 0.92	0.04	4.8%
Capital	10500	/	7600	= 1.38	12100	/	8250	= 1.47	0.09	6.2%
Energy	10500	/	83000	= 0.13	12100	/	88000	= 0.14	0.01	8.7%

CHAPTER 2: OPERATIONS STRATEGY FOR COMPETITIVE ADVANTAGE

TRUE/FALSE

1. An organization's mission statement is its broad statement of purpose.
   True (Identifying missions and strategies, easy)

2. Once an organization's mission has been decided upon, each functional area within the firm determines its own supporting mission.
   True (Identifying missions and strategies, easy)

3. Operations strategies are implemented in the same way in all types of organizations.
   False (Identifying missions and strategies, moderate)

4. An organization's behavior will be optimized if each of its departments optimizes their behaviors independently.
   False (Identifying missions and strategies, easy)

5. Top-level managers usually define the missions of each functional area, then merge these missions to define the mission of the organization.
   False (Identifying missions and strategies, moderate)

6. Strategies are mostly the same from one manufacturing company to another.
   False (Identifying missions and strategies, moderate)

7. An organization's mission and its strategy are basically the same thing.
   False (Identifying missions and strategies, easy)

8. An organization's mission statement provides a plan of action.
   False (Identifying missions and strategies, easy)

9. An organization's strategy provides the purpose of the organization.
   False (Identifying missions and strategies, easy)

10. Differentiation, cost, and response are the three strategies for achieving competitive advantage.
    True (Achieving competitive advantage through operations, moderate)

11. An organization's ability to generate unique advantages over competitors is central to a successful strategy implementation.
    True (Achieving competitive advantage through operations, moderate)

12. Errors made within the location decision area may overwhelm efficiencies in other areas.
    True (Ten strategic decision of OM, moderate)

13. Decisions regarding quality are among the ten decisions of operations management.
    True (Ten strategic decision of OM, easy)

14. Decisions regarding location are among the ten decisions of operations management.
    True (Ten strategic decision of OM, easy)

15. Decisions regarding maintenance are among the ten decisions of operations management.
    True (Ten strategic decision of OM, easy)

16. Decisions that involve what is to be made and what is to be purchased fall under the heading of supply-chain management.
    True (Ten strategic decision of OM, moderate)

17. The ten operations decisions are mostly used in manufacturing organizations, not services.
    False (Ten strategic decision of OM, moderate)

18. The fact that most services are tangible is key to how the ten decisions of operations management are handled differently for goods than for services.
    False (Ten strategic decision of OM, moderate)

19. The relative importance of each of the ten operations decisions depends on the ratio of goods and services in an organization.
    True (Ten strategic decision of OM, moderate)

20. The PIMS program has identified attributes shared by companies with high return on investment.
    True (Issues in operations strategy, easy)

21. Among the categories of strategic options, marketing and distribution offer an easier route to sustainable competitive advantage than operations management.
    False (Issues in operations strategy, moderate)

22. In order to maintain focus, an organization's strategy must not change during the product's life cycle.
    False (Issues in operations strategy, moderate)

23. Opportunities and threats are classified as internal factors of strategy development.
    False (Strategy development and implementation, moderate)

24. A strategy is established independently of the organization's SWOT analysis.
    False (Strategy development and implementation, easy)

25. Strategies change because an organization's internal strengths and weaknesses may change.
    True (Strategy development and implementation, moderate)

26. SWOT analysis identifies those activities that make a difference between having and not having a competitive advantage.
    False (Strategy development and implementation, moderate)

27. Critical success factors are those relatively few activities that make a difference between having and not having a competitive advantage.
True (Strategy development and implementation, moderate)

28. The operations function is most likely to be successful when the operations strategy is integrated with other functional areas.
True (Strategy development and implementation, moderate)

29. For the greatest chance of success, an organization's Operations Management strategy must support the company's strategy.
True (Strategy development and implementation, moderate)

MULTIPLE CHOICE

30. Which of the following is **true** about business strategies?
    a. All firms within an industry will adopt the same strategy.
    b. Well defined missions make strategy development much easier.
    c. Strategies are formulated independently of SWOT analysis.
    d. An organization should stick with its strategy for the life of the business.
    e. Organizational strategies depend on operations strategies.
    b (Identifying missions and strategies, moderate)

31. Which of the following statements about organizational missions is **false**?
    a. They reflect a company's purpose.
    b. They indicate what a company intends to contribute to society.
    c. They define a company's reason for existence.
    d. They provide guidance for functional area missions.
    e. They are formulated after strategies are known.
    c (Identifying missions and strategies, moderate)

32. Which of the following activities takes place once the mission has been developed?
    a. The firm develops alternative or back-up missions in case the original mission fails.
    b. The functional areas develop their functional area strategies.
    c. The functional areas develop their supporting missions.
    d. The ten OM decision areas are prioritized.
    e. The organization files SEC Form 1095, Formal Mission Statement.
    c (Identifying missions and strategies, moderate)

33. The fundamental purpose for the existence of any organization is described by its
    a. policies
    b. procedures
    c. strategy
    d. mission
    e. bylaws
    d (Identifying missions and strategies, moderate)

34. The impact of strategies on the general direction and basic character of a company is
   a. long range
   b. medium range
   c. short ranged
   d. temporal
   e. minimal
   a (Identifying missions and strategies, moderate)

35. Which of the following is **true**?
   a. Corporate strategy is shaped by functional strategies.
   b. Corporate mission is shaped by corporate strategy.
   c. Functional strategies are shaped by corporate strategy.
   d. External conditions are shaped by corporate mission.
   e. Corporate mission is shaped by functional strategies.
   c (Identifying missions and strategies, difficult)

36. The fundamental purpose of an organization's mission statement is to
   a. define the organization's purpose in society
   b. define the operational structure of the organization
   c. generate good public relations for the organization
   d. define the functional areas required by the organization
   e. create a good human relations climate in the organization
   a (Identifying missions and strategies, moderate)

37. Which of the following is **not** a key way in which business organizations compete with one-another?
   a. production cost
   b. quality
   c. product duplication
   d. flexibility
   e. time to perform certain activities
   c (Achieving competitive advantage through operations, moderate)

38. A strategy is
   a. a broad statement of purpose
   b. a simulation used to test various product line options
   c. a plan for cost reduction
   d. an action plan to achieve the mission
   e. a set of opportunities in the marketplace
   d (Achieving competitive advantage through operations, moderate)

39. Which of the following is **not** an operations strategy?
   a. response
   b. low cost
   c. differentiation
   d. technology
   e. all of the above are operations strategies
   d (Achieving competitive advantage through operations, moderate)

40. According to the authors, which of the following strategic concepts allow firms to achieve their missions?
    a. differentiation, cost leadership, and quick response
    b. differentiation, quality leadership, and quick response
    c. distinctive competency, cost leadership, and experience
    d. differentiation, distinctive competency, quality, leadership, and capacity
    e. productivity, efficiency, and quality leadership
    a (Achieving competitive advantage through operations, moderate)

41. The ability of an organization to produce goods or services that have some uniqueness in their characteristics is
    a. time-based competition
    b. competing on productivity
    c. competing on flexibility
    d. competing on differentiation
    e. mass customization
    d (Achieving competitive advantage through operations, moderate)

42. Which of the following is an example of competing on the basis of differentiation?
    a. A firm manufactures its product with less raw material waste than its competitors.
    b. A firm's products are introduced into the market faster than its competitors'.
    c. A firm's distribution network routinely delivers its product on time.
    d. A firm offers more reliable products than its competitors.
    e. A firm advertises more than its competitors.
    d (Achieving competitive advantage through operations, moderate)

43. Which of the following is the best example of competing on low-cost leadership?
    a. a firm produces its product with less raw material waste than its competitors
    b. a firm offers more reliable products than its competitors
    c. a firm's products are introduced into the market faster than its competitors'
    d. a firm's research and development department generates many ideas for new products
    e. a firm advertises more than its competitors
    a (Achieving competitive advantage through operations, difficult)

44. Which of the following statements best characterizes delivery **reliability**?
    a. a company that always delivers on the same day of the week
    b. a company that always delivers at the promised time
    c. a company that delivers more frequently than its competitors
    d. a company that delivers faster than its competitors
    e. a company that has a computerized delivery scheduling system
    b (Achieving competitive advantage through operations, difficult)

45. Which of the following statements best characterizes delivery **speed**?
    a. a company that uses airlines, not trucks, to move its goods
    b. a company that delivers frequently
    c. a company that delivers faster than its competitors
    d. a company that always delivers on the promised due date
    e. a company that has a computerized delivery scheduling system
    c (Achieving competitive advantage through operations, moderate)

46. Which of the following is an example of competing on quick response?
    a. a firm produces its product with less raw material waste than its competitors
    b. a firm offers more reliable products than its competitors
    c. a firm's products are introduced into the market faster than its competitors'
    d. a firm's research and development department generates many ideas for new products
    e. a firm advertises more than its competitors
    c (Achieving competitive advantage through operations, difficult)

47. Costs, quality, and human resource decisions interact strongly with the _____ decision.
    a. layout design
    b. process and capacity design
    c. maintenance
    d. goods and service design
    e. all of the above are correct
    d (Ten strategic decisions of OM, moderate)

48. Response-based competitive advantage can be
    a. flexible response
    b. reliable response
    c. quick response
    d. all of the above
    e. none of the above
    d (Ten strategic decisions of OM, moderate)

49. Which of the following is **not** an operations decision?
    a. scheduling
    b. layout design
    c. price
    d. quality
    e. inventory
    c (Ten strategic decisions of OM, moderate)

50. Which of the following OM decisions pertains to sensible location of processes and materials in relation to each other?
    a. goods and service design
    b. supply chain management
    c. production planning
    d. scheduling
    e. layout design
    e (Ten strategic decisions of OM, moderate)

51. Which of the following influences layout design?
    a. capacity needs
    b. personnel levels
    c. purchasing decisions
    d. inventory requirements
    e. all of the above influence layout decisions
    e (Ten strategic decisions of OM, moderate)

52. Which of these companies is most apt to have quality standards that are relatively subjective?
   a. Chrysler
   b. Dell Computer
   c. Harvard University
   d. Sanyo Electronics
   e. Whirlpool

   c (Ten strategic decision of OM, moderate)

53. Which of these organizations is most apt to have quality standards that are relatively objective?
   a. a chemical manufacturer
   b. a university
   c. a discount retailer
   d. a law firm
   e. a bookstore

   a (Ten strategic decisions of OM, moderate)

54. Which of the following statements concerning the operations management decision is relevant to services?
   a. There are many objective quality standards.
   b. Labor standards vary depending on customer requirements.
   c. The customer is not involved in most of the process.
   d. The work force's technical skills are very important.
   e. Ability to inventory may allow the leveling of the output rates.

   b (Ten strategic decisions of OM, moderate)

55. Which of these organizations is likely to have the most important inventory decisions?
   a. a marketing research firm
   b. a lobbying agency
   c. a management consulting firm
   d. a restaurant
   e. a law firm

   d (Ten strategic decisions of OM, moderate)

56. Which of the following will more likely locate near their customers?
   a. an automobile manufacturer
   b. a medical clinic
   c. an aluminum manufacturer
   d. an insurance company headquarters
   e. all of the above

   b (Ten strategic decisions of OM, moderate)

57. The PIMS program has identified
   a. the operations decisions all organizations must make
   b. the distinctive competencies any company needs
   c. the characteristics of firms with high "ROI"
   d. the corporate decisions any company needs to make
   e. all of the above

   c (Issues in operations strategy, moderate)

58. Which of the following is **not** one of the five PIMS characteristics of high Return on Investment organizations?
    a. high product quality
    b. high capacity utilization
    c. low direct cost per unit
    d. low investment intensity
    e. all of the above are PIMS characteristics
    e (Issues in operations strategy, moderate)

59. Standardization is an appropriate strategy in which stage of the product life cycle?
    a. introduction
    b. growth
    c. maturity
    d. decline
    e. incubation
    c (Issues in operations strategy, moderate)

60. Optimizing capacity would be most appropriate for which stage in the product life cycle?
    a. introduction
    b. growth
    c. maturity
    d. decline
    e. incubation
    c (Issues in operations strategy, moderate)

61. Competitive product improvements and options are best introduced in the _____ stage in the product life cycle
    a. introduction
    b. growth
    c. maturity
    d. decline
    e. incubation
    b (Issues in operations strategy, moderate)

62. Which of the following preconditions does **not** affect the formulation of an OM strategy?
    a. external economic and technological conditions
    b. the company's employment benefits
    c. competitors' strengths and weaknesses
    d. knowledge of the company's strategy
    e. knowledge of each product's life cycle
    b (Issues in operations strategy, moderate)

63. Which of the following changes does **not** result in strategy changes?
    a. change in the company's financial situation
    b. a company's adoption of new technology
    c. change in the product life cycle
    d. change in the competitive environment
    e. change in job scheduling techniques
    e (Issues in operations strategy, moderate)

64. Which of the following is **not** a key external factor that should be taken into account by a corporate strategy?
    a. economic conditions
    b. political conditions
    c. legal environments
    d. financial resources
    e. competition
    d (Strategy development and implementation, moderate)

65. All of these preconditions affect an operations management strategy **except**
    a. external economic and technological conditions
    b. competitors' strengths and weaknesses
    c. knowledge of the company's strategy
    d. knowledge of each product's life cycle
    e. maintenance policies
    e (Strategy development and implementation, moderate)

66. The acronym SWOT stands for
    a. Special Weapons for Operations Timeliness
    b. Services, Worldwide Optimization, and Transport
    c. Strengths, Weaknesses, Opportunities, and Threats
    d. Strengths Worldwide Overcome Threats
    e. none of the above
    c (Strategy development and implementation, easy)

67. The two internal elements of SWOT analysis are
    a. opportunities and threats
    b. strengths and opportunities
    c. weaknesses and threats
    d. strengths and weaknesses
    e. strengths and threats
    d (Strategy development and implementation, moderate)

68. One of the most important questions to ask when implementing a particular strategy is
    a. What will this strategy cost?
    b. Which elements can be done somewhat poorly and still have the strategy succeed?
    c. What activities must be done particularly well for this strategy to succeed?
    d. Which elements of this strategy affect the quality of the product?
    e. Which elements of this strategy enhance flexibility?
    c (Strategy development and implementation, moderate)

69. Which of the following statements is true about operations strategy?
    a. It should support the corporate strategy.
    b. It should help achieve the operation's mission.
    c. It should be integrated with the other functional areas' strategies.
    d. It should promote competitive advantage.
    e. all of the above are true
    e (Strategy development and implementation, moderate)

70. Which of these organizations is likely to have the most complex inventory decisions?
    a. a marketing research firm
    b. a stock brokerage firm
    c. a radio station
    d. a computer manufacturing company
    e. an elementary school
    d (Strategy development and implementation, moderate)

71. The three steps of the operations manager's job, in order, are
    a. develop the strategy, find the right staff, establish the organizational structure
    b. find the right staff, establish the organizational structure, develop the strategy
    c. find the right staff, develop the strategy, establish the organizational structure
    d. develop the strategy, establish the organizational structure, find the right staff
    e. establish the organizational structure, find the right staff, develop the strategy
    d (Strategy development and implementation, moderate)

72. A firm can effectively use its operations function to yield competitive advantage via all of the following **except**
    a. customization of the product
    b. set equipment utilization goals below the industry average
    c. speed of delivery
    d. constant innovation of new products
    e. maintain a variety of product options
    b (Achieving competitive advantage through operations, moderate)

73. When developing the operations strategy for a new manufacturing organization, one of the most important considerations is that
    a. it requires minimal capital investment
    b. it utilizes as much automation as possible
    c. it utilizes an equal balance of labor and automation
    d. it supports the overall competitive strategy of the company
    e. none of the above
    d (Strategy development and implementation, moderate)

FILL-IN-THE-BLANK

74. When making location decisions, companies providing services may need to be near _____, while companies producing goods will need to be near _____.
    customers; raw materials or labor force (Ten strategic decisions of OM, moderate)

75. In good producing organizations, _____,_____, and _____ may be inventoried.
raw materials, work-in-process, and finished goods (Ten strategic decisions of OM, moderate)

76. PIMS stands for _____. PIMS is a program of the _____.
Profit Impact of Market Strategy; Strategic Planning Institute. (Issues in operations strategy, moderate)

77. Strategy is not static, but dynamic because of changes in the _____ and _____.

   organization, environment (Issues in operations strategy, moderate)

78. The _____ is the purpose or rationale for an organization's existence.
mission (Identifying missions and strategies, moderate)

79. The _____ is how an organization expects to achieve its missions and goals.
strategy (Identifying missions and strategies, moderate)

80. The creation of a unique advantage over competitors is called a _____.
competitive advantage (Achieving competitive advantage through operations, moderate)

81. Competitive advantage in operations can be achieved by _____, _____, and/or _____.
differentiation, low cost, response (Achieving competitive advantage through operations, moderate)

82. In strategy development and implementation, the two <u>external</u> factors are _____ and _____; the two <u>internal</u> factors are _____ and _____.
opportunities and threats; strengths and weaknesses (Strategy development and implementation, moderate)

SHORT ANSWER

83. Define **mission**.
The organization's mission is its purpose - what it will contribute to society. (Identifying missions and strategies, moderate)

84. Define **strategy**.
Strategy is an organization's action plan to achieve the mission. (Identifying missions and strategies, moderate)

85. Describe how an organization's mission and strategy have different purposes.
An organization's mission specifies where it is going, whereas a strategy specifies how to get there. (Identifying missions and strategies, moderate)

86. What are the three conceptual ways to competitive advantage proposed by the authors?
Differentiation, cost leadership, and quick response. (Achieving competitive advantage through operations, moderate)

87. List five of the operations management decisions that support missions and implement strategies.
Any five of: quality, goods and service design, process and capacity design, location selection, layout design, people and work systems, supply chain management, inventory, scheduling, maintenance. (Ten strategic OM decisions, moderate)

88. How do goods and services differ with regard to handling the quality decision?
There are many objective quality standards for goods, whereas there are many subjective quality standards for services. (Ten strategic OM decisions, moderate)

89. For what type of organization might the location decision area be the least important of its ten decision areas? For what type of organization might the location decision be the most important of the ten decision areas? Discuss, augment your response with examples.
The relationship between the organization and its suppliers or its customers is key. If that relationship is very weak (as in no transportation costs, or customers can reach firm from any location), location diminishes in importance. If that relationship is strong (uniqueness of site, high transportation costs, customers will not travel far) location increases in importance. "Least" examples: Telemarketing firm, tax help-line, Internet sales. "Most" examples: gold mine, oil well, ski resort. (Ten strategic OM decisions, difficult)

90. With regard to the scheduling decision, how are goods-producing organizations different from service companies? Discuss.
Good-producing companies: the ability to inventory may allow leveling the output rates; service companies: primarily concerned with meeting the customer's immediate schedule. (Ten strategic OM decisions, difficult)

91. Cite an example of a service company that has a scheduling decision much like that of a goods-producing company. Discuss how this is possible.
Would be a firm that can level demand, as with reservations or appointments; perhaps delivers a standardized service. Vaccinations at a health clinic? (Ten strategic OM decisions, difficult)

92. List PIMS' five characteristics of high ROI firms.
High product quality; high capacity utilization; high operating effectiveness; low investment intensity; and low direct cost per unit. (Issues in operations strategy, moderate)

93. What are the main reasons why strategies must be dynamic?
Changes within the organization; and changes in the environment. (Strategy development and implementation, moderate)

94. List the four elements of SWOT analysis.
Strengths, weaknesses. opportunities, and threats. (Strategy development and implementation, easy)

95. List the three steps involved in an operations manager's job.
Develop strategy, group activities into an organizational structure, and staff it with personnel that will get the job done. (Strategy development and implementation, moderate)

CHAPTER 3: OPERATIONS IN A GLOBAL ENVIRONMENT

TRUE/FALSE

1. Boeing used international partners in building the Boeing 777 partly to attract demand from its competitor, Airbus.
    True (Global company profile: Boeing, easy)

2. The Boeing 777 has content from about a dozen countries in addition to the U.S.
    True (Global company profile: Boeing, easy)

3. The globalization of production simplifies the job of the operations manager.
    False (Global company profile: Boeing, easy)

4. The new standards for global competitiveness result in companies seeking exceptional partners, wherever they may be, for their enterprise.
    True (Global company profile: Boeing, moderate)

5. Globalization has led some organizations to seek methods of reducing distribution and shipping times.
    True (Introduction, easy)

6. Part of the increase in globalization is the rapid growth in emerging world markets such as China.
    True (Global company profile: Boeing, moderate)

7. Levi jeans and Coke are both cited as examples of domestic products.
    False (Introduction, moderate)

8. The acronym **MNC** stands for Multinational Corporation.
    True (Introduction, easy)

9. Dow Chemical, Gillette, and Nestle are all examples of MNCs for which over half of each firm's business takes place outside the organization's home country.
    True (Global operations strategies, moderate)

10. Production processes are being dispersed to take advantage of national differences in labor costs.
    True (Why global operations are important, moderate)

11. In global operations, cost cutting can take place because of less stringent regulations in foreign countries.
    True (Why global operations are important, moderate)

12. The major stated advantage of **maquiladoras** is lower costs of taxation.
    True (Why global operations are important, moderate)

13. NAFTA seeks to phase out all trade and tariff barriers in the United States and in Europe.
    False (Why global operations are important, moderate)

14. One of the several reasons for global operations is to gain improvements in supply.
   True (Why global operations are important, moderate)

15. Gaining nearness to foreign customers is an important part of providing better goods and services to them.
   True (Why global operations are important, moderate)

16. A product may be in its maturity phase of the product life cycle in one country, but in the introductory stage in another.
   True (Why global operations are important, moderate)

17. Reductions in communication and information processing costs are major contributors to organizations' abilities to manage globally dispersed operations.
   True (Achieving global operations, moderate)

18. Use of Critical Success Factors is one method to assist in determining the country in which to locate a new facility.
   True (Achieving global operations, moderate)

19. Critical Success Factors will generate the same answer, whether weighted or unweighted calculations are used.
   False (Achieving global operations, moderate)

20. Maytag is an example of an organization that has been highly successful in globalizing its organization.
   False (Achieving global operations, moderate)

21. One of the benefits of the World Trade Organization (WTO) is a growing uniformity in the definition of ethical conduct by managers in various cultures.
   True (Achieving global operations, moderate)

22. Bribery is an example of ethical and cultural considerations.
   True (Achieving global operations, moderate)

23. Protection of intellectual property rights is an important issue related to cultural and ethical variations among countries.
   True (Achieving global operations, moderate)

24. Global service operations are almost nonexistent.
   False (Global issues in service operations, moderate)

25. Four issues of special importance in managing global service operations are capacity planning, location planning, facilities design and layout, and scheduling.
   True (Global issues in service operations, moderate)

26. The multidomestic OM strategy maximizes local responsiveness.
   True (Global operations strategies, moderate)

27. Firms using the global strategy can be thought of as "world companies."
True (Global operations strategies, moderate)

28. The transnational strategy does poorly on cost reductions.
False (Global operations strategies, moderate)

MULTIPLE CHOICE

29. The "new standards of global competitiveness" include
   a. quality
   b. variety
   c. customization
   d. timeliness
   e. all of the above
   e (Global company profile: Boeing, moderate)

30. The "new standards of global competitiveness" include all of the following **except**
   a. quality
   b. maquiladora
   c. customization
   d. timeliness
   e. all of the above
   b (Global company profile: Boeing, moderate)

31. "Levi jeans" are described in the textbook as a _____ product.
   a. world
   b. global
   c. domestic
   d. service
   e. none of the above
   b (Introduction, moderate)

32. The acronym **MNC** stands for
   a. Mexican National Committee (for international trade)
   b. Maquiladora Negates Competition
   c. Multinational Corporation
   d. Maytag-Nestle Corporation
   e. none of the above
   c (Global operations strategies, easy)

33. Nestlé is described in the textbook as a _____ firm.
   a. domestic
   b. global
   c. subsidiary
   d. transnational
   e. all of the above
   d (Global operations strategies, moderate)

34. Which of the following are examples of transnational firms?
    a. Nestlé
    b. Bertelsmann
    c. Reuters
    d. Citicorp
    e. all of the above are transnationals
    e (Global operations strategies, moderate)

35. Firms are dispersing production processes to take advantage of national differences in
    a. labor cost
    b. facilities
    c. capital
    d. labor quality
    e. all of the above
    e (Why global operations are important, moderate)

36. Cost cutting in MNCs can take place because of
    a. lower wage scales
    b. lower indirect labor costs
    c. less stringent regulations
    d. lower taxes and tariffs
    e. all of the above
    e (Why global operations are important, moderate)

37. Multinational organizations can shop from country to country and cut costs through
    a. lower wage scales
    b. lower indirect labor costs
    c. less stringent regulations
    d. lower taxes and tariffs
    e. all of the above
    e (Why global operations are important, moderate)

38. The term **maquiladora** is most synonymous with
    a. Chinese forced labor camps
    b. free trade zones
    c. cheap labor zones
    d. areas that do not meet U.S. standards for workplace safety and pollution
    e. none of the above
    b (Why global operations are important, moderate)

39. Which of the following represent reasons for globalizing operations?
    a. reduce costs
    b. improve supply chain
    c. attract new markets
    d. attract and retain global talent
    e. all of the above are valid
    e (Why global operations are important, moderate)

40. NAFTA, passed in 1993, seeks to
    a. curb illegal immigration from Mexico to the United States
    b. substitute cheap labor in Mexico for expensive labor in the United States
    c. phase out all trade and tariff barriers between the United States and Mexico
    d. phase out all trade and tariff barriers between the United States, Canada, and Mexico
    e. all of the above are NAFTA goals
    d (Why global operations are important, moderate)

41. Which of the following was **not** suggested by the authors as a reason for globalizing operations?
    a. reduce costs
    b. improve supply chain
    c. attract new markets
    d. stockholder approval ratings
    e. all of the above are valid
    d (Why global operations are important, moderate)

42. Which of the following is associated with reducing the risk of "going global"?
    a. expanded product life cycle
    b. NAFTA
    c. lower wage scales
    d. culture and ethics
    e. none of the above
    b (Why global operations are important, moderate)

43. Which of the following is associated with reducing the risk of "going global"?
    a. maquiladora
    b. NAFTA
    c. protection of investment capital
    d. protection of intellectual property rights
    e. all of the above
    e (Why global operations are important, moderate)

44. Which of the following makes possible the effective management of a highly integrated, globally dispersed operation?
    a. Critical Success Factors
    b. increasing levels of education in the global work force
    c. rapid declines in information processing and communication costs
    d. all of the above are valid
    e. none of the above are true
    c (Achieving global operations, moderate)

45. Which of the following are major contributors to organizations' abilities to manage globally dispersed operations?
    a. rapid growth in emerging markets
    b. lower wage scales in third-world countries
    c. reductions in communication and information processing costs
    d. less stringent environmental regulations in certain countries
    e. all of the above
    c (Achieving global operations, moderate)

46. Which of the following are typical of the Critical Success Factors used for international facility location decisions?
   a. political and legal factors
   b. availability of technology
   c. economic factors
   d. culture and ethics
   e. all of the above
   e (Achieving global operations, moderate)

47. Which of the following are **not** typical of the Critical Success Factors used for international facility location decisions?
   a. political and legal factors
   b. economic factors
   c. culture and ethics
   d. capacity planning
   e. technology
   d (Achieving global operations, moderate)

48. Which of the following is true regarding Critical Success Factors (CSFs)?
   a. The list of critical success factors is the same from one organization to another.
   b. The critical success factors must be weighted equally.
   c. Critical Success Factors are relevant for strategic planning, but not for Global Operations.
   d. Use of CSFs is one method of determining the country in which to locate a new facility.
   e. All of the above are true.
   d (Achieving global operations, moderate)

49. Which of the following organizations is an example of a firm that has had difficulty with successful globalization?
   a. Maytag
   b. Nestlé
   c. Boeing
   d. Coca-Cola
   e. all of the above are successes in globalization
   a (Achieving global operations, moderate)

50. Which of the following is **not** true regarding global product design?
   a. firms must consider social and cultural differences
   b. packaging can help make a product seem domestic in origin
   c. packaging decisions include container size and dimensions
   d. very famous branded items may be formulated differently in other countries than in the U.S.
   e. all of the above are true
   e (Achieving global operations, moderate)

51. Which of the following is the best description of Maytag's experience with globalization?
    a. enormously successful
    b. generally successful
    c. mixed results
    d. earnings disaster
    e. resulted in bankruptcy
    d (Achieving global operations, moderate)

52. Which of the following represent issues of culture and ethics in international operations?
    a. bribery
    b. employee punctuality
    c. employee stealing
    d. protection of intellectual property rights
    e. all of the above are culture and ethics issues
    e (Achieving global operations, moderate)

53. Which of the following are of special importance to the managing of global service operations?
    a. capacity planning
    b. location planning
    c. facilities design and layout
    d. scheduling
    e. all of the above
    e (Global issues in service operations, moderate)

54. Which of the following are of special importance to the managing of global service operations?
    a. demographic factors
    b. economic factors
    c. culture and ethics
    d. capacity planning
    e. none of the above
    d (Global issues in service operations, moderate)

55. Which of the international operations strategies involves high cost reductions and high local responsiveness?
    a. International strategy
    b. Global strategy
    c. Transnational strategy
    d. Multidomestic strategy
    e. none of the above
    c (Global operations strategies, moderate)

56. Which of the international operations strategies uses import/export or licensing of existing products?
    a. International strategy
    b. Global strategy
    c. Transnational strategy
    d. Multidomestic strategy
    e. none of the above
    a (Global operations strategies, moderate)

57. Which of the international operations strategies uses the existing domestic model globally?
    a. International strategy
    b. Global strategy
    c. Transnational strategy
    d. Multidomestic strategy
    e. none of the above
    d (Global operations strategies, moderate)

58. Which of the following statements about global service operations is **true**?
    a. Global service operations are almost non-existent
    b. Global services, being tangible, can be transported from country to country
    c. Global service operations are responsible for about one-quarter of all international trade
    d. Global service operations offer a slower growth rate than manufacturing or agriculture
    e. None of the above are true
    c (Global issues in service operations, moderate)

FILL-IN-THE-BLANK

59. _____ are Mexican factories located along the U.S.-Mexico border that receive preferential tariff treatment.
    Maquiladoras (Why global operations are important, moderate)

60. _____ is a free trade agreement between Canada, Mexico, and the United States.
    NAFTA--North American Free Trade Agreement (Why global operations are important, moderate)

61. An _____ is a firm that transforms resources into a service-creating utility for its global customers.
    international service provider (Global issues in service operations, moderate)

62. An _____ is a firm that engages in cross-border transactions.
    international business (Global operations strategies, moderate)

63. A(n) _____ is a firm that has extensive involvement in international business, owning or controlling facilities in more than one country.
    MNC--multinational corporation (Global operations strategies, moderate)

64. The _____ strategy utilizes a standardized product across countries.
    Global (Global operations strategies, moderate)

65. The _____ strategy uses exports and licenses to penetrate globally.
    International (Global operations strategies, moderate)

66. The _____ strategy uses subsidiaries, franchises, or joint ventures with substantial independence.
    Multidomestic (Global operations strategies, moderate)

67. The _____ strategy describes a condition in which material, people, and ideas cross or transgress national boundaries.
Transnational (Global operations strategies, moderate)

SHORT ANSWER

68. Based on the descriptions and analysis of the textbook, would Boeing be better described as a global firm or a transnational firm? Discuss.
Global seems the better label, since authority and responsibility reside in the U.S.--the home country. (Global company profile: Boeing, moderate)

69. List six reasons to internationalize operations.
Reduce costs, improve supply chain, provide better goods and services, attract new markets, learn to improve operations, attract and retain global talent. (Why global operations are important, moderate)

70. List two organizations that have helped reduce tariffs.
WTO, NAFTA (Why global operations are important, moderate)

71. "Coke" is described in the text as a global product. Does this mean that Coke is formulated in the same way throughout the world? Discuss.
No. Sweetness is adjusted for the tastes of individual countries. (Achieving global operations, moderate)

72. The textbook listed several considerations for achieving global operations. Which of these are included in the "ten decision areas" of the previous chapter? Which are not on that list? Discuss.
Product design, process design and technology, facility location are included on both lists. Culture and ethics are not on the list of decisions; they are "considerations" not decisions. (Achieving global operations, moderate)

73. Describe how Critical Success Factors can be used to help with a global facility location decision.
Identify the CSFs, applying differential weights as appropriate; collect nation-specific data on them; build a factor rating scheme for all alternatives on all CSFs; choose the highest scoring alternative. (Achieving global operations, moderate)

74. Explain how falling information processing costs and communication costs enable organizations to more effectively manage dispersed global activities.
Organizations can afford better, faster networks; there is less time delay, less information quality loss associated with distance. Teams of workers need not be face to face. The organization becomes more virtual; with lower transaction costs, managing globally becomes less difficult. (Achieving global operations, moderate)

75. How might Hewlett-Packard achieve global product design in the design of its laser printers, in the presence of different voltages, plugs, building codes, and other national differences that impact how a laser printer plugs into the wall? Discuss.
(This is a critical-thinking question; a suggested answer follows) H-P could design its printers with switches to select incoming voltage differences; could provide voltage adapters; could sell printers without power cords; could sell battery-powered printers which would not be dependent on electrical codes. (Achieving global operations, difficult)

76. List the broad categories of Critical Success Factors. Under what broad category would you place each of the following? Are any of these so important as to warrant its own new category? Support your choices.
   a. child labor issues
   b. workplace safety issues
   c. collaboration with competitors or suppliers
   d. pollution emissions
   e. infrastructure--roads, bridges, airports, electricity, phone, etc.
   List is Technology, Education, Political/Legal, Social/Cultural, and Economic. (a) is part legal, part cultural; (b) is part legal, part education; (c) is mostly legal; (d) is political/legal; (e) may deserve its own category, or in the economic category. (Global issues in service operations, difficult)

77. Build a list of Critical Success Factors appropriate to an American fast food organization seeking new consumer markets overseas. Support your selections.
   (suggested answer) Elements related to workers--quantity, cost, literacy, work ethic--should be high; elements related to supply chain--infrastructure, taxes--should also be high; technology may not be on the list; cultural elements--tastes may influence the acceptance of American foods. (Achieving global operations, difficult)

78. State the list of steps for establishing a global service operation.
   (1) Determine if sufficient people or facilities exist to support the service; (2) identify foreign markets that are open; (3) determine what services are of most interest to foreign consumers; and (4) determine how to reach global customers. (Achieving global operations, moderate)

PROBLEMS

79. A global firm is attempting to penetrate new market areas, one at a time. Its major products sell best to affluent, educated, younger householders. The critical success factors for this venture are judged to be demographic factors, economic factors, social and cultural factors, and political and legal factors. Using a scale of 5=best to 1=worst, the following data were assembled.

Critical Success Factor	Country A	Country B	Country C
Demographic factors	2	5	3
Economic factors	4	2	4
Political/Legal	1	3	3
Social/Cultural	4	2	3

Which country has the most attractive score? If demographic factors are twice as important as each of the others, which country is now most attractive?
Unweighted, A=11, B=12, and C=13. C is highest. If demographics are doubled, the scores become 13, 17, and 16, and B is now preferred. (Achieving global operations, moderate)

80. A multinational firm is ready to build a very large chemicals plant. Three countries have the necessary raw materials. The CSFs for this project include labor skill, political stability, work culture, and infrastructure. Scored from 10=best to 1=worst, the following table summarizes the ratings of the three competing countries. Which country has the most attractive score? If the infrastructure CSF is weighted 0.4 and the others 0.2 each, which country is now most attractive?

Critical Success Factor	Country R	Country S	Country T
Labor skill	7	7	4
Political stability	8	6	5
Work culture	4	6	6
Infrastructure	4	5	6

Unweighted, R=23, S=24, and T=21. S is highest. Weighted, the scores become 5.4, 5.8, and 5.4, but S is still the highest rated country.

Candidate Country Ratings

CSF	Weights	Country R	Country S	Country T	calculations		
Labor skill	0.2	7	7	4	1.4	1.4	0.8
Political stability	0.2	8	6	5	1.6	1.2	1
Work culture	0.2	4	6	6	0.8	1.2	1.2
Infrastructure	0.4	4	5	6	1.6	2.0	2.4
	1				5.4	5.8	5.4

(Achieving global operations, moderate)

81. A financial services firm that is currently operating only in the U.S. and Canada is considering offering its services in other countries. The critical success factors have been identified, and are in the first column of the table below. On a scale of 1=worst to 5=best, which of the three country alternatives (A, B, C) is best if all factors are equal? If the five factors are weighted 0.2, 0.1, 0.4, 0.1, and 0.2, is the outcome the same?

Candidate Country Ratings

Critical Success Factors	Country A	Country B	Country C
Infrastructure (especially telecommunications)	4	5	1
Education (for worker and consumer literacy)	5	1	5
Legal (similarity to current U.S. system)	1	4	3
Social/Cultural	3	4	3
Economic factors (strong financial markets)	4	3	2

Unweighted, A and B are a dead heat at 17, with C at 14; weighted, B is much higher than A or C.

Candidate Country Ratings — **Calculations**

Weights	Country A	Country B	Country C			
0.2	4	5	1	0.8	1	0.2
0.1	5	1	5	0.5	0.1	0.5
0.4	1	4	3	0.4	1.6	1.2
0.1	3	4	3	0.3	0.4	0.3
0.2	4	3	2	0.8	0.6	0.4
1	17	17	14	2.8	3.7	2.6

(Achieving global operations, moderate)

CHAPTER 4: FORECASTING

TRUE/FALSE

1. Tupperware's use of forecasting is critical to the organization's success.
    True (Global company profile: Tupperware Corporation, easy)

2. Tupperware's use of forecasting involves both quantitative and qualitative forecasting tools.
    True (Global company profile: Tupperware Corporation, easy)

3. No single forecasting technique is appropriate under all conditions.
    True (What is forecasting? easy)

4. A medium-range forecast would be used for new product planning.
    False (What is forecasting? moderate)

5. Long-range forecasts tend to be more accurate than short-range forecasts.
    False (What is forecasting? easy)

6. Over the life cycle of a product, the time horizon and the forecasting techniques used tend to remain relatively constant.
    False (What is forecasting? moderate)

7. The weighted moving average technique is not well suited for forecasting the demand for a very new product.
    True (Time-series forecasting, moderate)

8. Demand forecasts drive decisions in many areas.
    True (The strategic importance of forecasting, easy)

9. Determining the objective of a forecast is the first of the seven steps in the forecasting system.
    True (Seven steps in the forecasting system, easy)

10. Forecasts of product families tend to be more accurate than forecasts of individual products.
    True (Seven steps in the forecasting system, moderate)

11. A combination of qualitative and quantitative forecasting techniques is usually the most effective approach.
    True (Forecasting approaches, moderate)

12. In the consumer market survey approach to forecasting, groups of 5 to 10 experts make the actual forecast.
    False (Forecasting approaches, moderate)

13. A time series is a collection of data taken at equal time intervals.
    True (Forecasting approaches, moderate)

14. Seasonal indexes adjust raw data for patterns that repeat at regular time intervals.
    True (Time-series forecasting, moderate)

15. A naive forecast for June sales of a product would be equal to the sales in May.
True (Forecasting approaches, easy)

16. The larger the number of periods in the simple moving average forecasting method, the greater the method's responsiveness to changes in demand.
False (Forecasting approaches, moderate)

17. A weighted moving average forecast will not lag behind a trend if the weights are set properly.
False (Forecasting approaches, moderate)

18. A disadvantage of exponential smoothing is the extensive record keeping involved.
False (Forecasting approaches, moderate)

19. Increasing the value of alpha in exponential smoothing makes the forecast more accurate.
False (Forecasting approaches, moderate)

20. Forecasting software routinely automates the selection of the smoothing constant and improves the accuracy of the forecasting model by choosing the alpha that provides the minimum forecast error.
True (Forecasting approaches, moderate)

21. Mean Absolute Deviation is a measure of the overall error of a forecasting model.
True (Forecasting approaches, easy)

22. The exponential smoothing with trend adjustment model allows exponential smoothing to deal with time series containing trends.
True (Forecasting approaches, easy)

23. In trend projection, the trend component is the slope of the regression equation.
True (Forecasting approaches, easy)

24. In trend projection, a negative regression slope is mathematically impossible.
False (Forecasting approaches, moderate)

25. The smaller the standard error of the estimate, the more accurate the forecasting model.
True (Associative forecasting methods: Regression and correlation analysis, easy)

26. A regression equation with a correlation coefficient of 0.82 means that for every unit rise in X, there is a 0.82 unit rise in Y.
False (Associative forecasting methods: Regression and correlation analysis, moderate)

27. In a regression equation where Y is product demand and X is advertising, a coefficient of determination (R^2) of .80 means that 80% of the variance in demand is explained by advertising.
True (Associative forecasting methods: Regression and correlation analysis, moderate)

28. Regression analysis, because it is limited to a single independent variable, has serious limitations as a forecasting device.
False (Associative forecasting methods: Regression and correlation analysis, moderate)

29. A Running Sum of Forecast Errors (RSFE) of zero indicates that the forecast has been perfect, with zero error in each period.
False (Monitoring and controlling forecasts, moderate)

30. Tracking limits should be within ± 8 MADs for low-volume stock items.
True (Monitoring and controlling forecasts, moderate)

31. Many service firms use point-of-sale computers to collect detailed records needed for accurate short-term forecasts.
True (Forecasting in the service sector, moderate)

MULTIPLE CHOICE

32. One purpose of short-range forecasts is to determine
    a. production plans
    b. inventory budgets
    c. job assignments
    d. research and demand plans
    e. facility location
    c (What is forecasting? moderate)

33. Forecasts are usually classified by time horizon into three categories
    a. finance/accounting, marketing, and operations
    b. strategic, tactical, and operational
    c. short-range, medium-range, and long-range
    d. exponential smoothing, regression, and time series
    e. departmental, organizational, and industrial
    c (What is forecasting? easy)

34. A forecast with a time horizon of about 3 months to 3 years is typically called a
    a. long-range forecast
    b. **medium-range forecast**
    c. short-range forecast
    d. weather forecast
    e. strategic forecast
    b (What is forecasting? moderate)

35. Forecasts
    a. become more accurate with longer time horizons
    b. are more accurate for individual items than for groups of items
    c. are rarely perfect
    d. all of the above
    e. none of the above
    c (What is forecasting? moderate)

36. Forecasts used for new product planning, capital expenditures, facility location or expansion, and R&D typically utilize a
   a. long-range time horizon
   b. medium-range time horizon
   c. short-range time horizon
   d. naive method, because there is no data history
   e. all of the above

   a (What is forecasting? moderate)

37. The three major types of forecasts used by business organizations are
   a. strategic, tactical, and operational
   b. economic, technological, and demand
   c. causal, time-series, and seasonal
   d. exponential smoothing, Delphi, and regression
   e. departmental, organizational, and territorial

   b (Types of forecasts, moderate)

38. Which of the following is **not** a step in the forecasting process?
   a. determine the purpose
   b. eliminate any assumptions
   c. establish a time horizon
   d. select a forecasting model
   e. implement the results

   b (The strategic importance of forecasting, moderate)

39. The two general approaches to forecasting are
   a. mathematical and statistical
   b. qualitative and quantitative
   c. judgmental and qualitative
   d. historical and associative
   e. judgmental and associative

   b (Forecasting approaches, easy)

40. Which of the following is **not** a type of qualitative forecasting?
   a. executive opinions
   b. sales force composites
   c. consumer surveys
   d. the Delphi method
   e. time series analysis

   e (Forecasting approaches, moderate)

41. Which of the following would be considered a possible disadvantage to using executive opinions to develop a forecast?
   a. difficult to interpret the results
   b. diffuses responsibility for the forecast
   c. often requires extensive use of computers
   d. brings together knowledge of top managers
   e. forecasters are sometimes overly influenced by recent events

   e (Forecasting approaches, moderate)

42. The forecasting model that pools the opinions of a group of experts or managers is known as the
    a. sales force composition model
    b. multiple regression
    c. consumer market survey model
    d. jury of executive opinion model
    e. management coefficients model
    d (Forecasting approaches, moderate)

43. Which of the following would be an advantage when using a sales force composite to develop a demand forecast?
    a. The sales staff is least affected by changing customer needs.
    b. The sales force can easily distinguish between customer desires and probable actions.
    c. The sales staff is often aware of customers' future plans.
    d. Salespeople are least likely to be influenced by recent events.
    e. Salespeople are least likely to be biased by sales quotas.
    c (Forecasting approaches, moderate)

44. Which of the following uses three types of participants: decision makers, staff, and respondents?
    a. executive opinions
    b. sales force composites
    c. consumer surveys
    d. the Delphi method
    e. time series analysis
    d (Forecasting approaches, moderate)

45. Which of the following statements about time series forecasting is **true**?
    a. It is based on the assumption that future demand will be the same as past demand.
    b. It makes extensive use of the data collected in the qualitative approach.
    c. Because it accounts for trends, cycles, and seasonal patterns, it is more powerful than causal forecasting.
    d. The analysis of past demand helps predict future demand.
    e. All of the above are true.
    d (Time-series forecasting, moderate)

46. Which of the following techniques uses variables such as price and promotional expenditures, which are related to product demand, to predict demand?
    a. exponential smoothing
    b. weighted moving average
    c. simple moving average
    d. associative models
    e. time series
    d (Forecasting methods, moderate)

47. Time series data may exhibit which of the following behaviors?
   a. random variations
   b. seasonality
   c. cycles
   d. trend
   e. all of the above
   e (Time-series forecasting, moderate)

48. Which of the following is **not** present in a time series?
   a. seasonality
   b. trend
   c. operational variations
   d. cycles
   e. random variations
   c (Time-series forecasting, moderate)

49. The fundamental difference between cycles and seasonality is
   a. the duration of the repeating patterns
   b. the magnitude of the variation
   c. the ability to attribute the pattern to a cause
   d. all of the above
   e. none of the above
   a (Time-series forecasting, moderate)

50. Gradual, long-term movement in time series data is called
   a. seasonal variation
   b. cycles
   c. exponential variation
   d. a trend
   e. random variation
   d (Time-series forecasting, moderate)

51. Which of the following is **not** true about time series decomposition?
   a. Trend and seasonal patterns are sought.
   b. Cycles and random fluctuations are identified.
   c. There is the assumption that future values can be directly predicted from past values of the same variable.
   d. Annual seasonal fluctuations are ignored.
   e. All of the above are true.
   d (Time-series forecasting, moderate)

52. In time series, which of the following cannot be predicted?
   a. random fluctuations
   b. large increases in demand
   c. technological trends
   d. seasonal fluctuations
   e. large decreases in demand
   a (Time-series forecasting, moderate)

53. Which time series model below assumes that demand in the next period will be equal to the most recent period's demand?
    a. naive approach
    b. moving average approach
    c. weighted moving average approach
    d. exponential smoothing approach
    e. regression analysis
    a (Time-series forecasting, easy)

54. Which of the following is **not** a characteristic of simple moving averages?
    a. smoothes random variations in the data
    b. weights each historical value equally
    c. lags changes in the data
    d. has minimal data storage requirements
    e. smoothes real variations in the data
    d (Time-series forecasting, moderate)

55. What is the approximate forecast for May using a four-month moving average?

	Nov.	Dec.	Jan.	Feb.	Mar.	April
	39	36	40	38	48	46

    a. 38
    b. 41
    c. 42
    d. 43
    e. 46
    d (Time-series forecasting, moderate)

56. A six-month moving average forecast is better than a three-month moving average forecast if
    a. demand is rather stable
    b. demand has been changing due to recent promotional efforts
    c. demand follows a downward trend
    d. demand follows a seasonal pattern that repeats itself twice a year
    e. demand follows an upward trend
    a (Time-series forecasting, moderate)

57. Which of the following statements comparing the weighted moving average technique and exponential smoothing is **true**?
    a. Exponential smoothing is more easily used in combination with the Delphi method.
    b. Exponential smoothing typically requires relatively less record-keeping of past data.
    c. More emphasis can be placed on recent values using the weighted moving average.
    d. Exponential smoothing is considerably more difficult to implement on a computer.
    e. Exponential smoothing allows one to develop forecasts for multiple periods, whereas weighted moving averages do not.
    b (Time-series forecasting, moderate)

58. Which time series model uses past forecasts and past demand data to generate a new forecast?
   a. naive
   b. moving average
   c. weighted moving average
   d. exponential smoothing
   e. regression analysis
   d (Time-series forecasting, moderate)

59. Increasing the number of periods in a moving average will accomplish greater smoothing, but at the expense of
   a. manager understanding
   b. accuracy
   c. responsiveness to changes
   d. stability
   e. all of the above are diminished when the number of periods increases
   c (Time-series forecasting, moderate)

60. Which is **not** a characteristic of exponential smoothing?
   a. smoothes random variations in the data
   b. weights each historical value equally
   c. easily altered weighting scheme
   d. has minimal data storage requirements
   e. smoothes real variations in the data
   b (Time-series forecasting, moderate)

61. Given an actual demand of 103, a previous forecast value of 97, and an alpha of .4, the exponential smoothing forecast for the next period would be
   a. 94.6
   b. 97.4
   c. 99.4
   d. 100.0
   e. 103.0
   c (Time-series forecasting, moderate)

62. A forecast based on the previous forecast plus a percentage of the forecast error is a(n)
   a. naive forecast
   b. moving average forecast
   c. weighted moving average forecast
   d. exponentially smoothed forecast
   e. qualitative forecast
   d (Time-series forecasting, moderate)

63. Given an actual demand of 64, a previous forecast of 59, and an α of .3, what would the forecast for the next period be using simple exponential smoothing?
   a. 36.9
   b. 57.5
   c. 60.5
   d. 62.5
   e. 65.5
   c (Time-series forecasting, moderate)

64. Which of the following smoothing constants would make an exponential smoothing forecast equivalent to a naive forecast?
   a. 0
   b. 1 divided by the number of periods
   c. 0.5
   d. 1.0
   e. cannot be determined
   d (Time-series forecasting, moderate)

65. Which of the following values of alpha would cause exponential smoothing to respond the most quickly to forecast errors?
   a. 0.0
   b. 0.1
   c. 0.20
   d. 0.5
   e. cannot be determined
   d (Time-series forecasting, moderate)

66. Given forecast errors of -1, 4, 8, and -3, what is the mean absolute deviation?
   a. 2
   b. 3
   c. 4
   d. 8
   e. 16
   d (Time-series forecasting, moderate)

67. A forecasting method has produced the following over the past five months. What is the mean absolute deviation?

Actual	Forecast	Error	|Error|
10	11	-1	1
8	10	-2	2
9	8	1	1
6	6	0	0
7	8	-1	1

    a. -0.2
    b. -1
    c. 1
    d. 1.25
    e. 8.6
    c (Time-series forecasting, moderate)

68. The primary purpose of the mean absolute deviation (MAD) in forecasting is to
    a. estimate the trend line
    b. eliminate forecast errors
    c. measure forecast accuracy
    d. seasonally adjust the forecast
    e. all of the above
    c (Time-series forecasting, moderate)

69. In trend-adjusted exponential smoothing, the forecast including trend (FIT) consists of
    a. an exponentially smoothed forecast and a smoothed trend factor
    b. an exponentially smoothed forecast and an estimated trend value
    c. the old forecast adjusted by a trend factor
    d. the old forecast and a smoothed trend factor
    e. a moving average and a trend factor
    a (Time-series forecasting, moderate)

70. Which of the following is **true** regarding the two smoothing constants of the Forecast Including Trend (FIT) model?
    a. They are called alpha and beta, Producer's Risk and Consumer's Risk.
    b. Their values are determined independently.
    c. Alpha is always smaller than beta.
    d. All of the above are true.
    e. None of the above are true.
    b (Time-series forecasting, moderate)

71. For a given product demand, the time series trend equation is $25.3 + 2.1 X$. What is your forecast of demand for period 7?
    a. 23.2
    b. 25.3
    c. 27.4
    d. 40
    e. cannot be determined
    d (Time-series forecasting, moderate)

72. The degree or strength of a linear relationship is shown by the
    a. alpha
    b. correlation coefficient
    c. mean
    d. mean absolute deviation
    e. RSFE
    b (Associative forecasting methods: regression and correlation analysis, moderate)

73. If two variables were perfectly correlated, the correlation coefficient r would equal
    a. 0
    b. less than 1
    c. exactly 1
    d. -1 or +1
    e. greater than 1
    d (Associative forecasting methods: regression and correlation analysis, moderate)

74. The percent of variation in the dependent variable that is explained by the regression equation is measured by the
    a. mean absolute deviation
    b. coefficient of determination
    c. slope
    d. correlation coefficient
    e. intercept
    b (Associative forecasting methods: regression and correlation analysis, moderate)

75. The tracking signal is
    a. the running sum of forecast errors (RSFE)
    b. the mean absolute deviation (MAD)
    c. the ratio RSFE/MAD
    d. the standard error of the estimate
    e. the mean absolute percentage error (MAPE)
    c (Monitoring and controlling forecasts, moderate)

FILL-IN-THE-BLANK

76. _____ is the art and science of predicting future events.
    Forecasting (What is forecasting? easy)

77. _____ forecasts address the business cycle by predicting inflation rates, money supplies, housing starts, and other planning indicators.
Economic (Types of forecasts, moderate)

78. _____ forecasts are concerned with rates of technological progress, which can result in the birth of exciting new products, requiring new plants and equipment.
Technological (Types of forecasts, moderate)

79. _____ forecasts are projections of demand for a company's products or services.
Demand (Types of forecasts, moderate)

80. _____ forecasts employ one or more mathematical models that rely on historical data and/or causal variables to forecast demand.
Quantitative (Forecasting approaches, moderate)

81. _____ forecasts incorporate such factors as the decision maker's intuition, emotions, personal experiences, and value system.
Qualitative (Forecasting approaches, moderate)

82. _____ is a forecasting technique that takes the opinions of a small group of high-level managers and results in a group estimate of demand.
Jury of executive opinion (Forecasting approaches, moderate)

83. _____ is a forecasting technique based upon salespersons' estimates of expected sales.
Sales force composite (Forecasting approaches, moderate)

84. _____ is a forecasting method that solicits input from customers or potential customers regarding future purchasing plans.
Consumer market survey (Forecasting approaches, moderate)

85. _____ forecasts use a series of past data points to make a forecast.
Time-series (Forecasting approaches, moderate)

86. The _____ approach to forecasting assumes that demand in the next period is equal to demand in the most recent period.
naive (Forecasting approaches, moderate)

87. A _____ forecast uses an average of the most recent periods of data to forecast the next period.
moving average (Forecasting approaches, moderate)

88. The _____ is a weighting factor used in exponential smoothing.
smoothing constant (Forecasting approaches, moderate)

89. _____ is a measure of overall forecast error for a model.
MAD, Mean Absolute Deviation (Forecasting approaches, moderate)

90. _____ is a time-series forecasting method that fits a trend line to a series of historical data points and then projects the line into the future for forecasts.

Trend projections (Forecasting approaches, moderate)

91. The _____ measures the strength of the relationship between two variables.

coefficient of correlation (Associative forecasting methods: regression and correlation analysis, moderate)

92. _____ measure how well the forecast is predicting actual values.

Tracking signals (Monitoring and controlling forecasts, moderate)

93. _____ forecasting tries a variety of computer models and selects the best one for a particular application.

Focus (Monitoring and controlling forecasts, moderate)

SHORT ANSWER

94. A skeptical manager asks what short-range forecasts can be used for. Give her three possible uses/purposes.

Any three of: planning purchasing, job scheduling, work force levels, job assignments, production levels. (What is forecasting? moderate)

95. List the three forecasting time horizons. State an approximate duration for each.

Short-range (under 3 months), medium-range (3 to 18 months), and long-range (over 18 months). (What is forecasting? easy)

96. A skeptical manager asks what medium-range forecasts can be used for. Give her three possible uses/purposes.

Any three of: sales planning, production planning and budgeting, cash budgeting, analyzing various operating plans. (What is forecasting? moderate)

97. A skeptical manager asks what long-range forecasts can be used for. Give her three possible uses/purposes.

Any three of: planning new products, capital expenditures, facility location or expansion, research and development. (What is forecasting? moderate)

98. Identify and briefly describe the three major types of forecasts.

The three types are economic, technological, and demand; economic refers to macroeconomic, growth and financial variables; technological refers to forecasting amount of technological advance, or futurism; demand refers to product demand. (Types of forecasts, moderate)

99. List the seven steps involved in forecasting.
    1. determine the use of the forecast
    2. select the items that are to be forecast
    3. determine the time horizon of the forecast
    4. select the forecasting model(s)
    5. gather the data needed to make the forecast
    6. make the forecast
    7. validate the forecasting mode and implement the results.
    (Seven steps in the forecasting process, moderate)

100. Identify and briefly describe the two general forecasting approaches.
    Approaches are qualitative and quantitative. Qualitative is relatively subjective; quantitative uses numeric models. (Forecasting approaches, moderate)

101. List the qualitative forecasting methods.
    Jury of executive opinion, sales force composite, Delphi method, and consumer market surveys. (Forecasting approaches, moderate)

102. List the four quantitative forecasting methods.
    Moving averages, exponential smoothing, trend projection/ linear regression, and causal model. (Forecasting approaches, moderate)

103. List the time series models.
    Naive, moving averages, exponential smoothing, and trend projection. (Time-series forecasting, moderate)

104. What is the primary difference between a time series model and a causal model?
    A time series model predicts on the basis of the assumption that the future is a function of the past, whereas a causal model incorporates into the model the variables or factors that might influence the quantity being forecast. (Time-series forecasting, moderate)

105. Define time series.
    A sequence of evenly spaced data points with the four components of trend, seasonality, cyclical, and random variation. (Time-series forecasting, moderate)

106. List the four components of a time series.
    Trend, seasonality, cycles, and random variation. (Time-series forecasting, moderate)

107. Compare seasonal effects and cyclical effects.
    A cycle is longer (typically several years) than a season (typically days, weeks, months, or quarters). A cycle has variable duration, while a season has fixed duration and regular repetition. (Time-series forecasting, moderate)

108. Distinguish between a **moving average** model and an **exponential smoothing** model.
    Exponential smoothing is a weighted moving average model wherein previous values are weighted in a specific manner--in particular, <u>all</u> previous values are weighted with a set of weights which decline exponentially. (Time-series forecasting, moderate)

109. What methods are used to determine the accuracy of any given forecasting method? Specifically, how would you determine whether time series regression or exponential smoothing is better in a specific application?
MAD and MSE are common measures of forecast accuracy. To find the more accurate forecasting model, forecast with each tool for several periods where the demand outcome is known, and calculate MSE and/or MAD for each. The smaller error indicates the better forecast. (Time-series forecasting, difficult)

110. Explain why such forecasting devices as Moving Averages, Weighted Moving Averages, and Exponential Smoothing are not well suited for data series that have trends.
There is no mechanism for growth in these models; they are built exclusively from historical demand values. Such methods will always lag trends. (Time-series forecasting, moderate)

111. A firm is considering the use of several competing forecasting techniques. They are all judged appropriate techniques for the problem at hand. It is your task to determine the forecast accuracy of each of the techniques, and then to recommend one technique. How would you go about the process of determining which of the techniques was the most accurate?
MAD and MSE are common measures of forecast accuracy. To find the more accurate forecasting model, forecast with each tool for several periods where the demand outcome is known, and calculate MSE and/or MAD for each. The smaller error indicates the better forecast. (Time-series forecasting, moderate)

112. Explain the role of regression models (time series and otherwise) in forecasting. That is, how is trend projection able to forecast? How is causal regression able to forecast? You may wish to construct a simple example.
The trend projection equation has a slope that is the increase in demand per period. To forecast the demand for period t, perform the calculation a + bt. (Time-series forecasting, difficult)

113. Explain the value of seasonal indexes in forecasting. How are seasonal patterns different from cyclical patterns?
Seasonal patterns are of fixed duration and repeat regularly. Cycles vary in length and regularity. Seasonal indexes allow "generic" forecasts to be made specific to the month, week, etc., of the application. (Time-series forecasting, moderate)

114. Distinguish a dependent variable from an independent variable.
The independent variable causes some behavior in the dependent variable; the dependent variable shows the effect of changes in the independent variable. (Associative forecasting methods: regression and correlation, moderate)

115. Explain, in your own words, the meaning of the correlation coefficient. Discuss the meaning of a negative value of the correlation coefficient.
The correlation coefficient measures the degree to which the independent and dependent variables move together. A negative value would mean that as X increases, Y tends to fall. The variables move together, but move in opposite directions. (Associative forecasting methods: regression and correlation, moderate)

116. Explain, in your own words, the meaning of the coefficient of determination.
The coefficient of determination measures the amount (percent) of total variation in the data that is explained by the model. (Associative forecasting methods: regression and correlation, moderate)

117. Explain the purpose of a **tracking signal**.
Monitor forecasts to ensure they are performing well. (Monitoring and controlling forecasts, moderate)

118. In your own words, explain **adaptive forecasting**.
Adaptive forecasting refers to computer monitoring of tracking signals and self-adjustment if a signal passes its preset limit. (Monitoring and controlling forecasts, moderate)

Problems

119. What is the forecast for May based on a weighted moving average applied to the following past demand data and using the weights: 4, 3, 2 (last weight is for most recent data)?

Nov.	Dec.	Jan.	Feb.	Mar.	April
37	36	40	42	47	43

44.1 (Time-series forecasting, easy)

120. Weekly sales of ten-grain bread at the local Whole Foods Market are in the table below. Based on this data, forecast week 9 using a three-week moving average.

Week	Sales
1	415
2	389
3	420
4	382
5	410
6	432
7	385
8	408

408.3 (Time-series forecasting, easy)

54

121. Weekly sales of copy paper at Cubicle Suppliers are in the table below. Forecast week 8 with a three-period moving average and with a four-period moving average. Compute MAD for each forecast. Which model is more accurate?

Week	Sales (cases)
1	17
2	22
3	27
4	32
5	19
6	18
7	22

The forecast with 3ma is 19.7; with 4ma the forecast is 22.8 The four-week moving average is more accurate.

Week	Sales (cases)	3MA	|error|	4MA	|error|
1	17				
2	22				
3	27				
4	32	22	10		
5	19	27	8	24.5	5.5
6	18	26	8	25	7
7	22	23	1	24	2
8		19.7		22.8	
		MAD =	6.75		4.8

(Time-series forecasting, moderate)

122. Two weeks ago, the actual demand for vegetarian sausage at Healthy R Us was 30, and the forecast was 35. Last week, demand was 40. Using exponential smoothing with ‡ = 0.3, what is this week's forecast (rounded to the first decimal point)?
35.5 (Time-series forecasting, easy)

123. A management analyst is using exponential smoothing to predict merchandise returns at an upscale branch of a department store chain. Given an actual number of returns of 148 items in the most recent period completed, a forecast of 172 items for that period, and a smoothing constant of 0.4, what is the forecast for the next period? How would the forecast be changed if the smoothing constant were 0.8? Explain the difference in terms of alpha and responsiveness.
162.4; 152.8 (Time-series forecasting, easy)

124. Given the following data, calculate the three-year moving averages for years 4 through 10.

Year	Demand
1	71
2	94
3	57
4	92
5	133
6	87
7	119
8	127
9	96

Year	Demand	3ma
1	71	
2	94	
3	57	
4	92	74
5	133	81
6	87	94
7	119	104
8	127	113
9	96	111
10		114

(Time-series forecasting, moderate)

125. Use exponential smoothing with $\alpha = 0.2$ to calculate smoothed averages and a forecast for period 7 from the data below. Assume the forecast for the initial period is 7.

Period	Demand
1	11
2	9
3	8
4	9
5	13
6	8

Period	Demand	Forecast	Average
1	11	7	7.8
2	9	7.8	8.04
3	8	8.04	8.03
4	9	8.03	8.23
5	13	8.23	9.18
6	8	9.18	8.94
7		8.94	

(Time-series forecasting, moderate)

126. The following trend projection is used to predict quarterly demand: $Y = 350 - 2.5t$, where $t = 1$ in the first quarter of 1998. Seasonal (quarterly) relatives are Quarter 1 = 1.5; Quarter 2 = 0.8; Quarter 3 = 1.1; and Quarter 4 = 0.6. What is the seasonally adjusted forecast for the four quarters of 2000?

Period	Projection	Adjusted
9	327.5	491.25
10	325	260
11	322.5	354.75
12	320	192

(Time-series forecasting, moderate)

127. Sales of music stands at the local music store over the past ten days are shown in the table below. Forecast demand, including period 10 using exponential smoothing with an alpha of .5 (initial forecast = 30). Compute the MAD. Compute the tracking signal. What do you recommend for this forecasting process?

Period	Demand
1	13
2	21
3	28
4	37
5	25
6	29
7	36
8	22
9	25
10	28

Period	Demand	Forecast	Average	RSFE	|error|
1	13	30	21.50		
2	21	21.5	21.25	-0.50	0.50
3	28	21.25	24.63	6.75	6.75
4	37	24.63	30.81	12.38	12.38
5	25	30.81	27.91	-5.81	5.81
6	29	27.91	28.45	1.09	1.09
7	36	28.45	32.23	7.55	7.55
8	22	32.23	27.11	-10.23	10.23
9	25	27.11	26.06	-2.11	2.11
10	28	26.06	27.03	1.94	1.94
			RSFE	11.06	5.4 MAD
			Tracking	2.05	

(Time-series forecasting, moderate)

128. Use exponential smoothing with trend adjustment to forecast deliveries for period 10. Let alpha = 0.3, beta = 0.2; let the initial trend value be 5 and the initial forecast be 200.

Period	Deliveries
1	200
2	214
3	211
4	228
5	235
6	222
7	248
8	241
9	253
10	267

alpha =		0.3	beta =	0.2	
		Forecast	Actual	Trend	FIT
Initial		200	200	5	
	2	200	214	4	204
	3	204.2	211	4.039999	208.24
	4	206.24	228	3.640001	209.88
	5	212.768	235	4.217601	216.9856
	6	219.4376	222	4.708001	224.1456
	7	220.2063	248	3.920146	224.1265
	8	228.5444	241	4.803737	233.3482
	9	232.2811	253	4.590322	236.8714
	10	238.4968	267	4.915391	243.4122

(Time-series forecasting, moderate)

129. A restaurant uses a multiple regression model to schedule manpower requirements. The model used is $Y = 12 + 0.1*T + 0.2*D$. where Y is number of employees needed, T is time (measured in days from the present, which is a Monday), and D is customer demand. These forecasts need to be seasonalized because each day of the week has its own demand pattern. The seasonal relatives for each day of the week are Monday: 0.903; Tuesday, 0.791; Wednesday, 0.927; Thursday, 1.033; Friday, 1.422; Saturday, 1.478; and Sunday 0.445. Average daily demand is 94 patrons. What is the deseasonalized forecast manpower requirement for day 100?

If Day 1 is a Monday, then day 100 is a Wednesday. The regression model calculates manpower requirements at 12 + 0.1*100 + 0.2 * 94 = 40.8. This value must be adjusted by multiplying by the Wednesday relative of 0.927. The seasonalized result is 37.8. (Associative forecasting methods: regression and correlation, moderate)

(Associative forecasting methods: regression and correlation, moderate)

130. Favors Distribution Company purchases small imported trinkets in bulk, packages them, and sells them to retail stores. They are conducting an inventory control study of all their items. The following data are for one such item, which is not seasonal.
    a. Use trend projection to estimate the relationship between time and sales (state the equation).
    b. Calculate forecasts for the first four months of the next year.

	1	2	3	4	5	6	7	8	9	10	11	12
Month	Jan	Feb	Mar	Apr	May	Jun	Jul	Aug	Sep	Oct	Nov	Dec
Sales	51	55	54	57	50	68	66	59	67	69	75	73

The trend projection equation is Y = 48.32 + 2.105 T. The next four months are forecast to be 75.68, 77.79, 79.89, and 82.00. (Time-series forecasting, moderate)

131. A local restaurant bases its manpower scheduling on the anticipated customer demand. Customer demand shows little trend, but shows substantial variability among the days of the week. The restaurant therefore wants to build a forecasting system that will enable it to adequately predict the number of customers for any given day in the near future. The restaurant has collected data for the past four weeks, as shown in the data below. Calculate the seasonal (daily) indexes for the restaurant.

Mon., 9/9	84	Mon., 9/16	82	Mon., 9/23	93	Mon., 9/30	80
Tue., 9/10	82	Tue., 9/17	71	Tue., 9/24	77	Tue., 10/1	67
Wed., 9/11	78	Wed., 9/18	89	Wed., 9/25	83	Wed., 10/2	98
Thu., 9/12	95	Thu., 9/19	94	Thu., 9/26	103	Thu., 10/3	96
Fri., 9/13	130	Fri., 9/20	144	Fri., 9/27	135	Fri., 10/4	125
Sat., 9/14	144	Sat., 9/21	135	Sat., 9/28	140	Sat., 10/5	136
Sun., 9/15	42	Sun., 9/22	48	Sun., 9/29	37	Sun., 10/6	40

Day of week	Day average	Day relative
Monday	84.75	0.903
Tuesday	74.25	0.791
Wednesday	87.00	0.927
Thursday	97.00	1.033
Friday	133.50	1.422
Saturday	138.75	1.478
Sunday	41.75	0.445
	93.86	

(Time-series forecasting, moderate)

132. A firm has modeled its experience with industrial accidents and found that the number of accidents per year (Y) is related to the number of employees (X) by the regression equation $Y = -1.3 + 0.19*X$. R-Square is 0.68; the standard error of the estimate is 2.0. The regression is based on 20 annual observations. The firm intends to employ 86 workers next year. How many accidents do you project? How much confidence do you have in that forecast?

$Y = 1.3 + 0.19 * 86 = 17.6$ accidents. This is not a time series, so next year = year 21 is of no relevance. Confidence stems in part from the coefficient of determination; the model explains 68 percent of the variation in number of accidents, which seems respectable. Confidence also follows from the standard error, which appears small compared to the number of accidents forecast.

(Associative forecasting methods: regression and correlation, moderate)

133. Marie Bain is the production manager at a company that manufactures hot water heaters. Marie needs a demand forecast for the next few years to help decide whether to add new production capacity. The company's sales history (in thousands of units) is shown in the table below. Use exponential smoothing with trend adjustment, to forecast demand for period 6. The initial forecast for period 1 was 10 units; the initial estimate of trend was 0. The smoothing constants are $\alpha = .4$ and $\beta \cdot = .3$

Period	Actual
1	12
2	15
3	16
4	16
5	18
6	20

Period	Forecast	Actual	Trend	FIT
1	10	12	0	
2	12	15	0.6	12.6
3	13.28	16	0.87	14.15
4	14.52	16	1.02	15.54
5	16.03	18	1.22	17.25
6	17.80	20	1.44	19.24

(Time-series forecasting, moderate)

134. The quarterly sales for specific educational software over the past three years are given in the following table. Compute the four seasonal factors.

	YEAR 1	YEAR 2	YEAR 3
Quarter 1	1690	1800	1850
Quarter 2	940	900	1100
Quarter 3	2625	2900	2930
Quarter 4	2500	2360	2615

	Avg.	Relative
Quarter 1	1780	0.882
Quarter 2	980	0.486
Quarter 3	2818.33	1.397
Quarter 4	2491.66	1.235
Grand Average	2017.5	

(Time-series forecasting, moderate)

135. Arnold Tofu owns and operates a chain of 12 vegetable protein "hamburger" restaurants in northern Louisiana. Sales figures and profits for the stores are in the table below. Sales are given in millions of dollars; profits are in hundred of thousands of dollars. Calculate a regression line for the data. What is your forecast of profit for a store with sales of $24 million? $30 million?

Store	Sales	Profits	Store	Sales	Profits
1	7	15	7	16	24
2	2	10	8	12	20
3	6	13	9	14	27
4	4	15	10	20	44
5	14	25	11	15	34
6	15	27	12	7	17

Students must recognize that sales is the independent variable and profits is dependent. Store number is not a variable, and the problem is not a time series. The regression equation is Y = 5.0601 + 1.593 X (Y = profit, X = sales). A store with $24 sales is estimated to profit $43.3; $30 in sales should yield $52.85 in profit.
(Associative forecasting methods: regression and correlation, moderate)

136. Sales of vegetable dehydrators at a discount department store over the past year are shown below. Management prepared a forecast using a combination of exponential smoothing and manager's judgment for the upcoming four months (March, April, May, and June of 2000).
a. Compute MAD for the manager's technique
b. Do the manager's results outperform (have smaller MAD than) a naive forecast?
c. Which forecast do you recommend, based on lower forecast error?

Month	1999-2000 Unit Sales	Management's forecast
Jul.	100	
Aug.	93	
Sept.	96	
Oct.	110	
Nov.	124	
Dec.	119	
Jan.	92	
Feb.	83	
Mar.	101	120
Apr.	96	114
May	89	110
Jun.	108	108

Students must determine the naive forecast for the four months. The naive forecast for March is the February actual of 83, etc. MAD for the manager's technique is 14.5, while MAD for the naive forecast is only 12.25

	Actual	Forecast	Error	Naive	error
Mar.	101	120	19	83	18
Apr.	96	114	18	101	5
May	89	110	21	96	7
Jun.	108	108	0	89	19
		MAD=	14.5		12.25

(Monitoring and controlling forecasts, moderate)

CHAPTER 5: DESIGN OF GOODS AND SERVICES

TRUE/FALSE

1. One example of product strategy is customization.
    True (Introduction, easy)

2. The goal of the product decision is to develop and implement a product strategy that meets the needs of the marketplace and creates a competitive advantage.
    True (Introduction, moderate)

3. One factor influencing market opportunities for new products is political/legal change.
    True (Goods and services selection, easy)

4. Once a product is successful in the marketplace, its design should not be changed.
    False (Goods and services selection, moderate)

5. Most new product ideas become successfully marketed products.
    False (Goods and services selection, moderate)

6. The four phases of the product life cycle are introduction, growth, maturity, and decline.
    True (Goods and services selection, moderate)

7. In the maturity stage of the product life cycle, operations managers will be concerned with keeping sufficient capacity available for the product.
    False (Goods and services selection, moderate)

8. One environmentally friendly approach to product design is to use lighter components.
    True (Issues for product design, moderate)

9. The traditional product design approach for product development uses development teams.
    False (Goods and services selection, moderate)

10. Representatives from the OM area typically dominate product development teams.
    False (Product development, moderate)

11. Robust design is a method that ensures that small variation in production or assembly does not adversely affect the product.
    True (Issues for product design, moderate)

12. The use of product development teams is also called concurrent engineering.
    True (Goods and services selection, moderate)

13. Faster product development is one source of competitive edge.
    True (Goods and services selection, moderate)

14. Modular design exists only in tangible products; it makes no sense in services.
    False (Issues for product design, moderate)

15. A disadvantage of CAD is that it increases the cost of the product due to the expensive technology.
False (Issues for product design, moderate)

16. Value engineering typically increases costs.
False (Goods and services selection, moderate)

17. An engineering change notice lists the components, their descriptions, and the quantity of each required to make one unit of a product.
False (Defining the product and Document for products, moderate)

18. The "Make-or-Buy" decision distinguishes between what an organization chooses to produce and what it chooses to purchase from suppliers.
True (Defining the product, moderate)

19. One of the benefits of using Group Technology is improved design.
True (Defining the product, moderate)

20. Group technology enables the grouping of parts into families based on similar processing requirements.
True (Defining the product, moderate)

21. The customer may participate in the design and in delivery of services.
True (Service design, moderate)

22. Quality Function Deployment refers to first, determining what will satisfy the customer, and second, translating those customer desires into a target design.
True (Product development, moderate)

23. An assembly drawing lists the operations necessary to produce the component.
False (Documents for production, moderate)

24. The moment-of-truth is the crucial moment between the service provider and the customer that exemplifies, enhances, or detracts from the customer's expectation.
True (Service design, moderate)

25. Decision trees are only useful for product decisions.
False (Application of decision trees to product design, moderate)

26. The payoff is the objective of the decision tree.
False (Application of decision trees to product design, moderate)

27. QFD (Quality Function Deployment) is used to help determine what will satisfy the customer.
True (Product development, moderate)

28. Ideas are constantly reviewed during a brainstorming session.
False (Product development, moderate)

29. The House of Quality is a graphic technique for defining the relationship between customer desires and product.
True (Product development, moderate)

30. Concurrent engineering uses teams for design and engineering activities.
True (Product development, moderate)

MULTIPLE CHOICE

31. The three major subdivisions of the product decision are
   a. goods, services, and hybrids
   b. strategy, tactics, and operations
   c. selection, definition, and design
   d. cost, differentiation, and speed of response
   e. legislative, judicial, and executive
   c (Goods and services selection, moderate)

32. Operations managers must be able to anticipate changes in which of the following?
   a. product opportunities
   b. the products themselves
   c. product volume
   d. product mix
   e. all of the above
   e (Goods and services selection, moderate)

33. Which of the following are likely to influence market opportunities in the auto industry?
   a. sustained economic growth
   b. changing demographics
   c. the development of stronger materials
   d. suppliers
   e. all of the above may influence market opportunities
   e (Goods and services selection, moderate)

34. In which stage of the product life cycle should product strategy focus on process modifications?
   a. introduction
   b. growth
   c. maturity
   d. decline
   e. none of the above
   a (Goods and services selection, moderate)

35. Which of the following would likely cause a change in market opportunities based upon levels of income and wealth?
   a. economic change
   b. technological change
   c. political change
   d. sociological and demographic change
   e. legal change
   a (Goods and services selection, moderate)

36. In which stage of the product life cycle should product strategy focus on forecasting capacity requirements?
   a. introduction
   b. growth
   c. maturity
   d. decline
   e. none of the above
   b (Goods and services selection, moderate)

37. In which stage of the product life cycle should product strategy focus on improved cost control?
   a. introduction
   b. growth
   c. maturity
   d. decline
   e. none of the above
   c (Goods and services selection, moderate)

38. A product's life cycle is divided into four stages, which are
   a. introduction, growth, maturity, and decline
   b. introduction, growth, saturation, and maturity
   c. introduction, growth, stability, and decline
   d. introduction, maturity, saturation, and decline
   e. none of the above
   a (Goods and services selection, easy)

39. Among the elements that make products more friendly to the environment are
   a. less harmful ingredients
   b. more recycled materials
   c. using less energy
   d. ability to recycle product
   e. all of the above
   e (Issues for product design, moderate)

40. Which of the following is **true** regarding value engineering?
   a. Value engineering is oriented toward improvement of design.
   b. Value engineering occurs only after the product is selected and designed.
   c. Value engineering is the same as value analysis.
   d. Value engineering occurs during production when it is clear the product is a success.
   e. Value analysis can save substantial amounts of product cost, but quality suffers.
   a (Product development, moderate)

41. The benefits of Computer Aided Design include all of the following **except**
   a. product quality improvement
   b. shorter design time
   c. production cost reductions
   d. lesser need for interaction with the marketing and operations functions
   e. design database availability
   d (Issues for product design, moderate)

42. Value analysis takes place
    a. during the initial stages of production when something needs to be done to assure product success
    b. when the product is selected and designed
    c. when the product is first conceived
    d. during the production process when it is clear the product is a success
    e. when the product cost is very low
    d (Issues for product design, moderate)

43. Which of the following helps operations managers direct their efforts toward those items that show the greatest promise?
    a. value analysis
    b. value engineering
    c. financial analysis
    d. product-by-value analysis
    e. product cost justification
    d (Issues for product design, moderate)

44. An engineering drawing shows
    a. the dimensions, tolerances, materials, and finishes of a component
    b. the dimensions, tolerances, cost, and sales or use volume of a component
    c. the materials, finishes, machining operations, and dimensions of a component
    d. the cost, materials, tolerances, and lead-time for a component
    e. the cost, dimensions, and machining operations for a component
    a (Defining the product, moderate)

45. The dimensions, tolerances, materials, and finishes of a component are typically shown on
    a. an engineering drawing
    b. a bill of material
    c. an assembly drawing
    d. an assembly chart
    e. a route sheet
    a (Defining the product, moderate)

46. Which of the following typically shows the components, their description, and the quantity of each required to make one unit of a product?
    a. an engineering drawing
    b. a bill of material
    c. an assembly drawing
    d. an assembly chart
    e. a route sheet
    b (Defining the product, moderate)

47. Which of the following shows in schematic form how a product is assembled?
    a. an engineering drawing
    b. an assembly drawing
    c. an assembly chart
    d. a route sheet
    e. a process sheet
    b (Defining the product, moderate)

48. Which of the following does **not** result from the effective use of group technology?
    a. improved design
    b. simplified training
    c. reduced raw materials and purchases
    d. simplified production planning and control
    e. improved layout, routing, and machine loading
    b (Defining the product, moderate)

49. Which of the following is documented on a bill of materials?
    a. the tolerances for each component
    b. the cost of the product
    c. the components, their description, and the quantity of each required to make one unit of a product
    d. the existing inventory level for the product
    e. none of the above
    c (Defining the product, moderate)

50. Group technology requires that
    a. each component be identified by a coding scheme that specifies the type of processing and the parameters of the processing
    b. a specific series of engineering drawings be prepared
    c. all bill of material be prepared using the same format
    d. engineering change notices be linked to each of the bill of material and engineering notices
    e. the final products be standardized
    a (Defining the product, moderate)

51. An assembly drawing
    a. shows, in schematic form, how the product is assembled
    b. shows an exploded view of the product
    c. lists the operations, including assembly and inspection, necessary to produce the component with the material specified in the bill of material
    d. provides detailed instructions on how to perform a given task
    e. describes the dimensions and finish of each component
    b (Documents for production, moderate)

52. An assembly chart
    a. shows graphically how the product is assembled
    b. shows an exploded view of the product
    c. lists the operations, including assembly and inspection, necessary to produce the component with the material specified in the bill of material
    d. provides detailed instructions on how to perform a given task
    e. describes the dimensions and finish of each component
    a (Documents for production, moderate)

53. A route sheet provides
    a. an exploded view of the product
    b. a schematic showing how the product is assembled
    c. a sequence of operations necessary to produce the component
    d. an instruction to make a given quantity of a particular item
    e. a set of detailed instructions about how to perform a task
    c (Documents for production, moderate)

54. A process sheet is a type of
    a. assembly drawing
    b. assembly chart
    c. route sheet
    d. work order
    e. bill of materials
    c (Documents for production, moderate)

55. Which of the following documents lists the operations (including assembly and inspection) necessary to produce the component with the material specified in the bill of material?
    a. an engineering drawing
    b. an assembly drawing
    c. a route sheet
    d. an assembly chart
    e. an operations chart
    c (Documents for production, moderate)

56. Which of the following is **not** a service design technique?
    a. automation
    b. increasing customer participation
    c. customizing as late in the process as possible
    d. modularizing the product
    e. reducing customer interaction
    b (Service design, moderate)

57. The list of food items that your restaurant customers want the kitchen to prepare is an example of
    a. a route sheet
    b. an assembly chart
    c. a bill of materials
    d. a work order
    e. configuration management
    d (Documents for production, moderate)

58. The work order
   a. shows, in schematic form, how the product is assembled
   b. gives the instruction to make a given quantity of a particular item, usually to a given schedule
   c. lists the operations, including assembly and inspection, necessary to produce the component with the material specified in the bill of material
   d. provides detailed instructions on how to perform a given task
   e. is used to signal a change in work priorities
   b (Documents for production, moderate)

59. Which service design technique(s) would ordinarily **not** be appropriate for full-service restaurant meals?
   a. reduced customer interaction
   b. modularizing the product
   c. customization as late in the process as possible
   d. the moment of truth
   e. all of the above are appropriate
   a (Service design, moderate)

60. Which of the following examples involves customer participation in the design of the service?
   a. investing in a Fidelity mutual fund
   b. buying a life insurance policy
   c. providing the stockbroker with the desired distribution of the portfolio
   d. seeing a movie at the theater
   e. eating at a fast-food restaurant
   c (Service design, moderate)

61. Which of the following scenarios illustrates a moment that **exceeds** the customer's expectations?
   a. an express mail service that guarantees overnight delivery
   b. a flight attendant that responds shortly after being called
   c. a professor that contacts people in several companies to find you a job
   d. a hairdresser that cuts your hair at the right length
   e. a bank that sends you monthly account statements
   c (Service design, difficult)

62. Which of the following scenarios illustrates a moment that **meets** the customer's expectations?
   a. an express mail service that guarantees same day delivery
   b. a flight attendant that responds shortly after being called
   c. a professor that contacts people in several companies to find you a job
   d. a sales clerk that called you by your name on your second visit to the store
   e. a sales clerk at the clothing store that asked you to wait for a minute as soon as a wealthy-looking customer entered the store
   b (Service design, difficult)

63. Which of the following moments of truth exemplifies the customer's standard expectations?
    a. You had to visit more than once to reach your academic advisor.
    b. Your advisor was competent, helpful, and understanding.
    c. Your advisor failed to keep her appointment with you.
    d. Your advisor offered to work with you at your convenience.
    e. Your advisor made you wait, even though you had an appointment.
    b (Service design, difficult)

64. Which of the following product development strategies has the highest risk?
    a. alliances
    b. joint ventures
    c. acquiring the developer
    d. new internally developed products
    e. none of the above, they all are low risk strategies
    d (Time-based competition, moderate)

65. Which of the following is **not** an example of an internal product development strategy?
    a. new internally developed products
    b. alliances
    c. enhancements to existing products
    d. migrations of existing products
    e. all of the above are examples of internal product development strategy
    b (Time-based competition, moderate)

FILL-IN-THE-BLANK

66. In the _____ phase of the product life cycle, the product design has begun to stabilize.
    growth (Goods and services selection, moderate)

67. _____ lists products in descending order of the individual dollar contribution to the firm.
    Product-by-value analysis (Goods and service selection, moderate)

68. _____ is a process for determining customer requirements and translating them into attributes that each functional area can understand and act upon.
    Quality Function Deployment (QFD) (Goods and service selection, moderate)

69. The _____ is a part of the quality function deployment process that utilizes a planning matrix to relate customer "wants" to "how" the firm is going to meet those "wants."
    House of Quality (Goods and service selection, moderate)

70. A _____ is a design that can be produced to requirements even with unfavorable conditions in the production process.
    robust design (Issues for product design, moderate)

71. Products designed in easily segmented components are known as _____.
    modular designs (Issue for product design, moderate)

72. The use of a computer to interactively develop, design, and document products is called _____.
Computer-Aided Design (CAD) (Issues for product design, moderate)

73. _____ reviews successful products for improvement during the production process.
Value analysis (Issues for product design, moderate)

74. Sensitivity to a wide variety of environmental issues in production processes is referred to as _____.
green manufacturing (Issues for product design, moderate)

75. Rapidly developing products and moving them to the market is referred to as _____.
time-based competition (Issues for product design, moderate)

76. A drawing that shows the dimensions, tolerances, materials, and finishes of a component is a(n) _____.
engineering drawing (Defining the product, moderate)

77. A listing of the components, their description, and the quantity of each required to make one unit of product is the _____.
bill of materials (Defining the product, moderate)

78. An exploded view of the product is a(n) _____.
assembly drawing (Defining the product, moderate)

79. An _____ is a correction or modification of an engineering drawing or bill of materials.
engineering change notice (ECN) (Documentation for production, moderate)

80. The _____ is the crucial moment between the service provider and the customer that exemplifies, enhances, or detracts from the customer's expectations.
moment-of-truth (Service Design, moderate)

Short Answers

81. In what ways is product strategy linked to product decisions?
Investment, market share, product life cycle, and breadth of the product line. (Introduction, moderate)

82. Your text states that, to maximize the potential for success, top companies focus on only a few products. Why do you think this is so? State an example of this phenomenon. Can you state a counter-example?
Text cites Honda, Intel, and Microsoft. There are many others. Most students will offer "to take advantage of what the company does well." A counter-example might be Procter and Gamble, with its very many household products, or any conglomerate. Students might relate to make-or-buy decisions. (Introduction, moderate)

83. What is the objective of the product decision?
Develop and implement a product strategy that meets the demands of the marketplace with a competitive advantage. (Goods and services selection, moderate)

84. What are the three primary subdivisions of the product strategy?
Product selection, product definition, and product design. (Goods and services selection, moderate)

85. List the factors that influence new product opportunities.
Economic change, sociological and demographic change, technological change, political change, and other changes brought about through market practice, professional standards, suppliers, and distributors. (Goods and services selection, moderate)

86. Your text lists five factors that influence opportunities for new products. List them. Compare this list to the list of typical Critical Success Factors in making global location decisions in Chapter 3. What are the similarities? The differences? Explain.
Text list is economic change, sociological and demographic change, technological change, political/legal change, and other changes. From Chapter 3, the list is Education level, Political/Legal, Economic, Social and Cultural, and Technological. Education from one list may be included in the other list as part of demographics. The lists are quite similar, except that the "opportunities" list focuses on change, not extent or value. Both lists are probably drawn from a common list of forces that act on organizations. (Goods and services selection, difficult)

87. Your authors write, with respect to the product decision, that managers "must be able to accept risk and tolerate failure." Why is this necessary given all the powerful tools and carefully built systems that support the product decision?
The vast majority of new product ideas do not become marketable products, and most marketable products are failures. Perhaps 500 designs accompany each success. (Goods and services selection, moderate)

88. How is it possible for the stage of a product's life cycle to affect its product strategy? In particular, describe how a product in **growth** and a product in **maturity** might differ in appropriate product strategy.
There is no reason for the strategy to be static through the life cycle stages. Clearly, organizations will treat very new products differently than much older ones, in terms of support for changes, aggressiveness in pursuit of market, etc. In particular, growth is associated with stabilization of design, and with ensuring that sufficient capacity exists. Maturity is a time for high-volume operations and cost control. (Goods and services selection, moderate)

89. List four methods of product design. Which of these is generally thought to be best?
Traditional--different phases of development done in distinct departments; Champion--a manager shepherds the product through the development process; Teams--product development teams, design for manufacturability teams, value engineering teams. This last version seems best. (Product development, moderate)

90. List the stages of product development.
Ideas; firm ability to carry out idea; customer requirements; functional specifications; product specifications; design review; test market; introduction; and evaluation of success. (Product development, moderate)

91. List the benefits associated with value engineering.
Immediate cost reductions; reduced product complexity; additional standardization of components; improvement of functional aspects of the products; improved job design and job safety; improved maintainability (serviceability) of the product; and robust design. (Product development, moderate)

92. Explain the difference between value analysis and value engineering.
Value engineering is concerned with reducing cost and improving function in a <u>preproduction</u> setting; value analysis, with similar aims, takes place <u>during production</u>, when the product has shown that it will succeed. Techniques are the same. (Product development and Issues for product design, moderate)

93. List the general benefits derived from CAD/CAM.
Product quality (better adherence to standards); shorter design time; production cost reductions (from better design); database availability (for new products); and new range of capabilities (ease programming of CNC machines). (Issues for product design, moderate)

94. Explain what is meant by robust design.
The product is designed so that small variations in production or assembly do not adversely affect the product. (Issues for product design, moderate)

95. Discuss the advisability of using modular assemblies in manufacturing. (What are the advantages and disadvantages?) To what extent can these arguments be utilized in service products?
Modules are easily segmented components; they add flexibility to production and marketing; allows mix-and-match of components (customization at point of customer contact). Use of modules usually means fewer parts, less design and tooling expense. Disadvantages include using a module in a product for which a more specific component would have been better. Modules exist in services, as in fast food meals built to customer specification. (Issues for product design, difficult)

96. List three specific ways in which Computer Aided Design (CAD) benefits the design engineer.
Determine various kinds of engineering data; check interference on parts that must fit together; and efficiently analyze existing and new designs. (Issues for product design, difficult)

97. What information is contained in a bill of materials?
A bill of materials lists the components, their description, and the quantity of each required to make one unit of the product. (Defining the product, easy)

98. What information is contained in an engineering drawing?
An engineering drawing shows the dimensions, tolerances, materials, and finishes of a component. (Defining the product, easy)

99. State the benefits of implementing group technology.
Improved design; reduced raw materials and purchases; simplified production planning and control; improved routing and machine loading; reduced tooling setup time, work-in-process, and production time; and development of work cells. (Defining the product, moderate)

100. What information is contained in an assembly chart? In a process sheet?
An assembly chart shows in schematic form how a product is assembled. Along with a list of the operations necessary to produce a component, the process sheet includes specific methods of operation and labor standards. (Documentation for production, moderate)

101. List the four methods of service design that can reduce costs and enhance the product.
Customizing as late in the process as possible; modularizing the product; identifying the service parts that lend themselves to automation or reduced customer interaction; and focusing design on the moment of truth. (Service design, moderate)

102. Explain what is meant by service design by the "moment of truth."
The moment of truth is the moment that exemplifies, detracts from, or enhances the customer's expectations. (Service design, moderate)

103. Explain how decision trees can be used in the product design process.
Decision trees assist in problems that have multiple, successive decisions, as product decisions do. Decision trees are useful in problems that have discrete, probabilistic outcomes, as many product decision problems can be assumed to have. Decision trees are useful in problems involving expected monetary value. (Application of decision trees to product design, moderate)

104. Explain how the House of Quality translates customer desires into product/service attributes.
Quality Function Deployment is a rigorous method aimed at that specific result. It identifies customer wants, and relates them to product attributes and firm abilities. It orders the wants and measures the strength of the links between wants and attributes. (Product development, moderate)

105. List the steps involved in building the House of Quality?
Identify customers' wants, identify product/service attributes, relate the customers' wants to the product/service hows, conduct an evaluation of competing products, develop performance specifications for product or service hows, and assign hows to the appropriate place in the transformation process. (Product development, moderate)

106. The House of Quality approach is often a **sequence** of houses. Explain.
The first house of design characteristics is important, but does not complete the problem. Design characteristics of the first house lead to specific components of the next, to production processes of a third, and finally to a quality plan. (Product development, moderate)

CHAPTER 6: MANAGING QUALITY

TRUE/FALSE

1. Productivity usually increases at the expense of quality.
   False (Quality and strategy, moderate)

2. An improvement in quality increases costs.
   False (Quality and strategy, moderate)

3. For most, if not all organizations, quality is a tactical rather than a strategic issue.
   False (Quality and strategy, moderate)

4. The definition of quality adopted by The American Society for Quality Control is a customer-oriented definition.
   True (Defining quality, moderate)

5. Measurement is the focus of the product-based definition of quality.
   True (Defining quality, moderate)

6. Prevention costs are associated with evaluating products.
   False (Defining quality, moderate)

7. The ISO 9000 series standards say nothing about the actual quality of the product.
   True (Defining quality, moderate)

8. ISO 14000's primary focus is with environmental management standards.
   True (Defining quality, moderate)

9. TQM is important because quality influences all of the ten decisions made by operations managers.
   True (Total quality management, moderate)

10. Quality is mostly the business of the Quality Control staff, not ordinary employees.
    False (Total quality management, moderate)

11. Operations is concerned with TQM, but accounting need not be.
    False (Total quality management, moderate)

12. Generally, the employees producing the product or providing the service are not to blame for quality problems.
    True (Total quality management, moderate)

13. Kaizen is similar to TQM in that both are focused on continuous improvement.
    True (Total quality management, moderate)

14. The Japanese use the term "poka-yoke" to refer to continuous improvement.
    False (Total quality management, moderate)

15. Quality circles empower employees to improve productivity by finding solutions to work-related problems.
    True (Total quality management, moderate)

16. Benchmarks are relevant only when the companies you compare yourself with are in the same industry as your organization.
    False (Total quality management, moderate)

17. Waste reduction is central to the Just-in-Time philosophy.
    True (Total quality management, moderate)

18. Line employees need the knowledge of TQM tools; managers, more concerned with other strategic issues, do not.
    False (Total quality management, moderate)

19. The quality loss function indicates that costs related to poor quality are low as long as the product is within acceptable specification limits.
    False (Total quality management, moderate)

20. The essence of Pareto's rule is that eighty percent of the causes are responsible for twenty percent of the problems.
    False (Tools of TQM, moderate)

21. A fishbone chart helps identify the source of a problem.
    True (Tools of TQM, moderate)

22. As long as sample measurements fall within the control limits, the process is in control.
    False (Tools of TQM, moderate)

23. When and where to inspect depends upon the type of product involved and upon the processes that make it.
    False (The role of inspection, moderate)

24. Source inspection is inferior to inspection before costly operations.
    False (Tools of TQM, moderate)

25. Customer expectation is the standard against which the service is judged.
    True (TQM in services, moderate)

26. Use of "poka-yoke" should lead to use of fewer inspection points.
    True (Tools of TQM, moderate)

MULTIPLE CHOICE

27. According to the manufacturing-based definition of quality,
    a. quality is the degree of excellence at an acceptable price and the control of variability at an acceptable cost
    b. quality depends on how well the product fits patterns of consumer preferences
    c. quality is the degree to which a specific product conforms to standards
    d. even though quality cannot be defined, you know what it is
    e. quality lies in the eyes of the beholder
    c (Defining quality, moderate)

28. "Quality is defined by the customer" is
    a. an unrealistic definition of quality
    b. a manufacturing-based definition of quality
    c. a product-based definition of quality
    d. a user-based definition of quality
    e. the definition proposed by the American Society for Quality Control
    d (Defining quality, moderate)

29. ISO 9000 seeks standardization in terms of
    a. products
    b. production procedures
    c. procedures to manage quality
    d. suppliers' specifications
    e. all of the above
    c (Defining quality, moderate)

30. Which of the following is **true** about ISO 14000 certification?
    a. it is a prerequisite for ISO 9000 certification
    b. it deals with environmental management
    c. it indicates a higher level of adherence to standards than ISO 9000
    d. it is only sought by companies exporting their goods
    e. it is of little interest to European companies
    b (Defining quality, moderate)

31. Which of the following is **true** about ISO 14000 certification?
    a. it is not a prerequisite for ISO 9000 certification
    b. it deals with environmental management
    c. it offers a good systematic approach to pollution prevention
    d. one of its core elements is life-cycle assessment
    e. all of the above are true
    e (Defining quality, moderate)

32. Total Quality Management emphasizes
    a. ISO 14000 certification
    b. the responsibility of the Quality Control staff to identify and solve all quality-related problems
    c. a commitment to quality that goes beyond internal company issues to suppliers and customers
    d. a system where strong managers are the only decision makers
    e. a process where mostly statisticians get involved
    c (Total quality management, moderate)

33. A successful TQM program incorporates all of the following **except**
    a. continuous improvement
    b. employment involvement
    c. benchmarking
    d. centralized decision making authority
    e. knowledge of tools
    d (Total quality management, moderate)

34. A successful TQM program does **not** require which of the following?
    a. continuous improvement
    b. employment involvement
    c. benchmarking
    d. knowledge of tools
    e. ISO 14000 certification
    e (Total quality management, moderate)

35. The philosophy of zero defects is
    a. unrealistic
    b. prohibitively costly
    c. an ultimate goal; in practice, 1 to 2% defects is acceptable
    d. consistent with the commitment to continuous improvement
    e. the result of Deming's research
    d (Total quality management, moderate)

36. "Kaizen" is a Japanese term meaning
    a. a foolproof mechanism
    b. Just-in-Time (JIT)
    c. continuous improvement
    d. a fishbone diagram
    e. setting standards
    c (Total quality management, moderate)

37. Based on his 14 Points, Deming is a strong proponent of
    a. inspection at the end of the production process
    b. an increase in numerical quotas to boost productivity
    c. training and knowledge
    d. looking for the cheapest supplier
    e. all of the above
    c (Total quality management, moderate)

38. Quality Circles members
    a. are paid according to their contribution to quality
    b. are external consultants designed to provide training in the use of Quality tools
    c. are always machine operators
    d. are all trained to be facilitators
    e. none of the above, all of the statements are false

    e (Total quality management, moderate)

39. The process of identifying other organizations that are best at some facet of your operations and then modeling your organization after them is known as
    a. continuous improvement
    b. employee empowerment
    c. benchmarking
    d. copycatting
    e. industrial espionage

    c (Total quality management, moderate)

40. Inspection, scrap, and repair are examples of
    a. internal costs
    b. external costs
    c. costs of dissatisfaction
    d. prevention costs
    e. societal costs

    a (Defining quality, moderate)

41. A quality loss function utilizes all of the following costs **except**
    a. the cost of scrap and repair
    b. sales costs
    c. the cost of customer dissatisfaction
    d. inspection, warranty, and service costs
    e. costs to society

    b (Tools of TQM, moderate)

42. Costs of dissatisfaction, repair costs, and warranty costs are elements of cost in the
    a. Pareto Chart
    b. Taguchi Loss Function
    c. ISO 9000 Quality Cost Calculator
    d. Process Chart
    e. none of the above

    b (Total quality management, moderate)

43. All of the following costs are likely to decrease as a result of better quality **except**
    a. customer dissatisfaction costs
    b. inspection costs
    c. scrap costs
    d. warranty and service costs
    e. maintenance costs

    e (Defining quality, moderate)

44. The "four Ms" of cause-and-effect diagrams are
    a. material, methods, men, and mental attitude
    b. named after four quality experts
    c. material, management, manpower, and motivation
    d. material, machinery/equipment, manpower, and methods
    e. none of the above
    d (Tools of TQM, moderate)

45. Pareto charts are used to
    a. identify inspection points in a process
    b. organize errors, problems or defects
    c. outline production schedules
    d. show an assembly sequence
    e. all of the above
    b (Tools of TQM, moderate)

46. A service goes through several steps. The supervisor is concerned about long delays for customers of this service. In order to identify where time might be lost, which of the following tools would you suggest?
    a. Fishbone chart
    b. Pareto chart
    c. Process chart
    d. House of Quality diagram
    e. Top 40 chart
    c (Tools of TQM, moderate)

47. Pareto charts are used to
    a. identify inspection points in a process
    b. organize errors, problems or defects
    c. outline production schedules
    d. show an assembly sequence
    e. provide guidelines for quality training
    b (Tools of TQM, moderate)

48. The process improvement technique that sorts the "vital few" from the "trivial many" is
    a. Pareto analysis
    b. benchmarking
    c. brainstorming
    d. Yamaguchi analysis
    e. Taguchi analysis
    a (Tools of TQM, moderate)

49. Among the tools of TQM, the tool ordinarily used to aid in understanding the sequence of events through which a product travels is
   a. a process chart
   b. a Pareto chart
   c. a check sheet
   d. a Taguchi map
   e. a poka-yoke
   a (Tools of TQM, moderate)

50. Process charts include symbols for which processes?
   a. operation, transportation, inspection, delay, and storage
   b. methods, materials, manpower, and machinery
   c. lead, direct, control, staff, and manage
   d. cost control, market share gain, productivity increase, rework decrease, and scrap reduction
   e. none of the above
   a (Tools of TQM, moderate)

51. A process chart is used for all of the following **except**
   a. to identify the best data collection points
   b. to help translate consumers' wants into product attributes
   c. to isolate and track the origin of problems
   d. to identify the best place for process audits
   e. to identify opportunities for travel distance reduction
   b (Tools of TQM, moderate)

52. If a sample of parts is measured and the mean of the measurements is outside the control limits
   a. the process is in control, but not capable of producing within the established control limits
   b. the process is out of control and the process should be investigated for assignable variation
   c. the process is within the established control limits with only natural causes of variation
   d. the process is monitored closely to see if the next sample mean will also fall outside the control limits
   e. none of the above
   b (Tools of TQM, moderate)

53. When a sample measurement falls inside the control limits, it means that
   a. each unit manufactured is good enough to sell
   b. if there is no other pattern in the samples, the process is in control
   c. the process limits cannot be determined statistically
   d. the process output exceeds the requirements
   e. no investigation is necessary until another sample value falls outside the control limits
   b (Tools of TQM, moderate,)

54. A fishbone diagram is also known as
   a. a cause-and-effect diagram
   b. a poka-yoke diagram
   c. a Kaizen diagram
   d. a Kanban diagram
   e. a Taguchi diagram
   a (Tools of TQM, moderate)

55. A quality circle holds a brainstorming session and attempts to identify the factors responsible for flaws in a product. Which tool do you suggest they use to organize their findings?
   a. Ishikawa diagram
   b. Pareto chart
   c. process chart
   d. control charts
   e. activity chart
   a (Tools of TQM, moderate)

56. Which of the following is **true** regarding control charts?
   a. Control charts are built so that new data can be quickly compared to past performance data.
   b. Control charts graphically present data.
   c. Control charts plot data over time.
   d. Values above the upper and lower control limits indicate points out of adjustment.
   e. All of the above are true.
   e (Tools of TQM, moderate)

57. The goal of inspection is
   a. to detect a bad process immediately
   b. to add value to a product or service
   c. to correct deficiencies in products
   d. to correct system deficiencies
   e. all of the above
   a (Role of inspection, moderate)

58. Which of the following is **not** a typical inspection point?
   a. upon receipt of goods from your supplier
   b. during the production process
   c. before the product is shipped to the customer
   d. after a costly process
   e. at the supplier's plant while the supplier is producing
   d (Role of inspection, moderate)

59. A good description of "source inspection" is inspecting
   a. materials upon delivery by the supplier
   b. the goods at the production facility before they reach the customer
   c. the goods as soon as a problem occurs
   d. goods at the supplier's plant
   e. one's own work, as well as the work done at the previous work station
   e (Role of inspection, moderate)

60. "Poka-yoke" is the Japanese term for
   a. card
   b. continuous improvement
   c. foolproof device
   d. fishbone diagram
   e. frequency of defects
   c (Role of inspections, moderate)

61. A worker operates a shear press. She notices that the metal sheets she is cutting have curled edges. Who should get the first "shot" at solving the problem?
    a. the foreman
    b. a member of the Quality Control department
    c. the operator herself
    d. an engineer
    e. the employee's supervisor
    c (Role of inspection, moderate)

62. A recent consumer survey conducted for a car dealership indicates that, when buying a car, customers are primarily concerned with the salesperson's ability to explain the car's features, the salesperson's friendliness, and the dealer's honesty. The dealership should be **especially** concerned with which dimensions of service quality?
    a. communication, courtesy, and credibility
    b. competence, courtesy, and security
    c. competence, responsiveness, and reliability
    d. communication, responsiveness, and reliability
    e. understanding/knowing customer, responsiveness, and reliability
    a (TQM in services, moderate)

FILL-IN-THE-BLANK

63. _____ costs result from production of defective parts or services before delivery to the customer.
    Internal failure (Defining quality, moderate)

64. _____ is a set of quality standards developed by the International Standards Organization.
    ISO 9000 (Defining quality, moderate)

65. _____ is a set of environmental standards developed by the International Standards Organization.
    ISO 14000 (Defining quality, moderate)

66. _____ is the Japanese word for the ongoing process of incremental improvement.
    Kaizen (Total quality management, moderate)

67. Enlarging employee jobs so that the added responsibility and authority is moved to the lowest level possible in the organization is called _____.
    employee empowerment (Total quality management, moderate)

68. _____ selects a demonstrated standard of performance that represents the very best performance for a process or activity.
    Benchmarking (Total quality management, moderate)

69. _____ is a philosophy of continuous improvement to bring the product exactly on target.
    Target-oriented quality (Total quality management, moderate)

70. _____ diagrams show the relationship between two measurements.
Scatter (Tools of TQM, moderate)

71. _____ diagrams use a schematic technique to discover possible locations of quality problems.
Cause-and-effect (Tools of TQM, moderate)

72. _____ are a graphical method to identify the critical few from the trivial many.
Pareto charts (Tools of TQM, moderate)

73. _____ use symbols to analyze the movement of people or materials.
Process charts (Tools of TQM, moderate)

74. _____ show the range of values of a measurement and the frequency with which each value occurs.
Histograms (Tools of TQM, moderate)

75. _____ are graphical presentations of data over time that show upper and lower control limits for processes we want to control.
Control charts (Tools of TQM, moderate)

76. _____ is a means of ensuring that an operation is producing at the quality level expected.
Inspection (The role of inspection, moderate)

77. A _____ is a foolproof device or technique that ensures production of good units every time.
poka-yoke (The role of inspection, moderate)

SHORT ANSWER

78. Explain in a short paragraph how higher quality can lead to lower costs.
Higher quality leads to greater demand, to greater market share, to greater economies of scale, and finally to lower costs. (Defining quality, moderate)

79. Explain in a short paragraph how higher quality can lead to higher productivity.
Higher quality leads to less scrap, rework, and warranty cost, hence to less input required for same output. (Defining quality, moderate)

80. List four ways in which quality affects a company.
It affects strategy through costs and market share; company's reputation, product liability, and international implications. (Defining quality, moderate)

81. State the ASCQ definition of quality. Of the three "flavors" or categories of quality definitions, which type is it? Explain.
Quality is the totality of features and characteristics of a product or service that bear on its ability to satisfy stated or implied needs. This is user-based, as evidenced by the reference to needs, not to specifications or ingredients. (Defining quality, moderate)

82. Quality has at least three categories or types of definitions; list them. Provide a brief explanation of each.
User-based (in the eyes of the beholder), manufacturing-based (conforming to standards), and product-based (measurable content of product). (Defining quality, moderate)

83. List the five core elements of ISO14000.
Environmental management, auditing, performance evaluation, labeling, and life cycle assessment. (Defining quality, moderate)

84. List the six concepts that are necessary for an effective TQM program. How are these related to Deming's 14 points?
Continuous improvement, employee involvement, benchmarking, Just-in-Time, Taguchi concepts, and knowledge of TQM tools. The 14 points were Deming's way of showing how he implemented TQM. (Total quality management, moderate)

85. Name three of the important people associated with the quality concepts of this chapter. In each case, write a short sentence about each one summarizing their primary contribution to the field of quality management.
Deming (14 points, leadership and training; good workers cannot overcome bad processes); Crosby (Quality is Free--the cost of poor quality is underestimated); and Juran (top management involvement in quality is vital). (Total quality management, moderate)

86. What steps can be taken to develop benchmarks?
Determine what to benchmark, form a benchmarking team, identify benchmarking partners, collect and analyze benchmarking information, and take action to match or exceed the benchmark. (Total quality management, moderate)

87. List the seven tools of Total Quality Management.
Check sheet, scatter diagram, cause-and-effect diagram, Pareto charts, process charts, histogram, and statistical process control. (Total quality management, moderate)

88. Explain how Just-In-Time processes relate to the quality of an organization's outputs.
Cuts costs of quality, by lowering waste and scrap; improves quality by shortening the time between error detection and error correction; better quality means less inventory and better JIT system. (Total quality management, moderate)

89. List the three concepts central to Taguchi's approach?
Quality robustness, quality loss factor, and target-oriented quality. (Total quality management, moderate)

90. Explain how a Pareto chart can identify the most important causes of errors in a process.
There will generally be some causes with much higher frequencies than others. The frequency plot will clearly show which cause has the highest frequency. (Tools of TQM, moderate)

91. List four benefits associated with the use of process charts.
Help identify the best data collection points, isolate and track the origin of problems, identify the best place for process checks, and identify opportunities for travel distance reduction. (Tools of TQM, moderate)

92. In the textbook illustrations of an Ishikawa diagram or cause-and-effect diagram, there are four broad categories of "causes". Name them.
Material, machinery/equipment, methods, and manpower. (Tools of TQM, moderate)

93. A process is said to be operating in statistical control when _____.
The only source of variation is natural variation, not assignable variation. (Tools of TQM, moderate)

94. Of the several points where inspection is likely to take place, which apply especially well to manufacturing?
Inspect at your supplier's plant while the supplier is producing, inspect at your facility upon receipt of goods from your supplier, inspect before costly or irreversible processes, inspect during the step-by-step production process, inspect when production or service is complete, and inspect before delivery from your facility all work well in manufacturing. Inspect at point of customer contact does not. (Role of inspection, moderate)

95. State the two basic decisions associated with inspection.
When to inspect, and where to inspect. (Role of inspection, moderate)

96. Explain, in your own words, what is meant by **source inspection**.
Consistent with the concept of employee empowerment, individual employees self-check their work and that of the employee preceding them. (Role of inspection, moderate)

97. What are the two types of sampling? Name them; provide a brief description or example of each.
Attribute sampling (present or absent); variables sampling (measured amount). (Role of inspection, moderate)

98. What roles do operations managers play in addressing the major aspects of service quality?
The design and delivery of service can make a difference on the tangible components of service, containing the determinants of service quality in the process design, managing expectations, and having alternate plans for exceptions. (TQM in services, moderate)

99. List the ten determinants of service quality.
Reliability, responsiveness, competence, access, courtesy, communication, credibility, security, understanding/knowing the customer, and tangibles. (TQM in services, difficult)

CHAPTER 6 SUPPLEMENT: STATISTICAL PROCESS CONTROL

TRUE/FALSE

1. In the context of statistical process control, all processes are subject to some degree of variability.
    True (Statistical Process Control (SPC), moderate)

2. The control chart has its origins in the work of the OM pioneer Walter Shewhart.
    True (Statistical Process Control (SPC), moderate)

3. Statistical process control has been popular since the early 1900s.
    False (Statistical Process Control (SPC), moderate)

4. The purpose of process control is to detect when natural causes of variation are present.
    False (Statistical Process Control (SPC), moderate)

5. A normal distribution is generally described by its two parameters: the mean and the range.
    False (Statistical Process Control (SPC), moderate)

6. A process is said to be in statistical control when assignable causes are the only sources of variation.
    False (Statistical Process Control (SPC), moderate)

7. A mistake stemming from an operator's inadequate training is an example of an assignable cause of variation.
    True (Statistical Process Control (SPC), moderate)

8. Averages of small samples, not individual measurements, are generally used in statistical process control.
    True (Statistical Process Control (SPC), moderate)

9. The Central Limit Theorem states that when the sample size increases, the distribution of the sample means will approach the normal distribution.
    True (Statistical Process Control (SPC), moderate)

10. In statistical process control, the range often substitutes for the standard deviation.
    True (Statistical Process Control (SPC), moderate)

11. If the process average is in control, then the process range must also be in control.
    False (Statistical Process Control (SPC), moderate)

12. A process range chart illustrates the amount of variation within the samples.
    True (Statistical Process Control (SPC), moderate)

13. Mean charts and range charts complement one another, one detecting shifts in process average, the other detecting shifts in process dispersion.
    True (Statistical Process Control (SPC), moderate)

14. A c-chart is appropriate to plot the number of typographic errors per page.
    True (Statistical Process Control (SPC), moderate)

15. To classify batteries as "good" or "bad," one would sample by variables.
    False (Statistical Process Control (SPC), moderate)

16. To measure the voltage of batteries, one would sample by attributes.
    False (Statistical Process Control (SPC), moderate)

17. The c-chart, like the x-bar chart, is based on the normal distribution.
    False (Statistical Process Control (SPC), moderate)

18. The C_{pk} index is based on the notion that a process in control may or may not be capable of producing to desired standards.
    True (Statistical Process Control (SPC), moderate)

19. A run test is a method to examine the points in a control chart to see if nonrandom variation is present.
    True (Statistical Process Control (SPC), moderate)

20. A C_{pk} index value of zero indicates that a process is both in control and capable of producing to desired dimensions.
    False (Statistical Process Control (SPC), moderate)

21. Acceptance sampling accepts or rejects the entire lot based on the information contained in the sample.
    True (Acceptance sampling, moderate)

22. If statistical process control is used effectively by your suppliers, some acceptance sampling may be eliminated.
    True (Acceptance sampling, moderate)

23. Every sample runs the risk of an erroneous conclusion because the sample was not representative of the population it was drawn from.
    True (Acceptance sampling, moderate)

24. The probability of rejecting a good lot is known as Consumer's Risk.
    False (Acceptance sampling, moderate)

25. The average level of quality we are willing to accept is known as the acceptable quality level (AQL).
    False (Acceptance sampling, moderate)

26. An acceptance sampling plan must define "good lots" and "bad lots" and specify the risk level associated with each one.
    True (Acceptance sampling, moderate)

27. The steeper an OC curve, the better it discriminates between good and bad lots.
True (Acceptance sampling, moderate)

28. A lot that is accepted by acceptance sampling has no defects present.
False (Acceptance sampling, moderate)

29. An Average Outgoing Quality (AOQ) value of 1 is ideal, because all defects have been removed.
False (Acceptance sampling, moderate)

MULTIPLE CHOICE

30. If a sample of items is measured and the mean of the sample is outside the control limits
    a. the process is out of control and the cause should be established
    b. the process is in control, but not capable of producing within the established control limits
    c. the process is within the established control limits with only natural causes of variation
    d. the process is monitored closely to see if the next sample mean will also fall outside the control limits
    a (Statistical Process Control (SPC), moderate)

31. Control charts for variables are based on data that comes from
    a. individual items
    b. averages of small samples
    c. averages of large samples
    d. the entire lot
    e. acceptance sampling
    b (Statistical Process Control (SPC), moderate)

32. Assignable causes
    a. are causes of variation that can be identified and removed
    b. are not as important as natural causes
    c. are within the limits of a control chart
    d. depend on the inspector assigned to the job
    e. are also referred to as "chance" causes
    a (Statistical Process Control (SPC), moderate)

33. The purpose of an $\overline{X}$ chart is to determine whether there has been a
    a. gain or loss in uniformity
    b. change in the percent defective in a sample
    c. change in the number of defects in a sample
    d. change in the central tendency of the process output
    e. change in the AOQ
    d (Statistical Process Control (SPC), moderate)

34. Statistical Process Control charts
    a. display the measurements on every item being produced
    b. display upper and lower limits for process variables or attributes, and signal when a process is no longer in control
    c. indicate to the process operator the average outgoing quality of each lot
    d. indicate to the operator the true percent defective of each lot
    e. none of the above
    b (Statistical Process Control (SPC), moderate)

35. Up to three standard deviations above or below centerline is the amount of variation that statistical process control allows for
    a. Type I errors
    b. about 95.5% variation
    c. all types of variation
    d. assignable variation
    e. natural variation
    e (Statistical Process Control (SPC), moderate)

36. A sample of parts is measured. The mean of this sample is in the middle of the control limits, but some individual parts measure too low for design specifications and other parts measure too high. Which of the following is true?
    a. The process is out of control, and the cause should be established.
    b. The process is in control, but not capable of producing within the established control limits.
    c. The process is within the established control limits with only natural causes of variation.
    d. The process is outside the established control limits with only natural causes of variation.
    e. The process is in control, and there is nothing to worry about.
    b (Statistical Process Control (SPC), difficult)

37. The x-bar chart tells us
    a. whether a gain or loss in dispersion has occurred
    b. whether there has been a change in the percent defective in a sample
    c. whether there has been a change in the central tendency of the process output
    d. whether there has been a change in the number of defects in a sample
    e. none of the above
    c (Statistical Process Control (SPC), moderate)

38. The type of inspection that classifies items as being either good or defective is
    a. variable inspection
    b. attribute inspection
    c. fixed inspection
    d. all of the above
    e. none of the above
    b (Statistical Process Control (SPC), moderate)

39. The mean and standard deviation for a process for which we have a substantial history are $\bar{x} = 160$ and $\sigma = 2$. For the variable control chart, a sample size of 16 will be used. What is the mean of the sampling distribution?
    a. 1/8 (0.125)
    b. 0.5
    c. 2
    d. 40
    e. none of the above
    e (Statistical Process Control (SPC), moderate)

40. If $\bar{x} = 23$ ounces, $\sigma = 0.5$ ounces, and n = 16, the $\pm 3\sigma$ control limits will be _____.
    a. 21.5 to 24.5 ounces
    b. 3 ounces
    c. 22.625 to 23.375 ounces
    d. 22.25 to 23.75 ounces
    e. none of the above
    c (Statistical Process Control (SPC), moderate)

41. Jars of pickles are sampled and weighed. Sample measures are plotted on control charts. The ideal weight should be precisely 11 oz. Which type of chart(s) would you recommend?
    a. x - and R-charts
    b. p- harts
    c. c-charts
    d. x -, but not R-charts
    e. both p- and c-charts
    a (Statistical Process Control (SPC), moderate)

42. The usual purpose of an R-chart is to signal whether there has been a
    a. gain or loss in uniformity
    b. change in the percent defective in a sample
    c. change in the central tendency of the process output
    d. change in the number of defects in a sample
    e. change in the AOQ
    a (Statistical Process Control (SPC), moderate)

43. Plots of sample ranges indicate that the most recent value is below the lower control limit. What course of action would you recommend?
    a. Since there is no obvious pattern in the measurements, variability is in control.
    b. One value outside the control limits is insufficient to warrant any action.
    c. Variation is not in control; investigate what created this condition.
    d. Lower than expected dispersion is a desirable condition; there is no reason to investigate.
    e. The process is out of control; reject the last units produced.
    c (Statistical Process Control (SPC), difficult)

44. To set $\bar{x}$-chart upper and lower control limits, one must know the process central line, which is
   a. the average of the sample means
   b. the total number of defects in the population
   c. the percent defects in the population
   d. the size of the population
   e. the average range
   a (Statistical Process Control (SPC), moderate)

45. According to the text, the most common choice for limits for control charts is usually
   a. ± 1 standard deviation
   b. ± 2 standard deviations
   c. ± 3 standard deviations
   d. ± 1 standard deviation for means and ± 2 standard deviations for ranges
   e. none of the above
   c (Statistical Process Control (SPC), moderate)

46. The normal application of a p-chart is in
   a. process sampling by variables
   b. acceptance sampling by variables
   c. process sampling by attributes
   d. acceptance sampling by attributes
   e. none of the above
   c (Statistical Process Control (SPC), moderate)

47. Which of the following is true of a p-chart?
   a. The lower control limit may be below zero.
   b. The lower control limit may be at zero.
   c. The lower control limit is found by subtracting a fraction from the average number of defects.
   d. The lower control limit indicates the minimum acceptable number of defects.
   e. The lower control limit is the same as the lot tolerance percent defective.
   b (Statistical Process Control (SPC), moderate)

48. The c-chart signals whether there has been a
   a. gain or loss in uniformity
   b. change in the number of defects per unit
   c. change in the percent defective in a sample
   d. change in the central tendency of the process output
   e. change in the AOQ
   b (Statistical Process Control (SPC), moderate)

49. The statistical process chart used to control the number of defects per unit of output is the
   a. $\bar{x}$-chart
   b. R-chart
   c. p-chart
   d. c-chart
   e. AOQ chart
   d (Statistical Process Control (SPC), moderate)

50. The local newspaper receives several complaints per day about typographic errors. Over a seven-day period, the publisher has received calls from readers reporting the following number of errors: 4, 3, 2, 6, 7, 3, and 9. Based on these data alone, what type of control chart(s) should the publisher use?
    a. p-chart
    b. c-chart
    c. x-chart
    d. R-chart
    e. x- and R-charts
    b (Statistical Process Control (SPC), moderate)

51. A manufacturer uses statistical process control to control the quality of the firm's products. Samples of 50 of Product A are taken, and a defective/acceptable decision is made on each unit sampled. For Product B, the number of flaws per unit is counted. What type(s) of control charts should be used?
    a. p-charts for A and B
    b. p-chart for A, c-chart for B
    c. c-charts for both A and B
    d. p-chart for A, mean and range charts for B
    e. c-chart for A, mean and range charts for B
    b (Statistical Process Control (SPC), difficult)

52. A nationwide parcel delivery service keeps track of the number of late deliveries (more than 30 minutes past the time promised to clients) per day. They plan on using a control chart to plot their results. Which type of control chart(s) would you recommend?
    a. x- and R-charts
    b. p-charts
    c. c-charts
    d. x-, but not R-charts
    e. both p- and c-charts
    c (Statistical Process Control (SPC), moderate)

53. Which of the following is **true** regarding process capability?
    a. Process capability is based on measurements of individual units, not averages of samples.
    b. Capability and "in control" are usually shown on the same chart.
    c. Capability and "in control" mean the same thing.
    d. A process is "capable" if its R-chart is in control.
    e. None of the above are true.
    a (Statistical Process Control (SPC), moderate)

54. Which of the following is true regarding the process capability index C_{pk}?
    a. A C_{pk} index value of 1 is ideal, meaning all units meet specifications.
    b. The larger the C_{pk} the more units meet specifications.
    c. The C_{pk} index can only be used when the process centerline is also the specification centerline.
    d. Positive values of the C_{pk} index are good, negative values are bad.
    e. None of the above are true.
    b (Statistical Process Control (SPC), moderate)

55. A run test is used
   a. to examine variability in acceptance sampling plans
   b. in acceptance sampling to establish control
   c. to examine points in a control chart to check for natural variability
   d. to exmaine points in a control chart to check for nonrandom variability
   e. none of the above
   d (Statistical Process Control (SPC), moderate)

56. An acceptance sampling plan's ability to discriminate between low quality lots and high quality lots is described by
   a. a Gantt chart
   b. an Operating Characteristics curve
   c. the Central Limit Theorem
   d. a process control chart
   e. a range chart
   b (Acceptance sampling, moderate)

57. Acceptance sampling's primary purpose is to
   a. estimate process quality
   b. estimate lot quality
   c. detect and eliminate defectives
   d. decide if a lot meets predetermined standards
   e. determine whether defective items found in sampling should be replaced
   d (Acceptance sampling, moderate)

58. Which of the following statements on acceptance sampling is **true**?
   a. Acceptance sampling draws samples from a population of items, tests the sample, and accepts the entire population if the sample is good enough, and rejects it if the sample is poor enough.
   b. The sampling plan contains information about the sample size to be drawn and the critical acceptance or rejection numbers for that sample size.
   c. The steeper an operating characteristic curve, the better its ability to discriminate between good and bad lots.
   d. All of the above are true.
   e. All of the above are false.
   d (Acceptance sampling, moderate)

59. Acceptance sampling
   a. may involve inspectors taking random samples (or batches) of finished products and measuring them against predetermined standards
   b. may involve inspectors taking random samples (or batches) of incoming raw materials and measuring them against predetermined standards
   c. is more economical than 100% inspection
   d. may be either of a variable or attribute type, although attribute inspection is more common in the business environment
   e. all of the above are true
   e (Acceptance sampling, moderate)

60. Which of the following statements on statistical process control is **true**?
    a. Consumers' risk is the risk that a buyer would incorrectly reject a lot that is actually good.
    b. Producer's risk is the probability that a lot or population that is actually out of control is accepted as "good."
    c. The term Type I error can be properly used to refer to producer's risk and to consumer's risk.
    d. All of the above are true.
    e. All of the above are false.
    e (Acceptance sampling, moderate)

61. Acceptance sampling is usually used to control
    a. incoming lots of purchased products
    b. the number of units output from one stage of a process which are then sent to the next stage
    c. the number of units delivered to the customer
    d. the quality of work-in-process inventory
    e. none of the above
    a (Acceptance sampling, moderate)

62. An operating characteristics curve shows
    a. product quality under different manufacturing conditions
    b. how the probability of accepting a lot varies with the population percent defective
    c. when product specifications don't match process control limits
    d. how operations affects certain characteristics of a product
    e. upper and lower product specifications
    b (Acceptance sampling, moderate)

63. An Operating Characteristic (OC) curve describes
    a. the sample size necessary to distinguish between good and bad lots
    b. the most appropriate sampling plan for a given incoming product quality level
    c. how well an acceptance sampling plan discriminates between good and bad lots
    d. how many defects per unit are permitted before rejection occurs
    e. none of the above
    c (Acceptance sampling, moderate)

64. Producer's risk is the probability of
    a. accepting a good lot
    b. rejecting a bad lot
    c. accepting a bad lot
    d. rejecting a good lot
    e. none of the above
    d (Acceptance sampling, moderate)

65. Which of the following is true regarding the relationship between AOQ and the true population percent defective?
    a. AOQ is greater than true percent defective.
    b. AOQ is the same as the true percent defective.
    c. AOQ is less than the true percent defective.
    d. There is no relationship between AOQ and true percent defective.
    e. The relationship between these two cannot be determined.
    c (Acceptance sampling, difficult)

66. A Type I error occurs when
    a. a good lot is rejected
    b. a bad lot is accepted
    c. the number of defectives is very large
    d. the population is worse than the AQL
    e. none of the above
    a (Acceptance sampling, moderate)

67. A Type II error occurs when
    a. a good lot is rejected
    b. the population is worse than the LTPD
    c. the proportion defectives is very small
    d. none of the above
    b (Acceptance sampling, moderate)

68. Average outgoing quality (AOQ) usually
    a. improves with inspection
    b. stays the same with inspection
    c. worsens with inspection
    d. may either improve or worsen with inspection
    e. is the average quality before inspection
    a (Acceptance sampling, moderate)

69. In most acceptance sampling plans, when a lot is rejected, the entire lot is inspected and all
    defective items are replaced. When using this technique the AOQ
    a. worsens (AOQ becomes a larger fraction)
    b. improves (AOQ becomes a smaller fraction)
    c. is not affected, but the AQL is improved
    d. is not affected
    e. falls to zero
    b (Acceptance sampling, moderate)

70. An acceptance sampling plan is to be designed to meet the organization's targets for product quality
    and risk levels. Which of the following is true?
    a. AQL, LTPD, α and β collectively determine n and c.
    b. n and c determine the AOL.
    c. n and c are determined from the values of AQL and LTPD.
    d. α and β are determined from the values of AQL and LTPD.
    e. None of the above are true.
    a (Acceptance sampling, moderate)

71. Which of the following statements about acceptance sampling is **true**?
    a. Acceptance sampling removes all defective items.
    b. Acceptance sampling of incoming lots is replacing statistical process control at the supplier.
    c. The steeper an OC curve, the better it discriminates between good and bad lots.
    d. Acceptance sampling occurs continuously along the assembly line.
    e. All of the above are true.
    c (Acceptance sampling, moderate)

72. A lot that is accepted by acceptance sampling
    a. has more defects than existed before the sampling
    b. has had all its defects removed by 100% inspection
    c. will have the same defect percentage as the LTPD
    d. has no defects present
    e. all of the above are false
    e (Acceptance sampling, moderate)

73. Which of the following is true regarding the Average Outgoing Quality Level?
    a. An AOQ value of 1 is ideal, because all defects have been removed.
    b. AOQ is always greater than AQL but less than LTPD.
    c. AOQ rises (worsens) following inspection of failed lots.
    d. AOQ is very low (very good) for extremely poor quality lots.
    e. None of the above is true.
    d (Acceptance sampling, difficult)

FILL-IN-THE-BLANK

74. _____ are a graphical presentation of process data over time.
    Control charts ((Statistical Process Control (SPC), moderate)

75. _____ is variation in a production process that can be traced to specific causes.
    Assignable variation (Statistical Process Control (SPC), moderate)

76. The _____ is a quality control chart that indicates when changes occur in the central tendency of a production process.
    x-bar chart (Statistical Process Control (SPC), moderate)

77. The _____ is the chief way to control attributes.
    P-chart (Statistical Process Control (SPC), moderate)

78. The _____ is a quality control chart used to control the number of defects per unit of output.
    c-chart (Statistical Process Control (SPC), moderate)

79. _____ is a method of measuring samples of lots or batches of product against predetermined standards.
    Acceptance sampling (Acceptance sampling, moderate)

80. An _____ is a graph that describes how well an acceptance plan discriminates between good and bad lots.
    OC or Operating Characteristics curve (Acceptance sampling, moderate)

81. The _____ is the poorest level of quality that we are willing to accept.
    AQL or Acceptable Quality Level (Acceptance sampling, moderate)

82. The _____ is the percent defective in an average lot of goods inspected through acceptance sampling.
    AOQ or Average Outgoing Quality (Acceptance sampling, moderate)

SHORT ANSWER

83. List Shewhart's two types of variation. What are they now called?
Common and special causes are now called natural and assignable variation. (Statistical Process Control (SPC), moderate)

84. Define "in statistical control."
A process is said to be operating in statistical control when the only source of variation is common causes. (Statistical Process Control (SPC), moderate)

85. What is the basic objective of a process control system?
It is to provide a statistical signal when assignable causes of variation are present. (Statistical Process Control (SPC), moderate)

86. List three possible causes of assignable variation given in your text. What are some others?
Text list includes machine wear, misadjusted equipment, fatigued or untrained workers, new batches of raw materials, etc. Others might be bad measuring device, workplace lighting, other ergonomic conditions, etc. (Statistical Process Control (SPC), difficult)

87. What are the three possible results (or findings) from the use of control charts?
The results of a control chart can indicate (a) in control and capable, (b) in control but not capable, and (c) out of control. (Statistical Process Control (SPC), moderate)

88. Explain briefly what an x-bar chart and an R chart do.
The x-bar chart indicates whether changes have occurred in the central tendency of a process; the R-chart indicates whether a gain or a loss in uniformity has occurred. (Statistical Process Control (SPC), moderate)

89. Briefly explain what the Central Limit Theorem has to do with control charts.
The CLT underlies the distribution of sample means and the standard deviation of sample means. It leads to the usability of the normal distribution in control charts. (Statistical Process Control (SPC), moderate)

90. Explain how a person using 2-sigma control charts will more easily find samples "out of bounds" than 3-sigma control charts. What are some possible consequences of this fact?
2-sigma covers only 95.5% of all natural variation; even in the absence of assignable cause, points will fall outside the control limits 4.5% of the time. (Statistical Process Control (SPC), moderate)

91. List the five steps in developing and using x-bar and R-charts.

1. Collect 20 to 25 samples of n=4 or 5 each; compute the mean and range of each sample.
2. Compute the overall means ($\bar{\bar{x}}$ and $\bar{R}$), set appropriate control limits, usually at the 99.7% level, and calculate the preliminary upper and lower control limits. If the process is not currently stable, use the desired mean, μ, instead of $\bar{\bar{x}}$ to calculate limits.
3. Graph the sample means and ranges on their respective control charts and determine whether they fall outside the acceptable limits.
4. Investigate points or patterns that indicate the process is out of control. Try to assign causes for the variation and then resume the process.
5. Collect additional samples and, if necessary, revalidate the control limits using the new data. (Statistical Process Control (SPC), moderate)

92. Briefly explain the difference between a p-chart and a c-chart.

The p-chart and the c-chart are both used for attribute inspection. A p-chart indicates whether changes in the proportion defective have occurred. A c-chart indicates whether changes in the number of defects per unit have occurred. (Statistical Process Control (SPC), moderate)

93. Examine the POM for Windows outputs below. Answer the following questions.
   a. What is the sample size?
   b. What is the number of samples?
   c. What is the mean of sample 8; what is the range of sample 10?
   d. What is the probability that, if the process is in control, a sample will falsely indicate "out of control"?
   e. Is this process in control? Explain--a simple Yes or No is insufficient.
   f. What additional steps should the quality assurance team take?

Chester's Pickles Solution

2 sigma	X-bar	Range
UCL (Upper control limit)	12.6856	1.0193
CL (Center line)	12.36	0.67
LCL (Lower Control Limit)	12.0344	0.

Method
2 sigma

Chester's Pickles

Sample Number	Item 1	Item 2	Item 3	Item 4
Sample 1	12.2	12.6	12.	12.1
Sample 2	11.9	12.5	12.4	12.7
Sample 3	12.	12.2	12.9	13.1
Sample 4	12.5	12.5	12.4	12.8
Sample 5	12.2	12.8	12.7	12.
Sample 6	12.1	12.5	11.8	12.3
Sample 7	12.3	12.4	12.8	12.4
Sample 8	12.	12.1	12.4	12.2
Sample 9	12.1	12.8	12.4	11.9
Sample 10	12.6	12.4	12.1	12.3

The sample size is 4; ten samples were taken. The mean of sample 8 is 12.175; the range of sample 10 is 0.5. This chart is built on 2-sigma limits, so the probability of a false signal is about 4.5%. The process is not in control-while all means are within limits, the range for sample 3 is too large. Investigate for assignable cause and eliminate that cause.

		Mean	Range
UCL (Upper control limit)		12.6856	1.0193
CL (Center line)		12.36	0.67
LCL (Lower Control Limit)		12.0344	0

Sample Number	Item1	Item2	Item3	Item4	Mean	Range
Sample 1	12.2	12.6	12	12.1	12.225	0.6
Sample 2	11.9	12.5	12.4	12.7	12.375	0.8
Sample 3	12	12.2	12.9	13.1	12.55	1.1
Sample 4	12.5	12.5	12.4	12.8	12.55	0.4
Sample 5	12.2	12.8	12.7	12	12.425	0.8
Sample 6	12.1	12.5	11.8	12.3	12.175	0.7
Sample 7	12.3	12.4	12.8	12.4	12.475	0.5
Sample 8	12	12.1	12.4	12.2	12.175	0.4
Sample 9	12.1	12.8	12.4	11.9	12.3	0.9
Sample 10	12.6	12.4	12.1	12.3	12.35	0.5

(Statistical Process Control (SPC), difficult)

94. Is a process that is in control also a process that is capable of making parts to required standards? Explain.

No; the two concepts are independent. A process can be in control but not capable. (Statistical Process Control (SPC), moderate)

95. Can "in control" and "capable" be shown on the same chart?

Only indirectly. The chart illustrating control plots the averages of small samples, while "Capability" is based on the dimensions of individual units. Figure S6.2 suggests that an overly wide range for sample means implies an overly large range for individual values as well. (Statistical Process Control (SPC), moderate)

96. Define Producer's Risk. How does it relate to the errors of hypothesis testing? What is the symbol for its value?

Producer's risk is the probability of rejecting a good lot. It is a Type I error; its value is alpha. (Acceptance sampling, moderate)

97. Define Consumer's Risk. How does it relate to the errors of hypothesis testing? What is the symbol for its value?

The consumer's risk is the probability of accepting a bad lot. It is a Type II error; its value is beta. (Acceptance sampling, moderate)

98. What are the acceptable quality level (AQL) and the lot tolerance percent defective (LTPD)? How are they used?

The AQL is the quality level of a lot considered to be good. The LTPD is the quality level of a lot we consider bad. These are combined with risk levels to determine an acceptance sampling plan. (Acceptance sampling, moderate)

99. What four elements determine the value of average outgoing quality? Why does this curve rise, peak, and fall?

The four elements are the true percent defective of the lot, the probability of accepting the lot, the number of items in the lot, and the number of items in the sample. AOQ is near zero for very good output (which has few defects to find) and for very bad output (which often fails inspection and has its defects removed). AOQ has higher values for output of intermediate quality, for which the probability of rejection is not very high. (Acceptance sampling, moderate)

100. Pierre's Motorized Pirogues and Mudboats is setting up an acceptance sampling plan for the special air cleaners he manufactures for his boats. His specifications, and the resulting plan are shown on the POM for Windows output below. In relatively plain English (someone else will translate for Pierre), explain exactly what he will do when performing the acceptance sampling procedure, and what actions he might take based on the results.

Quality Control Results				
			Pierre Solution	
Parameter	Value		Result	Plan 1
AQL	0.015		Sample Size	175.
LTPD	0.06		Critical Value	5.
ALPHA	0.05		Actual Producer's risk	0.0495
BETA	0.1		Actual Consumer's risk	0.0456

Pierre should select samples of size 175 from his lots of air cleaners. He should count the number of defects in each sample. If there are 4 or fewer defects, the lot passes inspection. If there are 5 or more defects, the lot fails inspection. Lots that fail can be handled several ways: they can be 100% inspected to remove defects, they can be sold at a discount, they can be destroyed, they can be sent back for rework, etc. (Acceptance sampling, moderate)

101. Pierre's Motorized Pirogues and Mudboats is setting up an acceptance sampling plan for the special air cleaners he manufactures for his boats. His specifications, and the resulting plan are shown on the POM for Windows output below. Pierre is a bit confused. He mistakenly thinks that acceptance sampling will reject all bad lots and accept all good lots. Explain why this will not happen.

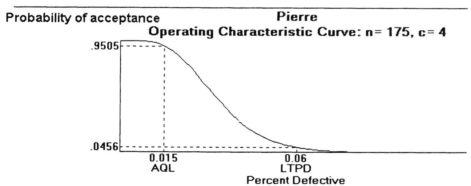

Acceptance sampling cannot discriminate perfectly between good and bad lots; this is illustrated by the OC curve that is not straight up and down. In this example, "good" lots will still be rejected almost 5% of the time. "Bad" lots will still be accepted almost 5% of the time. (Acceptance sampling, moderate)

102. Pierre's Motorized Pirogues and Mudboats is setting up an acceptance sampling plan for the special air cleaners he manufactures for his boats. His specifications, and the resulting plan are shown on the POM for Windows output below. Pierre wants acceptance sampling to remove ALL defects from his production of air cleaners. Explain carefully why this won't happen.

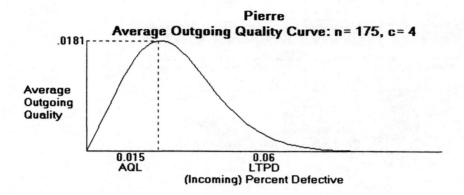

Pierre
Average Outgoing Quality Curve: n= 175, c= 4

Acceptance sampling is not intended to remove all defects, nor will it. Consider a lot with a defect rate of 0.005 in this example. If the sample is representative, the lot will pass inspection--which means that no one will inspect the lot for defects. The defects that were present before sampling are still there. Generally, acceptance sampling passes some lots and rejects others. Defects can only be removed from those lots that fail inspection. (Acceptance sampling, moderate)

PROBLEMS

103. In the table below are selected values for the OC curve for the acceptance sampling plan n=92, c=3. (Watch out--the points are not evenly spaced.) Assume that upon failed inspection, defective items are replaced. Calculate the AOQ for each data point. (You may assume that the population is much larger than the sample.) Plot the AOQ curve. At approximately what population defective rate is the AOQ at its worst? Explain how this happens. How well does this plan meet the specifications of AQL=0.015, α=0.05; LTPD=0.08, β=0.10? Discuss.

Population percent defective	Probability of acceptance
0.005	0.99877
0.010	0.98607
0.015	0.94986
0.020	0.88673
0.030	0.70166
0.040	0.49543
0.060	0.19075
0.080	0.05743
0.100	0.01451

The plan meets the α specification very well, but misses the β somewhat (not 10% but 5.7 percent).

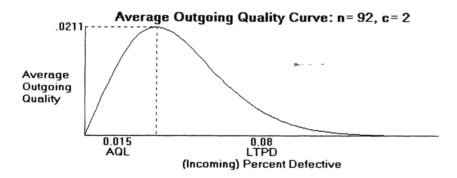

Average Outgoing Quality Curve: n= 92, c= 2

Population percent defective	Probability of acceptance	AOQ	
0.005	0.99877	0.004994	
0.010	0.98607	0.009861	
0.015	0.94986	0.014248	at AQL
0.020	0.88673	0.017735	
0.030	0.70166	0.02105	maximum
0.040	0.49543	0.019817	
0.060	0.19075	0.011445	
0.080	0.05743	0.004595	at LTPD
0.100	0.01451	0.001451	

(Acceptance Sampling, moderate)

In the table below are selected values for the OC curve associated with the acceptance sampling plan n=50, c=1. (Watch out--the points are not evenly spaced.) Assume that upon failed inspection, defective items are replaced. Calculate the AOQ for each data point. (You may assume that the population is much larger than the sample.) Plot the AOQ curve. At approximately what population defective rate is the AOQ at its worst? Explain how this happens. How well does this plan meet the specifications of AQL=0.0050, α=0.05; LTPD=0.05, $\cdot\beta$=0.10? Discuss.

Population percent defective	Probability of acceptance
0.005	0.97387
0.01	0.91056
0.02	0.73577
0.03	0.55528
0.04	0.40048
0.05	0.27943
0.06	0.19000
0.08	0.08271

This plan does not meet the specification very well. At .005 defective, the probability of acceptance is not 95 percent but over 97. At 0.05 defective, the acceptance rate is not 5% but 28.

Parameter	Value		Result	Value
AQL	0.005			
LTPD	0.05			
n	50.		Actual Producer's risk	0.0261
c	1.		Actual Consumer's risk	0.2794

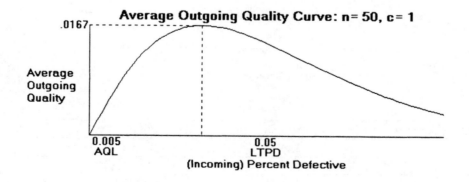

Average Outgoing Quality Curve: n= 50, c= 1

Average Outgoing Quality

.0167

0.005
AQL

0.05
LTPD

(Incoming) Percent Defective

Population percent defective	Probability of acceptance	AOQ	
0.005	0.97387	0.004869	at AQL
0.01	0.91056	0.009106	
0.02	0.73577	0.014715	
0.03	0.55528	0.016658	maximum
0.04	0.40048	0.016019	
0.05	0.27943	0.013972	at LTPD
0.06	0.19000	0.0114	
0.08	0.08271	0.006617	

(Acceptance sampling, moderate)

104. A state department of tourism and recreation collects data on the number of cars with out-of-state license plates in a state park. (The group's position is that more out-of-state plates means the state's advertising programs are working.) The sample size is fixed at n=100 each day. Data from the previous 20 days indicate the following number of out-of-state license plates:

Day	1	2	3	4	5	6	7	8	9	10
Out-of-state plates	24	35	16	21	26	31	13	15	23	12

Day	11	12	13	14	15	16	17	18	19	20
Out-of-state plates	22	13	25	33	16	22	34	9	23	13

a. Calculate the overall proportion of "tourists" (cars with out-of-state plates).
b. Calculate the LCL and UCL for these data.
c. Are all points within the control limits?
d. What action do you suggest for improving this process?
(a) 0.213; (b) 0.0902 to 0.3358; (c) No; two points are above UCL, and one is below LCL; (d) Investigate the cause of the one day below LCL and the two days above UCL. Perhaps the out-of-control points are due to holidays or other assignable cause. (Statistical Process Control (SPC), moderate)

105. Small boxes of Caesar salad croutons are labeled "net weight 2.5 ounces." To construct control charts, random samples of 4 boxes were weighed. Five hours of observation yielded:

Sample	mean	range
1	2.4	0.3
2	2.6	0.2
3	2.5	0.2
4	2.7	0.3
5	2.4	0.6

a. What is the upper control limit for the $\bar{x}$ chart?
b. What is the lower control limit for the $\bar{x}$ chart?
c. What are the upper and lower limits for the Range chart?
d. Is this process in control? Explain-a simple yes or no is insufficient
(a) 2.7533; (b) 2.2867; (c) 0 to 0.7302; (d) All points are in control on means chart; all points are in control in range chart, no pattern or trend. Therefore the process is in control.
(Statistical Process Control (SPC), moderate)

106. Len Liter is attempting to monitor a filling process that has an overall average of 705 cc. The average range is 6 cc. If you use a sample size of 10, what are the upper and lower control limits for the mean and range?

From table, $A_2 = 0.308$, $D_4 = 1.777$, $D_3 = 0.223$

$UCL\bar{x} = \bar{\bar{x}} + A_2 * \bar{R}$	$LCL\bar{x} = \bar{\bar{x}} - A_2 * \bar{R}$	$UCL_R = D_4 * \bar{R}$	$LCL_R = D_3 * \bar{R}$
$= 705 + 0.308 * 6$	$= 705 - 0.308 * 6$	$= 1.777 * 6$	$= 0.223 * 6$
$= 706.848$	$= 703.152$	$= 10.662$	$= 1.338$

(Statistical Process Control (SPC), moderate)

107. Cartons of Plaster of Paris are supposed to weigh exactly 32 oz. Inspectors want to develop process control charts. They take ten samples of six boxes and weigh them. Based on the following data, compute the lower and upper control limits and determine whether the process is in control.

Sample	mean	range
1	33.8	1
2	34.4	0.3
3	34.5	0.5
4	34.1	0.7
5	34.2	0.2
6	34.3	0.4
7	33.9	0.5
8	34.0	0.8
9	33.8	0.3
10	34.0	0.3

$n = 6$; $\bar{x} = 341/10 = 34.1$; $\bar{R} = 5.0/10 = 0.5$. The process is not in control, since the mean values for samples 1, 2, 3, and 9 fall outside the control limits. Although all the sample ranges fall within 0 and 1.002, the assignable causes should be investigated and eliminated. (Statistical Process Control (SPC), moderate)

Method		Sample Size				
3 sigma ▼		◄	⌐	►	6	

			Paris Solution			
Sample	Mean	Range		3 sigma	X-bar	Range
Sample 1	33.8	1.	UCL (Upper control limit)	34.3415	1.002	
Sample 2	34.4	0.3	CL (Center line)	34.1	0.5	
Sample 3	34.5	0.5	LCL (Lower Control Limit)	33.8585	0.	
Sample 4	34.1	0.7				
Sample 5	34.2	0.2				
Sample 6	34.3	0.4				
Sample 7	33.9	0.5				
Sample 8	34.	0.8				
Sample 9	33.8	0.3				
Sample 10	34.	0.3				

108. McDaniel Shipyards wants to develop control charts to assess the quality of its steel plate. They take ten sheets of 1" steel plate and compute the number of cosmetic flaws on each roll. Each sheet is 20' by 100'. Based on the following data, develop limits for the control chart and determine whether the process is in control.

Sheet	Number of flaws
1	6
2	1
3	3
4	2
5	1
6	2
7	1
8	0
9	0
10	2

Sheet number 1 has too many flaws; investigate the cause.

Use c-chart $UCL_c = 1.8 + 3\sqrt{1.8}$ $LCL_c = 1.8 - 3\sqrt{1.8}$
$\bar{c}$ = **total defects/**   = **1.8 + 4.02**   = **1.8 - 4.02**
  number of sheets = 1.8   = **5.82**   **converts to zero**

(Statistical Process Control (SPC), moderate)

109. Rancho No Tengo Orchards wants to establish control limits for its mangos before they are sent to the retailers. They randomly take six containers (assume it is enough) of one hundred mangos in an attribute testing plan and find some mangos with blemishes. What should be the limits on the control chart? Is the process in control?

Container	Number of mangos with blemishes
1	5
2	3
3	1
4	3
5	4
6	2

Limits are LCL = 0 and UCL = 0.081. All six points are in control; there is no pattern or trend in the data.

$$UCL = 0.03 + 3\sqrt{\frac{(0.03*0.97)}{100}} \qquad LCL = 0.03 - 3\sqrt{\frac{(0.03*0.97)}{100}}$$

= 0.03 + (3 * 0.017)   **= 0.03 - (3 * 0.017)**
= 0.081   **= -0.021 converts to 0**

(Statistical Process Control (SPC), moderate)

110

110. Whole Grains LLC uses statistical process control to ensure that their health-conscious, low-fat, multi-grain sandwich loaves have the proper weight of 6 oz. Based on a previously stable and in-control process, the control limits of the x and R charts are: UCL x = 6.56, LCL x = 5.84, UCL_R= 1.141, LCL_R= 0. Over the past few days, they have taken five random samples of four loaves and have found the following. Is the process still in control?

Sample	Net Weight			
	Loaf #1	Loaf #2	Loaf #3	Loaf #4
1	6.3	6.0	5.9	5.9
2	6.0	6.0	6.3	5.9
3	6.3	4.8	5.6	5.2
4	6.2	6.0	6.2	5.9
5	6.5	6.6	6.5	6.9

The process is no longer in control. Sample 3 lies outside the range limits; Sample 5 is outside the mean limits. The assignable causes should be determined and eliminated. Perhaps there is a new baker's assistant who lacks good judgment about weight of the loaves. (Statistical Process Control (SPC), moderate)

	Mean	Range
Sample 1	6.025	0.4
Sample 2	6.05	0.4
Sample 3	5.475	1.5
Sample 4	6.075	0.3
Sample 5	6.625	0.4

111. The average strengths of spring from a process are found in the following table. The sample means and sample ranges are based on a sample of 4. Construct a control chart to determine if the process is in control.

Sample Number	Sample Average	Sample Range
1	324	6
2	321	8
3	327	5
4	330	7
5	331	4
6	330	4
7	332	5
8	334	5

Samples 1, 2, and 8 are outside the control limits on the x-bar chart. Consequently, action should be taken to identify the cause of the out of control signal. (Statistical Process Control (SPC), moderate)

▦ Quality Control Results　　　　　　　　　　　　　　　　　　　　　　　　_ □ ✕

			\<untitled> Solution		
Sample	Mean	Range	3 sigma	X-bar	Range
Sample 1	324.	6.	UCL (Upper control limit)	332.6345	12.551
Sample 2	321.	8.	CL (Center line)	328.625	5.5
Sample 3	327.	5.	LCL (Lower Control Limit)	324.6155	0.
Sample 4	330.	7.			
Sample 5	331.	4.			
Sample 6	330.	4.			
Sample 7	332.	5.			
Sample 8	334.	5.			

112. The defect rate for a product has historically been about 1.5%. What are the upper and lower control chart limits if you wish to use a sample size of 100 and 3 sigma limits?

$$\text{UCL}_p = p + 3 \cdot \sqrt{\frac{p \cdot q}{n}} \qquad = 0.015 + 3 \cdot \sqrt{(0.015 * 0.985)/100} = 0.0515$$

$$\text{LCL}_p = p - 3 \cdot \sqrt{\frac{p \cdot q}{n}} \qquad = 0.015 - 3 \cdot \sqrt{(0.015 * 0.985)/100} = \text{-0.0215, or zero.}$$

(Statistical Process Control (SPC), moderate)

113. The mean and standard deviation for a process are $\bar{x} = 90$ and $\sigma = 8$. For the variable control chart, a sample size of 16 will be used. Calculate the standard deviation of the sampling distribution.
$8/\sqrt{16} = 2$
(Statistical Process Control (SPC), moderate)

114. If $\bar{x} = 9$ ounces, $\sigma = 0.5$ ounces, and n = 16, calculate the 3-sigma control limits.
8.625 to 9.375 ounces
(Statistical Process Control (SPC), moderate)

115. A hospital-billing auditor has been inspecting patient bills. While almost all bills contain some errors, the auditor is looking now for large errors (errors in excess of $250). Among the last 100 bills inspected, the defect rate has been 18%. Calculate the upper and lower limits for the billing process for 99.7% confidence.
0.18 plus or minus 3 x 0.03842, or 0.0647 to 0.2953
(Statistical Process Control (SPC), moderate)

116. Repeated sampling of a certain process shows that the average of all sample ranges to be 1.0 cm. The sample size has been constant at n = 4. What are the 3-sigma control limits for this R-chart?
zero to 2.28
(Statistical Process Control (SPC), moderate)

117. A woodworker is concerned about the quality of the finished appearance of her work. In sampling units of a split-willow hand-woven basket, she has found the following number of finish defects in ten units sampled: 4, 0, 3, 0, 1, 0, 1, 1, 0, 2.
a. Calculate the average number of defects per basket
b. If 3-sigma control limits are used, calculate the lower control limit, centerline, and upper control limit.
(a) 1.2; (b) 0, 1.2, and 4.5.
(Statistical Process Control (SPC), moderate)

118. The intended width of a bronze bar is intended to be one-eighth of an inch (0.125 inches). Inspection samples contain four rods each. The average range of these samples is 0.01 inches. What are the upper and lower control limits for this process, using 3-sigma limits?
LCL = .1177; UCL =.1323.
(Statistical Process Control (SPC), moderate)

119. The specifications for a plastic liner for concrete highway projects calls for a thickness of 3.0 mm $\pm$ .1mm. The standard deviation of the process is estimated to be 0.02 mm. What are the upper and lower specification limits for this product? The process is known to operate at a mean thickness of 3.0 mm. What is the C_{pk} for this process? About what percent of all units of this liner will meet specifications?
LSL = 2.9 mm, USL = 3.1 mm. C_{pk} = (3.1-3.0)/(3*0.02) = 1.67. The upper specification limit lies about 5 standard deviations from the centerline, so practically 100 percent of units will meet specifications. (Statistical Process Control (SPC), moderate)

120. The specifications for a plastic liner for concrete highway projects calls for a thickness of 6.0 mm $\pm$ 0.1 mm. The standard deviation of the process is estimated to be 0.02 mm. What are the upper and lower specification limits for this product? The process is known to operate at a mean thickness of 6.04 mm. What is the C_{pk} for this process? About what percent of all units of this liner will meet specifications?
LSL = 5.9 mm, USL = 6.1 mm. C_{pk} is the lesser of (6.1-6.04)/(3*0.02) = 1.00 and (5.9 - 6.04)/(3*0.02) = 2.33. The upper specification limit lies about 3 standard deviations from the centerline, and the lower specification limit is further away, so practically all units will meet specifications. (Statistical Process Control (SPC), moderate)

CHAPTER 7: PROCESS STRATEGY AND CAPACITY PLANNING

TRUE/FALSE

1. A firm's process strategy is the organization's approach to transforming resources into goods and services.
   True (Introduction, easy)

2. A very large percentage of production is accomplished in job shops.
   True (Four process strategies, easy)

3. Intermittent processes are organized around a product.
   False (Four process strategies, easy)

4. In process-focused facilities, such as restaurants, equipment utilization is low.
   True (Four process strategies, moderate)

5. The typical full-service restaurant is product focused.
   False (Four process strategies, moderate)

6. Process focus, intermittent process, and job shop all refer to the same thing.
   True (Four process strategies, moderate)

7. Harley-Davidson, because it has so many possible combinations of products, is process oriented.
   False (Four process strategies, moderate)

8. While flexibility is normally highest in process-oriented facilities, it remains very important in repetitive focus plants and product focus plants as well.
   True (Four process strategies, moderate)

9. High-volume, low-variety processes are continuous processes.
   True (Four process strategies, moderate)

10. Changing from one process to another is so difficult that it means, in the extreme, starting over.
    True (Four process strategies, moderate)

11. Mass customization is only recently possible, the result of advances in computers and electronic controls.
    True (Four process strategies, moderate)

12. Mass customization relies on modular design.
    True (Four process strategies, moderate)

13. Scheduling is least complex in the repetitive focus.
    False (Four process strategies, moderate)

14. A process map, with a time axis added, becomes a process chart.
    False (Process analysis and design, moderate)

15. Mass customization provides a process that caters to constant customer desires.
    False (Four process strategies, moderate)

16. Successful process reengineering focuses on departmental areas where small, continuous improvements can be made.
    False (Process Reengineering, moderate)

17. Time-function mapping is a flow process chart with time added to the horizontal axis.
    True (Process analysis and design, moderate)

18. Process charts use a schematic or drawing to show the movement of material, product, or people.
    False (Process analysis and design, moderate)

19. Service blueprinting is a process analysis technique.
    True (Process analysis and design, moderate)

20. Service typically implies some customization.
    True (Service process design, moderate)

21. Professional services typically require low levels of labor intensity.
    False (Service process design, moderate)

22. One technique for improving service productivity is postponement.
    True (Service process design, moderate)

23. Process reengineering involves the fundamental rethinking and radical redesign of business processes.
    True (Service process design, moderate)

24. Processes can be environmentally friendly and socially responsible while still contributing to profitable strategies.
    True (Service process design, moderate)

25. Flexibility is the ability to respond with little penalty in time, cost, or customer value.
    True (Selection of equipment and technology, moderate)

26. Capacity is the maximum output of a system in a given period.
    True (Selection of equipment and technology, moderate)

27. Effective capacity is capacity adjusted for efficiency.
    False (Selection of equipment and technology, moderate)

28. Changes in capacity may lead or lag the demand.
    True (Selection of equipment and technology, moderate)

29. Changes in capacity may be incremental or large.
   True (Selection of equipment and technology, moderate)

30. If forecasts indicate uneven demand, there is little a firm can do to balance demand with capacity.
   False (Selection of equipment and technology, moderate)

31. Variable costs are those that continue even if no units are produced.
   False (Break-even analysis, moderate)

32. Break-even analysis helps identify the volume at which fixed costs and revenue are equal.
   False (Break-even analysis, moderate)

33. The net present value of $10,000 to be received in exactly three years is considerably greater than $10,000.
   False (Strategy-driven investments, easy)

34. A crossover chart indicates at what quantity profit changes from negative to positive.
   False (Break-even analysis, moderate)

35. One limitation of the net present value approach to investments is that investments with identical net present values may have very different cash flows.
   True (Break-even analysis, moderate)

MULTIPLE CHOICE

36. An organization's process strategy
   a. is the same as its transformation strategy
   b. must meet various constraints, including cost
   c. will have long-run impact on efficiency and production
   d. is concerned with how resources are transformed into goods and services
   e. all of the above are true
   e (Introduction, moderate)

37. Three types of processes are:
   a. goods, services, and hybrids
   b. manual, automated, and service
   c. intermittent, repetitive, and continuous
   d. modular, continuous, and technological
   e. input, transformation, and output
   c (Four process strategies, moderate)

38. A job shop is an example of a(n)
   a. repetitive process
   b. intermittent process
   c. continuous process
   d. line process
   e. specialized process
   b (Four process strategies, moderate)

39. Which of the following industries is likely to have low equipment utilization?
    a. auto manufacturing
    b. hospitals
    c. beer making
    d. paper manufacturing
    e. chemical processing
    b (Four process strategies, moderate)

40. Which one of the following products is most likely made in a job shop environment?
    a. graphite pencils
    b. personal computers
    c. cigarettes
    d. McDonald's hamburgers
    e. custom furniture
    e (Four process strategies, moderate)

41. A continuous process is commonly used to produce
    a. high-volume, high-variety products
    b. low-volume, high-variety products
    c. high-volume, low-variety products
    d. low-variety products at either high- or low-volume
    e. high-volume products of either high- or low-variety
    c (Four process strategies, moderate)

42. Which of the following products is likely to be assembled on a repetitive process line?
    a. automobiles
    b. personal computers
    c. dishwashers
    d. television sets
    e. all of the above
    e (Four process strategies, moderate)

43. An assembly line is an example of a(n)
    a. repetitive process
    b. intermittent process
    c. continuous process
    d. line process
    e. specialized process
    a (Four process strategies, moderate)

44. Which of the following is **false** regarding repetitive processes?
    a. They use modules.
    b. They are the classic assembly lines.
    c. They have more structure and less flexibility than a job shop layout.
    d. They allow easy switching from one product to the other.
    e. They include the assembly of basically all automobiles.
    d (Four process strategies, moderate)

45. Which of the following transformations generally has the highest equipment utilization?
   a. repetitive process
   b. intermittent process
   c. continuous process
   d. line process
   e. modular process
   c (Four process strategies, moderate)

46. Which of the following is **true** regarding the concept of **flexibility**?
   a. It is the ability to change production rates with little penalty in time, cost, or customer value.
   b. It can be accomplished with sophisticated electronic equipment.
   c. It may involve modular, movable, even cheap equipment.
   d. All of the above are true.
   e. None of the above are true.
   d (Selection of equipment and technology, moderate)

47. Which of the following is **true** regarding **mass customization**?
   a. It is a form of mass production, but with individualized products.
   b. It is a form of agile production, but at assembly line speed.
   c. It blurs the distinctions among the traditional three process models.
   d. It allows for individualized products, such as custom-fitted bicycles, without sacrificing the speed of an assembly line.
   e. All of the above are true.
   e (Four process strategies, moderate)

48. Mass customization, when done correctly,
   a. helps eliminate the guesswork that comes with sales forecasting
   b. drives down inventories
   c. increases pressure on scheduling
   d. increases pressure on supply chain performance
   e. all of the above
   e (Four process strategies, moderate)

49. A drawing of the movement of material, product, or people is a(n)
   a. process chart
   b. service blueprinting
   c. process map
   d. flow diagram
   e. none of the above
   d (Process analysis and design, moderate)

50. Which of the following characteristics best describes **repetitive focus**?
   a. uses modules
   b. falls between product and process focus
   c. widely used for the assembly of automobiles
   d. has more structure than process-focused facilities
   e. all of the above
   e (Four process strategies, moderate)

51. Which of the following characteristics best describes **process focus**?
    a. low volume, high variety
    b. Finished goods are usually made to order.
    c. Processes are designed to perform a wide variety of activities.
    d. All of the above are true.
    e. Non of the above are true.

    d (Four process strategies, moderate)

52. Service blueprinting
    a. provides the basis to negotiate prices with suppliers
    b. mimics the way people communicate
    c. focuses on the provider's interaction with the customer
    d. determines the best time for each step in the process
    e. can only be successful with two-dimensional processes

    c (Process analysis and design, moderate)

53. Process reengineering
    a. is the fundamental rethinking and radical redesign of business processes
    b. tries to bring about dramatic improvements in performance
    c. focuses on activities that cross functional lines
    d. can focus on any process
    e. all of the above

    e (Process reengineering, moderate)

54. Flexibility can be achieved with
    a. moveable equipment
    b. inexpensive equipment
    c. sophisticated electronic equipment
    d. all of the above
    e. none of the above

    d (Selection of equipment and technology, moderate)

55. Which one of the following services involves high interaction and low labor intensity?
    a. hospital care
    b. air travel
    c. fast food
    d. catalog sales
    e. postal services

    a (Service process design, moderate)

56. In mass service and professional service, the operations manager should focus on
    a. automation
    b. equipment maintenance
    c. human resources
    d. sophisticated scheduling
    e. all of the above

    c (Service process design, moderate)

57. In mass service and service factory quadrants of the service process matrix, the operations manager could focus on all of the following **except**
    a. automation
    b. standardization
    c. tight quality control
    d. customization
    e. removing some services
    d (Service process design, moderate)

58. Strategies for improving productivity in services are
    a. lean production, strategy-driven investments, automation, and process focus
    b. reduce inventory, reduce waste, reduce inspection, and reduce rework
    c. high interaction, mass customization, service factory, and just-in-time
    d. separation, automation, scheduling, and training
    e. none of the above
    d (Service process design, moderate)

59. Which of the following is **true** regarding opportunities to improve service processes?
    a. Layout is of little consequence, since services seldom use an assembly line.
    b. If a work force is strongly committed, it need not be cross-trained and flexible.
    c. Automation can do little to improve service processes, because services are so personal.
    d. All of the above are true.
    e. None of the above are true.
    e (Service process design, moderate)

60. Making environmentally sound products through efficient processes
    a. is unprofitable, as long as recyclable materials prices are soft
    b. can still be profitable
    c. is known as lean manufacturing
    d. is easier for repetitive processes than for product-focused processes
    e. none of the above
    b (Environmentally friendly processes, moderate)

61. Capacity is
    a. the average output that can be achieved under ideal conditions
    b. the actual production over a specified time period
    c. a measure of the maximum usable capacity of a particular facility
    d. the maximum output of a system in a given period
    e. the sum of all of the organization's inputs
    d (Selection of equipment and technology, moderate)

62. Effective capacity is
    a. the maximum output of a system in a given period
    b. the percent of design capacity actually expected
    c. the average output that can be achieved under ideal conditions
    d. a measure of the minimum usable capacity of a particular facility
    e. none of the above
    b (Selection of equipment and technology, moderate)

63. The Academic Computing Center has five trainers available in its computer labs to provide training sessions to students. Assume that the capacity of the system is 1800 students and the utilization is 90%. If the number of students who actually got their orientation session is 1500, what is the efficiency of the system?
    a. 92.6%
    b. 1620 students
    c. 1350 students
    d. 90%
    e. 75%

    a (Selection of equipment and technology, moderate)

64. Organizations have four approaches for capacity expansion. Which of the following is **not** one of them?
    a. lead demand with incremental expansion
    b. lag demand with incremental expansion
    c. lead demand with one-step expansion
    d. lag demand with one-step expansion
    e. average capacity with incremental expansion

    d (Selection of equipment and technology, moderate)

65. Which of the following is **false** regarding capacity expansion?
    a. "Average" capacity sometimes leads demand, sometimes lags it.
    b. If "lagging" capacity is chosen, excess demand can be met with overtime or subcontracting.
    c. Capacity may only be added in large chunks.
    d. Total cost comparisons are a rather direct method of comparing capacity alternatives.
    e. All of the above are true.

    c (Selection of equipment and technology, moderate)

66. Break-even is the number of units at which
    a. total revenue equals price times quantity
    b. total revenue equals total variable cost
    c. total revenue equals total fixed cost
    d. total profit equals total cost
    e. total revenue equals total cost

    e (Break-even analysis, moderate)

67. Basic break-even analysis typically assumes that
    a. revenues increase in direct proportion to the volume of production, while costs increase at a decreasing rate as production volume increases
    b. both costs and revenues are made up of fixed and variable portions
    c. variable costs and revenues increase in direct proportion to the volume of production
    d. costs increase in direct proportion to the volume of production, while revenues increase at a decreasing rate as production volume increases because of the need to give quantity discounts
    e. all of the above are assumptions in the basic break-even model

    c (Break-even analysis, difficult)

68. DuLarge Fabricators wants to increase capacity by adding a new machine. The fixed costs for Machine A are $70,000, and its variable cost is $15 per unit. The revenue is $22 per unit. The break-even point for Machine A is
   a. $70,000 dollars
   b. 70,000 units
   c. 10,000 units
   d. $10,000 dollars
   e. cannot be calculated from the information provided
   c (Break-even analysis, moderate)

69. Which of the following costs would be incurred even if no units are produced?
   a. raw material costs
   b. building rental costs
   c. direct labor costs
   d. transportation costs
   e. purchasing costs
   b (Break-even analysis, moderate)

70. DuLarge Fabricators wants to increase capacity by adding a new machine. The firm is considering proposals from vendor A and vendor B. The fixed costs for machine A are $90,000 and for machine B, $75,000. The variable cost for A is $15.00 per unit and for B, $18.00. The revenue generated by the units processed on these machines is $22 per unit. If the estimated output is 5000 units, which machine should be purchased?
   a. machine A
   b. machine B
   c. either Machine A or Machine B
   d. no purchase because neither machine yields a profit at that volume
   e. purchase both machines since they are both profitable
   d (Break-even analysis, moderate)

71. DuLarge Fabricators wants to increase capacity by adding a new machine. The firm is considering proposals from vendor A and vendor B. The fixed costs for machine A are $90,000 and for machine B, $70,000. The variable cost for A is $6.00 per unit and for B, $8.00. The revenue generated by the units processed on these machines is $22 per unit. The crossover between machine A and machine B is
   a. 10,000 units, with A more profitable at low volumes
   b. 10,000 dollars, with A more profitable at low volumes
   c. 10,000 units, with B more profitable at low volumes
   d. 13,333 for A and 8,750 for B
   e. none of the above
   c (Break-even analysis, moderate)

72. DuLarge Fabricators wants to increase capacity by adding a new machine. The firm is considering proposals from vendor A and vendor B. The fixed costs for machine A are $90,000 and for machine B, $75,000. The variable cost for A is $15.00 per unit and for B, $18.00. The revenue generated by the units processed on these machines is $22 per unit. If the estimated output is 15,000 units, which machine should be purchased?
    a. machine A
    b. machine B
    c. either machine A or machine B
    d. no purchase because neither machine yields a profit at that volume
    e. purchase both machines since they are both profitable

    a (Break-even analysis, moderate)

73. The basic break-even model can be modified to handle more than one product. This extension of the basic model requires
    a. price and sales volume for each product
    b. sales volume for each product
    c. price and cost for each product, as well as the percent of total sales that each product represents
    d. three-dimensional graphing software
    e. at least a Pentium computer

    c (Break-even analysis, moderate)

74. Which of the following represent "strategy-driven investments"--the integration of a firm's investments with its strategic decisions, including the process decision?
    a. Select investments as part of a coordinated strategic plan.
    b. Choose investments that yield competitive advantage.
    c. Choose investments that consider product life cycles.
    d. Test investments in the light of several revenue projections.
    e. All of the above are strategy driven.

    e (Strategy-driven investments, moderate)

75. Which of the following does **not** represent "strategy-driven investments"--the integration of a firm's investments with its strategic decisions, including the process decision?
    a. Select investments as part of a coordinated strategic plan.
    b. Choose investments that yield competitive advantage.
    c. Choose investments that minimize cost.
    d. Test investments in the light of several revenue projections.
    e. All of the above are strategy driven.

    c (Strategy-driven investments, moderate)

76. Net present value
    a. is gross domestic product less depreciation
    b. is sales volume less sales and excise taxes
    c. is profit after taxes
    d. is the discounted value of a series of future cash receipts
    e. ignores the time value of money

    d (Strategy-driven investments, moderate)

77. Net present value will be greater
    a. as a fixed set of cash receipts occurs later rather than earlier
    b. for a 6% discount rate than for a 9% discount rate
    c. as the total of the cash receipts, made in same time periods, is smaller
    d. for one end-of-year receipt of $1200 than for twelve monthly receipts of $100 each
    e. all of the above are true
    b (Strategy-driven investments, moderate)

FILL-IN-THE-BLANK

78. An organization's approach to tranform resources into goods and services is called its

    _____.
    process strategy (Introduction, moderate)

79. The process strategy that is organized around processes to facilitate low-volume, high-variety processes is called a _____.
    process focus (Four process strategies, moderate)

80. _____ is a process strategy that uses a product-oriented production process that uses modules.
    Repetitive focus (Four process strategies, moderate)

81. _____ is a rapid, low-cost production process that caters to constantly changing unique customer desires.
    Mass customization (Four process strategies, moderate)

82. A _____ is a drawing used to analyze movement of people or material.
    flow diagram (Process analysis and design, moderate)

83. A _____ uses symbols to analyze the movement of people or material.
    process chart (Process analysis and design, moderate)

84. _____ is a process analysis technique that focuses on the producer's interaction with the customer.
    Service blueprinting (Process analysis and design, moderate)

85. _____ is the fundamental rethinking and radical redesign of business processes to bring about dramatic improvements in performance.
    Process reengineering (Process reengineering, moderate)

86. _____ involves the ability to respond with little penalty in time, cost, or customer value.
    Flexibility (Selection of equipment and technology, moderate)

87. _____ is actual output as a percent of design capacity.
    Utilization (Selection of equipment and technology, moderate)

88. _____ is actual output as a percent of effective capacity.
    Efficiency (Selection of equipment and technology, moderate)

89. _____ analysis finds the point at which cost equals revenues.
    Break-even (Break-even analysis, moderate)

90. _____ cost is the cost that continues even if no units are produced.
    Fixed (Break-even analysis, moderate)

91. _____ is a means of determining the discounted value of a series of future cash receipts.
    Net present value or NPV (Strategy-driven investments, moderate)

SHORT ANSWERS

92. What is process strategy?
    Process strategy is the organization's approach to transform resources into goods and services. (Introduction, easy)

93. What is the objective of a process design?
    To develop a process that will produce goods and services that meet the product specifications within cost and other managerial constraints. (Introduction, easy)

94. Name and describe briefly the three basic process strategies.
    Process focus, product focus, and repetitive focus. Process is a job shop--high variety and low volume; Repetitive is an assembly line--relatively standardized products with options from modules; Product is for high-volume, low variety, such as oil refining, flour milling. Additionally, mass customization, high volume, high variety. (Four process strategies, moderate)

95. Why is equipment utilization in process-focused service industries often low?
    Excess capacity to meet peak demand loads is often desirable; and scheduling is typically difficult. (Four process strategies, moderate)

96. The textbook described four basic process models, and hinted that there are others. Construct an example of a hybrid process. Can this process be applied in any well-known organization? How common do you think hybrid processes are?
    Most students will graft elements of process onto elements of product or repetitive. Examples may include food service, where "process" may typify most operations, but salad bars add an element of "repetitive." In health care, hybrids of process and repetitive can readily be found. (Four process strategies, moderate)

97. Compare an intermittent process to a continuous process on the basis of variety, volume, equipment utilization, and inventory.
    Intermittent has high variety, low volume, low utilization, general purpose equipment. Since most output is made to order, there is little inventory of raw materials or finished goods. Continuous has low variety, high volume, high utilization, and specialized equipment. Just-in-time practices keep inventory very low. (Four process strategies, moderate)

98. What are the four questions that represent the issues of process analysis and design?
Is the process designed to achieve competitive advantage in terms of differentiation, response, or low cost? Does the process eliminate steps that do not add value? Does the process maximize customer value as perceived by the customer? Will the process win orders? (Four process strategies, moderate)

99. What is service blueprinting?
Service blueprinting is a process analysis technique that focuses on the provider's interaction with the customer. (Process analysis and design, moderate)

100. What is process reengineering?
Process reengineering is the rethinking and radical design of business processes to bring about dramatic improvements in performance. (Process reengineering, moderate)

101. Name the four quadrants of the Service Process Matrix. Discuss how it is used to classify services into categories.
1. mass service (low interaction/customization; high labor intensity)
2. professional service (high interaction/customization; high labor intensity)
3. service factory (low interaction/customization; low labor intensity)
4. service shop (high interaction/customization; low labor intensity)
(Service process strategy, moderate)

102. What are the techniques to improve service productivity?
Separation, self-service, postponement, focus, modules, automation, scheduling, and training. (Service process strategy, moderate)

103. How are environmental issues linked to the process choice? Won't being an environmentally conscious firm drive up costs and take away any competitive advantage? Discuss, with examples to support your position.
Environmental issues are directly on point in the process decision. The process choice selects equipment that has emissions; creates waste in work or in packaging, etc. Not all environmentally conscious activities are cost-adding. But even if they were, cost is not the only thing affected. Customers may be attracted to products that are made from recycled materials, or that are more recyclable. This translates into revenue enhancement, not an element of cost. The competitive advantage centers on the customer, not the cost. (Environmentally friendly processes, moderate)

104. What is the fundamental distinction between design capacity and effective capacity? Provide a brief example.
Capacity is the same as design capacity. Effective capacity, or utilization, is the ratio of expected capacity to capacity. (Selection of equipment and technology, moderate)

105. Under what conditions would a firm want its capacity to lag demand? To lead demand?
Lagging is preferred when short-term options like overtime and subcontracting are relatively low cost and/or easy to use. Leading is preferred when a firm could not afford to lose customers for lack of demand, and overtime, etc., were not available. (Selection of equipment and technology, moderate)

106. Define **fixed costs**.
    Fixed costs are those that continue even if no units are produced. (Break-even analysis, moderate)

107. Define **variable costs**. What special assumption is made about variable costs in the textbook?
    Variable costs are those that vary with the number of units produced, linearity or proportionality. (Break-even analysis, moderate)

108. What are the **internal** actions that adjust processes to match capacity with demand?
    Staffing changes; adjusting equipment and processes; improving methods to increase throughput; and redesigning the product to facilitate more throughput. (Selection of equipment and technology, moderate)

109. Define break-even and crossover. Explain how they differ.
    Break-even is defined as the volume for which cost equals revenue. Crossover is the volume at which two alternatives have the same total cost, or the same total revenue, or the same profit. Break-even is absolute; crossover is comparative. (Break-even analysis, moderate)

110. What are the suggested actions to make a firm's investments supportive of its strategic decisions?
    Be made as part of a strategic plan; yield a competitive advantage; consider product life cycles; be evaluated based upon a variety of operating factors; and be tested in light of several revenue projections. (Strategy-driven investment, moderate)

111. Explain how net present value is an appropriate tool for comparing investments in processes.
    NPV works with the time value of money, comparing cost and income streams over perhaps long periods of time. Process decisions may incur much of their expense early in the life of the equipment, but the stream of revenues may follow for decades. NPV is the appropriate analytical tool for that situation. (Strategy-driven investment, moderate)

PROBLEMS

112. Huge University's Executive MBA program has the facilities and faculty to handle an enrollment of 2000 students per semester. However, in an effort to limit class sizes to a "reasonable" level (under 200, generally), they placed a ceiling on enrollment to 1500 students. Although there was ample demand for business courses last semester, conflicting schedules allowed only 1450 students to take business courses. What are the utilization and efficiency of this system?
    Design Capacity = 2,000 students
    Effective Capacity = 1500 students
    Actual Output = 1450 students

$$\text{Utilization} = \frac{\text{actual capacity}}{\text{design capacity}} = \frac{1450}{2000} = 72.5\%$$

$$\text{Efficiency} = \frac{\text{actual capacity}}{\text{effective capacity}} = \frac{1450}{1500} = 96.7\%$$

(Selection of equipment and technology, moderate)

113. A fleet repair facility has the capacity to repair 800 trucks per month. However, due to scheduled maintenance of their equipment, management feels that they can repair no more than 500 trucks per month. Last month, two of the employees were absent several days each, and only 300 trucks were repaired. What are the utilization and efficiency of the repair shop?

Design Capacity = 800 trucks
Effective Capacity = 500 trucks
Actual Output = 300 trucks

$$\text{Utilization} = \frac{\text{acutal output}}{\text{design capacity}} = \frac{300}{800} = 37.5\%$$

$$\text{Efficiency} = \frac{\text{actual output}}{\text{effective capacity}} = \frac{300}{500} = 60\%$$

(Selection of equipment and technology, moderate)

114. The owner of Ha'Peppas! is considering a new oven in which to bake the firm's signature dish, vegetarian pizza. Oven type A can handle 20 pizzas an hour. The fixed costs associated with oven A are $20,000 and the variable costs are $2.00 per pizza. Oven B is larger and can handle 40 pizzas an hour. The fixed costs associated with Oven B are $30,000 and the variable costs are $1.25 per pizza. The pizzas sell for $14 each, average.
a. What is the break-even point for each oven?
b. If the owner expects to sell 9,000 pizzas, which oven should she purchase?
c. If the owner expects to sell 12,000 pizzas, which oven should she purchase?
Answer:

(a) $\text{BEPA} = \dfrac{20000}{14 - 2} = 1667$ pizzas; $\quad \text{BEPB} = \dfrac{30000}{14 - 1.25} = 2353$ pizzas

(b) For both quantities, oven A is slightly more profitable (but oven B is catching up).

(c)

	Oven A	Oven B	At sales of:	Profit A =	Profit B =
Fixed cost	$20,000.00	$30,000.00	9000 →	88000	84750
Revenue	$ 14.00	$ 14.00	12000 →	124000	123000
Variable cost	$ 2.00	$ 1.25			

(Break-even analysis, moderate)

115. A manufacturer is currently producing an item that has a variable cost of $0.75 per unit and a selling price of $2.00 per unit. Fixed costs are $20,000. Current volume is 40,000 units. The firm can produce what they believe is a better product by adding a new piece of equipment to the process line. This equipment represents an increase of $5,000 in fixed cost. The variable cost would decrease $0.25 per unit. Volume for the new and improved product should rise to 50,000 units. Should the company invest in the new equipment?
Total profit now: 40,000 * (2.00 - 0.75) - $20,000 = $30,000
Total profit with new machine: 50,000 * (2.00 - .50) - $25,000 = $50,000
(Break-even analysis, moderate)

116. Grand Isle, Louisiana, is a popular resort, but regularly faces a shortage of fresh water. Marie Bain has the entrepreneurial spirit and plans to open a business shipping barges of fresh water to the town. They estimate their fixed cost to be $2,500,000, and their variable cost (water, labor, fuel) to be $50,000 per barge load. Selling price is expected to average $75,000 per barge load.
   a. What is her break-even point in units?
   b. What is her break-even point, in dollars?
   If she anticipates demand for 20 barges during the next year, should she enter this business? Break-even occurs at 2,500,000/(75,000-50,000)=100 barge loads. Break-even in dollars is $7,500,000 in revenue (costs will be $2,500,000 fixed and 100 * 50,000 variable). Demand of 20 is clearly not enough for profitability. (Break-even analysis, moderate)

117. A firm is about to undertake the manufacture of a product, and is weighing the process configuration options. There are two different job shop processes under consideration, as well as a repetitive focus. The small job shop has Fixed Costs of $2,000 per month, and Variable Costs of $20 per unit. The larger job shop has Fixed Costs of $10,000 per month and variable costs of $1 per unit. A repetitive focus plant has Fixed Costs of $60,000 and Variable Costs of $0.40 per unit.
   a. If demand were 1,000 units per month, what would cost be under each process configuration?
   b. At what level of demand does the small job shop become cheaper than the larger job shop?
   c. At what level of demand does the repetitive shop become cheaper than the larger job shop?
   (a) Small: $22,000, Large: $11000, Repetitive: $60,400; (b) at 421, the small job shop becomes cheaper than the larger job shop; (c) at 83,333 units, the repetitive shop is cheaper than the larger job shop. (Break-even analysis, moderate)

118. A product is currently made in a process-focused shop, where Fixed Costs are $8,000 per year and Variable Cost is $40 per unit. The firm sells the product for $200 per unit. What is the break-even point for this operation? What is the profit (or loss) on a demand of 200 units per year?
   BEP = 50 units; TR = $40,000, TC = $16,000, therefore Profit = $24,000. (Break-even analysis, moderate)

119. A product is currently made in a process-focused shop, where Fixed Costs are $8,000 per year and Variable Cost is $40 per unit. The firm currently sells 200 units of the product at $200 per unit. A manager is considering a repetitive focus to lower costs (and lower prices, thus raising demand). The costs of this proposed shop are Fixed Costs = $24,000 per year and Variable Costs = $10 per unit. If a price of $80 will allow 400 units to be sold, what profit (or loss) can this proposed new process expect? Do you anticipate that the manager will want to change the process? Explain.
   Old: TR = $40,000, TC = $16000, therefore Profit = $24,000.
   New: TR = $80 x 400 = $32,000, TC = $24,000 + $10 x 400 = $28,000, for a profit of $4,000. Most will say NO; the larger repetitive process is less profitable than the smaller process-focused shop. (Break-even analysis, moderate)

120. Health Care of the South is about to buy an expensive piece of diagnostic equipment. The company estimates that it will generate uniform revenues of $400,000 for each of the next eight years. What is the present value of this stream of earnings, at an interest rate of 7%? What is the present value if the machine lasts only six years, not eight? If the equipment cost $2,000,000, should the company purchase it?
   S = R * X = 400,000 * 5.971 = $2,388,400; S = R * X = 400,000 * 4.766 = $1,906,400
   The company should purchase the equipment if it believes it will last eight years, but not if it fears that it will last only six. (Strategy-driven investments, moderate)

121. Advantage Milling Devices is preparing to buy a new machine for precision milling of special metal alloys. This device can earn $300 per hour, and can run 3,000 hours per year. The machine is expected to be this productive for four years. If the interest rate is 8%, what is the present value? What is the present value if the interest rate is not 8%, but 10%? Why does present value fall when interest rates rise?

S = R * X = 300 * 3,000 * 3.312 = $2,980,800; S = R * X = 300 * 3,000 * 3.17 = $2,853,300
NPV falls because higher interest rates create a greater discount on future receipts.
(Strategy-driven investments, moderate)

122. A new machine tool is expected to generate receipts as follows: $5,000 in year one; $3,000 in year two, nothing in the next year, and $2000 in the fourth year. At an interest rate of 6%, what is the present value of these receipts? Is this a better present value than $2500 each year over four years? Explain.

5,000 x .943 + 3,000 x .890 + 2,000 x .792 = $8,969 using table ($8,971.16 using Excel). The steady stream generates NPV of 2,500 x 3.465 = $8,662.5 ($8,662.76 using excel). The irregular stream has the higher present value because the large receipts are early. (Strategy-driven investments, moderate)

CHAPTER 7 SUPPLEMENT: OPERATIONS TECHNOLOGY

TRUE/FALSE

1. The new production technologies, in both manufacturing and services, are based largely on the electronic flow of information.
    True (Introduction, moderate)

2. The Internet has become a great source of technical resources for companies.
    True (The Internet, moderate)

3. Design for Manufacture and Assembly (DFMA) focuses on the effect of design upon assembly.
    True (Design technology, moderate)

4. Computer-Aided Design is the use of computers to interactively design products and prepare engineering documentation.
    True (Design technology, moderate)

5. Computer-aided manufacturing (CAM) refers to the use of specialized computer programs to direct and control manufacturing equipment.
    True (Design technology, moderate)

6. Computer Numeric control (CNC) refers to the use of specialized computer programs to direct and control a specific piece of manufacturing equipment.
    True (Design technology, moderate)

7. Virtual reality technology can simulate the experience of driving a car not yet manufactured.
    True (Design technology, moderate)

8. Virtual reality technology can improve designs less expensively than the use of physical models or prototypes.
    True (Design technology, moderate)

9. Process control is the use of information technology to monitor and control a physical process.
    True (Production technology, moderate)

10. Periodic measurements, computer analysis of digitized data, resulting in feedback or signals are activities typical of process control systems.
    True (Production technology, moderate)

11. Vision systems are less consistent than their human counterparts.
    False (Production technology, moderate)

12. One advantage of the use of robots is improved consistency.
    True (Production technology, moderate)

13. Flexible manufacturing systems, because of easily changed control programs, are able to perform such tasks as manufacturing one-of-a-kind parts economically.
True (Production technology, moderate)

14. Automated storage and retrieval systems are commonly used in distribution facilities of retailers.
True (Production technology, moderate)

15. Computer-integrated manufacturing involves DNC machines linked together by an automated material handling system.
False (Production technology, moderate)

16. Production technology has had a major impact on services, but as yet there has been little reduction in service labor requirements.
False (Technology in services, moderate)

17. Point-of-sale terminals, optical checkout scanners, and ATMs are examples of technology's impact on services.
True (Technology in services, moderate)

18. Expert systems are modeled on the architecture of the brain and can perform pattern recognition.
False (Information sciences in operations, moderate)

19. Neural networks are designed to speed the flow of information from country to country in global organizations.
False (Information sciences in operations, moderate)

20. Enterprise resource planning allows companies to automate and integrate the majority of their business processes.
True (Enterprise Resource Planning (ERP), moderate)

21. Enterprise resource planning systems are stand-alone systems that limit the sharing of information.
False (Enterprise Resource Planning (ERP), moderate)

22. ERP systems are easily installed.
False (Enterprise Resource Planning (ERP), moderate)

23. ERP systems use client/server networks.
True (Enterprise Resource Planning (ERP), moderate)

24. ERP requires major changes in the company that installs it.
True (Enterprise Resource Planning (ERP), moderate)

25. ERP systems cannot be used in service industries.
False (Enterprise Resource Planning (ERP), moderate)

MULTIPLE CHOICE

26. The Internet
    a. is an international computer network connecting millions of companies and people
    b. is still in its infancy
    c. has already had a significant impact on operations management
    d. enhances communications between organizations
    e. all of the above

    e (The Internet, moderate)

27. "The use of computers to interactively design products and prepare engineering documentation" is a statement describing
    a. CNC machines
    b. computer-aided manufacture
    c. vision systems
    d. computer-aided design
    e. flexible manufacturing systems

    d (Design technology, moderate)

28. Which of the following is true regarding Computer-Aided Design?
    a. It is the use of computers to interactively design products and prepare engineering documentation.
    b. It is too expensive to use in most manufacturing and design settings.
    c. It is an old technology, no longer in significant use.
    d. It results in longer development cycles for virtually all products.
    e. All of the above are true.

    a (Design technology, moderate)

29. DFMA is an extension of CAD that
    a. contributes to improved designs and faster product development
    b. focuses on the effect of design upon assembly
    c. allows for significant reductions in manufacturing costs
    d. all of the above
    e. none of the above

    d (Design technology, moderate)

30. Which of the following is **true** concerning CAD?
    a. Most product costs are determined at the design stage.
    b. Design options are easier to review before final commitments are made.
    c. Virtually all products have their development cycle shortened.
    d. Accurate information flows to other departments.
    e. All of the above.

    e (Design technology, moderate)

31.	Which of these statements best describes virtual reality technology?
	a.	the use of special computer programs to direct and control manufacturing equipment
	b.	the ability to depict objects in three-dimensional form
	c.	a visual form of communication in which images substitute for the real thing
	d.	to monitor and control a physical process
	e.	none of the above
	c (Design technology, moderate)

32.	Two extensions of CAD technology are
	a.	DFMA and 3-D object modeling
	b.	CAM and CIM
	c.	vision systems and robots
	d.	NC and CNC machines
	e.	none of the above
	a (Design technology, moderate)

33.	Which of these is **not** a benefit of CAD/CAM?
	a.	shorter design time
	b.	production cost reductions
	c.	new range of capabilities
	d.	images substitute for the real product
	e.	database availability
	d (Design technology, moderate)

34.	Which of the following are among those technology advances that enhance production?
	a.	automated storage and retrieval systems
	b.	flexible manufacturing systems
	c.	computer integrated manufacturing
	d.	vision systems
	e.	all of the above
	e (Design technology, moderate)

35.	Which of the following are production-enhancing technology advances?
	a.	standard for the exchange of product data
	b.	flexible manufacturing systems
	c.	virtual reality systems
	d.	computer-aided design
	e.	all of the above
	b (Design technology, difficult)

36.	Which of the following are typical of process control systems?
	a.	they have sensors
	b.	their sensors take measurements on a periodic basis
	c.	the sensors' measurements are digitized
	d.	the digitized data are analyzed by computer, which generates feedback
	e.	all of the above
	e (Production technology, moderate)

37. The use of information technology to monitor and control a physical process is known as
    a. computer-aided design
    b. information numeric control
    c. numeric control
    d. process control
    e. none of the above
    d (Production technology, moderate)

38. Which of the following is **true** regarding vision systems?
    a. They do not become bored.
    b. They are consistently accurate.
    c. They are modest in cost.
    d. All of the above are true.
    e. None of the above are true.
    d (Production technology, moderate)

39. Which of the following statements regarding robots is **true**?
    a. they are now cost competitive for a wide range of tasks
    b. communication between robot and operator is typically provided by a computer
    c. instructions to robots provide complete task control
    d. robots can be used in continuous processes
    e. all of the above are true
    e (Production technology, difficult)

40. "Automatic placement and withdrawal of parts and products into and from designated places in a warehouse" describes
    a. ASRS
    b. AGV
    c. CAD/CAM
    d. CIM
    e. FMS
    a (Production technology, moderate)

41. Which of the following statements regarding automated guided vehicles is **false**?
    a. They are used to move mail in offices.
    b. They are used to move workers from one side of the plant to the other.
    c. They are used to deliver meals in hospitals and jails.
    d. They are an alternative to monorails, conveyors, and robots in automated material handling.
    e. They are electronically guided and controlled carts used to move parts and equipment.
    b (Production technology, moderate)

42. A flexible manufacturing system is known as a(n)
    a. direct numerical control (DNC) machine
    b. robot
    c. automatic guided vehicle
    d. automated work cell
    e. automated production system
    d (Production technology, moderate)

43. A system that can economically produce low-volume, high variety products is
   a. computer-aided manufacturing
   b. computer-integrated manufacturing
   c. an automated robotic system
   d. a flexible manufacturing system
   e. none of the above
   d (Production technology, moderate)

44. Computer-integrated manufacturing (CIM) includes manufacturing systems that have
   a. computer-aided design, a flexible manufacturing system, inventory control, warehousing and shipping integrated
   b. transaction processing, management information systems and decision support systems integrated
   c. automated guided vehicles, robots, and process control
   d. robots, automated guided vehicles, and transfer equipment
   e. all of the above
   a (Production technology, moderate)

45. An automated production system in which the DNC machines are linked together by an automated material handling system is known as a(n)
   a. adaptive control system
   b. robotics
   c. flexible manufacturing system
   d. automatic guided vehicle (AGV) system
   e. manufacturing cell
   c (Production technology, moderate)

46. Which one of the following technologies is used **only** for material handling, **not** actual production or assembly?
   a. Robots
   b. CNC
   c. AGV
   d. CAD
   e. FMS
   c (Production technology, moderate)

47. "Operators simply load new programs, as necessary, to produce different products" describes
   a. CAD
   b. automated guided vehicles
   c. vision systems
   d. robots
   e. flexible manufacturing systems
   e (Production technology, moderate)

48. Examples of the impact of technology on services include
    a. ATM machines
    b. supermarket scanners
    c. ticketless air travel
    d. electronic hotel key/lock systems
    e. all of the above
    e (Technologies in services, moderate)

49. Which of the following is modeled on the human brain's meshlike architecture, can perform pattern recognition, and can be programmed to learn?
    a. expert systems
    b. automated guided vehicles
    c. neural networks
    d. vision systems
    e. all of the above
    c (Information sciences in operations, moderate)

50. Which of the following is **true** regarding the impact of information sciences on service operations?
    a. Automatic identification systems, such as bar codes, allow operations data to be captured without workers keying in data.
    b. Management information systems provide much of the control information for a firm.
    c. The Internet has become a source of technical information for customers as well as companies.
    d. Expert systems mimic human logic to solve problems much as human experts would.
    e. All of the above are true.
    e (Information sciences in operations, moderate)

51. Enterprise Resource Planning (ERP)
    a. has existed for over a decade
    b. does not integrate well with functional areas other than operations
    c. automates and integrates the majority of business processes
    d. is inexpensive to implement
    e. all of the above
    c (Enterprise Resource Planning (ERP), moderate)

52. Which of the following is **false** concerning Enterprise Resource Planning (ERP)?
    a. It attempts to automate and integrate the majority of business processes.
    b. It shares common data and practices across the enterprise.
    c. It provides and accesses information in a real-time environment.
    d. It is inexpensive to implement.
    e All of the above are true.
    d (Enterprise Resource Planning (ERP), moderate)

53. Enterprise Resource Planning (ERP)
    a. has been made possible because of advances in hardware and software
    b. uses client/server networks
    c. creates commonality of databases
    d. uses business application-programming interfaces (BAPI) to access their database
    e. all of the above are true of ERP
    e (Enterprise Resource Planning (ERP), moderate)

54. All of the following are advantages of Enterprise Resource Planning (ERP) **except**
    a. creates commonality of databases
    b. increases communications and collaboration worldwide
    c. helps integrate multiple sites and business units
    d. requires major changes in the company and its processes to implement
    e. can provide a strategic advantage over competitor
    d (Enterprise Resource Planning (ERP), moderate)

FILL-IN-THE-BLANK

55. The _____ is reshaping how business thinks about delivering value to its customers, interacting with suppliers, and managing its employees.
    Internet (The Internet, moderate)

56. The _____ is an international computer network connecting people and organizations around the world.
    Internet (The Internet, easy)

57. An in-house Internet is called an _____
    intranet (The Internet, moderate)

58. The interactive use of a computer to develop and document a design is _____.
    computer-aided design or CAD (Design technology, moderate)

59. _____ provides a format allowing the electronic transmittal of three-dimensional data.
    Standard for the exchange of product data or STEP (Design technology, moderate)

60. The use of information technology to control machinery is called _____.
    computer-aided manufacturing or CAM (Design technology, moderate)

61. The control of machines by computer programs is called _____.
    numerical control or NC (Production technology, moderate)

62. _____ is the use of information technology to control a physical process.
    Process control (Production technolgy, moderate)

63. A _____ is a flexible machine with the ability to hold, move, or grab items.
    robot (Product technology, moderate)

64. _____ is a computer-controlled warehouse that provides for the automatic placement of parts into and from designated places within the warehouse.
Automated storage and retrieval system or ASRS (Production technology, moderate)

65. _____ is an electronically guided and controlled cart used to move materials.
Automated guided vehicle or AGV (Production technology, moderate)

66. A _____ uses an automated work cell controlled by electronic signals from a common centralized computer facility.
flexible manufacturing system or FMS (Production technology, moderate)

67. A _____ is a system that processes the transactions that occur within and between firms.
transaction processing system (Information sciences in operations, moderate)

68. An _____ is a computer program that mimics human logic and "solves" problems much as a human expert would.
expert system (Information sciences in operations, moderate)

69. A(n) _____ system is a packaged business software that automates and integrates the majority of their business processes, shares common data and practices across the entire enterprise, and produces and accesses information in a real-time environment.
enterprise resource planning or ERP (Enterprise Resource Planning (ERP), moderate)

SHORT ANSWERS

70. How has the Internet impacted operations management?
It enables integration of traditional information systems, as well as enhancing communication between organizations. Internet-based systems tie together global design, manufacturing, delivery, sales, and after-service activities. It reshapes how businesses deliver value to their customers, interact with suppliers, and manage employees. The Internet enhances communications, collaboration, and productivity. (The Internet, difficult)

71. List the tools provided by the information sciences that contribute to better, cheaper, and more rapidly designed products.
CAD, STEP, CAM, and virtual technology. (Design technology, easy)

72. List the benefits of CAD and CAM.
Product quality, shorter design time, production cost reductions, database availability, and new range of capabilities. (Design technology, moderate)

73. Describe how DFMA might help a designer of motorcycles.
It allows examination of designs before manufacturing, making changes easier and cheaper. Thus a new seat design could be examined for fit, strength, clearances with other parts on the electronic drawing before a manufacturing mistake is made. It allows for significant reductions in manufacturing costs. (Design technology, easy)

74. Explain, in your own words, how STEP can contribute to the globalization of an enterprise.
STEP is an international standard for electronic transfer of product design information; it can be exchanged internationally, so that product developers in New York can communicate with designers in India who can communicate easily with manufacturers in China. The organization can more easily be geographically dispersed if this information can so easily be exchanged. (Design technology, easy)

75. List the advances being made in technology to enhance production.
Numerical control, process control, vision systems, robots, automated storage and retrieval systems, automated guided vehicles, flexible manufacturing systems, and computer integrated manufacturing. (Production technology, moderate)

76. List the typical elements in a process control system.
Sensors collect data; analog devices read data on periodic basis; measurements are digitized and transmitted to a computer; data is analyzed; and output in the form of signals, diagrams, charts, messages, etc. (Production technology, moderate)

77. Explain, in your own words, what a robot is, within the context of production technology.
A robot is a mechanical device that may have a few electronic impulses stored on a semiconductor chip that will activate motors or switches. (Production technology, moderate)

78. List the benefits of flexible manufacturing systems.
Improved capital utilization, low direct labor cost, reduced inventory, and consistent quality. (Production technology, moderate)

79. Explain, in your own words, what a **Flexible Manufacturing System** is.
A system using an automated work cell controlled by electronic signals from a common centralized computer facility. (Production technology, moderate)

80. In what way does CIM connect CAD to FMS?
FMS connects backward to CAD, using engineering, production, and inventory data. CAD data generates instructions for NC machines. If this NC is connected to others in an FMS, the whole is CIM-integrated from design through machine control and material handling. (Production technology, moderate)

81. List five examples of technology's impact on services. Specifically, identify one of these which has led to labor cost reductions. Discuss briefly. Can you add an item, not identified in the textbook, to this list?
Textbook identifies about three dozen examples. Students may add examples like PointCast (or other "push" information technologies), Amazon.com (fully electronic Internet-based shopping), or examples from entertainment (video gaming, network gaming). (Technology in services, moderate)

82. Describe briefly what an Automatic Identification Systems is. Describe how service organizations could use AIS to reduce operating costs and, at the same time, increase the variety of services offered.

   Bar-codes, radio signals, and other optical signals automate data entry. Suggested: Costs are reduced because clerks spend much less time keying in prices and quantities; new services are possible because the added detail from AIS systems allows greater information about customers and products. (Information sciences in operations, moderate)

83. What does Enterprise Resource Planning (ERP) allow an organization to do?
   It allows them to automate and integrate the majority of their business processes, to share common data and practices across the entire enterprise, and to produce and access information in a real-time environment. (Enterprise Resource Planning (ERP), moderate)

84. What are the advantages of Enterprise Resource Planning (ERP)?
   It provides integration of the supply-chain, production, and administrative processes; creates commonality of databases, incorporates improved, redesigned, or "best" practices; increases communication and collaboration worldwide; helps integrate multiple sites and business units; comes with software core that is off-the-shelf coding; and provides a strategic advantage over competitors. (Enterprise Resource Planning (ERP), moderate)

85. What are the disadvantages of Enterprise Resource Planning (ERP)?
   It is very expensive to purchase, and even more costly to customize, requires major changes in the company and processes to implement; is such a complex program that many companies cannot adjust to it; it involves an ongoing process for implementation; which is often never completed; and expertise in ERP is limited, with staffing an ongoing problem. (Enterprise Resource Planning (ERP), moderate)

CHAPTER 8: LOCATION STRATEGIES

TRUE/FALSE

1. Generally, the objective of the location decision is to maximize the firm's profit.
    False (The strategic importance of location, easy)

2. When selecting a location, service organizations typically focus on minimizing costs.
    False (The strategic importance of location, easy)

3. When choosing a location, industrial firms typically focus on minimizing costs.
    True (The strategic importance of location, easy)

4. The ratio of labor cost per day to productivity, in units per day, is the labor cost per unit.
    True (Factors that affect location decisions, moderate)

5. For a location decision, labor productivity may be important in isolation, but low wage rates are a more important criterion.
    False (Factors that affect location decisions, moderate)

6. Unfavorable exchange rates can offset low wage rates and high productivity advantages in foreign countries.
    True (Factors that affect location decisions, moderate)

7. Tangible costs, as they relate to location decision making, include such items as utilities, labor, material, taxes, and depreciation.
    True (Factors that affect location decisions, moderate)

8. Intangible costs are easier to measure than tangible costs.
    False (Factors that affect location decisions, moderate)

9. Manufacturers may want to locate close to their customers, not their resources, if the transportation of finished goods is expensive or difficult.
    True (Factors that affect location decisions, moderate)

10. Companies like to locate close to competitors.
    True (Factors that affect location decisions, moderate)

11. Clustering occurs when a major resource is found in a region.
    True (Factors that affect location decisions, moderate)

12. A requirement of factor rating is that the sum of factor weights be 1.
    False (Methods of evaluating location alternatives, moderate)

13. The factor-rating method can consider both tangible and intangible costs.
    True (Methods of evaluating location alternatives, moderate)

14. Break-even analysis of location decisions considers both tangible and intangible cost factors.
    False (Methods of evaluating location alternatives, moderate)

15. The graphic approach to location break-even analysis displays the range of volume over which each location is preferable.
True (Methods of evaluating location alternatives, moderate)

16. The center-of-gravity method finds the location of a centralized facility, such as a distribution center that will maximize the organization's revenue.
False (Methods of evaluating location alternatives, moderate)

17. The center-of-gravity method considers the number of trips necessary, but not the distance per trip in calculating the optimal location.
False (Methods of evaluating location alternatives, moderate)

18. Quality of transportation facilities is ordinarily considered in the transportation method.
False (Methods of evaluating location alternatives, moderate)

19. The transportation model calculates an optimal shipping system between a central facility and several outlying customers.
False (Methods of evaluating location alternatives, moderate)

20. Service firms choose locations based, in part, on the revenue potential of a site.
True (Service location strategy, moderate)

21. Both service and industrial location decisions make extensive use of the factor rating method.
True (Service location strategy, moderate)

22. Industrial location decisions will generally pay more attention to parking, access, and traffic counts than will service location decisions.
False (Service location strategy, moderate)

23. Industrial location decisions often assume that costs are relatively constant for a given area.
False (Service location strategy, moderate)

24. Labor cost and labor availability often drive the location decision in the telemarketing industry.
True (Service location strategy, moderate)

MULTIPLE CHOICE

25. Service location decisions typically attempt to
    a. reduce purchasing costs
    b. minimize costs
    c. decrease labor costs
    d. be environmentally correct
    e. none of the above
    e (Strategic importance of location, easy)

26. Globalization of the location decision is the result of all of the following **except**
    a. better international communications
    b. higher quality of labor overseas
    c. ease of capital flow between countries
    d. high differences in labor costs
    e. more rapid travel and shipping
    b (Strategic importance of location, moderate)

27. Industrial location analysis typically attempts to
    a. reduce costs
    b. maximize sales
    c. focus more on human resources
    d. be environmentally correct
    e. none of the above
    a (Strategic importance of location, easy)

28. A location decision for a traditional department store (Macy's) would tend to have a(n)
    a. cost focus
    b. revenue focus
    c. labor focus
    d. environmental focus
    e. education focus
    b (Strategic importance of location, moderate)

29. A location decision for an appliance manufacturer would tend to have a(n)
    a. cost focus
    b. revenue focus
    c. labor focus
    d. environmental focus
    e. education focus
    a (Strategic importance of location, moderate)

30. Which of the following is usually **not** one of the top considerations in choosing a manufacturing location?
    a. availability of labor and labor productivity
    b. exchange rates
    c. attitude of governmental units
    d. entertainment opportunities
    e. zoning regulations
    d (Factors that affect location decisions, moderate)

31. In location planning, environmental regulations, cost and availability of utilities, and taxes are
    a. regional/community factors
    b. global factors
    c. site-related factors
    d. country factors
    e. none of the above
    a (Factors that affect location decisions, moderate)

32. When making a location decision at the country level, which of these would be considered?
    a. corporate desires
    b. land/construction costs
    c. air, rail, highway, waterway systems
    d. zoning restrictions
    e. cultural and economic issues
    e (Factors that affect location decisions, moderate)

33. When making a location decision at the region/community level, which of these would be considered?
    a. government rules, attitudes, stability, incentives
    b. cultural and economic issues
    c. labor availability and costs
    d. zoning restrictions
    e. air, rail, highway, waterway systems
    c (Factors that affect location decisions, moderate)

34. Which of these factors would be considered when making a location decision at the region/community level?
    a. government rules, attitudes, stability, incentives
    b. cultural and economic issues
    c. zoning restrictions
    d. proximity to raw materials and customers
    e. air, rail, highway, waterway systems
    d (Factors that affect location decisions, moderate)

35. Which of these factors would be considered when making a location decision at the site level?
    a. government rules, attitudes, stability, incentives
    b. cultural and economic issues
    c. cost and availability of utilities
    d. proximity to raw materials and customers
    e. air, rail, highway, waterway systems
    e (Factors that affect location decisions, moderate)

36. Tangible costs include which of the following?
    a. climatic conditions
    b. availability of public transportation
    c. quality and attitude of prospective employees
    d. utility costs such as electricity and gas
    e. zoning regulations
    d (Factors that affect location decisions, moderate)

37. Intangible costs include which of the following?
    a. quality of education
    b. availability of public transportation
    c. quality of prospective employees
    d. all of the above
    e. none of the above
    d (Factors that affect location decisions, moderate)

38. Evaluating location alternatives by comparing their composite (weighted-average) scores is
   a. cost-volume analysis
   b. transportation model analysis
   c. factor rating analysis
   d. linear regression analysis
   e. crossover analysis
   c (Methods of evaluating location alternative, moderate)

39. Which of the following methods best considers intangible costs related to a location decision?
   a. crossover methods
   b. locational break-even analysis
   c. the transportation method
   d. the assignment method
   e. none of the above
   e (Factors that affect location decisions, moderate)

40. A clothing chain is considering two different locations for a new retail outlet. They have identified the four factors listed in the following table as the basis for evaluation, and have assigned weights as shown on the left. The manager has rated each location on each factor, on a 100-point basis, as shown on the right.

Factor	Factor Description	Weight		Barclay	Chester
1	Average community income	.40		30	20
2	Community growth potential	.25		40	30
3	Availability of public transportation	.15		20	20
4	Labor cost	.20		10	30

   What is the score for Barclay?
   a. 10.00
   b. 24.50
   c. 25.75
   d. 27.00
   e. 100.00
   d (Factors that affect location decisions, moderate)

41. An approach to location analysis that includes both qualitative and quantitative considerations is
   a. locational cost-volume
   b. factor rating
   c. transportation model
   d. assignment method
   e. make or buy analysis
   b (Factors that affect location decisions, moderate)

42. Community attitudes, zoning restrictions, and quality of labor force are likely to be considered in which of the following location decision methods?
   a. factor rating method
   b. transportation method
   c. locational break-even analysis
   d. center-of-gravity method
   e. simulation
   a (Factors that affect location decisions, moderate)

43. A full-service restaurant is considering opening a new facility in a specific city. The table below shows its ratings of four factors at each of two potential sites.

Factor	Weight	Gary Mall	Belt Line
Affluence of local population	.20	30	30
Traffic flow	.40	50	20
Parking availability	.20	30	40
Growth potential	.20	10	30

   The score for Gary Mall is _____ and the score for Belt Line is _____.
   a. 120; 120
   b. 22; 24
   c. 18; 120
   d. 34; 28
   e. none of the above
   d (Factors that affect location decisions, moderate)

44. The crossover chart for location break-even analysis shows where
   a. fixed costs are equal for alternative locations
   b. variable costs are equal for alternative locations
   c. total costs are equal for alternative locations
   d. fixed costs equal variable costs
   e. none of the above
   c (Factors that affect location decisions, moderate)

45. The center of gravity method does **not** take into consideration
   a. the location of markets
   b. the volume of goods shipped to the markets
   c. the value of the goods shipped
   d. the combination of volume and distance
   e. the center of gravity method considers none of the above
   c (Factors that affect location decisions, moderate)

46. The center-of-gravity method is used primarily to determine what type of locations?
   a. service locations
   b. manufacturing locations
   c. distribution center locations
   d. supplier locations
   e. telemarketing locations
   c (Factors that affect location decisions, moderate)

47. A regional bookstore chain is about to build a distribution center that is centrally located for its eight retail outlets. It will most likely employ which of the following tools of analysis?
   a. assembly line balancing
   b. load-distance analysis
   c. center-of-gravity model
   d. linear programming
   e. all of the above
   c (Factors that affect location decisions, moderate)

48. East Texas Seasonings is preparing to build one processing center to serve its four sources of seasonings. The four source locations are at coordinates shown below. Also, the volume from each source is provided. What is the center of gravity?

	X-coordinate	Y-coordinate	Volume
Athens, Texas	30	30	100
Beaumont, Texas	20	10	400
Carthage, Texas	10	70	100
Denton, Texas	50	50	200

   a. X = 30; Y = 27.5
   b. X = 22000; Y = 24000
   c. X = 27.5; Y = 30
   d. center of gravity = 27
   e. none of the above
   c (Factors that affect location decisions, moderate)

49. The transportation method, when applied to location analysis
   a. minimizes total fixed cost
   b. minimizes total production and transportation cost
   c. minimizes total variable cost
   d. maximizes revenues
   e. minimizes the movement of goods
   b (Factors that affect location decisions, moderate)

50. Production and/or shipping costs are always considered in which of the following location decision methods?
   a. factor rating method
   b. locational break-even analysis
   c. center-of-gravity method
   d. transportation method
   e. crossover analysis
   d (Factors that affect location decisions, moderate)

51. Which of the following are among the eight components of revenue and volume for the service firm?
    a. quality of the competition
    b. competition in the area
    c. purchasing power of the drawing area
    d. uniqueness of the firm's and the competitor's locations
    e. all of the above
    e (Service location strategy, moderate)

52. Which of the following are **not** among the eight components of revenue and volume for the service firm?
    a. quality of the competition
    b. shipment cost of finished goods
    c. purchasing power of the drawing area
    d. uniqueness of the firm's and the competitor's locations
    e. competition in the area
    b (Service location strategy, moderate)

53. Traffic counts and demographic analysis of drawing areas are techniques associated with
    a. an industrial location decision
    b. a manufacturing location decision
    c. a retail or professional service location decision
    d. the factor rating method
    e. the transportation method
    c (Service location strategy, moderate)

54. LaQuinta Motor Inns has a competitive edge over its rivals because
    a. it picks better locations than its rivals
    b. it picks larger locations than its rivals
    c. it builds only along Interstate highways
    d. it uses regression analysis to determine which variables most influence profitability
    e. all of the above
    d (Service location strategy, moderate)

55. Location analysis techniques typically employed by service organizations include
    a. factor rating method
    b. center of gravity method
    c. break-even analysis.
    d. traffic counts
    e. all of the above
    e (Service location strategy, moderate)

56. Which one of the following factors does **not** affect the volume and revenue for a service firm?
    a. affluence of customer drawing area
    b. competition in the area
    c. physical qualities of facilities and neighboring businesses
    d. environmental regulations
    e. quality of the competition
    d (Service location strategy, moderate)

57. Which of the following is most likely to affect the location decision of a service firm rather than a manufacturing firm?
   a. energy and utility costs
   b. attitude toward unions
   c. cost of shipping finished goods
   d. labor costs
   e. parking and access
   e (Service location strategy, moderate)

58. Traffic counts and demographic analysis of drawing areas are associated with
   a. industrial location decisions
   b. manufacturing location decisions
   c. service location decisions
   d. the transportation method
   e. cost-volume analysis
   c (Service location strategy, moderate)

59. Which of the following is a location analysis technique typically employed by a service organization?
   a. linear programming
   b. queuing theory
   c. crossover charts
   d. purchasing power analysis
   e. cost-volume analysis
   d (Service location strategy, moderate)

60. Location analysis techniques typically employed by manufacturing organizations include
   a. locational break-even analysis
   b. queuing theory
   c. correlation analysis and traffic counts
   d. simulation
   e. demographic analysis
   a (Service location strategy, moderate)

61. A jewelry store is more likely than a jewelry manufacturer to consider _____ in making a location decision.
   a. cost of raw materials
   b. parking and access
   c. climate
   d. transportation costs
   e. taxes
   b (Service location strategy, moderate)

62. Which of these is usually **not** a major element of volume and revenue for the service firm?
    a. purchasing power of the customer drawing area
    b. taxes
    c. competition in the area
    d. quality of the competition
    e. quality of management
    b (Service location strategy, moderate)

63. Which of the following is most likely to affect the location strategy of a manufacturing firm?
    a. utility costs
    b. purchasing power of drawing area
    c. competition in the area
    d. parking availability
    e. appearance/image of the area
    a (Service location strategy, moderate)

64. Which of these assumptions is **not** associated with strategies for goods-producing location decisions?
    a. most major costs can be identified explicitly for each site
    b. focus on identifiable cost
    c. high customer contact issues are critical
    d. intangible costs can be evaluated
    e. location is a major determinant of cost
    c (Service location strategy, moderate)

65. Geographic Information Systems can assist the location decision by
    a. automating center of gravity problems
    b. computerizing factor rating analysis
    c. updating transportation method solutions
    d. giving good Internet placement for virtual storefronts
    e. combining geography with demographic analysis
    e (Service location strategy, moderate)

FILL-IN-THE-BLANK

66. _____ costs are readily identifiable and can be measured with precision.
    Tangible (Factors that affect location decision, easy)

67. _____ occurs when competing companies locate near each other because of a critical mass of information, talent, venture capital, or natural resources.
    Clustering (Methods of evaluating location alternatives, moderate)

68. The _____ method is popular because a wide variety of factors, from education to recreation to labor skills, can be objectively included.
    factor-rating (Methods of evaluating location alternatives, moderate)

69. _____ is a cost-volume analysis to make an economic comparison of location alternatives.
    Locational break-even analysis (Methods of evaluating location alternatives, moderate)

70. The _____ is a mathematical technique used for finding the best location for a single distribution point that services several stores or areas.

center-of-gravity method (Methods of evaluating location alternatives, moderate)

71. The _____ is used to determine the best pattern of shipments from several points of supply to several points of demand.

transportation method (Methods of evaluating location alternatives, moderate)

SHORT ANSWERS

72. What is the key concept to Fedex's location competitive advantage? Discuss.

The central hub concept, with Memphis selected for several reasons, including its being in the middle of the country and having very few hours of bad weather closures. (Global company profile: Federal Express, moderate)

73. Describe Motorola's approach to seeking low-cost overseas locations.

Motorola pursues a low-cost strategy, but rejects countries with insufficient infrastructure and education. That is in line with the notion that low wages cannot be taken in isolation of productivity and other considerations. (The strategic importance of location, moderate)

74. State the fundamental objective of a location strategy.

Maximize the benefit of location to the firm. (The strategic importance of location, moderate)

75. List the changes that have fostered globalization.

Better international communications; more rapid, reliable travel and shipping; ease of capital flow between countries; and high differences in labor costs. (The strategic importance of location, moderate)

76. While most organizations may make the location decision infrequently, there are some organizations that make the decision quite regularly and often. Provide one or two examples. How might their approach to the location decision differ from the norm?

Most franchise operations add many new units per year; Exxon, McDonald's, and Wal-Mart add hundreds of units per year, almost a daily location decision. For such organizations, the location decision becomes more structured, more routine. Perhaps they better discover what makes their strategic locations decisions successful. (The strategic importance of location, moderate)

77. State three reasons why companies may need new locations.

Demand has outgrown the current plant's capacity; changes in labor productivity, exchange rates, costs, or attitudes have occurred; and customer demand has shifted. (The strategic importance of location, moderate)

78. List those factors, other than globalization, that affect the location decision.

Labor productivity, foreign exchange, changing attitudes toward the industry, unions, employment, zoning, pollution, and taxes. (Factors that affect location decision, moderate)

79. Why shouldn't low wage rates alone be sufficient to select a location?
Productivity should be considered also. Employees with poor training, poor education, or poor work habits are not a good buy. Moreover, employees who cannot or will not reach their place of work are not much good to the organization. (Factors that affect location decision, moderate)

80. What is the impact of exchange rates on location decisions?
Exchange rates fluctuate, and can negate savings from low wage rates. (Factors that affect location decision, moderate)

81. List the textbook's quality of life issues in a community. Can you add any items to this list? Support your choices.
The basic list includes all levels of education, cost of living, health care, sports, cultural activities, transportation, housing, entertainment, and religious facilities. Additions could include clean air and water, perhaps diversity. (Factors that affect location decision, moderate)

82. List those items associated with site cost; with labor cost.
Site cost: land, expansion, parking, and drainage. Labor cost: wages, unionization, and productivity. (Factors that affect location decision, moderate)

83. List those state and local government fiscal policies that affect a location decision.
Incentives, taxes, and unemployment compensation. (Factors that affect location decision, moderate)

84. List six factors that affect location decisions at the country (national) level.
Government rules, attitudes, stability, incentives; cultural and economic issues; location of markets; labor availability, attitudes, productivity, and costs; availability of supplies, communications, energy; and exchange rate. (Factors that affect location decision, moderate)

85. List eight factors that affect location decisions at the region/community (area) level.
Corporate desires; attractiveness of region (culture, taxes, climate, etc.); labor availability, costs, attitudes toward unions; cost and availability of utilities; environmental regulations of state and town; government incentives; proximity to raw materials and customers; and land/construction costs. (Factors that affect location decision, moderate)

86. List five factors that affect location decisions at the site level.
Site size and cost; air, rail, highway, waterway systems; zoning restrictions; nearness of services/supplies needed; and environmental impact issues. (Factors that affect location decision, moderate)

87. An old location adage states "Manufacturers locate near their resources, retailers locate near their customers." Discuss, with reference to the **proximity to markets** arguments of your text. Can you think of a counterexample in each case? Support your choices.

The issue of weight gain and weight loss during processing is important, and supports the manufacturing side of the saying (weight loss during mining and refining, for example, suggests shipping after processing). But JIT may be more easily accomplished when suppliers are clustered near the customer. And some services can take place at tremendous distances without sacrificing close contact. (Internet sales) (Factors that affect location decision, moderate)

88. List the four major methods for solving location problems.

Factor rating method, locational break-even analysis, center-of-gravity method, and transportation method. (Methods of evaluating location alternative, moderate)

89. List, in order, the steps in the factor rating approach to evaluating locations.

1. develop a list of relevant factors
2. assign a weight to each factor to reflect its relative importance in the company's objectives
3. develop a scale for each factor
4. have management score each location on each factor
5. multiply scores times weight for each factor, and total the score for each location
6. make a recommendation based upon the maximum point score
(Methods of evaluating location alternative, moderate)

90. Are there any disadvantages to the use of factor rating schemes?

Factor rating is subject to sensitivity to small swings in weights and scores, and is subject to subjectivity (different judges see different scores for same site). (Methods of evaluating location alternative, moderate)

91. List, in order, three steps to locational break-even (crossover) analysis.

1. determine fixed and variable cost for each location
2. plot the costs for each location, with costs on the vertical axis of the graph and annual volume on the horizontal axis
3. select the location that has the lowest total cost for the expected production volume
(Methods of evaluating location alternative, moderate)

92. List the eight major components of volume and revenue for a service firm.

1. purchasing power of the customer drawing area
2. service and image compatibility with demographics of the customer drawing area
3. competition in the area
4. quality of the competition
5. uniqueness of the firm's and competitor's locations
6. physical qualities of facilities and neighboring business
7. operating policies of the firm
8. quality of management
(Service location strategy, moderate)

93. Contrast the location problems of a food distributor and a supermarket. (The distributor sends trucks of food, meat, produce, etc., to the supermarket). Show the relevant considerations (factors) they share; show those where they differ.

The distributor is more concerned with transportation and storage cost, and the supermarket more concerned with proximity to markets. The distributor will focus more on roads, overall population density (store density), while the supermarket will focus more on neighborhood affluence, traffic patterns, etc. The distributor will be concerned with speedy and reliable delivery, the supermarket with easy access. Both will have concerns over attitudes and zoning. Both will need access to similar labor forces; both will need similar measures of workforce education, etc. Many other comparisons can be drawn. (Methods of evaluating location alternative, difficult)

94. State the three basic assumptions in determining the optimum location for a service organization. **Location is a major determinant of revenue; issues manifesting from high customer contact dominate; and costs are relatively constant for a given area, thus the revenue function is critical. (Methods of evaluating location alternative, moderate)**

95. State the four basic assumptions in determining the optimum location for a manufacturing organization.

Location is a major determinant of cost; most major costs can be identified explicitly for each site; low customer contact allows focus on the identifiable costs; and intangible cost can be objectively evaluated. (Methods of evaluating location alternative, moderate)

96. List the techniques used by service organizations to select locations. **Regression models to determine importance of various factors, factor rating method, traffic counts, demographic analysis of drawing area, purchasing power analysis of area, center-of-gravity method, and geographic information system. (Methods of evaluating location alternative, moderate)**

97. List the techniques used by industrial organizations to select locations. **Transportation method, factor rating method, locational break-even analysis, and cross-over charts. (Methods of evaluating location alternative, moderate)**

PROBLEMS

98. A clothing chain is considering two different locations for a new retail outlet. The organization has identified the four factors listed in the following table as the basis for evaluation, and has assigned weights as shown on the right side of this table. The manager has rated each location on each factor, on a 100-point basis (higher scores are better), as shown in the right-hand table.
    a. Calculate the composite score for each alternative location.
    b. Which site should be chosen?
    c. Are you concerned about the sensitivity and subjectivity of this solution? Comment.

Factor	Factor Description	Weight		Barclay	Chester
1	Average community income	.40		80	70
2	Community growth potential	.25		65	80
3	Availability of public transportation	.15		50	90
4	Labor cost	.20		60	65

The higher rated site is Chester, 74.5 to 67.75. There is a margin of several points, which should overcome most levels of subjectivity. The site factor scores are quite different, so that a small swing in weights could produce swings in scores of a few points, but probably not the seven necessary to reverse the findings. POM for Windows solution appears below.

Location Results

		clothing chain Solution	
	Weights	Barclay	Chester
Averge community income	0.4	80.	70.
Communty growth potential	0.25	65.	00.
Avail of public transport	0.15	50.	90.
Labor cost	0.2	60.	65.
Total	1.		
Weighted Total		67.75	74.5
Weighted Average		67.75	74.5

(Methods of evaluating location alternatives, moderate)

99. East Texas Seasonings is preparing to build one processing center to serve its four sources of seasonings. The four source locations are at coordinates shown below. Also, the volume from each source is provided.
    a. What is the center of gravity?
    b. How many distance units is it from this center of gravity to Athens?
    c. What is the rectilinear distance from center to Athens?

	X-coordinate	Y-coordinate	Volume
Athens, Texas	30	40	100
Beaumont, Texas	20	10	400
Carthage, Texas	50	60	100
Denton, Texas	10	70	200

Center of gravity is X = 22.5, Y = 35. From center to Athens is 9.014 units (not miles). City block distance is (30-22.5)+(40-35) = 12.5 units. POM for Windows solution appears below.

Location Results					
East Texas Seasonings Solution					
	Weight/# trips	x-coord	y-coord	X multiplied	Y multiplied
Athens	100.	30.	40.	3,000.	4,000.
Beaumont	400.	20.	10.	8,000.	4,000.
Carthage	100.	50.	60.	5,000.	6,000.
Denton	200.	10.	70.	2,000.	14,000.
Total	800.	110.	180.	18,000.	28,000.
Average		27.5	45.		
Weighted Average				22.5	35.
Median	400.			20.	10.

(**Methods of evaluating location alternatives, moderate**)

100. A manufacturing company preparing to build a new plant is considering three potential locations for it. The fixed and variable costs for the three alternative locations are presented below.
a. Complete a numeric locational cost-volume analysis.
b. Indicate over what range each of the alternatives A, B, C is the low-cost choice.
c. Is any alternative never preferred? Explain.

Costs	A	B	C
Fixed	2,000,000	1,500,000	3,000,000
Variable	$20/unit	$25/unit	$16/unit

B is cheapest up to 100,000 units; C is cheapest after 166,667 units. A is cheapest in between. The B-C crossover is not relevant (is above the A cost curve). Thus each alternative has an attractive range. POM for Windows solution appears below.

Breakeven/Cost-Volume Analysis Results

	Cost Type	Location A	Location B	Location C
		Manufacturing location Solution		
	Fixed	2,000,000.	1,500,000.	3,000,000.
	Variable	20.	25.	16.
BREAKEVEN POINTS	Units	Dollars		
Location A vs Location B	100,000.	4,000,000.		
Location A vs Location C	250,000.	7,000,000.		
Location B vs Location C	166,667.	5,666,675.		

(Methods of evaluating location alternatives, moderate)

101. A manufacturing company is considering two alternative locations for a new facility. The fixed and variable costs for the two locations are found in the table below. For which volume of business would the two locations be equally attractive? If the company plans on producing 50,000 units, which location would be more attractive?

	Glen Rose	Mesquite
Fixed Costs	$1,000,000	$1,300,000
Variable Costs	$25/unit	$20/unit

Crossover is at 60,000 units. Below the crossover, Glen Rose must be cheaper as it has the lower fixed cost. Thus for an estimated unit volume of 50,000, Glen Rose should be chosen. POM for Windows solution appears below.

⊞ Breakeven/Cost-Volume Analysis Results

	Cost Type	Glen Rose	Mesquite
		Manufacturing Location Solution	
	Fixed	1,000,000.	1,300,000.
	Variable	25.	20.
BREAKEVEN POINTS	Units	Dollars	
Glen Rose vs Mesquite	60,000.	2,500,000.	

(Methods of evaluating location alternatives, moderate)

102. Using the factor ratings shown below, determine which location alternative should be chosen on the basis of maximum composite score.

		Location		
Factor	Weight	A	B	C
Easy access	.15	84	71	91
Parking facilities	.20	72	76	92
Display area	.18	88	90	90
Shopper (walking) traffic	.21	94	86	80
Neighborhood wealth	.16	98	90	82
Neighborhood safety	.10	96	85	75

A is best (87.86), followed by C (86.03). B is somewhat further behind (83.01)

⊞ Location Results

	Weights	Location A	Location B	Location C
		Retail location Solution		
Easy access	0.15	84.	71.	91.
Parking facilities	0.2	72.	76.	92.
Display area available	0.18	88.	90.	92.
Shopper (walking) traffic	0.21	94.	86.	80.
Neighborhood wealth	0.16	98.	90.	82.
Neighborhood safety	0.1	96.	85.	75.
Total	1.			
Weighted Total		87.86	83.01	86.03
Weighted Average		87.86	83.01	86.03

(Methods of evaluating location alternatives, moderate)

103. A manager has received an analysis of several cities being considered for a new order fulfillment center (warehouse) for Shop at Home Network. The scores (scale is 10 points = best) are contained the table below.

a. If the manager weights the factors equally, how would the locations be ranked?

b. If transportation costs and operating costs are given weights that are double the weights of the others, should the locations be ranked differently?

	Location			
Factor	W	X	Y	Z
Business services	7	9	5	5
Community services	6	7	6	7
Real estate cost	7	3	8	7
Construction costs	8	5	6	5
Operating costs	7	4	7	6
Business taxes	6	9	5	4
Transportation costs	6	6	7	8

The locations are ranked W, Y, X, Z with equal weights; but W, Y, Z, X as revised. POM for Windows solution appears below.

Location Results

		Shop at Home Warehouse Solution			
	Weights	W	X	Y	Z
Business services	1.	7.	9.	5.	5.
Community services	1.	6.	7.	6.	7.
Real estate cost	1.	7.	3.	8.	7.
Construction cost	1.	8.	5.	6.	5.
Operating cost	1.	7.	4.	7.	6.
Business taxes	1.	6.	9.	5.	4.
Transportation costs	1.	6.	6.	7.	8.
Total	7.				
Weighted Total		47.	43.	44.	42.

Location Results

		Shop at Home Warehouse Solution			
	Weights	W	X	Y	Z
Business services	1.	7.	9.	5.	5.
Community services	1.	6.	7.	6.	7.
Real estate cost	1.	7.	3.	8.	7.
Construction cost	1.	8.	5.	6.	5.
Operating cost	2.	7.	4.	7.	6.
Business taxes	1.	6.	9.	5.	4.
Transportation costs	2.	6.	6.	7.	8.
Total	9.				
Weighted Total		60.	53.	58.	56.

(**Methods of evaluating location alternatives, moderate**)

160

104. Mil-Mill, which produces specialty textile fabrics or military uniforms, has plants in Syracuse and Philadelphia, will add a third such plant in either Athens, Baltimore, or Chapel Hill. The company has collected the following economic and noneconomic data.

The factor-rating scheme used by Mil-Mill is the following: For each site, the cost score is the ratio of minimum weekly cost to actual weekly cost, times 100. The weights are: cost, 0.35; finishing material supply, 0.20; maintenance facilities, 0.15; and community attitude, 0.30.

Factor	Athens	Baltimore	Chapel Hill
Economic factors			
Transportation cost/week	$780	$640	$560
Labor cost/week	$1200	$1020	$1180
Noneconomic factors			
Finishing material supply	35	85	70
Maintenance facilities	60	25	30
Community attitude	50	85	70

The cost ratio may seem a puzzle, but it generates a 0 to 100 scale, where the location with lowest cost gets 100. Example: Athens' total cost is $1980. Minimum cost is Baltimore, $1660. The ratio of 1660 to 1980 is .838. On composites, Baltimore is clearly best.

FACTOR	Weight	A	B	C	A	B	C
Transportation cost/week		$780	$640	$560			
Labor cost/week		$1,200	$1,020	$1,180			
Total cost	0.35	$1,980	$1,660	$1,740	83.8	100.0	95.4
Finishing material supply	0.2	35	85	70	35	85	70
Maintenance facilities	0.15	60	25	30	60	25	30
Community attitude	0.3	50	85	70	50	85	70
Multiplications		29.3	35.0	33.4			
		7	17	14			
		9	3.75	4.5			
		15	25.5	21			
Composite		**60.3**	**81.3**	**72.9**			

(Methods of evaluating location alternatives, moderate)

105. A small producer of machine tools wants to move to a larger building. Two alternatives have been identified. Bonham would have fixed costs of $800,000 per year and variable costs of $14,000 per standard unit produced. McKinney would have annual fixed costs of $920,000 and variable costs of $13,000 per standard unit. The finished items sell for $29,000 each.

a. At what volume of output would the two locations have the same profit?

b. For what range of output would Bonham be superior (have higher profits)?

c. For what range would McKinney be superior?

d. What is the relevance of break-even points for these cities?

$Profit_{Bonham} = -800000 + (29000-14000)X = -800000 + 15000X$

$Profit_{McKinney} = -920000 + (29000-13000)X = -920000 + 16000X$

Crossover is where $Profit_{Bonham} = Profit_{McKinney}$, or $-800000 + 15000X = -920000 + 16000X$

Crossover is at 120 units. McKinney is preferable beyond 120 units, Bonham below 120 units. Bonham has break even at about 53 units; McKinney about 58, so both are beyond break even at the crossover.

(Methods of evaluating location alternatives, moderate)

106. Location A would result in annual fixed costs of $300,000, variable costs of $55 per unit, and revenues of $68 per unit. Annual fixed costs at Location B are $600,000, with variable costs of $32 per unit, and revenue of $68 per unit. Sales volume is estimated to be 25,000 units per year. Which location is most attractive?

Profit A is 25000 x (68-55) - 300000 = $25,000.

Profit B is 25000 x (68-32) - 600000 = $300,000.

B is clearly more profitable at the estimated volume

(Methods of evaluating location alternatives, moderate)

107. A telecommunications firm is planning to lay fiber optic cable from several community college distance learning sites to a central studio, in such a way that the miles of cable is minimized. Some locations require more than one set of cables (these are the loads). Where should the studio be located to accomplish the objective? How many distance units (coordinates are not in miles) of cable need to be placed?

College	Map Coordinate (x, y)	Load
A	(2,10)	1
B	(6,8)	2
C	(4,9)	4
D	(9,5)	1
E	(8,1)	3
F	(3,2)	2
G	(2,6)	1

This is a center of gravity problem, even though it is not about shipping tangible items. X = 4.86, Y = 5.86. Distance units of cable equals 56.26. POM for Windows solution appears below.

Location Results

			Telecommunications Cables Solution		
	Weight/# trips	x-coord	y-coord	X multiplied	Y multiplied
A	1.	2.	10.	2.	10.
B	2.	6.	8.	12.	16.
C	4.	4.	9.	16.	36.
D	1.	9.	5.	9.	5.
E	3.	8.	1.	24.	3.
F	2.	3.	2.	6.	4.
G	1.	2.	6.	2.	6.
Total	14.	34.	41.	71.	80.
Average		4.8571	5.8571		

	Center	Weighted Center
A	5.0325	5.2727
B	2.4286	2.4671
C	3.2576	3.456
D	4.2306	3.993
E	5.7853	5.5499
F	4.281	4.2529
G	2.8607	3.0847
Total	27.8763	28.0762
Weighted total	55.9293	56.2639

(Methods of evaluating location alternatives, moderate)

108. The owner of a millwork shop is considering three alternative locations for a new plant for building embossed-and-clad steel exterior doors for residences. Fixed and variable costs follow. Since the plant ships nationwide, revenue is assumed the same regardless of plant location. Plot the total cost lines in the chart provided below, and identify the range over which each location is best.

| Costs | Location | | |
	A	B	C
Fixed	$750,000	$1,000,000	$1,100,000
Variable	$30	$18	$20

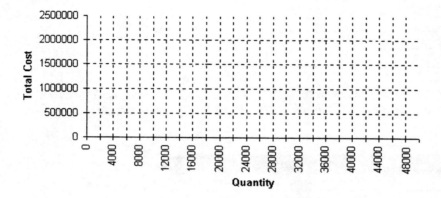

A is cheapest from 0 to about 21,000 units. B is cheapest thereafter. C can never be preferred.

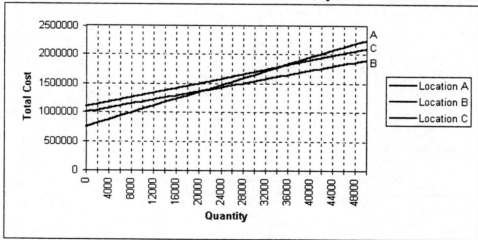

(Methods of evaluating location alternatives, moderate)

164

109. A manufacturing firm is considering three potential locations for a new parts manufacturing facility. A consulting firm has assessed three sites based on the four factors supplied by management as critical to the location's success. Given the management-supplied factor weights and the consultant team scores, which location should be selected? Scores are based on 50 = best. Do the results surprise you in any way? Comment.

Factor	Weight	Location		
		A	B	C
Labor Climate	20	35	40	40
Taxes	30	30	40	10
Utilities	10	25	10	45
Wages	40	10	30	25

B is clearly better than either A or C. This problem illustrates the importance of having good scores on important factors. POM for Windows solution appears below. C has scores that are about as high as those of B, but in the wrong places.

Location Results

	Weights	Location A	Location B	Location C
		Parts Facility Location Solution		
Labor climate	20.	35.	40.	40.
Taxes	30.	30.	40.	10.
Utilities	10.	25.	10.	45.
Wages	40.	10.	30.	25.
Total	100.			
Weighted Total		2,250.	3,300.	2,550.
Weighted Average		22.5	33.	25.5

(Methods of evaluating location alternatives, moderate)

110. Environmental Glass Products, Inc., wants to build a new centralized facility to receive household, commercial, and industrial glass for recycling. This center will be supplied by trucks coming from four "collection points," where recyclable glass is dropped off by individuals and businesses. The volume and the map coordinates for the four collection centers are shown below. Where should the collection center be located?

Collection points	Load	(X,Y) Coordinates
A	8000	(3,8)
B	5000	(7,2)
C	1000	(4,1)
D	4000	(6,2)

The center should be built near coordinates (5,5). POM for Windows solution appears below.

Location Results

Recycling Collection Center Solution					
	Weight/# trips	x-coord	y-coord	X multiplied	Y multiplied
Location 1	8,000.	3.	8.	24,000.	64,000.
Location 2	5,000.	7.	2.	35,000.	10,000.
Location 3	1,000.	4.	1.	4,000.	1,000.
Location 4	4,000.	6.	2.	24,000.	8,000.
Total	18,000.	20.	13.	87,000.	83,000.
Average		5.	3.25		
Weighted Average				4.8333	4.6111
Median	9,000.			4.	2.

(Methods of evaluating location alternatives, moderate)

166

111. A manufacturer of stamped metal auto parts has four parts factories in one city at the location coordinates shown below. Each coordinate unit represents a city block (roughly 100 meters). The yearly demand at each factory is also given.

Factories	(X,Y) Coordinates	Demand
Rayburn Industrial Park	(30,120)	18,000
Port of Zavalla	(60,40)	3,000
Henderson Mfg. Center	(70,100)	5,000
Wax Mills Site	(90,30)	4,000

Management has decided to build a new sheet metal mill, to supply these factories, at a location central to these plants. What should be the map coordinates of the new plant? What is the straight line distance from center to each factory? Why isn't the mill located near any one of the four factory sites?

The mill should be located near (48, 97). The distances are approximately 29 to Rayburn, 58 to Zavalla, 23 to Henderson, and 79 to Wax Mills, and 189 total (one-way). The center-of-gravity model does not favor any single data point; it is the weighted average of them all. In this case, being central does not mean being close to any single factory, but it is closer to the collection of all four than any other mill location could be. POM for Windows solution appears below.

Location Results

	Weight/# trips	x-coord	y-coord	X multiplied	Y multiplied
Rayburn Industrial Park	18,000.	30.	120.	540,000.	2,160,000.
Port of Zavalla	3,000.	60.	40.	180,000.	120,000.
Henderson Mfg. Center	5,000.	70.	100.	350,000.	500,000.
Wax Mills Site	4,000.	90.	30.	360,000.	120,000.
Total	30,000.	250.	290.	1,430,000.	2,900,000.
Average		62.5	72.5		
Weighted Average				47.6667	96.6667
Median	15,000.			30.	120.

Distance Table (Air/Straight line)

Sheet Metal Mill Solution

	Center	Weighted Center
Rayburn Industrial Park	57.5543	29.267
Port of Zavalla	32.596	57.9933
Henderson Mfg. Center	28.5044	22.5807
Wax Mills Site	50.6211	78.9719
Total	169.2759	188.8129
Weighted total	1,478,772.	1,129,577.

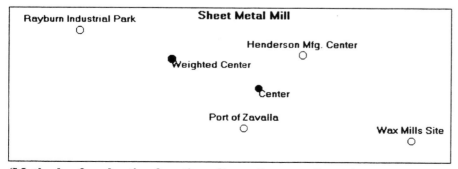

(Methods of evaluating location alternatives, moderate)

112. A contractor for the military is looking for a new location for a supply depot. The depot will supply four bases whose tonnage (demand) and map coordinates are shown below. If management wants the depot to have a central location, what should be its map coordinates?

Bases	(X,Y) Coordinates	Tonnage
Fort Able	(35,120)	40,000
Base Baker	(70,45)	50,000
Camp Charlie	(100,15)	25,000
Camp Delta	(60,90)	80,000

The depot should be located near X = 63, Y = 75. POM for Windows solution appears below.

Location Results					
Supply Depot Solution					
	Weight/# trips	x-coord	y-coord	X multiplied	Y multiplied
Able	40,000.	35.	120.	1,400,000.	4,800,000.
Baker	50,000.	70.	45.	3,500,000.	2,250,000.
Charlie	25,000.	100.	15.	2,500,000.	375,000.
Delta	80,000.	60.	90.	4,800,000.	7,200,000.
Total	195,000.	265.	270.	12,200,000.	14,625,000.
Average		66.25	67.5		
Weighted Average				62.5641	75.
Median	97,500.			60.	90.

(**Methods of evaluating location alternatives, moderate**)

113. A location analysis for a small manufacturer of parts for high-technology cable systems has been narrowed down to four locations. The manufacturer will need to train assemblers, testers, and robotics maintainers in local training centers. The manufacturer has asked each potential site to offer training programs, tax breaks, and other industrial incentives. The critical factors, their weights, and the ratings for each location are shown in the table below. High scores represent favorable values.

Factor	Weight	Location			
		Akron, OH	Biloxi, MS	Carthage, TX	Denver, CO
Labor availability	.15	90	80	90	80
Technical school quality	.10	95	75	65	85
Operating cost	.30	80	85	95	85
Land and construction cost	.15	60	80	90	70
Industrial incentives	.20	90	75	85	60
Labor cost	.10	75	80	85	75

Compute the composite (weighted average) rating for each location. Which site would you choose? Would you reach the same conclusion if the weights for operating cost and labor cost were reversed? Recompute as necessary and explain.

Carthage (87.5) is preferred rather strongly over the others (second place is 81.5) in the initial scenario. In the second scenario, all four scores fall, Carthage more than the others, but it is still firmly in first place. All scores fall because all sites had operating cost scores better than labor cost scores. When labor cost takes on the higher weight, the lower scores have more influence on the total. POM for Windows solution appears below.

Location Results

High Tech Cable Systems Solution					
	Weights	Akron	Biloxi	Carthage	Denver
Labor availabilty	0.15	90.	80.	90.	80.
Technical school	0.1	95.	75.	65.	85.
Operating cost	0.3	80.	85.	95.	85.
Land and construcion	0.15	60.	80.	90.	70.
Industrial incentives	0.2	90.	75.	85.	60.
Labor cost	0.1	75.	80.	85.	75.
Total	1.				
Weighted Total		81.5	80.	87.5	76.
Weighted Average		81.5	80.	87.5	76.

Location Results

High Tech Cable Systems Solution					
	Weights	Akron	Biloxi	Carthage	Denver
Labor availabilty	0.15	90.	80.	90.	80.
Technical school	0.1	95.	75.	65.	85.
Operating cost	0.1	80.	85.	95.	85.
Land and	0.15	60.	80.	90.	70.
Industrial	0.2	90.	75.	85.	60.
Labor cost	0.3	75.	80.	85.	75.
Total	1.				
Weighted Total		80.5	79.	85.5	74.
Weighted Average		80.5	79.	85.5	74.

(Methods of evaluating location alternatives, moderate)

114. A highway contractor needs to locate a single supply point to provide road building materials to four projects. The four projects, which are all approximately the same magnitude, are located at the following coordinates. Coordinate units are in miles.

	X (East)	Y (North)
Project A	60	10
Project B	15	60
Project C	20	50
Project D	30	35

a. Plot the locations of the four road-building sites. Properly label all points.
b. What is the center of gravity. Plot that point as well.
c. If a single truck were sent from center to each project and back (four round trips), how many miles would be traveled?

The supply point should be at (31.25, 38.75). Distance to each: 41 to A, 27 to B, 16 to C, and 4 to D; 87 total miles. POM for Windows solution appears below (Note that the graph compresses the Y dimension differently than the X dimension; also center and weighted center are the same in this problem).

Location Results

	Weight/# trips	x-coord	y-coord	X multiplied	Y multiplied
Project A	1.	60.	10.	60.	10.
Project B	1.	15.	60.	15.	60.
Project C	1.	20.	50.	20.	50.
Project D	1.	30.	35.	30.	35.
Total	4.	125.	155.	125.	155.
Average		31.25	38.75		
Weighted Average				31.25	38.75
Median	2.			20.	35.

Highway Contractor Solution

Distance Table (Air/Straight line)

Highway Contractor Solution

	Weighted Center
Project A	40.6586
Project B	26.7512
Project C	15.9099
Project D	3.9528
Total	87.2726
Weighted total	87.2726

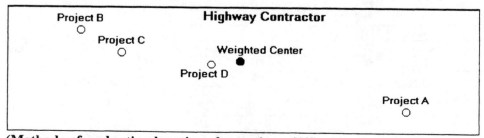

(Methods of evaluating location alternatives, difficult)

170

CHAPTER 9: LAYOUT STRATEGY

TRUE FALSE

1. Layout is a strategic decision because layout determines the long-run efficiency of an operations system.
    True (The strategic importance of layout decisions, easy)

2. The office layout allocates employee desk space and responds to customer behavior.
    False (Types of layout, moderate)

3. Layout strategies can help an organization achieve a strategic advantage.
    True (The strategic importance of layout decisions, moderate)

4. A process-oriented layout deals with low-volume, high-variety production.
    True (Process-oriented layout, easy)

5. The dominant problem associated with the fixed-position layout is that workers are fixed in position, and cannot be reassigned.
    False (Fixed-position layout, moderate)

6. Most hospitals tend to use the office layout model.
    False (Process-oriented layout, moderate)

7. The disadvantages of a process-oriented layout come from its specialized equipment and conveyor lines.
    False (Product-oriented layout, moderate)

8. CRAFT and MULTIPLE are software for balancing assembly lines.
    False (Process-oriented layout, moderate)

9. The work cell improves process layouts by reducing floor space.
    True (Process-oriented layout, moderate)

10. The work cell improves process layouts by reducing direct labor cost.
    True (Process-oriented layout, moderate)

11. A **focused work center** is well suited to the production of a large family of products requiring similar processing, even if their demands are not very stable.
    False (Process-oriented layout, moderate)

12. In Japan as well as in the U.S., the guideline in office layout design is to allocate 100 square feet per person.
    False (Office layout, moderate)

13. While offices move information rather than tangible goods, an office layout in some respects is like a factory layout in that production depends upon the flow of material.
    True (Office layout, moderate)

14. An office relationship chart positions workspaces by avoiding as many U relationships as possible.
False (Office layout, moderate)

15. Exposing customers to as many products as possible is an important consideration in the design of retail store layouts.
True (Retail layout, moderate)

16. Servicescape refers to the physical surrounding in which the service is delivered.
True (Retail layout, moderate)

17. Utilization of the total "cube" is an important consideration in warehouse layout decisions.
True (Warehousing and storage layout, moderate)

18. SLIM and COSMOS are geosynchronous satellites that aid with bar-code scanning and automatic identification systems.
False (Retail layout, moderate)

19. **Crossdocking** is a concept that helps explain why "warehouses" are now called "distribution centers."
True (Warehousing and storage layout, moderate)

20. Home appliances are typically manufactured using process layouts.
False (Repetitive and product-oriented layout, moderate)

21. An assembly line is an example of a product-oriented layout.
True (Repetitive and product-oriented layout, moderate)

22. A fabrication line is usually machine-paced and requires mechanical and engineering changes to facilitate balancing.
True (Repetitive and product-oriented layout, moderate)

23. The biggest advantage of a product layout is its flexibility to handle a varied product mix.
False (Repetitive and product-oriented layout, moderate)

24. The minimum number of workstations depends upon the set of task times and the precedence chart, but not the product demand.
False (Repetitive and product-oriented layout, moderate)

25. If the sum of the task times required to make one unit of product K is 11 minutes, and the desired cycle time is 2 minutes, then 22 workstations will be needed.
False (Repetitive and product-oriented layout, moderate)

26. If the demand for a product is 80 units per day and 480 minutes of production time are available per day, the cycle time is 6 minutes.
True (Repetitive and product-oriented layout, moderate)

27. For an assembly line to operate at 100% efficiency, there must be no idle time.
True (Repetitive and product-oriented layout, moderate)

MULTIPLE CHOICE

28. The layout strategy that deals with **low-volume, high-variety** production is
    a. fixed-position layout
    b. retail/service layout
    c. warehouse layout
    d. all of the above
    e. none of the above
    e (Types of layout, moderate)

29. A good layout requires determining
    a. capacity and space requirements
    b. material handling requirements
    c. environment and aesthetics
    d. flows of information
    e. all of the above
    e (The strategic importance of layout decision, moderate)

30. For which of the following operations would a fixed-position layout be most appropriate?
    a. assembly of an automobile
    b. production of cameras and TV sets
    c. construction of a ship
    d. refining of crude oil
    e. grocery store
    c (Fixed-position layout, difficult)

31. The **fixed-position** layout would be most appropriate in which of the following cases?
    a. constructing a Boeing 777
    b. a fast food restaurant
    c. a doctor's office
    d. a gourmet restaurant
    e. none of the above
    a (Fixed-position layout, difficult)

32. One factor impacting the fixed-position layout strategy is
    a. the movement of material to the limited storage areas around the site
    b. minimizing difficulties caused by material flow varying with each product
    c. requiring frequent contact close to one another
    d. the provision of low-cost storage with low-cost material handling
    e. balancing product flow from one work station to the next
    a (Fixed-position layout, moderate)

33. Because the fixed-position layout problem is so difficult to solve on-site, operations managers
    a. virtually never employ this layout strategy
    b. utilize this approach only for construction projects such as bridges and office towers
    c. increase the size of the site
    d. often complete as much of the project as possible off-site
    e. utilize this layout only for defense contractors
    d (Fixed-position layout, moderate)

34. The type of layout which features departments or other functional groupings in which similar activities are performed is
   a. process
   b. product
   c. fixed-position
   d. mass
   e. unit
   a (Process-oriented layout, moderate)

35. The main issue in designing process layouts concerns the relative positioning of
   a. work stations
   b. raw materials
   c. departments
   d. entrances, loading docks, etc.
   e. manufacturing cells
   c (Process-oriented layout, moderate)

36. One of the major advantages of process-oriented layouts is
   a. high equipment utilization
   b. large work-in-process inventories
   c. smooth and continuous flow of work
   d. flexibility in equipment and labor assignment
   e. none of the above
   d (Process-oriented layout, moderate)

37. A **process** layout would be most appropriate in which of the following cases?
   a. constructing a Boeing 777 aircraft
   b. a gourmet restaurant
   c. a fast-food restaurant
   d. an automobile factory
   e. a steel mill
   b (Process-oriented layout, moderate)

38. The major problem addressed by the process-oriented layout strategy is
   a. the movement of material to the limited storage areas around the site
   b. minimizing difficulties caused by material flow varying with each product
   c. requiring frequent contact close to one another
   d. the provision of low-cost storage with low-cost material handling
   e. balancing product flow from one work station to the next
   b (Process-oriented layout, moderate)

39. Which of the following is **not** an information requirement for solving a load-distance problem?
   a. a list of departments or work centers
   b. a projection of work flows between the work centers
   c. a list of product cycle times
   d. the distance between locations
   e. the cost per unit of distance to move loads
   c (Process-oriented layout, moderate)

40. The most common tactic followed in process-layout planning is to arrange departments or work centers so they
   a. minimize the cost of skilled labor
   b. maximize the machine utilization
   c. minimize the costs of material handling
   d. allocate the available space equally to all the departments
   e. none of the above
   c (Process-oriented layout, moderate)

41. Which of the following is **true** for process layouts, but **false** for product layouts?
   a. low in-process inventories
   b. low variety of products
   c. high volume of output
   d. often solved by assembly line balancing
   e. flexibility in equipment and labor assignments
   e (Process-oriented layout, moderate)

42. A process-oriented layout is best suited for
   a. the assembly of products like automobiles and appliances
   b. the mass production of uniform products
   c. low-volume, high-variety production
   d. high-volume, low-variety production
   e. construction of a ship
   c (Process-oriented layout, moderate)

43. The disadvantages of process-oriented layouts arise from
   a. the use of special purpose equipment
   b. machine maintenance, which tends to seriously degrade the capacity of the entire system
   c. the use of the general purpose machines and equipment
   d. the use of specialized material handling equipment
   e. the need for stable demand
   c (Process-oriented layout, moderate)

44. A big advantage of a process-oriented layout is
   a. its low cost
   b. its flexibility for variety
   c. the simplified scheduling problem presented by this layout strategy
   d. the ability to employ low-skilled labor
   e. its high equipment utilization
   b (Process-oriented layout, moderate)

45. A common method of developing a process-oriented layout strategy attempts to
   a. minimize the distance between adjacent departments
   b. maximize the number of different tasks which can be performed by an individual machine
   c. minimize the level of operator skill necessary
   d. minimize the material handling costs
   e. maximize job specialization
   d (Process-oriented layout, moderate)

46. According to Heizer and Render, an office layout
    a. groups workers, their equipment, and spaces/offices to provide for movement of information
    b. addresses the layout requirements of large, bulky projects such as ships and buildings
    c. seeks the best personnel and machine utilization in repetitive or continuous production
    d. allocates shelf space and responds to customer behavior
    e. deals with low-volume, high-variety production
    a (Office layout, moderate)

47. Which of the following is true of a **focused factory**?
    a. They may be focused in ways other than by product or layout.
    b. They may be focused only by processing requirements.
    c. They are much like a product facility within an otherwise process facility.
    d. All of the above are true.
    e. None of the above are true.
    a (Process-oriented layout, moderate)

48. Which rating reflects the highest importance for two departments' closeness to each other?
    a. A
    b. E
    c. I
    d. U
    e. X
    a (Process-oriented layout, moderate)

49. In the use of relationship charts for office layouts, the code "U" means the closeness between two departments is
    a. (U)nknown
    b. (U)nusually important
    c. of (U)sual importance
    d. (U)nimportant
    e. (U)ndesirable
    d (Process-oriented layout, moderate)

50. Which of the following constitutes a major trend influencing office layouts?
    a. downsizing
    b. globalization
    c. virtual companies
    d. environmental issues
    e. health issues
    c (Office layout, moderate)

51. According to Heizer and Render, a retail/service layout
    a. groups workers, their equipment, and spaces/offices to provide for movement of information
    b. addresses the layout requirements of large, bulky projects such as ships and buildings
    c. seeks the best personnel and machine utilization in repetitive or continuous production
    d. allocates space and responds to customer behavior
    e. deals with low-volume, high-variety production
    d (Retail layout, moderate)

52. Balancing low-cost storage with low-cost material handling is important in
   a. a fixed-position layout
   b. a process-oriented layout
   c. an office layout
   d. a product-oriented layout
   e. a warehouse layout
   e (Warehousing and storage layouts, moderate)

53. Which of the following does **not** support the retail layout objective of maximizing customer exposure to products?
   a. locate high-draw items around the periphery of the store
   b. use prominent locations for high-impulse and high-margin items
   c. maximize exposure to expensive items
   d. distribute "power items" to both sides of the aisle
   e. convey the store's mission with the careful positioning of the lead-off department
   c (Retail layout, moderate)

54. Which type of layout is used to achieve a smooth and rapid flow of large volumes of output?
   a. process
   b. batch
   c. product
   d. unit
   e. fixed-position
   b (Repetitive and product-oriented layout, moderate)

55. Which of the following layouts generally has the best machine utilization?
   a. a fixed-position layout
   b. a process-oriented layout
   c. an office layout
   d. a warehouse layout
   e. a product-oriented layout
   e (Repetitive and product-oriented layout, moderate)

56. The major problem addressed by the warehouse layout strategy is
   a. the movement of material to the limited storage areas around the site
   b. minimizing difficulties caused by material flow varying with each product
   c. requiring frequent contact close to one another
   d. the provision of low-cost storage with low-cost material handling
   e. balancing product flow from one work station to the next
   d (Warehousing and storage layouts, moderate)

57. Which of the following are strongly associated with "crossdocking"?
   a. non-value-adding activities such as receiving and storing
   b. multi-modal transportation facilities at seaports
   c. processing items as soon as they are received into a distribution center
   d. use of manual product identification systems
   e. all of the above
   c (Warehousing and storage layouts, moderate)

58. The concept of customizing in a warehouse layout
    a. cannot be considered seriously in today's high efficiency factories
    b. is theoretically sound, but several years away in practice
    c. is a new trend in value-added activities in warehouses
    d. is possible, but causes serious loss of oversight of the quality function
    e. none of the above

    c (Warehousing and storage layouts, moderate)

59. Which one of the following is **not** common to product layouts?
    a. a high rate of output
    b. specialization of labor
    c. low unit costs
    d. ability to adjust to changes in demand
    e. all are common

    d (Repetitive and product-oriented layout, moderate)

60. A major assumption of stability of demand is important for justifying which of the following layout types?
    a. product layout
    b. process layout
    c. fixed-position layout
    d. all of the above
    e. none of the above

    a (Repetitive and product-oriented layout, moderate)

61. A **product** layout would be most appropriate in which of the following cases?
    a. constructing a Boeing 777 aircraft
    b. a fast food restaurant
    c. a doctor's office
    d. a gourmet restaurant
    e. a grocery store

    b (Repetitive and product-oriented layout, moderate)

62. An adequate volume for high equipment utilization is an assumption for which of the following layout types?
    a. product layout
    b. process layout
    c. fixed-position layout
    d. retail layout
    e. warehouse

    a (Repetitive and product-oriented layout, moderate)

63. The assumptions necessary for a successful product layout include all **except**
   a. adequate volume for high equipment utilization
   b. volatile product demand
   c. standardized product
   d. all of the above are appropriate assumptions
   e. none of the above are appropriate assumptions
   b (Repetitive and product-oriented layout, moderate)

64. A product layout would be most appropriate for which one of the following businesses?
   a. fast food
   b. insurance sales
   c. clothing alterations
   d. steel-making
   e. a grocery store
   d (Repetitive and product-oriented layout, moderate)

65. Which of these layouts is most suitable for processing sugar from sugar beets or sugar cane?
   a. process layout
   b. fixed-position layout
   c. focused factory
   d. product layout
   e. cell layout
   d (Repetitive and product-oriented layout, moderate)

66. Which of the following is **true** regarding fabrication lines?
   a. They are the same thing as assembly lines.
   b. They are the same thing as focused factories.
   c. Balancing their assembly line is more technological than worker oriented.
   d. They are a special type of process layout.
   e. None of the above.
   c (Repetitive and product-oriented layout, moderate)

67. The central problem in product-oriented layout planning is
   a. minimizing material handling within workstations
   b. minimizing labor movement between workstations
   c. minimizing the imbalance in the work loads among workstations
   d. equalizing the space allocated to the different workstations
   e. maximizing equipment utilization
   c (Repetitive and product-oriented layout, moderate)

68. The **disadvantages** of product layout include
   a. high volume is required because of the large investment needed to set up the process
   b. work stoppage at any one point ties up the whole operation
   c. there is a lack of flexibility in handling a variety of products or production rates
   d. all of the above
   e. none of the above
   d (Repetitive and product-oriented layout, moderate)

69. The main advantage of a product-oriented layout is typically
   a. low raw material cost
   b. employability of highly skilled labor
   c. low capital cost
   d. low variable cost per unit
   e. high flexibility
   d (Repetitive and product-oriented layout, moderate)

70. In a product layout the process of deciding how to assign tasks to work stations is referred to as
   a. process balancing
   b. task allocation
   c. line balancing
   d. work allocation
   e. station balancing
   c (Repetitive and product-oriented layout, moderate)

71. In assembly line balancing, cycle time (the ratio of production time to demand), is
   a. the maximum time that a product is available at each work station
   b. the minimum time that a product is available at each work station
   c. the optimum time that a product is available at each work station
   d. the desired cycle time that a product is available at each work station
   e. all of the above
   a (Repetitive and product-oriented layout, moderate)

72. In assembly line balancing, the minimum number of workstations is
   a. the ratio of the sum of all task times to cycle time
   b. the ratio of demand times sum of task times to production time per day
   c. is always rounded upward to the next larger integer value
   d. all of the above
   e. none of the above
   d (Repetitive and product-oriented layout, moderate)

73. A production line is to be designed to make 500 El-More dolls per day. Each doll requires 11 activities totaling 16 minutes of work. The factory operates 1000 minutes per day. The desired cycle time for this assembly line is
   a. one-half minute
   b. two minutes
   c. 8,000 minutes
   d. 5,500 minutes
   e. cannot be determined
   b (Repetitive and product-oriented layout, moderate)

74. A production line is to be designed for a job with four tasks. The task times are 2.3 minutes, 1.4 minutes, 0.9 minutes, and 1.7 minutes. The maximum cycle time is _____ and the minimum cycle time is _____ minutes.
   a. 1.8; 1.4
   b. 1.4; 5.3
   c. 6.3; 2.3
   d. 2.3; 0.9
   e. none of these
   c (Repetitive and product-oriented layout, moderate)

75. Cycle time is computed as
   a. daily operating time divided by the desired output
   b. desired output divided by the daily operating time
   c. daily operating time divided by the product of desired output and the sum of job times
   d. the product of desired output and the sum of job times divided by daily operating time
   e. 1.00 minus station time
   a (Repetitive and product-oriented layout, moderate)

76. Daily capacity of a product layout is determined by
   a. cycle time divided by operating time
   b. operating time divided by cycle time
   c. operating time divided by total task time
   d. total task time divided by cycle time
   e. cycle time divided by total task time
   b (Repetitive and product-oriented layout, moderate)

77. Four hundred and eighty minutes of production time are available per day. The demand for the product is 80 units per day. What is the cycle time?
   a. 4 minutes
   b. 5 minutes
   c. 6 minutes
   d. 7 minutes
   e. 8 minutes
   c (Repetitive and product-oriented layout, moderate)

78. A production line is to be designed for a product whose completion requires 21 minutes of work. The factory works 400 minutes per day. Can an assembly line with five workstations make 100 per units per day?
   a. yes, with exactly 100 minutes to spare
   b. no, it will fall short even with a perfectly balanced line
   c. no, but four workstations would be sufficient
   d. yes, but the line's efficiency is very low
   e. cannot be determined from the information given
   b (Repetitive and product-oriented layout, moderate)

79. Four hundred and eighty minutes of production time are available per day. The demand for the product is 80 units per day. Each unit of the product requires 30 minutes of work. What is the theoretical minimum number of workstations?
   a. 2
   b. 3
   c. 4
   d. 5
   e. 6
   d (Repetitive and product-oriented layout, moderate)

80. Which of the following is **not** a heuristic rule for assigning tasks to work stations in a product layout?
   a. longest tasks first
   b. median tasks first
   c. in order of most number of following tasks
   d. in order of most number of preceding tasks
   e. in accordance with positional weight
   b (Repetitive and product-oriented layout, moderate)

81. Which of the following is a common heuristic for assembly line balancing?
   a. debits near the windows, credits near the door
   b. manufacturers locate near materials, retailers locate near customers
   c. earliest due date first
   d. ranked positional weight
   e. none of the above
   d (Repetitive and product-oriented layout, moderate)

82. If a layout problem is solved by use of "heuristics," this means that
   a. there was no other way to solve the problem
   b. no computer software was available
   c. the problem has only a few alternatives to evaluate
   d. no optimum solution exists
   e. a "satisfactory" solution is acceptable
   e (Repetitive and product-oriented layout, moderate)

FILL-IN-THE-BLANK

83. _____ layouts deal with low- volume, high-variety production with like machines and equipment grouped together.
   Process-oriented (Process-oriented layout, easy)

84. A _____ is a temporary product-oriented arrangement of machines and personnel in what is ordinarily a process-oriented facility.
   process-oriented (Process-oriented layout, moderate)

85. A _____ is designed to produce similar products or components.
   focused factory (Process-oriented layout, moderate)

86. An _____ groups workers, their equipments, and spaces/offices to provide for comfort, safety, and movement of information.
office layout (Office layout, moderate)

87. A _____ addresses flow, allocates space, and responds to customer behavior.
retail layout (Retail layout, moderate)

88. _____ refers to the physical surrounding in which a service takes place, and how they affect customers and employees.
Servicescape (Retail layout, moderate)

89. _____ avoids placing materials or supplies in storage by processing them as they are received for shipment.
Crossdocking (Warehousing and storage layouts, moderate)

90. A _____ line is a machine-paced product-oriented facility for building components.
fabrication (Repetitive and product-oriented layout, moderate)

91. A(n) _____ is an approach that puts fabricated parts together at a series of workstations.
assembly line (Repetitive and product-oriented layout, moderate)

92. _____ is the maximum time that the product is available at each workstation.
Cycle time (Repetitive and product-oriented layout, moderate)

SHORT ANSWERS

93. In what specific areas does the layout decision establish a firm's competitive priorities?
Processes, flexibility, cost, capacity, and quality of work life. (The strategic importance of layout decisions, moderate)

94. List the six fundamental layout strategies. Describe the use of each one very briefly.
**1. Fixed-position layout: for large bulky products such as ships and buildings
2. Process layout: for low-volume, high-variety production
3. Product oriented layout: assembly line
4. Retail-service layout: allocates shelf space and responds to customer behavior
5. Warehouse layout: addresses tradeoffs between space and material handling
6. Office layout: positions workers, their equipment, and space/offices to provide for transfer of information (Types of layout, moderate)**

95. What are the three factors that complicate a fixed-position layout?
There is limited space at virtually all sites; at different stages of the process, different materials are needed; and the volume of materials needed is dynamic. (Fixed position layout, moderate)

96. Explain how a load-distance model helps solve problems in process layout.
The problem in process layout is to hold down material movement and material handling. The load distance model calculates these movements from department to department, and can find that set of departmental space assignments that minimizes the aggregate material handling cost. This is an optimal layout for a process layout, given the pattern of loads and distances. (Process-oriented layout, moderate)

97. What are the three forms of "work cells" discussed in the textbook?
Work cell, focused work center, and focused factory. (Process-oriented layout, moderate)

98. List the advantages of work-cell layouts.
Reduction in work-in-process inventory; reduced raw materials and finished goods inventories; less floor space required; reduced direct labor cost; heightened sense of employee participation; increased utilization of equipment and machinery; and reduced investment in machinery and equipment. (Process-oriented layout, moderate)

99. What are the requirements for cellular production?
Group technology codes or their equivalent; a high level of training and flexibility on the part of employees; and either staff support or flexible, imaginative employees to establish the work cell initially. (Process-oriented layout, moderate)

100. What are the requirements for a focused work center or focused factory to be appropriate?
The requirements are identification of a large family of similar products, a stable demand, and adequate volume to justify the capital investment. (Process-oriented layout, moderate)

101. What design guidelines help retail layouts to maximize customer exposure to products?
**1. locating the high-draw items around the periphery of the store
2. using prominent locations for high-impulse and high-margin items
3. distributing what are known in the trade as "power items" to both sides of an aisle, and dispersing them to increase the viewing of other items
4. using end aisle locations because they have a very high exposure rate
5. conveying the image of the store by careful selection in the positioning of the lead-off department (Retail layout, moderate)**

102. What are the two major trends influencing office layout?
Technology and virtual companies. (Office layout, moderate)

103. What are the four assumptions or preconditions of establishing layout for high-volume, low-variety products?
**1. volume is adequate for high equipment utilization
2. product demand is stable enough to justify high investment in specialized equipment
3. the product is standardized or approaching a phase of its life cycle that justifies investment in specialized equipment
4. supplies of raw material and components are adequate and of uniform quality to ensure that they will work with the specialized equipment. (Repetitive and product-oriented layout, moderate).**

104. What is crossdocking? Why is it appropriate for some forms of warehouse layout?
Crossdocking avoids placing materials or supplies in storage by processing them as they are received for shipment. It avoids storing the product, saves space and receiving time, and speeds up shipment to the ultimate destination. (Warehousing and storage layouts, moderate)

105. What are the two basic types of product layouts? Explain how they are alike, and how they are different.
The two types are fabrication lines and assembly lines. Fabrication lines build components on a series of machines, while assembly lines put the fabricated parts together at a series of work stations. Fabrication lines tend to be machine paced and require mechanical changes to facilitate balance, while assembly lines tend to be paced by work tasks assigned to individuals or to workstations and are therefore balanced by moving tasks from one individual to another. (Repetitive and product-oriented layout, difficult)

106. Explain what the purpose of assembly line balancing is. Describe briefly how it is done. Explain how assembly line balancing supports the needs of product layout.
Assembly line balancing attempts to put equal amounts of work into each of the workstations that assemble a product. The technique begins with a task list and precedence chart; to this is added demand data, from which cycle time can be computed. This is the speed at which the line must move. Then the theoretical number of stations is calculated. Each required task is then assigned into one workstation. This approach holds down the amount of idle time in a product layout, and leads to higher utilization of the plant, and to higher volume of output. (Repetitive and product-oriented layout, difficult)

107. Define the following terms which occur in assembly line balancing: cycle time, minimum number of workstations, and efficiency.
Cycle time is the ratio of available work time to units demand. The theoretical minimum number of work stations in an assembly line is determined by dividing the total task-duration time for the product by the cycle time. The efficiency of a line balance is determined by dividing the total task time assigned by the product of the number of work stations times the cycle time. (Repetitive and product-oriented layout, moderate)

108. For each of the following products or operations indicate the most appropriate type of layout.

Product / operations	Type of layout
1. Custom picture framing	
2. Chemical processing	
3. Construction of a subway tunnel	
4. Insurance claims processing	
5. A regional distribution center	
6. Assembly of automobiles	

1. process-oriented; 2. product-oriented; 3. fixed-position; 4. office; 5. warehouse; and 6. product-oriented. (Repetitive and product-oriented layout, difficult)

109. Some of the decision-making models you have studied were **optimizing** models, while others were **satisficing** models. Give an example of each from this chapter on layout.
Load-distance models are solved optimally; office relationship and assembly line balance problems reach satisfactory, but not guaranteed optimal solutions. (Office layout, and Repetitive and product-oriented layout, moderate)

110. What is the role of heuristics in solving layout problems? Provide a brief example, drawing from manufacturing situations, retailing situations, or other service situations.
Heuristics are used in problems too complex to model explicitly, such as assembly line balancing problems, fixed-position layouts, office layouts and retail layouts. All of these layout types are quite complex, featuring very large numbers of alternative solutions and no single numeric objective for evaluating them. (Repetitive and product-oriented layout, moderate)

111. Consider the five ideas for determining the overall arrangement of most retail stores. How are these ideas implemented (a) in a supermarket, and (b) in a fine department store? (Please consider the entire store--not just the areas where merchandise is displayed.)
(Suggested response) The five ideas are: 1. locating the high-draw items around the periphery of the store, 2. using prominent locations for high-impulse and high-margin items 3. distributing what are known in the trade as "power items" to both sides of an aisle, and dispersing them to increase the viewing of other items, 4. using end aisle locations because they have a very high exposure rate, 5. conveying the image of the store by careful selection in the positioning of the lead-off department. Supermarkets make more use of aisles, where ideas 3 and 4 are featured. Department stores are meandering, so there's less use of end-caps. Both types of retail seem to follow idea 1 and 5. Idea 2 seems to be implemented with impulse items near the checkouts for both retail types. The supermarket's straight lines convey its strategy of low cost; the department store's display areas convey its focus on image, browsing, etc. (Retail layouts, difficult)

112. "Having a focused work center is like having a factory within a factory." Discuss. Include in your discussion what conditions make focused work centers appropriate.
A focused work center is a permanent product-oriented set of equipment within a process-oriented facility. It requires group technology or equivalent, a high level of staff training and flexibility, and good support or imagination to get started. (Process-orienteds, moderate)

113. A facilities manager at an insurance company headquarters once said, "I'd like to use Muther's office relationship chart to solve our office layout problem, but it can't optimize--it can't resolve all the conflicts." Discuss.
The office relationship chart shows several levels of importance associated with departmental closeness. These ratings are not necessarily transitive, in that a high positive between departments PQ and QR does not translate into a high goodness for PR. It may not be possible to meet all of the A conditions without generating some undesirable X conditions. And this does not reach to the lower levels (E, I, etc.). (Office layout, moderate)

114. Assembly line balancing has just been used to solve a product layout problem. Two solutions look especially attractive to the plant managers. Both solutions make the same output per day, and both have the same number of workstations. The managers were going to break the tie by looking at line efficiency, but discovered that both lines had the same efficiency as well. Should they have been surprised at this? Explain.

No, they should not be surprised. Efficiency is the ratio of actual work needed per unit to time available. Work needed is clearly the same in both cases as the product is the same. Work available is also the same, since both lines have the same number of stations and the same cycle time. Once cycle time and number of stations are known, so is efficiency, no matter what tasks are assigned to what stations within that framework. (Repetitive and product-oriented layout, difficult)

PROBLEMS

115. Develop a solution for the following line balancing problem, allowing a cycle time of 5 minutes.
    a. Draw the precedence diagram for the set of tasks.
    b. Calculate the theoretical minimum number of workstations.
    c. Balance this line using the longest task time heuristic.
    d. What tasks are assigned to which stations?
    e. Does the solution have the minimum number of stations? Explain.
    f. How much work is spent at work in each workstation?
    g. How much idle time is there, summed over all workstations?
    h. What is the efficiency of that line?

Work Task	Task Time (minutes)	Task Predecessor(s)
A	1.5	-
B	1	A
C	2.5	B
D	1	-
E	4	C, D
F	1.5	A
G	3	E, F

The minimum number of workstations is 3. Balance places ABDF in station 1, C in station 2, E in station 3, and G in station 4. The solution uses four stations, not three. POM for Windows solutions below. Idle time is distributed 0, 2.5, 1, and 2 minutes per station. There are 5.5 minutes idle time in the system. Efficiency is only 72.5%.

9.1
Precedence Graph

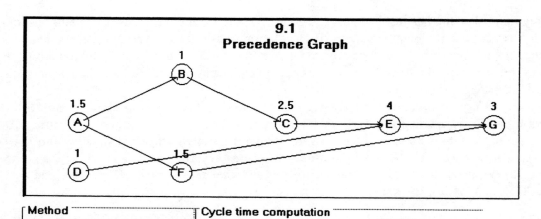

Method		Cycle time computation		
Longest operation time ▼		◉ Given ○ Computed		5

<table>
<tr><td colspan="5" align="center">9.1 Solution</td></tr>
<tr><td>Station</td><td>Task</td><td>Time
(minutes)</td><td>Time left
(minutes)</td><td>Ready tasks</td></tr>
<tr><td></td><td></td><td></td><td></td><td>A,D</td></tr>
<tr><td>1</td><td>A</td><td>1.5</td><td>3.5</td><td>D,B,F</td></tr>
<tr><td></td><td>F</td><td>1.5</td><td>2.</td><td>D,B</td></tr>
<tr><td></td><td>D</td><td>1.</td><td>1.</td><td>B</td></tr>
<tr><td></td><td>B</td><td>1.</td><td>0.</td><td>C</td></tr>
<tr><td>2</td><td>C</td><td>2.5</td><td>2.5</td><td>E</td></tr>
<tr><td>3</td><td>E</td><td>4.</td><td>1.</td><td>G</td></tr>
<tr><td>4</td><td>G</td><td>3.</td><td>2.</td><td></td></tr>
</table>

Summary Statistics		
Cycle time	5	minutes
Time allocated (cyc*sta)	20	minutes/cycle
Time needed (sum task)	14.5	minutes/unit
Idle time (allocated-needed)	5.5	minutes/cycle
Efficiency (needed/allocated)	72.5%	
Balance Delay (1-efficiency)	27.5%	
Min (theoretical) # of stations	3	

(Repetitive and product-oriented layout, moderate)

116. An assembly line has been designed to make battery-powered beverage mixers. Task details are shown in the table below:

Station	Task Assigned	Task Time (minutes)
1	1	3.0
2	3; 4	1.5; 2.0
3	2; 5; 6	0.5; 1.5; 1.0
4	7	3.0
5	8	2.5
6	9; 10; 11	2.0; 1.0; 0.5

a. What is the assigned cycle time (in minutes)?
b. What is the maximum output rate of this line in mixers per hour?
c. What is the total idle time per cycle?
d. What is the assembly line's efficiency?
Cycle time is 3.5 minutes (governed by stations 2 and 6). Maximum output is 60/3.5 = 17.14 units per hour. Idle time is 0.5 + 0 + 0.5 + 0.5 + 1.0 + 0 = 2.5 minutes. Efficiency is 18.5/21 = 88.1%. (Repetitive and product-oriented layout, moderate)

117. Departments A, B, C, and D need to be assigned to four rooms 1, 2, 3, and 4. These rooms are arranged in a row, in that order, and 20 meters between each. The departmental work flows are contained in the table below.
a. What is the material handling total of assigning A-1, B-2, C-3, D-4?
b. What is the material handling total of assigning A-1, B-4, C-3, D-2?

Flow Matrix				
	Dept. A	Dept. B	Dept. C	Dept. D
Dept. A	0	20	5	20
Dept. B	5	0	30	10
Dept. C	0	10	0	40
Dept. D	10	5	0	0

The material handling total of A-1, B-2, C-3, D-4 is 4700. The material handling total of A-1, B-4, C-3, D-2 is 4500 (which is also optimal). (Process-oriented layout, moderate)

118. Given the following flow and distance data, what is the appropriate layout?

9.4

Flow Table	A	B	C	D	Fixed room
A	0	3	6	2	
B	0	0	6	6	
C	0	2	0	8	
D	10	1	4	0	

Distance Table	Room1	Room2	Room3	Room4	
Room1	0	30	60	80	
Room2	30	0	30	50	
Room3	60	30	0	20	
Room4	80	50	20	0	

The appropriate assignment of departments to rooms is

Distances
- ◉ Symmetric
- ○ Not Symmetric

Method

Explicit enumeration ▼

Operations Layout Results

Room assignments

Department	Room
Total Movement	1800
A	Room4
B	Room1
C	Room2
D	Room3

119. Cyclone Appliances has developed a new European-style convection oven that will be made on an assembly line. The schedule requires 100 ovens in an 8-hour day. The assembly includes seven tasks. The table below indicates the performance time and the sequence requirements for each task.

Task	Performance Time (minutes)	Task must follow Task listed below
A	1	
B	2	A
C	3	B
D	2	B
E	4	C, D
F	1	E
G	2	F

a. What is the desired cycle time in seconds for this assembly operation?
b. What is the minimum number of work stations?
c. Group the tasks into the minimum number of work stations using the longest task time heuristic to minimize idle time at each station.
d. What is the total idle time for your solution?
e. What is the efficiency of the line?

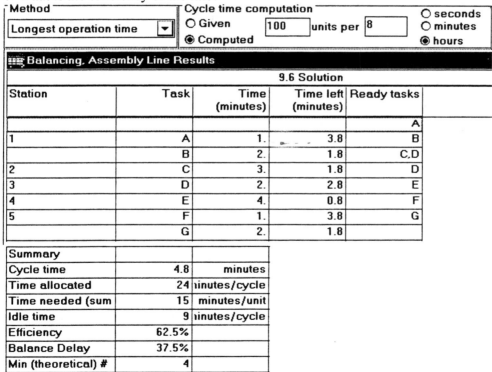

Method

Longest operation time ▼

Cycle time computation
○ Given   100 units per 8
● Computed

○ seconds
○ minutes
● hours

Balancing, Assembly Line Results

9.6 Solution

Station	Task	Time (minutes)	Time left (minutes)	Ready tasks
				A
1	A	1.	3.8	B
	B	2.	1.8	C,D
2	C	3.	1.8	D
3	D	2.	2.8	E
4	E	4.	0.8	F
5	F	1.	3.8	G
	G	2.	1.8	

Summary		
Cycle time	4.8	minutes
Time allocated	24	minutes/cycle
Time needed (sum	15	minutes/unit
Idle time	9	minutes/cycle
Efficiency	62.5%	
Balance Delay	37.5%	
Min (theoretical) #	4	

(Repetitive and product-oriented layout, moderate)

120. An electronics manufacturer makes remote control devices for interactive-cable-TV systems. The following assembly tasks must be performed on each device.

Task	Description	Predecessor(s)	Time (min.)
A	Place circuit into circuit frame	--	0.50
B	Solder circuit connections to central circuit control	A	0.70
C	Place circuit assembly in device frame	B	0.40
D	Attach circuit assembly to device frame	C	0.30
E	Place and attach display to frame	--	0.30
F	Place and attach keypad to frame	--	0.20
G	Place and attach top body of device to frame	E, F	0.35
H	Place and attach battery holder to frame	D	0.40
I	Place and attach bottom body of device to frame	G, H	0.60
J	Test device	I	0.30

a. Draw the precedence diagram for this problem.
b. What is the sum of the task times?
c. What cycle time will allow the production of 200 units over a ten hour day?
d. How many workstations will that require?

The sum of the task times is 4.05 minutes. The cycle time for 200 units output is 600/200 = 3 minutes. The minimum number of stations is 4.05/3 = 1.35 or 2. The diagram of this network appears below.

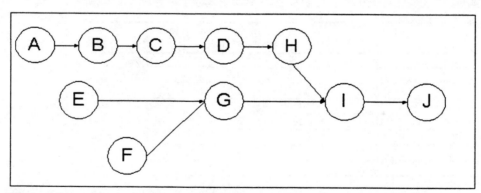

(Repetitive and product-oriented layout, moderate)

192

121. A company is designing a product layout for a new product. It plans to use this production line eight hours a day in order to meet projected demand of 400 units per day. The tasks necessary to produce this product are detailed in the table below.

Task	Predecessor	Time (seconds)
A	-	50
B	A	36
C	-	26
D	-	22
E	B, D	70
F	C, E	30

a. Draw the network described in the table.
b. Without regard to demand, what is the minimum possible cycle time (in seconds) for this situation; what is the maximum?
c. What is the required cycle time (in seconds) in order to meet the projected demand?
d. What is the minimum number of workstations needed to meet the projected demand?

The network diagram appears below. Minimum cycle time is 70 seconds (the longest task time); maximum cycle time is 234 seconds (sum of the task times). Cycle time is 480/400 = 1.2 minutes or 72 seconds (which is barely feasible). The number of stations required is at least 234/72 = 3.25 or 4.

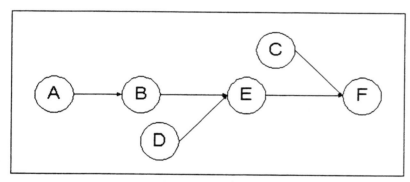

(Repetitive and product-oriented layout, moderate)

122. You have been asked to balance a flow shop assembly operation to achieve an output rate of 80 units per eight-hour day. Task times and precedence relationships are shown in the table below.

Task	Predecessor(s)	Duration
A	--	1.4
B	--	0.8
C	A, B	0.4
D	--	1.8
E	--	0.4
F	C	2.1
G	E, F	2.0
H	D, G	1.2

a. Draw the precedence diagram.
b. Determine the desired cycle time.
c. Determine the minimum number of stations needed.

The precedence diagram appears below. The desired cycle time for 80 units is 6 minutes. The minimum number of stations is 10.1 / 6 = 1.68 or 2.

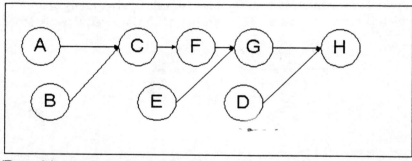

(Repetitive and product-oriented layout, moderate)

123. A firm operates a flow shop building kitchen cabinetry for recreational vehicles. The major activities of this process are listed below.

Method		Cycle time computation	
Most following tasks ▼		● Given ○ Computed	8

9.9

TASK	Hours	Predecessor 1	Predecessor 2	Predecessor 3	Predecesso 4
A	4				
B	6				
C	2	A			
D	6	A			
E	3	B	C		
F	3	B	C		
G	5	D	E	F	
H	1	G			

a. Draw the appropriate network for this project.

b. The goal is to produce 20 units per month (the plant operates 160 hours per month). How many stations are needed?

c. Balance with the most remaining tasks heuristic. What tasks are assigned to which stations?

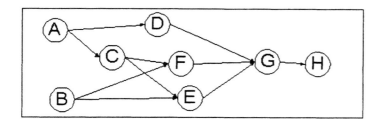

Method		Cycle time computation	
Most following tasks ▼		● Given ○ Computed	8

9.9 Solution

Station	Task	Time (hours)	Time left (hours)	Ready tasks (# followers)
				A(6),B(4)
1	A	4.	4.	B(4),C(4),D(2)
	C	2.	2.	B(4),D(2)
2	B	6.	2.	D(2),E(2),F(2)
3	D	6.	2.	E(2),F(2)
4	E	3.	5.	F(2)
	F	3.	2.	G(1)
5	G	5.	3.	H(0)
	H	1.	2.	

(Repetitive and product-oriented layout, moderate)

124. The table below details the tasks required for the Adams Industries' manufacture of a fully portable industrial vacuum cleaner. The times in the table are in minutes. Demand forecasts indicate a need to operate with a cycle time of 10 minutes.

Activity	Activity Description	Immediate Predecessors	Time
A	Attach wheels to tub	--	5
B	Attach motor to lid	--	1.5
C	Attach battery pack	B	3
D	Attach safety cutoff	C	4
E	Attach filters	B	3
F	Attach lid to tub	A, E	2
G	Assemble attachments	--	3
H	Function test	D, F, G	3.5
I	Final inspection	H	2
J	Packing	I	2

a. Draw the appropriate network for this project.

b. A POM for Windows solution is provided. Explain carefully which tasks are assigned to which workstation, and how much idle time is present.

c. Discuss how this balance could be improved to 100 percent.

See sketch below. Station 1 gets A, G, and B, and has 0.5 minutes left over. Station 2 gets C, D, and F with no time left over. Station 3 gets F, H ,I, and J, and has 0.5 minutes left over. Improvements in efficiency would seem impossible. The times are in 0.5 minute smallest increments, and can't be subdivided to achieve exact balance. Perhaps perversely, if tasks G and H each were 0.5 minute longer, the line would be 100% efficient.

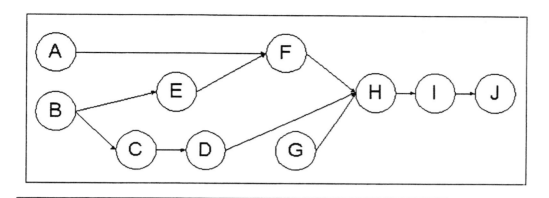

Method	Cycle time computation	
Longest operation time ▼	● Given	10
	○ Computed	

		9-10 Solution		
Station	Task	Time (minutes)	Time left (minutes)	Ready tasks
				A,B,G
1	A	5.	5.	B,G
	G	3.	2.	B
	B	1.5	0.5	C,E
2	C	3.	7.	E,D
	D	4.	3.	E
	E	3.	0.	F
3	F	2.	8.	H
	H	3.5	4.5	I
	I	2.	2.5	J
	J	2.	0.5	

Summary Statistics		
Cycle time	10	minutes
Time allocated (cyc*sta)	30	minutes/cycle
Time needed (sum task)	29	minutes/unit
Idle time (allocated-needed)	1	minutes/cycle
Efficiency (needed/allocated)	96.66666%	
Balance Delay (1-efficiency)	3.333333%	
Min (theoretical) # of stations	3	

(Repetitive and product-oriented layout, moderate)

125. As part of a major plant renovation project, the industrial engineering department has been asked to balance a revised assembly operation to achieve an output rate of 480 units per eight-hour day. Task times and precedence relationships are shown in the table below.

Task	Duration (minutes)	Follows task
A	0.1	--
B	0.2	a
C	0.1	b
D	0.2	--
E	0.1	--
F	0.6	c
G	0.5	d, e, f

a. Draw the precedence diagram.
b. Determine the desired cycle time.
c. Determine the minimum number of stations needed.
d. Assign tasks to stations on the basis of greatest number of following tasks;
e. Compute the percentage idle time for the above assignment.

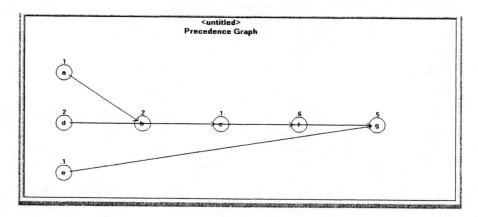

\<untitled\>
Precedence Graph

Balancing, Assembly Line Results

\<untitled\> Solution

Station	Task	Time	Time left	Ready tasks
1	a	0.1	0.9	d,e,b
	b	0.2	0.7	d,e,c
	c	0.1	0.6	d,e,f
	d	0.2	0.4	e,f
	e	0.1	0.3	f
2	f	0.6	0.4	g
3	g	0.5	0.5	

Summary Statistics	
Cycle time	1.
Time allocated (cyc*sta)	3.
Time needed (sum task)	1.8
Idle time (allocated-needed)	1.2
Efficiency (needed/allocated)	60.
Balance Delay (1-efficiency)	40.
Min (theoretical) # of stations	2.

(Repetitive and product-oriented layout, moderate)

198

126. Hemo-tech, Inc., a biomedical technology and research laboratory, produces a standard blood filtering device on an assembly line basis. Six basic tasks are performed along an assembly line. The time to perform each task and the tasks that must immediately precede each task are in the table below. Twenty pumps per 450-minute day must be produced by the assembly line.

Task	Preceding Task	Time to perform (min.)
A	--	5.40
B	A	3.20
C	--	1.50
D	B, C	2.80
E	D	17.10
F	E	12.80

a. Draw the network diagram of the precedence relationships.
b. Identify the absolute minimum and maximum cycle times.
c. How many workstations are required to meet the demand?
d. What is the cycle time required to meet demand?

The absolute minimum cycle time is 17.10 minutes (the longest operation). The absolute maximum cycle time is 42.80 minutes (the sum of all task times) The desired cycle time is 450/20 = 22.5 minutes. The number of stations required is 42.8/22.5 = 1.90 or 2.

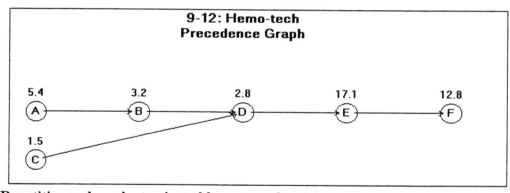

(Repetitive and product-oriented layout, moderate)

127. An assembly line with 11 tasks is to be balanced. The longest task is 2.4 minutes, the shortest task is 0.4 minutes, and the sum of the task times is 18 minutes. The line will operate for 600 minutes per day.
a. Determine the minimum and maximum cycle times.
b. What range of output is theoretically possible for the line?
c. What is the minimum number of stations needed if the maximum output rate is to be sought?
d. What cycle time will provide an output rate of 200 units per day?

Minimum cycle time is 2.4 minutes. Maximum cycle time is 18 minutes. Maximum output is 600/2.4 = 250; minimum output is 600/18 = 33.3. For maximum output, 18/2.4 = 7.5 or 8 stations will be needed. To produce 200 units per day requires a 3-minute cycle time.
(Repetitive and product-oriented layout, moderate)

128. A firm is planning to set up an assembly line to assemble 40 units per hour, and 57 minutes per hour are productive. The time to perform each task and the tasks which precede each task are:

Task	Preceding Task	Time to perform (min.)
A	--	.69
B	A	.55
C	B	.92
D	B	.59
E	B	.70
F	B	1.10
G	C, D, E	.75
H	G, F	.43
I	H	.29

a. Draw a network diagram of precedence relationships.
b. Compute the cycle time per unit in minutes.
c. Compute the minimum number of workstations required to produce 50 units per hour.
Cycle time is 57/40 = 1.425 minutes. The number of stations required is 6.02/1.425 = 4.22 or 5.

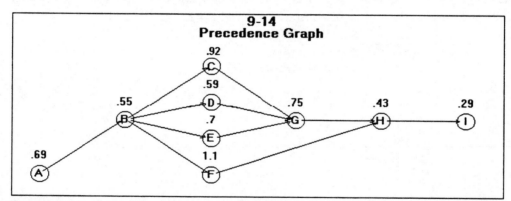

9-14
Precedence Graph

(Repetitive and product-oriented layout, difficult)

129. An insurance claims processing center has six work centers, any of which can be placed into any of six physical departmental locations. Call the centers 1, 2, 3, 4, 5, and 6, and the departments A, B, C, D, E, and F. The current set of assignments is A-3, B-1, C-6, D-2, E-4, and F-5.

The (symmetric) matrix of departmental distances, in meters is

	1	2	3	4	5	6
1	--	5	30	20	15	20
2		--	40	15	10	10
3			--	50	20	5
4				--	10	35
5					--	5
6						--

The matrix of work flow (estimated trips per day) is among centers

	A	B	C	D	E	F
A	--	15	20	0	30	0
B	20	--	50	0	160	10
C	0	50	--	30	0	30
D	30	60	20	--	70	0
E	40	0	0	10	--	60
F	0	0	30	20	50	--

The firm estimates that each trip costs approximately $4.
a. What is the cost of the current assignment?
b. Use trial-and-error to find one improved assignment.
c. What is that assignment, and what is its cost?

The current assignment costs 13,875. Optimal is 10,450, with A-3, B-5, C-4, D-1, E-6, and F-2. (Process-oriented layout, moderate)

130. There are three work centers (A, B, and C) behind the financial aid counter at a nearby university. They can each fit into any of three office spaces (1, 2, and 3) off the corridor behind the desk. There is no student contact in these areas, only workers. The distance 1-2 is 20 feet, 2-3 is 30 feet, and 1-3 is 50 feet. The matrix of work (trips per day) at the three centers is in the following table. Remember that each trip must be a round-trip (from 1 to 2 and back, for example).

	A	B	C
A	--	20	0
B	45	--	25
C	60	0	--

a. How many possible assignments are there? List them.
b. Calculate the total distance traveled in each of these assignments.
c. Which assignment minimizes distance traveled?
There are 3! = 6 assignments.

A	B	C	Cost
1	2	3	10100
1	3	2	10400
2	1	3	8700
2	3	1	8800
3	1	2	11100
3	2	1	10900

(Process-oriented layout, difficult)

CHAPTER 10: HUMAN RESOURCES AND JOB DESIGN

TRUE/FALSE

1. A reasonable quality of work life can be achieved in an organization solely by providing equitable pay to all employees.
    False (Human resource strategy for competitive advantage, moderate)

2. Labor planning deals with issues of employment stability and work schedules.
    True (Labor planning, easy)

3. The extreme cases of employment stability are "follow demand exactly" and "hold employment constant."
    True (Labor planning, moderate)

4. Flextime is a system that allows employees, within limits, to determine their own work schedules.
    True (Labor planning, moderate)

5. Labor specialization deals with worker skills and does not extend to the development of specialized tools.
    False (Job design, moderate)

6. An enriched job has more responsibility than the same job enlarged.
    True (Job design, moderate)

7. Psychological factors have little relevance in the design of assembly line jobs since they involve physical products and production technology.
    False (Job design, moderate)

8. Self-directed teams tend to be successful in work environments where there is little employee empowerment.
    False (Job design, moderate)

9. Expanded jobs are not suitable for all individuals.
    True (Job design, moderate)

10. Job expansion can lead to increased labor cost because of the extra workers hired in the expansion.
    False (Job design, moderate)

11. Profit-sharing is a motivation and incentive system where executives receive stock options.
    False (Job design, moderate)

12. The physical environment in which employees work may affect the quality of work life but it does not affect their performance and safety.
    False (Job design, moderate)

13. Ergonomics is a branch of economics that deals with costs of scheduling workers.
    False (Job design, moderate)

14. Techniques of methods analysis such as flow diagrams and activity charts are only useful in a factory or manufacturing environment.
    False (Job design, moderate)

15. An operations chart is used to study and improve the utilization of an operator (or crew) and a machine.
    False (Job design, moderate)

16. The visual workplace eliminates non-value-adding activities through devices such as **kanbans** and **andons**.
    True (The visual workplace, moderate)

17. The purpose of labor standards is to accurately define the skills required to complete a job.
    False (Labor standards, moderate)

MULTIPLE CHOICE

18. Which of the following best describes **mutual commitment** in an organization?
    a. an instance in which management is committed to the employees and the employees are committed to management
    b. both management and the employees are committed, but to different objectives
    c. management obtains the commitment of the employees to a stated objective
    d. both management and the employees are committed to the same objective
    e. both management and the employees can rely on each other
    d (Human resource strategy for competitive advantage, moderate)

19. Which of the following best describes **mutual trust**?
    a. that both management and the employees trust each other
    b. reasonable, documented employment policies, honestly and equitably implemented to the satisfaction of both management and the employees
    c. that management has gained the trust of the employees
    d. that management recognizes that the employees are competent, motivated people both able and willing to perform at the level required to produce a quality product
    e. management and the employees both agree on the objectives
    b (Human resource strategy for competitive advantage, moderate)

20. The objective of a human resource strategy is
    a. to produce the demand forecast at lowest labor cost
    b. to match employment levels with demand
    c. to achieve a reasonable quality of work life at low cost
    d. to manage labor and design jobs so people are effectively and efficiently utilized
    e. all of the above
    d (Human resource strategy for competitive advantage, moderate)

21. Which of the following is associated with work scheduling?
    a. flexible workweek
    b. job enlargement
    c. job enrichment
    d. meet demand exactly
    e. operations chart
    a (Labor planning, moderate)

22. The two most basic policies associated with employment stability are
    a. employment for life and guaranteed minimum wage
    b. follow demand exactly, and hold employment constant
    c. incentive plan and piece-rate plan
    d. job enrichment and job enlargement
    e. none of the above
    b (Labor planning, moderate)

23. Four of the seven components of job design are
    a. employment stability, work schedules, work sampling, motivation and incentive systems
    b. job specialization, job expansion, psychological components, ergonomics and work methods
    c. labor specialization and enrichment, motivation and incentive systems, employment stability, work sampling
    d. ergonomics and work methods, method time measurement, work schedules, motivation and incentive systems
    e. labor specialization, time studies, work sampling, and pre-determined time standards
    b (Job design, moderate)

24. The behavioral approach to job design which involves giving the worker a larger portion of the total task is
    a. job enlargement
    b. job enrichment
    c. job enhancement
    d. job rotation
    e. job involvement
    a (Job design, moderate)

25. Job rotation is an example of
    a. job enlargement
    b. job enrichment
    c. job scheduling
    d. job training
    e. job incentive
    a (Job design, moderate)

26. Which of the following terms implies an increase in responsibility and control?
    a. job enlargement
    b. job rotation
    c. job enrichment
    d. job re-design
    e. job satisfaction
    c (Job design, moderate)

27. When a worker has a say in the work methods that he/she wishes to utilize, his/her job is characterized by
    a. skill variety
    b. job identity
    c. job significance
    d. autonomy
    e. feedback
    d (Job design, moderate)

28. Which of the following statements describes job rotation?
    a. The job contains a larger number of similar tasks.
    b. The job includes some planning and control necessary for job accomplishment.
    c. The operator is allowed to move, for example, from one type of CNC machine to the other.
    d. The operator works on different shifts on a regular basis.
    e. The operator's schedule is flexible.
    c (Job design, moderate)

29. The difference between **job enrichment** and **job enlargement** is that
    a. enlarged jobs involve vertical expansion, while enriched jobs involve horizontal expansion
    b. enriched jobs involve vertical expansion, while enlarged jobs involve horizontal expansion
    c. enriched jobs enable an employee to do a number of boring jobs instead of just one
    d. job enlargement is more psychologically satisfying than job enrichment
    e. job enrichment is suitable for all employees, whereas job enlargement is not
    b (Job design, moderate)

30. When a worker obtains clear and timely information about his/her performance, his/her job is characterized by
    a. skill variety
    b. job identity
    c. job significance
    d. autonomy
    e. feedback
    e (Job design, moderate)

31. A job characterized by _____ allows a worker to use his/her dexterity, physical strength, and ability to plan and organize his/her work.
    a. skill variety
    b. job identity
    c. job significance
    d. autonomy
    e. feedback
    a (Job design, difficult)

32. Which of the following correctly describes the increasing reliance of employee contributions and increasing employee responsibility?
    a. Specialization is at the low end of the scale.
    b. Self-directed teams are at the high end of the scale.
    c. Job enlargement is lower-ranked than employee empowerment.
    d. All of the above are true.
    e. None of the above are true.
    d (Job design, difficult)

33. Ergonomics is **not** concerned with
    a. adequate compensation schemes
    b. levels of illumination, noise, temperature, and humidity
    c. adjusting and providing input to the machine
    d. feedback (providing information to the operator)
    e. the design of functional and comfortable office furniture
    a (Job design, moderate)

34. One of the elements of ergonomics is
    a. allocating work time based on economics studies
    b. the cost justification of technology
    c. the use of automation in a manufacturing organization
    d. the establishment of time standards
    e. designing tools and machines that facilitate human work
    e (Job design, moderate)

35. Management and labor share the labor cost reductions in which of these compensation schemes?
    a. bonus system
    b. quota system
    c. Scantron plan
    d. Scanlon plan
    e. measured day work plan
    d (Job design, moderate)

36. "Designed to show economy of motion by pointing out waste motion and idle time" describes
    a. an operations chart
    b. flow diagrams
    c. an activity chart
    d. all of the above
    e. none of the above
    a (Job design, moderate)

37. Which of the following is **not** an analytical target of methods analysis?
    a. body movement
    b. movement of capital
    c. movement of individuals
    d. movement of materials
    e. crew activity
    b (Job design, moderate)

38. Methods analysis focuses on
    a. the design of the machines used to perform a task
    b. issues such as the movement of individuals or materials
    c. establishing time standards
    d. reducing the number of skills needed for the completion of a task
    e. evaluating training programs to see if they are efficient
    b (Job design, moderate)

39. Which of the following statements regarding incentive systems is **false**?
    a. Bonuses are often used at the executive levels.
    b. About half of all American manufacturing firms use productivity incentives.
    c. Knowledge-based pay systems are increasing in. use
    d. The Scanlon plan is based on team productivity.
    e. Increasing use of cross-training has led to increasing use of knowledge-based pay systems.
    d (Job design, moderate)

40. Which of the following is used by methods analysis in analyzing body movement at the workstation level?
    a. MTM chart
    b. flow diagram
    c. operations chart
    d. process chart
    e. improvement chart
    c (Job design, moderate)

41. Method analysis employs which of the following charts in its analysis of the movement of workers and materials?
    a. micro-motion chart
    b. activity chart
    c. man-machine chart
    d. flow diagram
    e. movement chart
    d (Job design, moderate)

42. In a large aerospace company, it has been discovered that some insulators have been damaged. A methods specialist is sent out to follow the insulators through the production and storage processes and try to find out where in the process they are damaged. The specialist should use
    a. flow diagrams
    b. left- and right-hand charts
    c. program flowcharts
    d. job analysis charts
    e. activity charts
    a (Job design, difficult)

43. Flow diagrams are used to analyze:
    a. movement of people and materials
    b. utilization of an operator and machine
    c. body movements
    d. time taken by various activities
    e. unnecessary micro-motions
    a (Job design, moderate)

44. Activity charts help analyze
    a. movement of people and materials
    b. utilization of an operator and machine
    c. body movements
    d. activities that can cause injuries
    e. unnecessary micro-motions
    b (Job design, moderate)

45. "Schematic used to investigate movement of people or material" describes
    a. a flow chart
    b. an activity chart
    c. an operations chart
    d. a right-hand / left-hand chart
    e. none of the above
    a (Job design, moderate)

46. The visual workplace
    a. uses low-cost visual devices to share information
    b. includes statistical process control (SPC) charts
    c. includes kanbans
    d. all of the above
    e. none of the above
    d (The visual workplace, moderate)

47. **Labor standards** are defined as the
    a. preset activities required to perform a job
    b. amount of time required to perform a job or part of a job
    c. amount of space required by a specific crew to perform the job
    d. standard set of procedures to perform the job
    e. standard labor agreements
    b (Labor standards, moderate)

FILL-IN-THE-BLANK

48. _____ means a job that is not only reasonably safe and for which the pay is equitable, but which also achieves an appropriate level of both physical and psychological requirements.
Quality of work life (Human resource strategy for competitive advantage, moderate)

49. _____ is a means of determining staffing policies dealing with employment stability and work schedules.
Labor planning (Labor planning, moderate)

50. _____ refers to a work schedule that deviates from the normal or standard five 8-hour days.
Flexible workweek (Labor planning, moderate)

51. _____ is an approach that specifies the tasks that constitute a job for an individual or a group.
Job design (Job design, easy)

52. _____ is the grouping of a variety of tasks about the same skill level.
Job enlargement (Job design, moderate)

53. _____ is a method of giving an employee more responsibility that includes some of the planning and control necessary for job accomplishment.
Job enrichment (Job design, moderate)

54. A _____ is a group of empowered individuals working together to reach a common goal.
self-directed team (Job design, moderate)

55. _____ is a system providing some portion of any profit for distribution to employees.
Profit sharing (Job design, moderate)

56. _____ is the study of work, often called human factors.
Ergonomics (Job design, moderate)

57. _____ are drawings used to analyze movement of people or material.
Flow diagrams (Job design, moderate)

58. _____ are charts depicting right and left-hand motions.
Operations charts (Job design, moderate)

59. _____ is a call light that signals problems.
Andon (The visual workplace, moderate)

60. _____ are the amount of time required to perform a job or a part of a job.
Labor standards (Labor standards, easy)

SHORT ANSWER

61. Define quality of work life.
Quality of work life means a job that not only is reasonably safe and for which the pay is equitable, but also that adheres to an appropriate level of both physical and psychological requirements. (Human resource strategy for competitive advantage, moderate)

62. Define mutual trust.
Mutual trust is intended to mean reasonable, documented employment policies that are honestly and equitably implemented to the satisfaction of both management and employee. (Human resource strategy for competitive advantage, moderate)

63. What is flextime?
It is a system that allows employees, within limits, to determine their own work schedule. (Human resource strategy for competitive advantage, easy)

64. How does labor specialization assist in reducing labor costs (list three ways)?
Development of dexterity and faster learning by the employee because of repetition; less loss of time because the employee will not be changing jobs so frequently; development of specialized tools and a reduction in investment because each employee will require only a few tools for a particular task. (Job design, moderate)

65. List the limitations to job expansion.
Higher capital cost; many individuals prefer simpler jobs; higher wage rates are required; smaller labor pools exist; increased accident rates may occur; and current technology in some industries does not lend itself to job expansion. (Job design, moderate)

66. Explain how job expansion can lead to higher pay rates.
As expansion leads to workers having greater skills, they tend to be paid according to their highest skill. (Job design, moderate)

67. Explain how job expansion can lead to higher accident rates.
Expanded jobs have workers performing more tasks; they are less specialized; there's more to learn, which can lead to higher accident rates. (Job design, moderate)

68. List the constraints on human resource strategy.
Product strategy, process strategy, schedules, individual differences, location strategy, and layout strategy. (Human resource strategy for competitive advantage, moderate)

69. State the two major approaches to job expansion.
Job enlargement and job enrichment. (Job design, moderate)

70. What questions are answered once the set of job classifications and work rules are done?
Who can do what; when they can do it; under what conditions it is to be done. (Human resource strategy for competitive advantage, moderate)

71. List the seven components of job design.
Job specialization, job expansion, psychological components, self-directed teams, motivation and incentive systems, ergonomics and work methods, and visual workplace

72. List the techniques available for carrying out methods analysis.
Flow diagrams, process charts, activity charts, and operations charts. (Job design, moderate)

73. List the five desirable characteristics of job design, according to Hackman and Oldham.
Skill variety, job identity, job significance, autonomy, and feedback. (Job design, moderate)

74. Define vertical job expansion and horizontal job expansion. Explain clearly how they differ.
Vertical expansion refers to job enrichment that adds planning and control dimensions to the job; horizontal expansion refers to job enlargement which occurs when tasks of similar skills are added to the existing job. (Job design, moderate)

75. Describe how the "visual workplace" can increase information flow, improve efficiency, and eliminate non-value-adding activities. Support your argument with a few examples.
Visuals reduce the time spent sharing information, especially in signaling hazards, low-stock conditions, poor quality, etc. Time spent reading instructions or taking measurements are non-value-adding if a simple visual can replace them. Examples include graphs of stock conditions, painted warnings, markers, kanbans, andons, and others. (The visual workplace, moderate)

76. Define ergonomics. Discuss the role of ergonomics in job design.
Ergonomics is the study of human factors, the study of work. Ergonomics can make work safer, less damaging, by redesign of tools, workspaces, and worker motions. (Job design, moderate)

77. Describe the job design continuum. Specifically, explain how this relates to job expansion.
There are several forms of job expansion, some with greater levels of employee responsibility. At the low end are specialization, job enlargement and job enrichment. At the higher end are employee empowerment and self-directed teams. All are forms of job expansion. (Job design, moderate)

78. List the three forms of monetary rewards.
Pick three of the following: bonuses, profit sharing, gain sharing, incentive systems, and knowledge-based pay systems. (Job design, moderate)

CHAPTER 10 SUPPLEMENT: WORK MEASUREMENT

TRUE/FALSE

1. One use of labor standards is to determine what makes a fair day's work.
    True (Labor standards and work measurement, easy)

2. Labor standards based on historical experience are relatively inexpensive to obtain.
    True (Historical experience, easy)

3. Labor standards based on historical experience are questionable in terms of accuracy.
    True (Historical experience, easy)

4. Standard time may be greater than, or less than, actual cycle time.
    True (Time studies, moderate)

5. The allowance factor that increases normal time to standard time compensates for inadequate worker training and lack of worker dexterity.
    False (Time studies, moderate)

6. Normal time is always less than the actual cycle time.
    False (Time studies, moderate)

7. Standard time is always greater than normal time.
    True (Time studies, moderate)

8. Rest allowances can include amounts for the effects of lighting, heat and humidity, and noise.
    True (Time studies, moderate)

9. In constructing the standard time for a task, the elements that make up the task must use the same performance ratings factor.
    False (Time studies, moderate)

10. If a manager conducting a time study needed an accuracy of ± 0.1 minutes, rather than ± 0.2 minutes, the adequate sample size would have to be twice as large.
    False (Time studies, moderate)

11. Work sampling and time studies are similar in that the analyst in both cases records the time taken by the worker to accomplish each step of the task.
    False (Time studies, and Work sampling, moderate)

12. UPS may run the "tightest ship in the shipping business," but they got that high level of efficiency without time standards, because their contract with the Teamsters Union forbids them.
    False (Time studies, moderate)

13. Because service jobs are so much more variable than manufacturing jobs, time measurement standards similar to MTM do not exist for most services.
    False (Predetermined time standards, moderate)

14. An advantage of predetermined time standards is that no performance ratings are necessary.
True (Predetermined time standards, moderate)

15. An advantage of work sampling is that it completely breaks down work elements.
False (Work sampling, moderate)

16. Work sampling cannot be used to construct time standards.
False (Work sampling, moderate)

MULTIPLE CHOICE

17. Which of the following techniques may not provide reliable and accurate time standards?
    a. method time measurement (MTM)
    b. time studies
    c. work sampling
    d. historical experience
    e. pre-determined time standards
    d (Historical experience, moderate)

18. In stopwatch time study, the average time it takes a given worker to perform a task a certain number of times is the
    a. average actual cycle time
    b. standard time
    c. performance rating time
    d. normal time
    e. allowance time
    a (Time studies, moderate)

19. The average cycle time is calculated by
    a. the average observed time multiplied by the performance rating
    b. summing the times recorded to perform each element divided by the number of cycles observed
    c. normal time divided by allowance factor
    d. normal time divided by the number of cycles observed
    e. the average observed time divided by the allowance factor
    b (Time studies, moderate)

20. Which of the following are **true** regarding personal allowances and fatigue allowances?
    a. have a "constant" and a "variable" component
    b. allow for work conditions such as heating, lighting, and noise
    c. do not include delay allowances
    d. represent the adjustment between normal time and standard time
    e. all of the above are true
    e (Time studies, moderate)

21. The actual average cycle time for a given job is 11 minutes. The performance rating is 80%, and allowances are set by contract at 10%. What is the time standard?
    a. 9.78 minutes
    b. 11 minutes
    c. 13.75 minutes
    d. 15.2 minutes
    e. 88 minutes
    a (Time studies, moderate)

22. Personal time allowances in work measurement are often established in the range of
    a. 1 - 2%
    b. 3 - 5%
    c. 4 - 7%
    d. 6 - 10%
    e. 10-15%
    c (Time studies, moderate)

23. Sample observations of claims processor made over a 160-hour work month reveal that the worker produced a total of 384 completed claims forms. The performance rating was 90%. The worker was idle 20% of the time. The allowance factor is 8%. What is the normal time per unit?
    a. 0.42 minutes
    b. 16.6 minutes
    c. 18 minutes
    d. 20 minutes
    e. 115.2 hours
    c (Work sampling, moderate)

24. Sample observations of a claims processor made over a 160-hour work month reveal that the worker produced a total of 384 completed claims forms. The performance rating was 90%. The worker was idle 20% of the time. The allowance factor is 8%. What is the standard time per unit?
    a. 0.42 minutes
    b. 18 minutes
    c. 19.6 minutes
    d. 21.7 minutes
    e. 24.5 minutes
    c (Work sampling, moderate)

25. The data below represent time study observations for an assembly operation. Assume a 7% allowance factor. What is the normal time for element 3?

Element	Performance Rating	Observation (minutes per cycle)				
		1	2	3	4	5
1	100%	1.5	1.6	1.4	1.5	1.5
2	90%	2.3	2.2	2.1	2.2	2.4
3	115%	1.7	1.9	1.9	1.4	1.6
4	100%	3.5	3.6	3.6	3.6	3.2

   a. 1.7 min.
   b. 1.96 min.
   c. 2.10 min.
   d. 10.1 min.
   e. 11.2 min.
   b (Time study, moderate)

26. A bank manager wants to determine the percent of time its tellers are working and idle. He decides to use work sampling, and his initial estimate is that the tellers are idle 20% of the time. Approximately how many observations should be taken to be 95% confident that the results will not be more than 10% away from the true result?
   a. 6
   b. 10
   c. 44
   d. 62
   e. 384
   c (Work sampling, moderate)

27. For a time study, the three factors that determine how large a sample size to take are
   a. the level of confidence, the z-value, and normal time
   b. needed accuracy, desired confidence, and variation in the job elements
   c. the level of confidence, the z-value, and the work sampling idle percent
   d. actual time, normal time, and standard time
   e. actual time, standard time, and Greenwich Mean Time
   b (Time study, moderate)

28. An analyst recently prepared a labor standard. The accuracy is to be within 5%, and the confidence level is 90%. The standard deviation of the sample is 2 and the mean is 8. What sample size should the analyst have used?
   a. 14
   b. 27
   c. 68
   d. 136
   e. cannot be determined
   c (Time study, moderate)

29. Therbligs
     a. were invented by Frederick W. Taylor
     b. were named by Frank Gilbreth
     c. were used during the scientific management era, and are no longer in use
     d. are hyperactive rodent-like pets, whose name is associated with time standards
     e. none of the above
     b (Predetermined time standards, moderate)

30. Which of these is the most common predetermined time standard?
     a. CSD
     b. MTM
     c. TMU
     d. RCH
     e. SAE
     b (Predetermined time standards, moderate)

31. Predetermined time standards are an outgrowth of basic motions called
     a. flow diagrams
     b. activity charts
     c. therbligs
     d. SAE standards
     e. man-machine charts
     c (Predetermined time standards, moderate)

32. Which of the following best describes a **therblig**?
     a. the smallest unit of time used in methods time measurement exercises
     b. the largest unit of time used in method time measurement exercises
     c. the smallest unit of basic motion used in methods time measurement exercises
     d. the largest unit of basic motion used in methods time measurement exercises
     e. the smallest amount of time required to complete a job
     c (Predetermined time standards, moderate)

33. Which of the following is **true** regarding work sampling?
     a. The technique was developed in the 1890s.
     b. The method is used to estimate the percentage of time workers spend in unavoidable delays.
     c. Their use is accepted by unions as fair.
     d. The method makes extensive use of rest allowances.
     e. All of the above are false.
     b (Work sampling, moderate)

34. Among the advantages of predetermined time standards are all of the following **except**
     a. unions accept them as fair
     b. they are available before a task is actually performed
     c. they can be established in a laboratory setting
     d. they can only be determined after work actually takes place
     e. all of the above are advantages
     d (Predetermined time standards, moderate)

35. A technique for estimating the proportion of time a worker spends on various activities is
   a. stopwatch time study
   b. simultaneous motion study
   c. work sampling
   d. standard elemental (historical) times
   e. predetermined (published) time standards
   c (Work sampling, moderate)

36. All of the following are advantages of predetermined time standards **except**
   a. they are well accepted
   b. no performance ratings are necessary
   c. the standard can be set before the task is done and then can be used for planning
   d. they are customized to your company
   e. they are based on a large number of workers
   d (Predetermined time standards, moderate)

37. Timing a sample of a worker's performance and using it to set a standard is the work measurement technique of
   a. predetermined time standards
   b. time studies
   c. work sampling
   d. methods time measurement
   e. left-hand, right-hand charting
   b (Time studies, moderate)

38. The tally sheet data from a work sampling study provides information regarding
   a. the percent of time spent on various tasks
   b. the number of wasted motions
   c. the level of difficulty in a motion
   d. the quality of the work environment
   e. the number of micro-motions involved
   a (Work sampling, moderate)

39. An advantage of work sampling is that
   a. no observation is required
   b. it involves study of the equipment only
   c. the time spent observing the employee is relatively short
   d. a performance rating is necessary
   e. it is more effective than time studies when cycle times are short
   c (Work sampling, moderate)

FILL-IN-THE-BLANK

40. _____ involves timing a sample of a worker's performance and using it as a basis for setting a standard time.
   Time study (Time studies, easy)

41. _____ is the observed time adjusted for pace.
   Normal time (Time studies, moderate)

218

42. _____ divide manual work into small basic elements that have established and widely accepted times.
Predetermined time standards (Time studies, moderate)

43. _____ is an estimate, via sampling, of the percent of time that a worker spends on various tasks.
Work sampling (Work sampling, easy)

SHORT ANSWERS

44. Identify four ways in which labor standards are set.
Historical experience, time studies, pre-determined time standards, and work sampling. (Labor standards and work measurement, easy)

45. What are some of the uses to which labor standards are put?
1. to determine labor content of items produced
2. to determine staffing needs of organizations
3. to determine cost and time estimates prior to production
4. to determine crew size and work balance
5. to determine production expected
6. to determine the basis of wage-incentive plans
7. to determine efficiency of employees and supervision
(Labor standards and work measurement, moderate)

46. List the eight steps used to develop a time study-based labor standard.
Define the task to be studied, break down the task into precise elements, decide how many times to measure the task, time and record the elemental times and ratings of performance, compute the average actual cycle time, compute the normal time, compute the total normal time, and compute the standard time. (Time studies, moderate)

47. Define the average actual cycle time.
The actual average cycle time is computed by dividing the sum of the times recorded to perform each element by the number of cycles observed. It is adjusted for unusual influences. (Time studies, moderate)

48. Define normal time.
Normal time adjusts the observed time to what a normal worker could be expected to accomplish by multiplying the average actual cycle time by a performance rating factor. (Time studies, moderate)

49. What two broad categories do allowances fall into? Discuss why "allowances" are included to adjust normal time to standard time. Support your position with a few simple examples.
Allowances are categorized as "constant" and "variable." Allowances are for personal fatigue and other factors associated with ergonomics and other job conditions, including heat and humidity, lighting, noise, etc. These unavoidable factors influence productivity and need to be accounted for in determining fair time standards. (Time studies, moderate)

50. Define standard time.

   The standard time for a task provides allowances for personal needs, unavoidable delays, etc. The standard time is determined by dividing the normal time for a task by (1- allowance factor). (Time studies, moderate)

51. How is the statistical tool of adequate sample sizing used in work measurement?

   There are two applications: one in time studies, the other in work sampling. Both uses determine how many measurements need to be taken before specified levels of accuracy and confidence are achieved. This prevents users of time studies and work sampling from drawing faulty conclusions from too-small samples. (Time studies, and Work sampling, moderate)

52. State the three factors that influence the adequate sample size in work measurement.

   How accurate do we want the sample, the desired level of confidence, and the extent of variation in the job elements. (Time studies, and Work sampling, moderate)

53. State two disadvantages of time studies.

   They require a staff of trained analysts, and labor standards cannot be set before the task is actually performed. (Time studies, moderate)

54. List the seven steps in the work-sampling procedure.

   Take a preliminary sample to obtain an estimate of the parameter value, compute the sample size required, prepare a schedule for observing the worker at appropriate times, observe and record worker activities; rate worker performance, record the number of units produced during the applicable portion of the study, compute the normal time per part, and compute the standard time per part. (Work sampling, moderate)

55. What kind of circumstances call for the use of work sampling?

   Ratio delay studies, setting labor standards, measuring worker performance. (Work sampling, moderate)

56. What are the advantages of work sampling over time-study methods?

   Work sampling is less expensive since a single observer can observe several workers simultaneously, observers usually don't require much training, and no timing devices are needed, the study can be delayed temporarily at any time with little impact on the results. And because work sampling uses instantaneous observations over a long period, the worker has little chance of affecting the study's outcome. (Work sampling, moderate)

57. What are the disadvantages of work sampling?

   It does not break down work elements as completely as time studies; it can yield biased or incorrect results if the observer does not follow random routes of travel and observation, and it is less effective than time studies when cycle times are short. (Work sampling, moderate)

PROBLEMS

58. The cycle time for performing a certain task was measured to be 12 minutes. The performance rating of the worker timed was estimated at 105%. Common practice in this department is to allow 9% for constant allowances. In addition, it is estimated that there should be an extra variable allowance of 7% on this task.

a. Find the normal time for the operation.

b. Compute the allowance factor and the standard time for the operation.

Normal time = 12 minutes * 1.05 = 12.6 minutes

$$\text{Standard time} = \frac{\text{Normal allowance}}{1 - \text{Allowance factor}} = \frac{12.6}{1 - 0.16} = 15 \text{ minutes}$$

(Time studies, moderate)

59. A time study of a certain service task found an average cycle time of 15 minutes, with a standard deviation of 4 minutes. These figures were based on a sample of 100 measurements. Is the sample large enough that we are 95% confident that standard time is within 5% of its true value?

$$n = \left(\frac{zs}{h\bar{x}}\right)^2 = \left(\frac{1.96 * 4}{.05 * 15}\right)^2 = \left(\frac{7.84}{.75}\right)^2 = (10.45)^2 = 110$$

No, the sample was a bit too small. (Time studies, moderate)

60. How many observations would be necessary for a time studies analyst to be 99% confident that the average cycle time is within .1 minutes of the true value if the average cycle time is 10.5 minutes and the standard deviation of the cycle times is 2 minutes?

$$n = \left(\frac{zs}{h\bar{x}}\right)^2 = \left(\frac{2.58 * 2}{.1 * 10.5}\right)^2 = 24$$

(Time studies, moderate)

61. A hotel housekeeper was observed five times on each of four task elements. On the basis of these observations, find the standard time for the process. Assume a 10% allowance factor.

Element	Performance Rating	Observation (minutes per cycle)				
		1	2	3	4	5
1	100%	1.5	1.6	1.4	1.5	1.5
2	90%	2.3	2.5	2.1	2.2	2.4
3	120%	1.7	1.9	1.9	1.4	1.6
4	100%	3.5	3.6	3.6	3.6	3.2

Answer:

Element	Rating	Observation (units per minute)						
		1	2	3	4	5	Average	Normal
1	100%	1.5	1.6	1.4	1.5	1.5	1.5	1.50
2	90%	2.3	2.5	2.1	2.2	2.4	2.3	2.07
3	120%	1.7	1.9	1.9	1.4	1.6	1.7	2.04
4	100%	3.5	3.6	3.6	3.6	3.2	3.5	3.50

Normal time for process = 9.11

$$\text{Standard time for process} = \frac{\text{Normal time for process}}{1 - \text{Allowance factor}} = \frac{9.11}{1 - 0.10} = 10.12 \text{ minutes}$$

(Time studies, moderate)

62. In a preliminary work sample of an operation, out of 50 observations the operator was observed idle in 5 observations. What sample size is required for a work sampling study if the desired confidence level is 98% and the desired accuracy level is 4%? In a follow-up, the idle rate was 10 of the 50 observations. By how much does the adequate sample size change?

$$n = \frac{z^2 p(1-p)}{h^2} = \frac{2.33^2 * 0.1 * 0.9}{0.04^2} = 306$$

$$n = \frac{z^2 p(1-p)}{h^2} = \frac{2.33^2 * 0.2 * 0.8}{0.04^2} = 543, \quad \text{an increase of 237.}$$

(Work Sampling, moderate)

63. A work sample taken over a 100-hour work month produced the following results. What is the standard time for the job?

Units Produced	200	Performance Rating	110%
Idle Time	25%	Allowance Time	15%

$$\text{Cycle time} = \frac{100 \text{ hours x } 60 \text{ minutes x } 0.75}{200 \text{ units}} = 22.5 \text{ minutes}$$

Normal time = 22.5 minutes x 1.1 = 24.75 minutes

$$\text{Standard time for job} = \frac{\text{Normal time for process}}{1 - \text{Allowance fraction}} = \frac{24.75}{1 - 0.15} = 29.12 \text{ minutes/unit}$$

(Work sampling, moderate)

64. A brake system installer in an auto factory has an actual cycle time of 10 minutes on her task. The performance rating of the worker timed was estimated at 90%. Practice in this department is to allow 9% for the constant allowances. There is currently no variable allowance.
a. Find the normal time for the operation.
b. Compute the standard time for the operation.
c. Recompute the standard time if a variable allowance of 7% is factored in.
Normal time = 10 minutes * .90 = 9 minutes

$$\text{Standard time} = \frac{\text{Normal time}}{1 - \text{Allowance factor}} = \frac{9}{1 - 0.09} = 9.89 \text{ minutes}$$

$$\text{New standard time} = \frac{\text{Normal time}}{1 - \text{Allowance factor}} = \frac{9}{1 - 0.16} = 10.71 \text{ minutes}$$

(Time studies, moderate)

65. A work sample taken over a 100 hour work month produced the following results. 200 units were produced, with idle time percent of 25%. The worker is rated at 105% and allowances are 18%. What is the standard time for the job?

$$\text{Cycle time} = \frac{100 \text{ hours x } 60 \text{ minutes x } 0.75}{200 \text{ units}} = 22.5 \text{ minutes}$$

Normal time = 22.5 minutes x 1.05 = 23.625 minutes

$$\text{Standard time for job} = \frac{\text{Normal time}}{1 - \text{Allowance}} = \frac{23.625}{1 - 0.18} = 28.81 \text{ minutes/unit}$$

(Work sampling, moderate)

66. The data in the following table represent time-study observations on a new operation with three work elements. On the basis of these observations, find the standard time for the process. Assume an 8% allowance factor.

Element	Performance Rating	Observation (seconds per cycle)			
		1	2	3	4
1	100%	110.2	111	109.7	109
2	85%	114.7	114.9	115.2	113.8
3	110%	109	109.3	109.2	108.9

Answer:

Element	Rating	Observation (minutes per cycle)				Average	Normal Time
		1	2	3	4		
1	100%	110.2	111	109.7	109	109.975	109.98
2	85%	114.7	114.9	115.2	113.8	114.65	97.45
3	110%	109	109.3	109.2	108.9	109.1	120.01

Normal time for process = 327.44 seconds

$$\text{Standard time for job} = \frac{\text{Normal time}}{1 - \text{Allowance fraction}} = \frac{327.44}{1 - .08} = 355.9 \text{ seconds}$$

(Time studies, moderate)

67. Work sampling is being conducted on the activities of parcel delivery drivers. Details of that study are 600 units produced, with idle time of 20% over a 160 hour period. The drivers were rated at 115%, and allowances total 10%. Calculate the normal time and standard for the job.

$$\text{Cycle time} = \frac{160 \text{ hours x } 60 \text{ minutes x } 0.80}{600 \text{ units}} = 12.8 \text{ minutes}$$

Normal time = 12.8 minutes x 1.15 = 14.72 minutes

$$\text{Standard time for job} = \frac{\text{Normal time}}{1 - \text{Allowance fraction}} = \frac{14.72}{1 - .10} = 16.36 \quad \text{Minutes/unit}$$

(Time studies, moderate)

68. The manager of a claims processing contractor estimates that the claims processing clerks are idle 15% of the time. The manager would like to take a work sample that would be accurate within 4% and wants to have 95% confidence in the results. How many observations should be taken?

$$n = \frac{z^2 \cdot p \cdot (1 - p)}{h^2} = \frac{1.96^2 \cdot 0.15 \cdot .85}{0.04^2} = 307$$

(Work sampling, moderate)

69. A Methods and Measurements Analyst needs to develop a time standard for a certain task. The task involves use of ruler, square, and portable electric saw to mark and cut the "notch" in a rafter (a standard carpentry task of home construction). In a preliminary study, he observed one of his workers perform this task five times. The observations were made in an air-conditioned, well-lighted training facility, at ground level, with all tools and equipment clean and readily available.

Observation:	1	2	3	4	5
Task time (seconds):	82	74	80	83	76

a. What is the actual cycle time for this task?
b. What is the normal time for this task if the employee worked at a 15% faster pace than is typical for adequately trained workers?
c. What is standard time for this task if allowances are 7% constant and 4% variable?
d. If the analyst then thought more carefully about his experiment, and decided that the variable allowances needed to be increased to match the real (outside, unair-conditioned) work environment, and that the proper variable allowance was not 4% but 9%, what is the revised standard time?

Actual average cycle time is 79 seconds. Normal time is 77 * 1.15 = 90.85 seconds. Standard time is 90.85 / (1-.11) = 102.1 seconds. The revised standard time is 90.85 / (1-.16) = 108.2 seconds. (Time studies, difficult)

CHAPTER 11: SUPPLY CHAIN MANAGEMENT

TRUE/FALSE

1. Volkswagen's Rio de Janeiro plant is an illustration of a radical alteration of a supply chain.
    True (Global company profile: Volkswagen, easy)

2. Volkswagen's Rio de Janeiro plant achieves a new, high level of supply chain integration.
    True (Global company profile: Volkswagen, easy)

3. The key to effective supply chain management is to make the suppliers "partners" in the firm's strategy to satisfy an ever-changing marketplace.
    True (The strategic importance of the supply chain, moderate)

4. Supply chain management is the integration of the activities that procure materials, transform them into intermediate goods and final products, and deliver them to customers.
    True (The strategic importance of the supply chain, easy)

5. Activities of supply chain managers are generally limited to the operations function.
    False (The strategic importance of the supply chain, moderate)

6. Even though a firm may have a low cost strategy, supply chain strategy can select suppliers primarily on response or differentiation.
    False (The strategic importance of the supply chain, moderate)

7. McDonald's was able to utilize existing plants and transportation systems in preparing the supply chain for opening its stores in Moscow.
    False (Global supply chain issues, moderate)

8. Since the purchasing function in a business often spends more money than any other function, it provides a major opportunity to reduce cost and increase profit margins.
    True (Purchasing, moderate)

9. Purchasing is the least costly activity in most firms.
    False (Purchasing, easy)

10. Supply chain decisions are not generally strategic in nature, because purchasing is an ordinary expense to most firms.
    False (Purchasing, moderate)

11. The objective of the purchasing activity is, in part, to help identify the products and services that can be obtained externally.
    True (Purchasing, moderate)

12. Purchasing takes place in manufacturing environments, not service environments.
    False (Purchasing, easy)

13. In wholesale and retail firms, it is the buyer who usually has responsibility for both selection of the item to be purchased and sales and profit margins on the items to be resold.
False (Purchasing, moderate)

14. Make-or-buy decisions should be reviewed periodically.
True (Purchasing, moderate)

15. A reduction in inventory costs is a reason for making rather than buying.
False (Purchasing, moderate)

16. The need for special technical expertise is a reason for buying rather than making.
True (Purchasing, moderate)

17. With the many suppliers strategy, the order usually goes to the supplier that offers the best quality.
False (Supply-chain strategies, moderate)

18. The traditional American purchasing strategy is to develop long term, "partnering" relationships with a few suppliers.
False (Supply-chain strategies, moderate)

19. With few suppliers, the cost of changing partners is low.
False (Supply-chain strategies, moderate)

20. The biggest advantage of the "few suppliers" supply chain strategy may be the trust that comes with compatible corporate cultures.
True (Supply-chain strategies, moderate)

21. An organization that retails fast food and owns poultry plants and poultry feed mills is backward vertically integrated.
True (Supply-chain strategies, moderate)

22. A fast food retailer that acquired a spice manufacturer or a beverage distributor would be practicing forward vertical integration.
False (Supply-chain strategies, moderate)

23. Keiretsus offer a middle ground between few suppliers and vertical integration.
True (Supply-chain strategies, moderate)

24. Poka Yoke is the Japanese term for a company coalition of suppliers.
False (Supply-chain strategies, moderate)

25. A virtual company is an organization that exhibits high standards of ethical behavior in all countries in which it does business.
False (Supply-chain strategies, moderate)

26. In the vendor evaluation phase, most companies will use the same list of criteria and the same criteria weights.
False (Vendor selection, moderate)

27. The supply chain management opportunity called postponement involves delaying deliveries to avoid accumulation of inventory at the customer's site.
False (Managing the supply chain, moderate)

28. Drop shipping results in time and shipping cost savings.
True (Managing the supply chain, moderate)

29. Blanket orders are contracts to purchase certain items from the vendor including authorizations to ship them.
False (Managing the supply chain, moderate)

30. The Internet can replace more traditional electronic data interchange (EDI) for releasing orders to suppliers.
True (Managing the supply chain, moderate)

31. Internet purchasing may be part of an integrated Enterprise Resource Planning (ERP) system.
True (Managing the supply chain, moderate)

32. Materials Management is not likely to have much potential for competitive advantage.
False (Materials management, moderate)

33. With the growth of Just-in-Time practices, railroads have made large gains in the share of the nation's transport that they haul.
False (Materials management, moderate)

34. Waterways are an attractive distribution system when shipping cost is more important than speed.
True (Materials management, moderate)

35. Benchmark firms have driven down costs of supply chain performance.
True (Benchmarking supply-chain management, moderate)

MULTIPLE CHOICE

36. Which of the following is **not** a concern of the supply chain?
    a. transportation vendors
    b. credit and cash transfers
    c. suppliers
    d. distributors and banks
    e. maintenance scheduling
    e (The strategic importance of the supply chain, moderate)

37. One dollar saved in purchasing is
    a. equivalent to a dollar earned in sales revenue
    b. worth even more than a dollar earned in sales revenue
    c. worth slightly more than a dollar earned because of taxes
    d. worth from 35% in the technical instrument industry to 70% in the food products industry
    e. only worthwhile if you are in the 90% tax bracket and still have a low profit margin
    b (Purchasing, moderate)

38. Which one of the following statements about purchasing is **true**?
    a. The cost of purchases as a percent of sales is often small.
    b. Purchasing provides a major opportunity for price increases.
    c. Purchasing has an impact on the quality of the goods and services sold.
    d. Purchasing is always more efficient than making.
    e. Competitive bidding is a major factor in long-term cost reductions.
    c (Purchasing, moderate)

39. In a retail environment, the purchasing function is usually managed by
    a. an expediter
    b. a buyer
    c. a purchasing agent
    d. the keiretsu
    e. the store manager
    b (Purchasing, moderate)

40. The purpose of the expediter is to
    a. help the purchasing agent select the item to be purchased
    b. test the quality of the incoming order
    c. follow up on an order to ensure timely delivery
    d. gather the engineering documents, etc. necessary to describe the item to be purchased
    e. approve purchases made by the buyer
    c (Purchasing, moderate)

41. The role of purchasing is diminished in many service environments because
    a. the items to be purchased are very cheap
    b. the primary product is an intellectual one
    c. there is no trained professional to assume the purchasing function
    d. the items to be purchased are chosen in catalogs
    e. the issue of make (provide) or buy does not arise
    b (Purchasing, moderate)

42. Which one of the following is **not** a purchasing strategy?
    a. negotiation with many suppliers
    b. short-term relationships with few suppliers
    c. vertical integration
    d. keiretsu
    e. virtual companies
    b (Supply-chain strategies, moderate)

43. The purchasing approach that holds the suppliers responsible for maintaining the necessary technology, expertise, and forecasting ability plus cost, quality, and delivery competencies is
    a. vertical integration
    b. few suppliers
    c. many suppliers
    d. Keiretsu
    e. virtual companies
    c (Supply-chain strategies, moderate)

44. In the make-or-buy decision, one of the reasons for making is
   a. to assure adequate supply in terms of quantity
   b. to reduce inventory costs
   c. to obtain technical or management ability
   d. inadequate capacity
   e. reciprocity
   a (Purchasing, moderate)

45. In the make-or-buy decision, one of the reasons for buying is
   a. to assure adequate supply
   b. inadequate capacity
   c. to obtain desired quality
   d. to remove supplier collusion
   e. to maintain organizational talents
   b (Purchasing, moderate)

46. In the make-or-buy decision, which of the following is **not** a reason for buying?
   a. inadequate capacity
   b. patents or trade secrets
   c. lower inventory costs
   d. to obtain desired quality
   e. all of the above are reasons for buying
   d (Purchasing, moderate)

47. In the make-or-buy decision, which of the following is a reason for **making** an item?
   a. lower production cost
   b. inadequate capacity
   c. reduce inventory costs
   d. management can focus on its primary business
   e. none of the above is a reason for making an item
   a (Purchasing, moderate)

48. A disadvantage of the "few suppliers" strategy is
   a. the risk of not being ready for technological change
   b. the lack of cost savings for customers and suppliers
   c. possible violations of the Sherman Antitrust Act
   d. the high cost of changing partners
   e. all of the above are disadvantages of the "few suppliers" strategy
   d (Supply-chain strategies, moderate)

49. Which of the following is **not** an advantage of the few suppliers concept?
   a. suppliers' willingness to participate in JIT systems
   b. trust
   c. creation of value by allowing suppliers to have economies of scale
   d. suppliers' willingness to provide technological expertise
   e. vulnerability of trade secrets
   e (Supply-chain strategies, moderate)

50. Which of the following supply chain strategies creates value by allowing suppliers to have economies of scale?
    a. vertical integration
    b. long-term partnering with a few suppliers
    c. negotiating with many suppliers
    d. developing virtual companies
    e. suppliers becoming part of a company coalition
    b (Supply-chain strategies, moderate)

51. Which of the following best describes vertical integration?
    a. to develop the ability to produce products which complement the original product
    b. to produce goods or services previously purchased
    c. to develop the ability to produce the specified good more efficiently than before
    d. to sell products to a supplier or a distributor
    e. all of the above
    b (Supply-chain strategies, moderate)

52. Vertical integration will be less successful if this condition is present.
    a. availability of necessary capital
    b. availability of managerial talent
    c. required demand
    d. small market share
    e. current suppliers are unreliable
    d (Supply-chain strategies, moderate)

53. Vertical integration appears particularly advantageous when the organization has a
    a. a very specialized product
    b. a large market share
    c. a small market share
    d. a very common, undifferentiated product
    e. all of the above
    b (Supply-chain strategies, moderate)

54. A fried chicken fast food chain that acquired feed mills and poultry farms has performed
    a. forward vertical integration
    b. backward vertical integration
    c. current transformation
    d. horizontal integration
    e. job expansion
    b (Supply-chain strategies, moderate)

55. A rice mill in south Louisiana purchases the trucking firm that transports packaged rice to distributors. This is an example of
    a. forward vertical integration
    b. backward vertical integration
    c. current transformation
    d. horizontal integration
    e. keiretsu
    a (Supply-chain strategies, moderate)

56. The Japanese concept of a company coalition of suppliers is
    a. poka yoke
    b. kaizen
    c. dim sum
    d. illegal
    e. keiretsu
    e (Supply-chain strategies, moderate)

57. Japanese manufacturers often take a middle ground between purchasing from a few suppliers and vertical integration. This approach is
    a. kanban
    b. samurai
    c. poka yoke
    d. keiretsu
    e. kaizen
    d (Supply-chain strategies, moderate)

58. Which of the following is **not** an advantage of a virtual company?
    a. total control over every aspect of the organization
    b. specialized management expertise
    c. low capital investment
    d. flexibility
    e. speed
    a (Supply-chain strategies, moderate)

59. The three stages of vendor selection, in order, are
    a. vendor development, vendor evaluation, and vendor acquisition
    b. introduction, growth, and maturity
    c. vendor evaluation, vendor development, and negotiations
    d. vendor evaluation, negotiations, and vendor development
    e. vendor, vendi, venci
    c (Vendor selection, easy)

60. The three classic types of negotiation strategies are
    a. Theory X, Theory Y, and Theory Z
    b. many suppliers, few suppliers, and keiretsu
    c. cost-based price model, market-based price model, and competitive bidding
    d. vendor evaluation, vendor development, and vendor selection
    e. none of the above is correct
    c (Vendor selection, moderate)

61. A carpet manufacturer has delivered carpet directly to the end consumer rather than to the carpet dealer. The carpet manufacturer is practicing
    a. postponement
    b. drop shipping
    c. direct shipping
    d. passing the buck
    e. float reduction
    b (Managing the supply chain, moderate)

62. Hewlett-Packard withholds customization of its laser printers as long as possible. This is an example of
    a. channel assembly
    b. backward integration
    c. postponement
    d. timely customization
    e. standardization
    c (Managing the supply chain, moderate)

63. All of the following are "opportunities" for supply chain management **except**
    a. postponement
    b. channel assembly
    c. drop shipment
    d. blanket orders
    e. job enrichment
    e (Managing the supply chain, moderate)

64. Which of the following is **not** a component of negotiation strategies?
    a. cost-based price model
    b. market-based price model
    c. competitive bidding
    d. combination of the above negotiation techniques
    e. invoiceless bidding
    e (Vendor selection, moderate)

65. Advantages of the postponement technique typically include
    a. early customization of the product
    b. better quality of the product
    c. reduction in training costs
    d. reduction in inventory investment
    e. reduction in automation
    d (Managing the supply chain, moderate)

66. A furniture maker has delivered a dining set directly to the end consumer rather than to the furniture store. The furniture maker is practicing
    a. postponement
    b. drop shipment
    c. direct shipment
    d. passing the buck
    e. float reduction
    b (Managing the supply chain, moderate)

67. Which of the following best describes stockless purchasing?
    a. small lots are delivered frequently
    b. there is only one supplier for all units of a particular product
    c. the supplier delivers only what the customer needs
    d. there is minimal purchasing-oriented paperwork
    e. the supplier maintains the inventory for the customer
    e (Managing the supply chain, moderate)

68. Internet purchasing can be used
    a. to communicate order releases to suppliers
    b. to replace electronic data interchange (EDI)
    c. for comparison shopping
    d. as part of an integrated enterprise resource planning (EPR) system
    e. all of the above
    e (Managing the supply chain, moderate)

69. With the growth of JIT, which of the following distribution systems has been the biggest loser?
    a. trucking
    b. railroads
    c. waterways
    d. air freight
    e. pipelines
    b (Materials management, moderate)

70. Which one of the following distribution systems offers quickness and reliability when emergency supplies are needed overseas?
    a. trucking
    b. railroads
    c. waterways
    d. air freight
    e. pipelines
    d (Materials management, easy)

71. Which of the following is **true** regarding supply chain performance? Benchmark firms
    a. have more suppliers per purchasing agent
    b. have longer lead time
    c. use competitive bidding more often
    d. have far fewer shortages per year
    e. have slightly fewer shortages per year
    d (Benchmarking supply-chain management, moderate)

72. Which one of the following performance measures is **not** true of a world class firm?
    a. low number of suppliers per purchasing agent
    b. low purchasing costs as percent of purchases
    c. high lead time
    d. high percentage of on-time deliveries
    e. low number of shortages per year
    c (Benchmarking supply-chain management, moderate)

FILL-IN-THE BLANK

73. _____ is the management of activities that procure raw materials, transform those materials into intermediate goods and final products, and deliver the products through a distribution system.
    Supply-chain management (The strategic importance of the supply chain, easy)

74. _____ is the acquisition of goods and services.
    Purchasing (Purchasing, easy)

75. The _____ decision involves choosing between producing a component or a service or purchasing if from an outside source.
    make-or-buy (Purchasing, easy)

76. _____ is developing the ability to produce goods or services previously purchased or actually buying a supplier or a distributor.
    Vertical integration (Supply-chain strategies, moderate)

77. _____ is a Japanese term to describe suppliers who become part of a company coalition.
    Keiretsu (Supply-chain strategies, moderate)

78. _____ rely on a variety of supplier relationships to provide services on demand.
    Virtual companies (Supply-chain strategies, moderate)

79. _____ involves delaying any modifications or customization to the product as long as possible in the production process.
    Postponement (Managing the supply chain, moderate)

80. _____ postpones final assembly of a product so the distribution channel can assemble it.
    Channel assembly (Managing the supply chain, moderate)

81. _____ involves shipping directly from the supplier to the end consumer, rather than from the seller, saving both time and reshipping cost.
    Drop shipping (Managing the supply chain, moderate)

82. _____ involves reducing the number of variations in materials and components as an aid to cost management.
    Standardization (Managing the supply chain, moderate)

83. _____ is a standardized data-transmittal format for computerized communications between organizations.
Electronic Data Interchange (EDI) (Managing the supply chain, moderate)

84. _____ includes order releases communicated over the Internet or approved vendor catalogues available on the Internet for use by employees of the purchasing firm.
Internet purchasing or e-procurement (Managing the supply chain, moderate)

85. _____ is an approach that seeks efficiency of operations through the integration of all material acquisition, movement, and storage activities.
Materials management (Managing the supply chain, moderate)

SHORT ANSWER

86. Define supply chain management.
Supply chain management is the management of the activities that procure raw materials, transform them into intermediate goods and final products, and deliver the products to customers through a distribution system. (The strategic importance of the supply chain, moderate)

87. What are the special requirements of supply chain systems in global environments?
Flexible enough to react to sudden changes in parts availability and currency rates, etc.; able to use latest information technology to manage shipments; and staffed with specialists to handle duties, customs, political issues in other countries. (The strategic importance of the supply chain, moderate)

88. Why is the purchasing role in many service environments less important than in manufacturing?
The primary product in service is an intellectual one. (Purchasing, moderate)

89. What are the objectives of the purchasing function?
Help identify the products and services that can best be obtained externally; develop, evaluate, and determine the best supplier, price and delivery for them. (Purchasing, moderate)

90. List the reasons for making in the make-or-buy decision.
Lower production cost; unsuitable suppliers; ensure adequate supply; utilize surplus labor facilities and make a marginal contribution; obtain the desired quality; remove supplier collusion; obtain a unique item that would entail a prohibitive commitment for a supplier; maintain organizational talents; protect proprietary design or quality; and increase or maintain size of the company (management preference). (Purchasing, moderate)

91. List the reasons for **buying** in the make-or-buy decision.
Lower acquisition cost; preserve supplier commitment; obtain technical or managerial ability; inadequate capacity; reduce inventory costs; ensure alternative sources of supply; inadequate managerial or technical resources; reciprocity; item protected by patent or trade secret; and allow management to focus on primary business. (Purchasing, moderate)

92. List the five purchasing strategies.

1. the traditional American approach of negotiating with many suppliers and playing one supplier off against another

2. develop long, "partnering" relationships with a few suppliers who will work with the purchaser in satisfying the end customer

3. vertical integration where firms may decide to pursue backward integration by actually buying the supplier

4. Keiretsu where suppliers become part of a company coalition

5. develop virtual companies that use suppliers on an as-needed basis.

(Supply-chain strategies, moderate)

93. Can an organization's plans for vertical integration be supported by the tools of make-or-buy analysis? Explain; provide an example.

Yes; the decision to acquire a firm providing an upstream operation is the same as choosing to make whatever that upstream operation does. Not to acquire is the equivalent of "buy." The analysis also holds for downstream operations: the acquisition of a delivery fleet is equivalent to "make" in the downstream operation of distribution. (Supply-chain strategies, moderate)

94. What are the advantages of vertical integration?

Cost reduction; quality adherence; and timely delivery. (Supply-chain strategies, easy)

95. Using a T-account to display pros and cons, explore the advantages and disadvantages of using the few suppliers approach.

Advantages	Disadvantages
• long-term suppliers better understand firm	• concern about trade secrets and suppliers venturing out
• suppliers may gain economies of scale	• high cost of changing partners
• trust	• risk of poor supplier performance
• willingness to participate in JIT	

(Supply-chain strategies, moderate)

96. Between the "few suppliers" strategy and the vertical integration strategy lies the Japanese practice of keiretsu. Describe this practice. Would this activity be legal in U.S.?

Coalitions, long-term relationships between firms and their suppliers; exchange of expertise. Suggested: students should consider the anti-trust angle-that coalitions might be serving to restrict access and competition. (Supply-chain strategies, moderate)

97. State the three stages in the process to develop a vendor relationship.

Vendor evaluation; vendor development; and negotiations. (Vendor selections, easy)

98. What are the three classic types of vendor negotiation strategies?

Cost-base price model; market-based price model; and competitive bidding. (Vendor selection, moderate)

99. Why is channel assembly popular in the personal computer industry?
Better market response with less investment. This is possible because the late-stage assembly and customization is a natural part of a rapidly changing industry. (Managing the supply chain, moderate)

100. Define postponement.
Postponement is a technique that involves withholding any modifications or customization to the product as long as possible. (Managing the supply chain, moderate)

101. Define drop shipment.
Drop shipping means the supplier will ship directly to the end consumer, rather than to the seller, saving both time and reshipping costs. (Managing the supply chain, moderate)

102. Define EDI.
Electronic Data Interchange is a standardized data transmittal format for computerized communications between organizations. (Managing the supply chain, moderate)

103. What is the objective of materials management?
Obtain efficiency of operations through the integration of all material acquisition, movement, and storage activities in the firm. (Materials management, moderate)

104. What are the advantages of shipping by truck?
Flexibility, on-time behavior, no damage, paperwork in order, and low cost. (Materials management, moderate)

105. List the five major means of distribution.
Trucking; railways; air freight; waterways; and pipelines. (Materials management, moderate)

CHAPTER 11 SUPPLEMENT: E-COMMERCE AND OPERATIONS MANAGEMENT

TRUE/FALSE

1. E-commerce is the use of computer networks, primarily the Internet, to buy and sell products, services, and information.
   True (Electronic commerce, easy)

2. Business-to-business e-commerce applications include supply chain alliances.
   True (Electronic commerce, moderate)

3. Business-to-business e-commerce applications include benchmarking competitors.
   True (Electronic commerce, moderate)

4. E-commerce presents little security risk to organizations.
   False (Security in the e-commerce environment, easy)

5. E-commerce is revolutionizing operations management because it is so effective at reducing costs.
   True (Economics of e-commerce, moderate)

6. E-commerce increases economic efficiencies by matching buyers and sellers.
   True (Economics of e-commerce, easy)

7. One benefit of e-commerce is a lack of standards.
   False (Economics of e-commerce, easy)

8. One benefit of e-commerce is the opportunity to expand the market for both buyers and sellers.
   True (Economics of e-commerce, moderate)

9. One benefit of e-commerce is lower entry costs.
   True (Economics of e-commerce, moderate)

10. One benefit of e-commerce is increased flexibility of locations.
    True (Economics of e-commerce, moderate)

11. Integrating e-commerce software with existing software and databases is easily accomplished.
    False (Economics of e-commerce, easy)

12. Virtual teams yield better product design decisions.
    True (Product design, easy)

13. Virtual teams yield quicker product design decisions.
    True (Product design, easy)

14. E-commerce can support JIT by coordinating the supplier's inventory system with the service capabilities of the delivery firm.
True (Inventory reduction, moderate)

15. Online catalogues are quickly improving bidding processes.
True (E-procurement, moderate)

16. Large purchasers have developed their own online catalogues.
True (E-procurement, moderate)

17. Operations managers are finding online auctions a fertile area for disposing of excess inventory.
True (E-procurement, moderate)

18. The logistics vendor runs new e-commerce warehouses.
True (Inventory reduction, moderate)

19. E-commerce has the opportunity to reduce logistics costs substantially.
True (Inventory reductions, moderate)

MULTIPLE CHOICE

20. E-commerce can be used for
    a. tracking consumer behavior
    b. collaboration on product design
    c. speeding accounting transactions
    d. purchasing
    e. all of the above
    e (Electronic commerce, moderate)

21. Which of the following best describes consumer-to-consumer e-commerce?
    a. both sides of the transaction are businesses, non-profit organizations, or government
    b. transactions involve buyers who are individual customers
    c. customers sell directly to each other by electronic classified advertisements or auction sites
    d. individuals sell services or goods to businesses
    e. none of the above
    c (Electronic commerce, moderate)

22. Which of the following is **not** an application of business-to-business e-commerce?
    a. product design
    b. supply chain alliances
    c. competitor benchmarking
    d. forecasting
    e. all of the above are applications of B2B e-commerce
    e (Electronic commerce, moderate)

23. Which of the following is **not** an economic efficiency of e-commerce?
    a. new middlemen drive down transaction costs
    b. matches buyers and sellers
    c. facilitates the exchange of information
    d. increases barriers to entry
    e. time constraints in transactions are reduced
    d (Economics of e-commerce, moderate)

24. Which of the following is a limitation of e-commerce?
    a. reduces the cost of communication
    b. lowers entry costs
    c. reduces privacy
    d. expands availability of market
    e. all of the above are limitations of e-commerce
    c (Economics of e-commerce, moderate)

25. Which of the following is **not** a limitation of e-commerce?
    a. lack of system security
    b. difficulty integrating e-commerce software with existing software
    c. lower entry costs
    d. lack of trust
    e. lack of system standards
    c (Economics of e-commerce, moderate)

26. Online catalogues are generally **not** provided by
    a. buyers
    b. intermediaries
    c. agents
    d. sellers
    e. all of the above
    c (E-procurement, moderate)

FILL-IN-THE BLANK

27. _____ is the use of computer networks, primarily the Internet, to buy and sell products, services, and information.
    E-commerce (Electronic commerce, easy)

28. _____ e-commerce transactions involve individuals selling services or goods to businesses.
    Consumer-to-business (C2B) (Electronic commerce, easy)

29. _____ are information about products made available in electronic form via the Internet.
    Online catalogues (E-procurement, moderate)

30. _____ is the purchasing or order release communicated over the Internet or via approved online vendor catalogues.
    E-procurement (E-procurement, moderate)

SHORT ANSWER

31. What is electronic commerce?
   It is the use of computer networks, primarily the Internet, to buy and sell products, services, and information. (Electronic commerce, easy)

32. What are the four types of e-commerce transactions?
   Business-to-business (B2B), Business-to-consumer (B2C), Consumer-to-consumer (C2C), and Consumer-to-business (C2B). (Electronic commerce, moderate)

33. What type of information is shared in business-to-business (B2B) applications?
   Product, production processes, transportation, inventory, supply chain alliances, supply chain process and performance, competitor, sales and marketing, and customer. (Electronic commerce, moderate)

34. What economies are gained from e-commerce?
   New middlemen drive down transaction costs; matches buyers and sellers; facilitates the exchange of information, goods, and services; lowers the costs of transactions. (Economics of e-commerce, moderate)

35. What are the benefits of e-commerece?
   Improved, lower cost information that makes buyers and sellers more knowledgeable, lower entry cost increases information sharing, available 24 hours a day, virtually any place in the world enabling convenient transactions for those concerned, availability expands the market for both buyers and sellers, decreases the cost of creating, processing, distributing, storing, and retrieving paper-based information, reduces the costs of communication, richer communication than traditional paper and telephone communication because of video clips, voice, and demonstrations, fast delivery of digitized products such as drawings, documents, and software, and increased flexibility of lacations. (Economics of e-commerce, moderate)

36. What are the limitations of e-commerce?
   Lace of system security, reliability, and standards, lack of privacy, insufficient ban width, some transactions are still rather slow, integrating e-commerce software with existing software and databases is still a challenge, and lack of trust. (Economics of e-commerce, moderate)

37. What are the benefits of virtual teams in terms of product design?
   Cheaper, better, and quicker. (Product design, moderate)

38. What are the three versions of online catalogues?
   By vendor, by buyer, and by intermediaries. (E-procurement, moderate)

39. How does an e-commerce support JIT system?
   It can support JIT by coordinating the supplier's inventory system with service capabilities of the delivery firm. (Inventory reduction, moderate)

CHAPTER 12: INVENTORY MANAGEMENT

TRUE/FALSE

1. A major challenge in inventory management is to decrease the investment in inventory while satisfying customer demand.
   True (Introduction, easy)

2. The overall objective of inventory management is balancing the cost of inventory against the cost of providing reasonable levels of customer service.
   True (Introduction, easy)

3. Which item to order and with which supplier the order should be placed are the two fundamental issues in inventory management.
   False (Introduction, moderate)

4. The most important function of inventory is to provide a hedge against inflation.
   False (Introduction, easy)

5. ABC analysis classifies inventoried items into three groups, usually based on annual units or quantities used.
   False (Inventory management, easy)

6. Because ABC analysis emphasizes that all items in inventory are equally important, management resources must be equally devoted to all the items.
   False (Inventory management, moderate)

7. ABC analysis is based on the presumption that carefully controlling **all** items is necessary to produce important inventory savings.
   False (Inventory management, easy)

8. In ABC analysis, "C" Items are the most tightly controlled.
   False (Inventory management, moderate)

9. No matter what method of inventory management is used, record accuracy is of utmost importance.
   True (Inventory management, moderate)

10. Cycle counting is an inventory control technique exclusively used for cyclical items.
    False (Inventory management, moderate)

11. In cycle counting, the frequency of item counting and stock verification usually varies from item to item depending upon the item's classification.
    True (Inventory management, moderate)

12. Retail inventory that is unaccounted for between receipt and time of sale is known as shrinkage.
    True (Inventory management, moderate)

13. Service inventories don't really exist, since services are intangible.
    False (Inventory management, moderate)

14. Items like spark plugs inventoried by a lawnmower manufacturer for use in the production of lawnmowers have independent demand.
False (Inventory models, moderate)

15. Holding costs that amount to approximately 26% per year or more of the unit cost are not unusual.
True (Inventory models, moderate)

16. The EOQ model is best suited for items whose demand is dependent on other products.
False (Inventory models for independent demand, moderate)

17. An advantage of the basic EOQ model is that it always results in a small order size.
False (Inventory models for independent demand, moderate)

18. In the simple EOQ model, the EOQ would rise if the ordering cost were to decrease.
False (Inventory models for independent demand, moderate)

19. In the simple EOQ model, if the carrying cost were to double, the EOQ would also double.
False (Inventory models for independent demand, moderate)

20. In the simple EOQ model, if annual demand were to increase, the EOQ would increase proportionately.
False (Inventory models for independent demand, moderate)

21. At the Economic Order Quantity, holding costs are equal to purchasing costs.
False (Inventory models for independent demand, moderate)

22. The EOQ model is a Robust Model, meaning it operates automatically with artificial intelligence.
False (Inventory models for independent demand, moderate)

23. If demand and lead-time are uniform and constant, there is no need for safety stock.
True (Inventory models for independent demand, moderate)

24. A Production Order Quantity problem has a longer period between orders, compared to an Economic Order Quantity problem using the same inputs (except for the non-instantaneous receipt).
True (Inventory models for independent demand, moderate)

25. Inventory models cannot be used to develop an inventory strategy unless quantity discounts are absent.
False (Inventory models for independent demand, moderate)

26. In the quantity discount model, it is possible to have a cost-minimizing solution where annual ordering costs do not equal annual carrying costs.
True (Inventory models for independent demand, moderate)

27. Safety stock in inventory systems depends only on the average demand during the lead time.
False (Probabilistic models with constant lead time, moderate)

28. In a fixed-period inventory model, orders are placed for exactly what is needed when it is needed.
False (Fixed-period systems, moderate)

29. In a fixed-period inventory system, the quantity ordered is always equal to Economic Order Quantity.
False (Fixed-period systems, moderate)

MULTIPLE CHOICE

30. Which of the following is a reason for holding inventory?
    a. to meet customer demand
    b. to protect against shortages
    c. to decouple production from distribution
    d. to allow for smooth and flexible operations
    e. all of the above are motives for holding inventory
    e (Introduction, moderate)

31. Which of the following would **not** generally be a motive for a firm to hold inventories? To
    a. take advantage of quantity discounts
    b. minimize holding costs
    c. reduce stockout risks
    d. decouple production from distribution
    e. meet anticipated demand
    b (Introduction, moderate)

32. All of the following statements about ABC analysis are true **except**
    a. it states that all items require the same degree of control
    b. inventory may be categorized by measures other than dollar volume
    c. it categorizes on-hand inventory into three groups based on annual dollar volume
    d. it is an application of the Pareto principle
    e. it states that there are the critical few and the trivial many inventory items
    a (Inventory management, moderate)

33. Which of the following statements about ABC analysis is **false**?
    a. ABC analysis is based on the presumption that controlling the few most important items produces the vast majority of inventory savings.
    b. In ABC analysis, "A" Items are tightly controlled, have accurate records, and receive regular review by major decision makers.
    c. ABC analysis is based on the presumption that all items must be tightly controlled to produce important cost savings.
    d. In ABC analysis, "C" Items have minimal records, periodic review, and simple controls
    e. None of the above statements are true.
    c (Inventory management, moderate)

34. ABC analysis is based upon the principle that
    a. all items in inventory must be monitored very closely
    b. an item is critical if its usage is high
    c. there are usually a few critical items, and many items which are less critical
    d. the safety stock (in terms of volume) should be higher for A items than for C items
    e. an item is critical if its unit price is high

    c (Inventory management, moderate)

35. Cycle counting
    a. provides a measure of inventory accuracy
    b. provides a measure of inventory turnover
    c. assumes that all inventory records must be verified with the same frequency
    d. is a process by which inventory records are verified once a year
    e. assumes that the most frequently used items must be counted more frequently

    a (Inventory management, moderate)

36. ABC analysis divides on-hand inventory into three classes, generally based upon
    a. unit price
    b. the number of units on hand
    c. annual demand
    d. annual dollar volume
    e. item quality

    d (Inventory management, moderate)

37. Among the advantages of cycle counting is that it
    a. makes the annual physical inventory more acceptable to management
    b. allows more rapid identification of errors and consequent remedial action than is possible with annual physical inventory
    c. does not require the detailed inventory records necessary when annual physical inventory is used
    d. does not require highly trained people
    e. does not need to be performed for less expensive items

    b (Inventory management, moderate)

38. A certain type of computer costs $2,000, and the annual holding cost is 30%. Annual demand is 10000 units, and the order cost is $150 per order. What is the approximate economic order quantity?
    a. 14
    b. 70
    c. 100
    d. 140
    e. 600

    b (Inventory models for independent demand, easy)

39. The two most basic inventory questions answered by the typical inventory model are
    a. timing and cost of orders
    b. quantity and cost of orders
    c. timing and quantity of orders
    d. order quantity and service level
    e. ordering cost and carrying cost
    c (Inventory models for independent demand, moderate)

40. Most inventory models attempt to minimize
    a. the likelihood of a stockout
    b. the number of items ordered
    c. the number of orders placed
    d. total inventory based costs
    e. the safety stock
    d (Inventory models for independent demand, easy)

41. In the basic EOQ model, if the cost of placing an order doubles, and all other values remain constant, the EOQ will
    a. increase by 200%
    b. increase by 100%
    c. increase by about 41%
    d. increase, but more data is needed to say by how much
    e. either increase or decrease
    c (Inventory models for independent demand, moderate)

42. Which of the following statements about the basic EOQ model is **true**?
    a. If the ordering cost were to double, the EOQ would rise.
    b. If annual demand were to double, the EOQ would increase.
    c. If the carrying cost were to increase, the EOQ would fall.
    d. If annual demand were to double, the number of orders per year would decrease.
    e. All of the above statements are true.
    e (Inventory models for independent demand, moderate)

43. In the basic EOQ model, if D=6000 per year, S=$100, H=$10 per unit per month, the Economic Order Quantity is approximately
    a. 6000
    b. 60
    c. 346
    d. 100
    e. 35
    d (Inventory models for independent demand, moderate)

44. Which of the following statements about the basic EOQ model is **false**?
    a. If annual demand were to increase, the EOQ would increase.
    b. If the ordering cost were to increase, the EOQ would rise.
    c. If annual demand were to double, the EOQ would also double.
    d. If the setup cost were to decrease, the EOQ would fall.
    e. All of the above statements are false.
    c (Inventory models for independent demand, moderate)

45.   A product whose EOQ is 40 experiences a decrease in ordering cost from $90 per order to $10. The revised EOQ is
    a.   three times as large
    b.   one-third as large
    c.   nine times as large
    d.   one-ninth as large
    e.   cannot be determined
    b (Inventory models for independent demand, difficult)

46.   A product whose EOQ is 400 experiences a 50% increase in demand. The new EOQ is
    a.   unchanged
    b.   increased by 50%
    c.   increased by more than 50%
    d.   increased by less than 50%
    e.   cannot be determined
    d (Inventory models for independent demand, difficult)

47.   For a certain item, the cost-minimizing order quantity obtained with the basic EOQ model was 100 units and the total annual inventory cost was $400. The inventory carrying cost per unit per year for this item is
    a. $2.00
    b. $4.00
    c. $5.00
    d. $40.00
    e.   not enough data to determine
    b (Inventory models for independent demand, difficult)

48.   A product has demand of 1000 units per year. Ordering cost is $20 and holding cost is $4 per unit per year. The cost-minimizing solution for this product is to order
    a.   all 1000 units at one time
    b.   10 units per order
    c.   every 10 days
    d.   10 times per year
    e.   none of the above
    d (Inventory models for independent demand, moderate)

49.   A product has demand of 1000 units per year. Ordering cost is $20 and holding cost is $4 per unit per year. The EOQ model is appropriate. The cost-minimizing solution for this product will cost $_____ per year in total annual inventory costs.
    a. $4000
    b. $400
    c. $200
    d.   zero; this is a class C item
    e.   cannot be determined because unit price is not known
    b (Inventory models for independent demand, moderate)

50. The EOQ model with quantity discounts attempts to determine
    a. what is the lowest purchasing price?
    b. whether to use fixed-quantity or fixed period order policy?
    c. how many units should be ordered?
    d. what is the shortest lead time?
    e. what is the lowest amount of inventory necessary to satisfy a certain service level?
    c (Inventory models for independent demand, moderate)

51. An inventory decision rule states that "when the inventory level goes down to 14 gearboxes, 100 gearboxes will be ordered." Which of the following statements is true?
    a. 100 is the reorder point, and 14 is the order quantity.
    b. The number 100 is a function of demand during lead time.
    c. 14 is the safety stock, and 100 is the reorder point.
    d. 14 is the reorder point, and 100 is the order quantity.
    e. None of the above.
    d (Inventory models for independent demand, moderate)

52. The Production Order Quantity model
    a. relaxes the assumption of known and constant demand
    b. uses Ordering Cost, not Setup Cost, in its formula
    c. assumes instantaneous delivery
    d. results in larger average inventory than an equivalent EOQ model
    e. is appropriate when units are sold/used as they are produced
    e (Inventory models for independent demand, moderate)

53. Which of the following statements regarding the Production Order Quantity model is **true**?
    a. It applies only to items produced in the firm's own production departments.
    b. It relaxes the assumption that the demand rate is constant.
    c. It minimizes the total production costs.
    d. It relaxes the assumption that all the order quantity is received at one time.
    e. It minimizes inventory.
    d (Inventory models for independent demand, moderate)

54. Which of the following statements about quantity discounts is **false**?
    a. The cost-minimizing solution may, or may not, be where annual holding costs equal annual ordering costs.
    b. In inventory management, item cost becomes relevant to inventory decisions only when a quantity discount is available.
    c. The larger annual demand, the less attractive a discount schedule will be.
    d. The smaller the ordering cost, the less attractive a discount schedule will be.
    e. If carrying costs are expressed as a percentage of value, EOQ is larger at each lower price in the discount schedule.
    c (Inventory models for independent demand, moderate)

55. When quantity discounts are allowed, the cost-minimizing order quantity
    a. is an EOQ quantity
    b. minimizes the sum of holding and ordering costs
    c. minimizes the sum of holding, ordering, and product costs
    d. minimizes the unit purchase price
    e. may be a quantity below that at which one qualifies for that price
    c (Inventory models for independent demand, moderate)

56. A specific product has demand during lead time of 100 units, with a standard deviation of 20 units. What safety stock (approximately) provides a 95% service level?
    a. 33
    b. 40
    c. 133
    d. 140
    e. 165
    a (Probabilistic models with constant lead time, moderate)

57. If the standard duration of demand is five per week, demand is 50 per week, and the desired service level is 95%, approximately what is the statistical safety stock?
    a. 6 units
    b. 7 units
    c. 8 units
    d. 64 units
    e. cannot be determined without lead time data
    e (Probabilistic models with constant lead time, moderate)

58. Demand for dishwasher water pumps is 8 per day. The standard deviation of demand is 3, and the order lead time is four days. The service level is 95%. What should the reorder point be?
    a. about 18
    b. about 24
    c. about 32
    d. about 38
    e. more than 50
    e (Probabilistic models with constant lead time, moderate)

59. The purpose of safety stock is to
    a. eliminate the possibility of a stockout
    b. eliminate the likelihood of a stockout due to erroneous inventory tally
    c. control the likelihood of a stockout due to the variability of demand during lead time
    d. protect the firm from a sudden decrease in demand
    e. replace failed units with good ones
    c (Probabilistic models with constant lead time, moderate)

60. If demand is not uniform and constant, then stockout risks can be controlled by
    a. increasing the EOQ
    b. placing an extra order
    c. adding safety stock.
    d. raising the selling price to reduce demand
    e. reducing the reorder point
    c (Probabilistic models with constant lead time, moderate)

61. The proper quantity of safety stock is typically determined by
    a. minimizing an expected stockout cost
    b. setting the level of safety stock so that a given stockout risk is not exceeded
    c. carrying sufficient safety stock so as to eliminate all stockouts
    d. meeting 95% of all demands
    e. minimizing total costs
    b (Probabilistic models with constant lead time, moderate)

62. An advantage of the **fixed-period** inventory system is that
    a. there is no physical count of inventory items when an item is withdrawn
    b. no inventory records are required
    c. orders usually are for smaller order quantities
    d. the average inventory level is reduced
    e. the supplier will be more cooperative
    a (Fixed-period systems, moderate)

63. A disadvantage of the fixed-period inventory system is that
    a. additional inventory records are required
    b. the average inventory level is decreased
    c. since there is no count of inventory during the review period, a stockout is possible
    d. orders usually are for larger quantities
    e. it involves higher ordering costs than the fixed quantity inventory system
    c (Fixed-period systems, moderate)

FILL-IN-THE BLANK

64. _____ inventory is material that is usually purchased, but has yet to enter the manufacturing process.
    Raw material (Functions of inventory, easy)

65. _____ is a method for dividing on-hand inventory into three classifications based on annual dollar volume.
    ABC analysis (Inventory management, easy)

66. _____ is a continuing reconciliation of inventory with inventory records.
    Cycle counting (Inventory management, moderate)

67. _____ refers to a small amount of theft of inventory.
    Pilferage (Inventory management, moderate)

68. _____ is the amount of time required to prepare a machine or process for production.
   Setup time (Inventory management, moderate)

69. A _____ model gives satisfactory answers even with substantial variations in its parameters.
   robust (Inventory management, moderate)

70. The _____ is the inventory level (point) at which action is taken to replenish the stocked item.
   reorder point (ROP) (Inventory management, moderate)

71. _____ is extra stock that is carried to serve as a buffer.
   Safety stock (Inventory management, easy)

72. A _____ is a reduced price for items purchased in large quantities.
   quantity discount (Inventory management, easy)

73. _____ is the complement of the probability of a stockout.
   Service level (Probabilistic models with constant lead time, moderate)

74. A _____ system triggers inventory ordering on a uniform time frequency.
   Fixed-period (Fixed-period systems, moderate)

SHORT ANSWERS

75. List and describe briefly each of the several motives for holding inventory.
   To decouple or separate parts of the production process, to provide a stock of goods that will provide a selection for customers, to take advantage of quantity discounts, and to hedge against inflation. (Introduction, moderate)

76. What are the four types of inventory? Provide a simple example of each:
   raw material, work-in-process, maintenance/repair/operating supply (MRO), and finished goods. (Functions of inventory, easy)

77. What are MRO inventories? Why do they exist?
   MRO inventories are devoted to maintenance/repair/operating supplies. They exist because the need and timing for maintenance and repair of some equipment are unknown. (Introduction, easy)

78. List the advantages of cycle counting.
   **1. eliminating the shutdown and interruption of production necessary for annual physical inventories
   2. Eliminating annual inventory adjustments
   3. providing trained personnel to audit the accuracy of inventory
   4. allowing the cause of errors to be identified and remedial action to be taken
   5. maintaining accurate inventory records
   (Inventory management, moderate)**

79. Define shrinkage.
   Retail inventory that is unaccounted for between receipt and sale. (Inventory management,

easy)

80. What are the techniques to control service inventories?

    Good personnel selection, training, and discipline; tight control of incoming shipments; and effective control of all goods leaving the facility. (Inventory management, moderate)

81. List the typical components that constitute inventory holding or carrying costs.

    Housing costs, material handling costs, labor cost from extra handling, investment costs, pilferage, scrap, and obsolescence. (Inventory models, moderate)

82. List the typical cost components that constitute ordering costs in inventory systems.

    Cost of supplies, forms, order processing, clerical support, and so forth. (Inventory models, moderate)

83. State the major assumptions of the basic EOQ model.

    Demand is known and constant over time; lead time is known and constant; receipt of inventory is instantaneous; quantity discounts are not possible; the only variable costs are the costs of placing an order or setting up production and the cost of holding or storing inventory over time and if orders are placed at the right time, stockouts or shortages can be completely avoided. (Inventory models for independent demand, moderate)

84. Compare the assumptions of the production order quantity model to those of the basic EOQ model.

    All are the same, except the assumption that receipt of inventory is instantaneous, which holds for EOQ, but not POQ. (Inventory models for independent demand, moderate)

85. In some inventory models, the optimal behavior occurs where annual order costs and carrying costs are equal to one another. Illustrate this with an example.

    This is true in EOQ and POQ models. In an EOQ model DS/Q will equal $QH/2$. (Inventory models for independent demand, moderate)

86. Explain what is meant by the expression "Robust model." Specifically, what would you tell a manager who exclaimed "Uh-oh, we're in trouble! The calculated EOQ is wrong. Actual demand is 10% greater than estimated."

    The EOQ model gives quite good results under inexact inputs; a 10% error to alters the EOQ by less than 5%. (Inventory models for independent demand, moderate)

87. Explain why it is not necessary to include product cost (price, or price times quantity) in the EOQ model, but the Quantity Discount Model requires this information?

    Price times quantity is not variable in the EOQ model, but is in the discount model. When quality discounts are available, the unit purchase price of the item depends on the order quantity. (Inventory models for independent demand, moderate)

88. Define Service Level.

    The service level is the percentage of demand met by available stock; it is the complement of the probability of a stockout. (Probabilistic models with constant lead time, moderate)

89. What is "safety stock?" What is it providing safety against?

    Safety stock is inventory beyond average demand during lead time, held to control the level of shortages when demand and/or lead time are not constant; inventory carried to assure that

the desired service level is reached. (Probabilistic models with constant lead time, moderate)

90. In some inventory models, the optimal behavior occurs where ordering costs and carrying costs are equal to one another. Provide an example of a model where this "rule" does not hold; explain how the model's results are optimal anyway.

    This rule will not hold in all instances of quantity discount models. In order to take advantage of a discount, it may be cheaper to order a quantity that is not an EOQ. The goal in quantity discount models is to minimize the sum of ordering, carrying, and purchase costs. (Inventory models for independent demand, moderate)

91. When demand is not constant, the reorder point is a function of what four parameters?

    Demand per unit of time, lead time, customer service level, and standard deviation of demand. (Probabilistic models with constant lead time, moderate)

92. State a major advantage, and a major disadvantage, of a Fixed-Period System.

    Advantage-there is no physical count of inventory when items are withdrawn. Disadvantage-there is a possibility of stockout during the time between reviews. (Inventory models for independent demand, moderate)

PROBLEMS

93. Montegut Manufacturing produces a product for which the annual demand is 10,000. Production averages 100 per day, while demand is 40 per day. Holding costs are $1.00 per unit per year; set-up costs $200.00. If they wish to produce this product in economic batches, what size batch should be used? What is the maximum inventory level? How many order cycles are there per year? How much does management of this good in inventory cost the firm each year?

    This problem requires economic order quantity, non-instantaneous delivery.

$$Q = \sqrt{\frac{2DS}{H(1-d/p)}} = \sqrt{\frac{2* 10000* 200}{1.00(1-40/100)}} = 2582 \text{ units}$$

The maximum inventory level is 1549; there are almost four cycles per year; annual costs total $1,549. POM for Windows solution follows.

PARAMETER	VALUE		PARAMETER	VALUE
Demand rate(D)	10000		Optimal order quantity (Q*)	2,581.99
Setup/Ordering cost(S)	200		Maximum Inventory Level	1,549.19
Holding cost(H)	1		Average inventory	774.5967
Daily production rate(p)	100		Orders per period(year)	3.87
Days per year (D/d)	250		Annual Setup cost	774.6
Daily demand rate	40		Annual Holding cost	774.6
Unit cost	0			
			Unit costs (PD)	0.
			Total Cost	1,549.19

(Inventory models for independent demand, moderate)

94. Lead time for one of Montegut Manufacturing's fastest moving products is 3 days. Demand during this period averages 100 units per day. What would be an appropriate re-order point?

Re-order point = demand during lead time = 100 units/day * 3 days = 300 units.
(Inventory models for independent demand, easy)

95. Your company has compiled the following data on the small set of products that comprise the specialty repair parts division. Perform ABC analysis on the data. Which products do you suggest the firm keep the tightest control over? Explain.

SKU	Annual Demand	Unit Cost
R11	200	$250
S22	75	$100
T33	20	$ 50
U44	200	$150
V55	150	$ 75

R11 and U44 represent over 80% of the firm's volume in this area. R11 is classified A, U44 is classified B, and all others are C. The tightest controls go to R11, then U44 because of their high percentage of sales volume. POM for Windows solution follows.

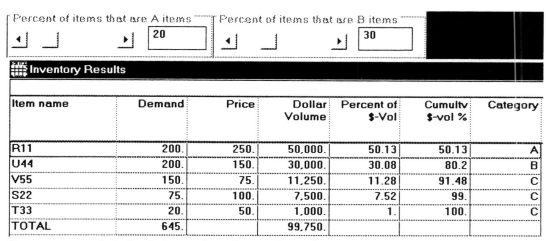

Item name	Demand	Price	Dollar Volume	Percent of $-Vol	Cumultv $-vol %	Category
R11	200.	250.	50,000.	50.13	50.13	A
U44	200.	150.	30,000.	30.08	80.2	B
V55	150.	75.	11,250.	11.28	91.48	C
S22	75.	100.	7,500.	7.52	99.	C
T33	20.	50.	1,000.	1.	100.	C
TOTAL	645.		99,750.			

(Inventory models for independent demand, moderate)

96. The annual demand, ordering cost, and the inventory carrying cost rate for a certain item are D = 600 units, S = $10/order and I = 30% of item price. Price is established by the following quantity discount schedule. What should the order quantity be in order to minimize the total annual cost?

Quantity	1 to 49	50 to 249	250 and up
Price	$5.00 per unit	$4.50 per unit	$4.10 per unit

Order 250 per order, paying $4.10 per unit. Holding costs are much larger than ordering costs, but this is offset by the unit price reduction. The annual total cost is $2,638. The EOQ value for the $4.50 price has an annual cost of $2,827, not much higher than this solution. POM for Windows solution follows.

Inventory Results

PARAMETER	VALUE				PARAMETER	VALUE
Demand rate(D)	600	xxxxxxx	xxxxxxx		Optimal order quantity	250.
Setup/Ordering	10	xxxxxxx	xxxxxxx		Maximum Inventory	250.
Holding		xxxxxxx	xxxxxxx		Average inventory	125.
					Orders per period(year)	2.4
	From	To	Price		Annual Setup cost	24.
	1	49.	5.		Annual Holding cost	153.75
	50	249.	4.5			
	250	999,999.	4.1		Unit costs (PD)	2,460.
	0	0.	0.		Total Cost	2,637.75

Details

Range	Quantity	Total Setup Cost	Total Holding Cost	Total Unit Cost	Total Cost
1 to 49					
50 to 249	94.2809	63.6396	63.6396	2,700.	2,827.279
250 to 999999	250.	24.	153.75	2,460.	2,637.75
0 to 0					

(Inventory models for independent demand, moderate)

97. Thomas' Bike Shop stocks a high volume item that has a normally distributed demand during the reorder period. The average daily demand is 50 units, the lead time is 4 days, and the standard deviation of demand during the reorder period is 10.

   a. How much safety stock provides a 95% service level to Thomas?

   b. What should the reorder point be?

   SS = 1.65 x 10 = 16.5 units or 17 units; ROP = (50* 4) + 17 = 217 units.

   (Probabilistic models with constant lead time, moderate)

98. The new office supply discounter, Paper Clips, Etc. (PCE), sells a certain type of ergonomically correct office chair which costs $300. The annual holding cost rate is 40%, annual demand is 600, and the order cost is $20 per order. The lead time is 4 days. Because demand is variable (standard deviation of daily demand is 2.4 chairs), PCE has decided to establish a customer service level of 90%. The store is open 300 days per year.

a. What is the optimal order quantity?

b. What is the safety stock?

c. What is the reorder point?

ROP= lead time demand + safety stock = (2 chairs/day * 4) + 1.282 * 2.4 x sqrt(4) = 14.15 chairs. POM for Windows solution follows.

Inventory Results

PARAMETER	VALUE	PARAMETER	VALUE
Demand rate(D)	600	Optimal order quantity (Q*)	14.14
Setup/Ordering cost(S)	20	Maximum Inventory Level	14.14
Holding cost(H)@40%	120	Average inventory	7.0711
Unit cost	300	Orders per period(year)	42.43
		Annual Setup cost	848.53
		Annual Holding cost	848.53
		Unit costs (PD)	180,000.
		Total Cost	181,697.1

(Probabilistic models with constant lead time, moderate)

99. Herbert Adams sells bicycles. One particular model is highly popular with annual sales of 2,000 units per year. The cost of one such bicycle is $800.00. Annual holding costs are 25% of the item's cost, and the ordering cost is $40. The store is open 250 days a year.

a. What is the economic order quantity?

b. What is the optimal number of orders?

c. What is the optimal number of days between orders?

d. What are the annual total costs?

The order size should be approximately 9 bicycles. There will be about 22 orders per year. Days between orders will be 250/22 = 11.18 Annual total costs = 894.43 + 894.43 = 1788.86 POM for Windows solution below.

Inventory Results

PARAMETER	VALUE	PARAMETER	VALUE
Demand rate(D)	200	Optimal order quantity (Q*)	8.94
Setup/Ordering cost(S)	40	Maximum Inventory Level	8.94
Holding cost(H)@25%	200	Average inventory	4.4721
Unit cost	800	Orders per period(year)	22.36
		Annual Setup cost	894.43
		Annual Holding cost	894.43

(Inventory models for independent demand, moderate)

100.   The soft goods department of a large department store sells 150 units per month of a certain large bath towel. The unit cost of a towel to the store is $2.50 and the cost of placing an order has been estimated to be $12.00. The store uses an inventory carrying charge of 27% per year. Determine the optimal order quantity, order frequency, and the annual cost of inventory management. If, through automation of the purchasing process, the ordering cost can be cut to $4.00, what will be the new economic order quantity, order frequency, and annual inventory management cost? Explain these results.

At S=$12, EOQ is 253, and there are about 7 orders per year. Annual costs of inventory management are $170.76. At S=$4, EOQ falls to 146, and order frequency rises to 12. Annual inventory management costs fall to $98.60. The lower order cost encourages smaller, more frequent orders. POM for Windows solutions follow.

Inventory Results

"Soft Goods Department" Solution			
PARAMETER	VALUE	PARAMETER	VALUE
Demand rate(D)	1800	Optimal order quantity (Q*)	252.98
Setup/Ordering cost(S)	12	Maximum Inventory Level	252.98
Holding cost(H)@27%	.675	Average inventory	126.4911
Unit cost	2.5	Orders per period(year)	7.12
		Annual Setup cost	85.38
		Annual Holding cost	85.38
		Unit costs (PD)	4,500.
		Total Cost	4,670.76

Inventory Results

"Soft Goods Department" Solution			
PARAMETER	VALUE	PARAMETER	VALUE
Demand rate(D)	1800	Optimal order quantity (Q*)	146.06
Setup/Ordering cost(S)	4	Maximum Inventory Level	146.06
Holding cost(H)@27%	.675	Average inventory	73.0297
Unit cost	2.5	Orders per period(year)	12.32
		Annual Setup cost	49.3
		Annual Holding cost	49.3
		Unit costs (PD)	4,500.
		Total Cost	4,598.59

(Inventory models for independent demand, moderate)

101. Central University uses $96,000 annually of a particular toner cartridge for laser printers in the student computer labs. The purchasing director of the university estimates the ordering cost at $45 and thinks that the university can hold this type of inventory at an annual storage cost of 22% of the purchase price. How many months' supply should the purchasing director order at one time to minimize the total annual cost of purchasing and carrying?

First, calculate the EOQ from the data provided. In this problem, the "units" are dollars, and the "price" of each is 1. One month's usage is 96000/12 = $8,000. EOQ = 6,267. Months usage = 6267/8000 = 0.78, or about three weeks usage. (This is supported by the order frequency of 15 per year). POM for Windows solution follows.

Toner Cartridges Solution

PARAMETER	VALUE	PARAMETER	VALUE
Demand rate(D)	96000	Optimal	6,266.8
Setup/Ordering cost(S)	45	Maximum	6,266.8
Holding cost(H)	.22	Average	3,133.398
Unit cost	1	Orders per	15.32
		Annual Setup	689.35
		Annual	689.35
		Unit costs	96,000.
		Total Cost	97,378.7

(Inventory models for independent demand, moderate)

102. A printing company estimates that it will require 750 reams of a certain type of paper in a given period. The cost of carrying one unit in inventory for that period is 40 cents. The company buys the insulators from a wholesaler in the same town, sending its own truck to pick up the orders at a fixed cost of $16.00 per trip. Treating this cost as the order cost, what is the optimum number of reams to buy at one time? How many times should lots of this size be bought during this period? What is the minimum cost of maintaining inventory on this item for the period? Of this total cost, how much is carrying cost and how much is ordering cost?

This is an EOQ problem, even though the time period is not a year. All that is required is that the demand value and the carrying cost share the same time reference.

$$EOQ = \sqrt{\frac{2 \cdot 750 \cdot 16}{0.40}} = 245$$

This will require slightly more than three orders per period. Other parts of the solution are shown in the POM for Windows solution. Setup costs and carrying costs are each $48.99, and the annual total is $97.90.

Inventory Results

PARAMETER	VALUE	PARAMETER	VALUE
Demand rate(D)	750	Optimal order quantity (Q*)	244.95
Setup/Ordering cost(S)	16	Maximum Inventory Level	244.95
Holding cost(H)	.4	Average inventory	122.4745
Unit cost	0	Orders per period(year)	3.06
		Annual Setup cost	48.99
		Annual Holding cost	48.99
		Unit costs (PD)	0.
		Total Cost	97.98

(Inventory models for independent demand, moderate)

103.   The Rushton Trash Company stocks, among many other products, a certain container, each of which occupies four square feet of warehouse space. The warehouse space currently available for storing this product is limited to 600 square feet. Demand for the product is 12000 units per year. Holding costs are $2 per container per year; Ordering costs are $5 per order.
   a. What is the cost-minimizing order quantity decision for Rushton?
   b. What is the total inventory-related cost of this decision?
   c. What is the total inventory-related cost of managing the inventory of this product, when the limited amount of warehouse space is taken into account?
   d. What would the firm be willing to pay for additional warehouse space?
   The warehouse will hold only 150 containers. The annual cost at Q=150 is 80 x 5 + 75 x 2 = $550. The EOQ is about 245, more than there is room to store. Total cost at Q=245 is $489.90 This cost is $61.1 less than current cost which reflects the limited storage space. Rushton would consider paying up to $61.1 for a year's rental of enough space to store 95 additional containers. (Inventory models for independent demand, difficult)

104.   A firm that makes electronic circuits has been ordering a certain raw material 160 ounces at a time. The firm estimates that carrying cost is 30% per year, and that ordering cost is about $20 per order. The current price of the ingredient is $200 per ounce. The assumptions of the basic EOQ model are thought to apply. For what value of annual demand is their action optimal?
   This problem reverses the unknown of a standard EOQ problem.

$$160 = \sqrt{\frac{2 \cdot D \cdot 20}{.3 \cdot 200}}; \text{ solving for D results in } D = \frac{160^2 \cdot .3 \cdot 200}{2 \cdot 20} = 38400$$

   (Inventory models for independent demand, difficult)

105.   A local firm has traditionally ordered a supply item 60 units at a time. The firm estimates that carrying cost is 40% of the $10 unit cost, and that annual demand is about 240 units per year. The assumptions of the basic EOQ model are thought to apply. For what value of ordering cost would their action be optimal?
   This problem reverses the unknown of a standard EOQ problem.

$$60 = \sqrt{\frac{2 \cdot 240 \cdot S}{.4 \cdot 10}}; \text{ solving for S results in S=\$30.}$$

   That is, if S were $30, then the EOQ would be 60. If the true ordering cost turns out to be much greater than $30, then the firm's order policy is ordering too little at a time. (Inventory models for independent demand, difficult)

106. Given the following data: D=72,000 units per year, S = \$120 per setup, P = \$4 per unit, and I = 25% per year, calculate the EOQ and calculate annual costs following EOQ behavior.

EOQ is 4157 units, for a total cost of \$4,156.92 POM for Windows solution follows.

Inventory Results

PARAMETER	VALUE		PARAMETER	VALUE
Demand rate(D)	72000		Optimal order quantity (Q*)	4,156.92
Setup/Ordering cost(S)	120		Maximum Inventory Level	4,156.92
Holding cost(H)@25%	1		Average inventory	2,078.461
Unit cost	4		Orders per period(year)	17.32
			Annual Setup cost	2,078.46
			Annual Holding cost	2,078.46
			Unit costs (PD)	288,000.
			Total Cost	292,156.9

(Inventory models for independent demand, moderate)

107. A toy manufacturer makes its own wind-up motors, which are then put into its toys. While the toy manufacturing process is continuous, the motors are intermittent flow. Data on the manufacture of the motors appears below.

Annual demand (D) = 50,000 units   Daily subassembly production rate = 1,000
Setup cost (S) = \$65 per batch   Daily subassembly usage rate = 200
Carrying cost = \$.10 per unit per year
a. To minimize cost, how large should each batch of subassemblies be?
b. Approximately how many days are required to produce a batch?
c. How long is a complete cycle?
d. What is the average inventory for this problem?
e. What is the total inventory cost (rounded to nearest dollar) of the optimal behavior in this problem?

Each batch should be 9014 units. It will take slightly over 9014 / 1000 =9 days to make these units. A complete cycle will last approximately 9014 / 200 = 45 days. Average inventory is 3,605 (not one-half of 9014) and the annual costs will total \$721.11.

Inventory Results

PARAMETER	VALUE		PARAMETER	VALUE
Demand rate(D)	50000		Optimal order quantity (Q*)	9,013.88
Setup/Ordering cost(S)	65		Maximum Inventory Level	7,211.1
Holding cost(H)	.1		Average inventory	3,605.551
Daily production rate(p)	1000		Orders per period(year)	5.55
Days per year (D/d)	250		Annual Setup cost	360.56
Daily demand rate	200		Annual Holding cost	360.56
Unit cost	0			
			Unit costs (PD)	0.
			Total Cost	721.11

(Inventory models for independent demand, moderate)

108.   Louisiana Specialty Foods can produce their famous Natchitoches (pronounced nak-a-tish-honest!) meat pies at a rate of 1650 cases of 48 pies each per day. The firm distributes the pies to regional stores and restaurants at a steady rate of 250 cases per day. The cost of setup, cleanup, idle time in transition from other products to pies, etc., is $320. Annual holding costs are $11.50 per case. Assume 250 days per year.

   a. Determine the optimum production run.

   b. Determine the number of production runs per year.

   c. Determine total inventory-related (setup and carrying) costs per year.

   d. Determine maximum inventory.

The optimum production run is 2,122 cases. The number of production runs will be 62500/2122 = 29.45. Total inventory management costs are $18,853.5, and maximum inventory is 1,639 (not 2,122) cases. POM for Windows solution follows.

Inventory Results

Louisiana Specialty Foods Solution				
PARAMETER	VALUE		PARAMETER	VALUE
Demand rate(D)	62500		Optimal order quantity (Q*)	2,121.62
Setup/Ordering cost(S)	320		Maximum Inventory Level	1,639.44
Holding cost(H)	11.5		Average inventory	819.7175
Daily production rate(p)	1100		Orders per period(year)	29.46
Days per year (D/d)	250		Annual Setup cost	9,426.75
Daily demand rate	250		Annual Holding cost	9,426.75
Unit cost	0			
			Unit costs (PD)	0.
			Total Cost	18,853.5

(Inventory models for independent demand, moderate)

109.   Holstein Computing manufactures an inexpensive audio card (Audio Max) for assembly into several models of its microcomputers. The annual demand for this part is 100,000 units. The annual inventory carrying cost is $4 per unit and the cost of preparing an order and making production setup for the order is $220. The company operates 250 days per year. The machine used to manufacture this part has a production rate of 2000 units per day.

   a. Calculate the optimum lot size.

   b. How many lots are produced in a year?

   c. What is the annual cost of preparing the orders and making the setups for Audio Max?

   d. What is the average inventory for Audio Max?

Problem requires the production order quantity model. The optimum lot size is 3708; this lot size will be repeated almost 27 times per year. The total inventory management cost will be $11,865.92, and average inventory will be 1,483 units. POM for Windows solution follows.

Inventory Results

Holstein Computing Solution				
PARAMETER	VALUE		PARAMETER	VALUE
Demand rate(D)	100000		Optimal order quantity (Q*)	3,708.1
Setup/Ordering cost(S)	220		Maximum Inventory Level	2,966.48
Holding cost(H)	4		Average inventory	1,483.24
Daily production rate(p)	2000		Orders per period(year)	26.97
Days per year (D/d)	250		Annual Setup cost	5,932.96
Daily demand rate	400		Annual Holding cost	5,932.96
Unit cost	0			
			Unit costs (PD)	0.
			Total Cost	11,865.92

(Inventory models for independent demand, moderate)

110.   Huckaby Motor Services, Inc., rebuilds small electrical items such as motors, alternators, and transformers, all using a certain type of copper wire. The firm's demand for this wire is approximately normal, averaging 20 spools per week, with a standard deviation of 6 spools per week. Cost per spool is $24; ordering costs are $10 per order; inventory handling cost is $4.00 per spool per year. Acquisition lead time is sixteen weeks. The company works 50, 5-day weeks per year.
   a. What is the optimal size of an order, if minimization of inventory system cost is the objective?
   b. What are the safety stock and reorder point if the risk of stockout is to be 10%?
   Answer:

$$EOQ = \sqrt{\frac{2 \cdot 20 \cdot 50 \cdot 10}{4}} = 70.7 \text{ spools}; SS = 1.29 \cdot 6 \cdot \sqrt{16} = 31 \text{ spools};$$

and ROP = 16 · 6 + 31 = 127 spools.

⊞ Inventory Results			
Huckaby Motor Services Solution			
PARAMETER	VALUE	PARAMETER	VALUE
Demand rate(D)	1000	Optimal order quantity (Q*)	70.71
Setup/Ordering cost(S)	10	Maximum Inventory Level	70.71
Holding cost(H)	4	Average inventory	35.3553
Unit cost	0	Orders per period(year)	14.14
		Annual Setup cost	141.42
		Annual Holding cost	141.42
		Unit costs (PD)	0.
		Total Cost	282.84

(Probabilistic models with constant lead time, moderate)

111.   Demand for ice cream at the Ouachita Dairy can be approximated by a normal distribution with a mean of 21 gallons per day and a standard deviation of 3 gallons per day. The new management desires a service level of 95%. Lead time is four days; the dairy is open seven days a week. What reorder point would be consistent with the desired service level?
   SS = 1.65 · 3 · $\sqrt{4}$ = 9.9 spools; and ROP = 21* 4 + 9.9 = 94 spools.
   (Probabilistic models with constant lead time, moderate)

112.   The Winfield Distributing Company has maintained an 80% service level policy for inventory of string trimmers. Mean demand during the reorder period is 130 trimmers, and the standard deviation is 80 trimmers. The annual cost of carrying one trimmer in inventory is $6. The area sales people have recently told Winfield's management that they could expect a $500 improvement in profit (based on current figures of cost per trimmer) if the service level were increased to 99%. Is it worthwhile for Winfield to make this change?
   This is solved with a cost comparison: total costs status quo compared to total costs at higher service, as amended by the increased profit. First calculate their safety stock. SS = 0.84 · 80 = 67.2 trimmers at $6 each, this safety stock policy costs about $403. At a service level of 99%, the safety stock rises to 2.33 · 80 = 186.4, which will cost $1118.4. The added cost is $715, which is more than the added profit, so Winfield should not increase its service level.
   (Probabilistic models with constant lead time, moderate)

113. Daily demand for a product is normally distributed with a mean of 200 units and a standard deviation of 30 units. The firm currently uses a reorder point system, and seeks a 75% service level during the lead time of 6 days.

a. What safety stock is appropriate for the firm?
b. What is the reorder point?

SS = 0.67 · 30 · $\sqrt{6}$ = 49.23; ROP = 200 · 6 + 49 = 1249

(Probabilistic models with constant lead time, moderate)

114. Daily demand for a product is normally distributed with a mean of 200 units and a standard deviation of 30 units. The firm currently uses a reorder point system. The lead time is 4 days.

a. what safety stock provides a 50% service level?
b. what safety stock provides a 90% service level?
c. what safety stock provides a 99% service level?

Standard deviation during lead time is 30 · $\sqrt{4}$ = 60 units. Z is 0 for 50% service level, 1.29 for 90%, and 2.33 for 99%. The resulting safety stocks are 0, 77.4, and 139.8.

(Probabilistic models with constant lead time, moderate)

115. Clement Bait and Tackle has been buying a chemical water conditioner for its bait (to help keep its baitfish alive) in an optimal fashion using EOQ analysis. The supplier has now offered Clement a discount of $0.50 off all units if the firm will make its purchases quarterly. Current data for the problem are: D=1800 units per year; S = $6.00, I = 15% per year; P = $25.

a. What is the EOQ at the current behavior?
b. What is the annual total cost of continuing their current EOQ-based behavior?
c. What is the annual total cost, if they accept the proposed discount?
d. At the cheaper of the two total costs, are carrying costs equal to ordering costs? Explain.

(a) approx. 76 units; (b) $45284.61; (c) Clement will have to purchase 450 units at a time to get the discount. Their cost would be $44,950.88 (d) They are not; accepting the discount requires an order quantity that is not EOQ. Purchasing 76 units at a time led to setup costs and holding costs of 142.30 each. With the discount, setup costs are $24 while holding costs are 826.88. POM for Windows solution follows.

Inventory Results

		Clement's Tackle Solution	
PARAMETER	VALUE	PARAMETER	VALUE
Demand rate(D)	1800	Optimal order quantity (Q*)	75.89
Setup/Ordering cost(S)	6	Maximum Inventory Level	75.89
Holding cost(H)@15%	3.75	Average inventory	37.9473
Unit cost	25	Orders per period(year)	23.72
		Annual Setup cost	142.3
		Annual Holding cost	142.3
		Unit costs (PD)	45,000.
		Total Cost	45,284.61

Details

			Clement's Tackle Solution		
Range	Quantity	Total Setup Cost	Total Holding Cost	Total Unit Cost	Total Cost
1 to 449	75.8947	142.3025	142.3025	45,000.	45,284.61
450 to 999999	450.	24.	826.875	44,100.	44,950.88
0 to 0					
0 to 0					

(Inventory models for independent demand, moderate)

116. The annual demand for an item is 10,000 units. The cost to process an order is $125 and the annual inventory holding cost is 20% of item cost. What is the optimal order quantity, given the following price breaks for purchasing the item? What price should the firm pay per unit? What is the total annual cost at the optimal behavior?

Quantity	Price
1-9	$2.95 per unit
10 - 999	$2.50 per unit
1,000 - 4,999	$2.30 per unit
5,000 or more	$1.85 per unit

The firm should pay $1.85 per unit by ordering 5000 units at a time. This is above the 2331 EOQ of the next higher price break. Since the firm is not ordering an EOQ amount, ordering costs and carrying costs will not be equal, but total costs are still minimized.

Inventory Results

PARAMETER	VALUE			PARAMETER	VALUE
Demand rate(D)	10000	xxxxxxx	xxxxxxx	Optimal order quantity	5,000.
Setup/Ordering	125	xxxxxxx	xxxxxxx	Maximum Inventory	5,000.
Holding		xxxxxxx	xxxxxxx	Average inventory	2,500.
				Orders per period(year)	2.
	From	To	Price	Annual Setup cost	250.
	1	9.	2.95	Annual Holding cost	925.
	10	999.	2.5		
	1000	4,999.	2.3	Unit costs (PD)	18,500.
	5000	999,999.	1.85	Total Cost	19,675.

Details

Range	Quantity	Total Setup Cost	Total Holding Cost	Total Unit Cost	Total Cost
1 to 9					
10 to 999					
1000 to 4999	2,331.262	536.1903	536.1902	23,000.	24,072.38
5000 to 999999	5,000.	250.	925.	18,500.	19,675.

(Inventory models for independent demand, moderate)

117. The annual demand for an item is 40,000 units. The cost to process an order is $20 and the annual inventory holding cost is $2 per item per year. What is the optimal order quantity, given the following price breaks for purchasing the item?

Quantity	Price
1-1,499	$2.50 per unit
1,500 - 4,999	$2.30 per unit
5,000 or more	$2.25 per unit

a. What is the optimal behavior?
b. Does the firm take advantage of the lowest price available? Explain.

Purchase 1500 units at a time, paying $2.30 each. It is not advantageous to pay $2.25 if that requires ordering 5000 units. The annual cost is $95,160 at the $2.25 price versus $94,033 annual cost at the $2.30 price. POM for Windows solution follows.

Inventory Results

PARAMETER	VALUE				PARAMETER	VALUE
Demand rate(D)	40000	xxxxxxx	xxxxxxx		Optimal order quantity	1,500.
Setup/Ordering	20	xxxxxxx	xxxxxxx		Maximum Inventory	1,500.
Holding cost(H)	2	xxxxxxx	xxxxxxx		Average inventory	750.
					Orders per period(year)	26.67
	From	To	Price		Annual Setup cost	533.33
	1	1,499.	2.5		Annual Holding cost	1,500.
	1500	4,999.	2.3			
	5000	999,999.	2.25		Unit costs (PD)	92,000.
	0	0.	0.		Total Cost	94,033.34

Details

Range	Quantity	Total Setup Cost	Total Holding Cost	Total Unit Cost	Total Cost
1 to 1499	894.4272	894.4272	894.4272	100,000.	101,788.9
1500 to 4999	1,500.	533.3333	1,500.	92,000.	94,033.34
5000 to 999999	5,000.	160.	5,000.	90,000.	95,160.
0 to 0					

(Inventory models for independent demand, moderate)

118.   A local artisan uses supplies purchased from an overseas supplier. The owner believes the assumptions of the EOQ model are met reasonably well. Minimization of inventory costs is her objective. Relevant data, from the files of the craft firm, are annual demand (D) =240 units, ordering cost (S) = $42 per order, and holding cost (H) = $4 per unit per year

    a. How many should she order at one time?

    b. How many times per year will she replenish its inventory of this material?

    c. What will be the total annual inventory costs associated with this material?

    d. If she discovered that the carrying cost had been overstated, and was in reality only $1 per unit per year, what is the corrected value of EOQ?

She should order 71 units at a time, 3.38 times per year. The inventory costs are 142 for holding and 142 for ordering, or 284 total. At the lower value for H, the EOQ will be cut exactly in half to 35.5 units, and order frequency will double to almost 7 orders per year. POM for Windows solution follows.

Inventory Results

PARAMETER	VALUE	PARAMETER	VALUE
Demand rate(D)	240	Optimal order quantity (Q*)	70.99
Setup/Ordering cost(S)	42	Maximum Inventory Level	70.99
Holding cost(H)	4	Average inventory	35.4965
Unit cost	0	Orders per period(year)	3.38
		Annual Setup cost	141.99
		Annual Holding cost	141.99
		Unit costs (PD)	0.
		Total Cost	283.97

(Inventory models for independent demand, moderate)

119.   Groundz Coffee Shop uses 3 pounds of a specialty tea weekly; each pound costs $16. Carrying costs are $2 per pound per week because space is very scarce. It costs the firm $7 to prepare an order. Assume the basic EOQ model with no shortages applies. Assume 52 weeks per year.

    a. How many pounds should Groundz to order at a time?

    b. What is total annual cost (excluding item cost) of managing this item on a cost-minimizing basis?

    c. In pursuing lowest annual total cost, how many orders should Groundz place annually?

    d. How many days will there be between orders (assume 310 operating days) if Main Street practices EOQ behavior?

Groundz should order 4.58 pounds per order, 34 times per year, (or a reasonable integer combination nearby). The firm will spend 476.59 managing this time in inventory. Days between orders will be 310/34 or approximately every 9 working days. POM for Windows solution follows.

Inventory Results

		Groundz Coffee Solution		
PARAMETER	VALUE		PARAMETER	VALUE
Demand rate(D)	156		Optimal order quantity (Q*)	4.58
Setup/Ordering cost(S)	7		Maximum Inventory Level	4.58
Holding cost(H)	104		Average inventory	2.2913
Unit cost	0		Orders per period(year)	34.04
			Annual Setup cost	238.29
			Annual Holding cost	238.29
			Unit costs (PD)	0.
			Total Cost	476.59

(Inventory models for independent demand, moderate)

120.   Pointe au Chien Containers, Inc. manufactures in batches; the manufactured items are placed in stock. Specifically, the firm is questioning how best to manage a specific wooden crate for shipping live seafood, which is sold primarily by the mail/phone order marketing division of the firm. The firm has estimated that carrying cost is $4 per unit per year. Other data for the crate are: annual demand 60000 units; setup cost $240. The firm currently plans to satisfy all customer demand from stock on hand. Demand is known and constant.

   a. What is the cost minimizing size of the manufacturing batch?
   b. What is the total cost of this solution?

The cost-minimizing batch size is 2683 crates. This will cost $10,733 per year in inventory management costs. POM for Windows solution follows.

Inventory Results

PARAMETER	VALUE	PARAMETER	VALUE
		Pointe au Chien Containers Solution	
Demand rate(D)	60000	Optimal order quantity (Q*)	2,683.28
Setup/Ordering cost(S)	240	Maximum Inventory Level	2,683.28
Holding cost(H)	4	Average inventory	1,341.641
Unit cost	0	Orders per period(year)	22.36
		Annual Setup cost	5,366.56
		Annual Holding cost	5,366.56
		Unit costs (PD)	0.
		Total Cost	10,733.13

(Inventory models for independent demand, moderate)

121.   Holding costs are $35 per unit per year, the ordering cost is $120 per order, and sales are relatively constant at 400 per month. What is the optimal order quantity?

Order size is 181; annual inventory expenses are $6,349.80

Inventory Results

PARAMETER	VALUE	PARAMETER	VALUE
Demand rate(D)	4800	Optimal order quantity (Q*)	181.42
Setup/Ordering cost(S)	120	Maximum Inventory Level	181.42
Holding cost(H)	35	Average inventory	90.7115
Unit cost	0	Orders per period(year)	26.46
		Annual Setup cost	3,174.9
		Annual Holding cost	3,174.9
		Unit costs (PD)	0.
		Total Cost	6,349.8

(Inventory models for independent demand, moderate)

122.　　The inventory management costs for a certain product are S=\$8 to order, and H=\$1 to hold for a year. Annual demand is 2400 units. Consider the following ordering plans.

　　a. Order all 2400 at one time
　　b. Order 600 once each quarter
　　c. Order 200 once each month

Calculate the annual costs associated with each plan. Plot these values. Is there another plan, cheaper than any of these? Calculate this, and plot it. Label your graph carefully.

Answer:

$$TC_{2400} = 8 \cdot 1 + 1 \cdot \frac{2400}{2} = 1208; \quad TC_{600} = 8 \cdot 4 + 1 \cdot \frac{600}{2} = 322; \quad TC_{200} = 8 \cdot 12 + 1 \cdot \frac{200}{2} = 196$$

$$EOQ = \sqrt{\frac{2 \cdot 2400 \cdot 8}{1}} = 196 \text{ is the cheapest solution.}$$

The graph cannot easily show the difference between Q = 196 and Q - 200, but the increase in cost for Q=600 and Q=2400 are dramatic.

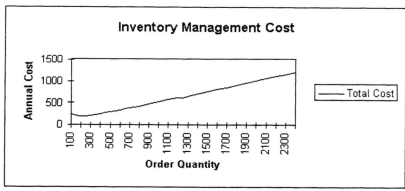

(Inventory models for independent demand, difficult)

CHAPTER 12 SUPPLEMENT: JUST-IN-TIME SYSTEMS

TRUE/FALSE

1. In the Just-in-time framework, waste is anything that does not add value.
    True (Just-in-time philosophy, easy)

2. In the Just-in-time framework, inventory is necessary to the elimination of variability.
    False (Just-in-time philosophy, moderate)

3. Product storage is an example of waste, in the sense that no value is added.
    True (Just-in-time philosophy, moderate)

4. Just-in-time is a philosophy that works well with continuous improvement philosophies.
    True (Just-in-time philosophy, moderate)

5. Just-in-time is push system, rather than a pull system.
    False (Just-in-time philosophy, moderate)

6. "Providing the next work station with exactly what is needed when it is needed" is a valid description of the push system.
    False (Just-in-time philosophy, moderate)

7. Things that do not add value can be seen from the perspective of the production floor or from the perspective of the consumer.
    True (Just-in-time philosophy, moderate)

8. Inventory exposes variability in production processes.
    False (Just-in-time philosophy, moderate)

9. Just-in-time systems attempt to reduce variability.
    True (Just-in-time philosophy, moderate)

10. Frequent deliveries in small lot quantities is characteristic of JIT partnerships.
    True (Suppliers, moderate)

11. In order for JIT to contribute to an organization's competitive advantage, inventory will require low setup times.
    True (Inventory, moderate)

12. JIT's contribution to competitive advantage is to achieve faster response to the customer regardless of cost.
    False (Just-in-time philosophy, moderate)

13. Many suppliers would feel that having a variety of customers is better than being tied to long-term contracts with one customer.
    True (Suppliers, moderate)

14. Organizations who would be JIT suppliers have concerns that the JIT firm's demands for small lot sizes are simply a way of transferring holding cost from manufacturer firm to the supplier firm.
True (Suppliers, moderate)

15. JIT techniques for dealing with inventory are not applicable to service organizations.
False (JIT in services, moderate)

16. Restaurants have such difficult forecasting problems that they are generally unable to use JIT.
False (JIT in services, moderate)

17. Once a good layout has been found, it should remain fixed.
False (JIT layout, moderate)

18. Poka yoke is a quality management tool, not relevant to JIT systems.
False (Quality, moderate)

19. Just-in-time inventory is zero inventory.
False (Inventory, moderate)

20. Hidden problems are generally uncovered during the process of reducing inventory.
True (Inventory, moderate)

21. Reducing lot size is of little help in reducing inventory costs.
False (Inventory, moderate)

22. Poka Kanban is the author of the phrase "Inventory is Evil."
False (Inventory, moderate)

23. Ordering in large quantities spreads the ordering cost over a large number of units.
True (Inventory, moderate)

24. Reducing setup times helps reduce inventory but decreases productivity, since fewer units are produced.
False (Inventory, moderate)

25. The best way to drive down lot sizes is by increasing carrying cost.
False (Inventory, moderate)

26. Lower average inventory is feasible only if setup times are short.
True (Inventory, moderate)

27. If setup times and costs can be reduced low enough, the JIT ideal of "Lot Size = 1" can be achieved.
True (Inventory, moderate)

28. With level material use schedules, a few large batches rather than frequent small batches, are processed.
False (Scheduling, moderate)

29. Because most services cannot be inventoried, there is little place for JIT to help service organizations achieve competitive advantage.
False (JIT in services, moderate)

MULTIPLE CHOICE

30. Which of the following is generally found in most JIT environments?
    a. push systems
    b. pull systems
    c. a push or pull system, depending upon the rate of demand
    d. a push system for high margin items and a pull system for low margin items
    e. a push system for purchased parts and a pull system for manufactured parts
    b (Just-in-time philosophy, moderate)

31. Which one of the following is **not** a benefit of the implementation of JIT?
    a. cost reduction
    b. work in process reduction
    c. quality improvement
    d. delay reduction
    e. variability increase
    e (Just-in-time philosophy, moderate)

32. The implementation of JIT offers several advantages, including
    a. reduced throughput
    b. decreased profit margins
    c. increase in variability to better respond to variable demand
    d. rework reduction
    e. work-in-process increases
    d (Just-in-time philosophy, moderate)

33. Which of the following illustrates an activity that does **not** add value?
    a. training employees
    b. ordering parts from a supplier
    c. a costly and lengthy operation
    d. accumulating parts in front of the next work center
    e. delivering the product to the customer
    d (Just-in-time philosophy, moderate)

34. In pull systems,
    a. the standardized container must hold exactly one part
    b. the standardized container should hold one days worth of inventory
    c. the supplier work center should set the pace for production
    d. the user work center should feel in control
    e. the usage rate should always slightly exceed the production rate
    c (Just-in-time philosophy, moderate)

35. Which of the following is **not** a reason for variability?
    a. employees, machines, and suppliers produce units late
    b. customer demand is unknownh
    c. engineering drawings are inaccurate
    d. production personnel tries to produce before drawings or specifications are complete
    e. employees, machines, and suppliers produce units that conform to standards
    e (Just-in-time philosophy, moderate)

36. Which of the following statements regarding a pull system is **true**?
    a. large lots are pulled from upstream stations.
    b. work is pulled to the downstream work stations before it is actually needed.
    c. manufacturing cycle time is increased.
    d. problems become more obvious.
    e. none of the above is true of a pull system
    d (Just-in-time philosophy, moderate)

37. In pull systems,
    a. the "supplier" work center sends parts to the "customer" work center as soon as a lot is completed
    b. the "supplier" work center is totally in charge
    c. the customer "work center" decides when inventory moves
    d. labor utilization is maximized
    e. inventory is pulled from the warehouse at a fast rate
    c (Just-in-time philosophy, moderate)

38. Manufacturing cycle time is best defined as the
    a. time it takes a unit to move from one workstation to the next
    b. time between the start of one unit and the start of the next unit
    c. sum of all the task times to make one unit of a product
    d. time from raw materials receipt to finished product exit
    e. length of the work shift, expressed in minutes per day
    d (Just-in-time philosophy, moderate)

39. Which one of the following does **not** exemplify JIT used for competitive advantage?
    a. Acme Foods decides to decrease the number of its suppliers to just a few.
    b. Cheramie Trucking trains workers to specialize and become very efficient in one job.
    c. Ajax, Inc. is proud to announce that incoming goods are delivered directly to the point of use.
    d. Ardoyne Builders has a scheduled preventive maintenance program.
    e. Cajun Contractors has reduced the amount of space for inventory.
    b (Just-in-time philosophy, moderate)

40. Which one of the following is **not** a requirement of JIT systems?
    a. quality deliveries on time
    b. strong job specialization
    c. low setup time
    d. training support
    e. employee empowerment
    b (Just-in-time philosophy, moderate)

41. In the quest for competitive advantage, which of the following is a JIT requirement?
    a. reduced number of vendors
    b. reduced space for inventory
    c. quality by suppliers
    d. small number of job classifications
    e. all of the above are JIT requirements
    e (Just-in-time philosophy, moderate)

42. Which one of the following is an example of JIT being used for competitive advantage?
    a. Jones Company has decreased the number of job classifications to just a few.
    b. Lafourche Metals increases the number of its suppliers to be less dependent on just a few.
    c. Houma Fabricators is proud to announce that incoming goods are inspected.
    d. Acme Company tells its maintenance department to intervene only if a machine breaks down.
    e. Caro Specialty Metals, Inc., has built a new, huge warehouse to store inventory.
    a (Just-in-time philosophy, moderate)

43. Great Lakes Barge and Baggage Company manufactures, among other things, battery-operated bilge pumps. Which of the following activities is **not** part of JIT? They
    a. communicate their schedules to suppliers
    b. use a pull system to move inventory
    c. produce in long production runs to reduce the impact of setup costs
    d. continuously work on reducing setup time
    e. produce in small lots
    c (Just-in-time philosophy, moderate)

44. A manufacturer took the following actions to reduce inventory. Which of these is generally **not** accepted as a JIT action? They
    a. used a pull system to move inventory
    b. produced in ever smaller lots
    c. required deliveries directly to the point of use
    d. picked the supplier that offered the lowest price based on quantity discounts
    e. worked to reduce their in-transit inventory
    d (Just-in-time philosophy, moderate)

45. Which one of the following is a characteristic of a JIT partnership?
    a. large number of suppliers
    b. steady output rate
    c. maximal product specifications imposed on supplier
    d. active pursuit of vertical integration
    e. frequent deliveries in large lot quantities
    b (Suppliers, moderate)

46. Characteristics of JIT partnerships with respect to suppliers include
    a. competitive bidding encouraged
    b. buyer plant pursues vertical integration to reduce the number of suppliers
    c. analysis to enable desirable suppliers to become/stay price competitive
    d. most suppliers at considerable distance from purchasing organization
    e. large number of suppliers to decrease dependence on just a few
    c (Suppliers, moderate)

47. Characteristics of Just-in-time suppliers do **not** include
    a. scheduling of inbound freight
    b. long-term contract agreements
    c. few suppliers
    d. an increase in release paperwork to obtain more detailed records
    e. the buyer actually helping the supplier to meet the quality requirements
    d (Suppliers, moderate)

48. Characteristics of JIT partnerships with respect to quantities include
    a. short-term contracts to ensure flexibility
    b. variable output rate
    c. suppliers package in variable quantities to meet exactly the customers' production requirements
    d. suppliers determine the quantities to be delivered based on their own production schedules
    e. suppliers increase production lot sizes in order to achieve economies of scale
    c (Suppliers, moderate)

49. A characteristic of JIT partnerships with respect to shipping is to
    a. use only full trucks to minimize freight costs
    b. use only air freight to speed up deliveries
    c. use public transportation to minimize costs
    d. use company-owned or contract shipping to gain control
    e. impose maximum product specifications on supplier
    d (Suppliers, moderate)

50. A characteristic of JIT partnerships with respect to quality is to
    a. help suppliers to meet quality requirement
    b. have 100% incoming inspection
    c. impose maximum product specifications on the supplier
    d. draw up strict contracts ensuring that all defectives will be immediately replaced
    e. maintain a steady output rate
    a (Suppliers, moderate)

51. Which of the following is **not** a goal of JIT partnerships?
    a. elimination of unnecessary activities
    b. elimination of in-plant inventory
    c. elimination of in-transit inventory
    d. elimination of poor suppliers
    e. all of the above are goals of JIT partnerships
    e (Suppliers, moderate)

52. Which of the following is **not** a goal of JIT partnerships?
    a. elimination of unnecessary activities
    b. elimination of in-plant inventory
    c. elimination of in-transit inventory
    d. elimination of engineering changes
    e. All of the above are goals of JIT partnerships
    d (Suppliers, moderate)

53. Which one of the following is a concern expressed by suppliers?
   a. elimination of in-plant inventory
   b. delivery to the point of use
   c. production with zero defects
   d. large lot sizes
   e. customers' infrequent engineering changes
   c (Suppliers, moderate)

54. Which one of the following is **not** a concern expressed by suppliers?
   a. desire for diversification
   b. poor customer scheduling
   c. customers' infrequent engineering changes
   d. small lot sizes
   e. proximity
   c (Suppliers, moderate)

55. Reduction of in-transit inventory can be encouraged through use of
   a. low setup costs
   b. low carrying costs
   c. use of trains, not trucks
   d. supplier location near plants
   e. low-cost, global suppliers
   d (Suppliers, moderate)

56. Just-in-Time systems make demands on layouts, including
   a. distance reduction
   b. increased flexibility
   c. reduced space and inventory
   d. cross-trained, flexible employees
   e. all of the above are JIT influences on layout
   e (JIT layout, moderate)

57. Which one of the following is **not** a layout tactic in a JIT environment?
   a. work cells for families of products
   b. distance minimized
   c. little space for inventory
   d. fixed equipment
   e. poka-yoke devices
   d (JIT layout, moderate)

58. Which of the following is **not** a JIT influence on layout design?
   a. distance reduction
   b. increased flexibility
   c. reduced space and inventory
   d. supplier location near the JIT firm
   e. all of the above are JIT influences on layout
   d (JIT layout, moderate)

59. Which of the following is **not** a benefit of small production lots?
    a. work-in-process inventory is smaller
    b. workstations can be placed closer together
    c. manufacturing cycle time is smaller
    d. fewer setups
    e. better product distribution (i.e. mix) available for customer demand
    d (Inventory, difficult)

60. Which of the following is the author of the phrase "Inventory is Evil"?
    a. Poka Yoke
    b. Shigeo Shingo
    c. Pat "Keiretsu" Morita
    d. Kanban Polka
    e. none of the above
    b (JIT layout, moderate)

61. Which of the following was a mistake, as Colorado Outfitters tried to reduce its setup time?
    a. They separated setup into preparation and actual setup, doing as much as possible while the machine/process was operating.
    b. They significantly reduced setup time and, satisfied with the results, they directed their efforts at other projects.
    c. They moved materials closer and improved material handling.
    d. They standardized and improved tooling.
    e. All of the above were proper actions.
    b (JIT layout, moderate)

62. Level schedules
    a. processes many small batches rather than one large one
    b. is known as "jelly bean" scheduling
    c. is based on meeting one day's demand with that day's production
    d. requires that schedules be met without variation
    e. all of the above are true regarding level scheduling
    e (Scheduling, moderate)

63. Kanban is associated with all of the following **except**
    a. meeting tight schedules
    b. reducing setup time
    c. increasing material handling
    d. reducing batch size
    e. signaling when it is time for the next batch
    c (Scheduling, moderate)

64. Which one of the following statements is **true** regarding JIT inventory?
    a. It exists just in case something goes wrong.
    b. It hides variability.
    c. It is minimized with large lot production.
    d. It is the minimum inventory necessary to keep a perfect system running.
    e. It increases if setup costs decrease.
    d (Inventory, moderate)

65. Which one of the following statements is **true** about the Kanban system?
    a. The quantities in the containers are usually large to reduce setup costs.
    b. It is associated with a push system.
    c. It is useful to smooth operations when numerous quality problems occur.
    d. The supplier work station signals to the customer work station as soon as a batch has been completed.
    e. The customer work station signals to the supplier work station when production is needed.
    e (Scheduling, moderate)

66. Which one of the following scenarios represents the use of a kanban to reduce inventories?
    a. A "supplier" work center signals to the downstream workstation that a batch has been completed.
    b. A supervisor signals to several work centers that the production rate should be changed.
    c. A "customer" work center signals to the "supplier" workstation that more parts are needed.
    d. An operator asks the next station's operator to help him fix his machine.
    e. A supervisor tells the operators to stay busy and start producing parts for next month.
    c (Scheduling, moderate)

67. The word "kanban" means
    a. low inventory
    b. employee empowerment
    c. continuous improvement
    d. lot size of one
    e. card
    e (Scheduling, moderate)

68. Which of the following is an illustration of employee empowerment?
    a. "no one knows the job better than those who do it"
    b. UPS drivers are trained to perform several motions smoothly and efficiently
    c. unionization of the workplace brings better morale and therefore better quality
    d. all of the above
    e. none of the above
    a (Employee empowerment, moderate)

69. Which of the following JIT principles is(are) **not** ordinarily applicable in restaurants?
    a. Close relationship with food suppliers.
    b. A kitchen set up to minimize wasteful movements.
    c. Food preparation in large batches
    d. Lean inventories of food
    e. All of the above are applicable to restaurants
    c (Scheduling, moderate)

70. The number of kanbans is
    a. one
    b. the same as EOQ
    c. one full day's production
    d. the ratio of the reorder point to container size
    e. none of the above
    d (Scheduling, moderate)

FILL-IN-THE-BLANK

71. _____ is a philosophy of continuous and forced problem solving that drives out waste.
    Just-in-time or JIT (Just-in-time philosophy, easy)

72. _____ is any deviation from the optimum process that delivers perfect product on time, every time.
    Variability (Just-in-time philosophy, moderate)

73. A _____ is a JIT concept that results in material being produced only when requested and moved to where it is needed just as it is needed.
    pull system (Just-in-time philosophy, moderate)

74. The _____ is the time between the arrival of raw materials and the shipping of finished products.
    manufacturing cycle time (Just-in-time philosophy, moderate)

75. A _____ is a system that pushes materials into downstream workstations regardless of their timeliness or availability of resources to perform the work.
    push system (Just-in-time philosophy, moderate)

76. _____ is an arrangement in which the supplier maintains title to the inventory until it is used.
    Consignment inventory (Just-in-time philosophy, moderate)

77. _____ is the minimum inventory necessary to keep a perfect system running.
    Just-in-time inventory (Inventory, moderate)

78. _____ involves scheduling products so that each day's production meets the demand for that day.
    Level scheduling (Scheduling, moderate)

79. _____ is the Japanese work for card that has come to mean "signal."
    Kanban (Scheduling, moderate)

SHORT ANSWERS

80. List five examples of operations situations that do not create value.
    Storage, inspection, delay, wait in queue, defective products. (Just-in-time philosophy, easy)

81. Define variability within the context of JIT.
    Variability is any deviation from the optimum process that delivers perfect products on time every time. (Just-in-time philosophy, moderate)

82. List four causes of variability in the workplace.
    1. employees, machine suppliers produce units that do not conform to standards, are late, or are not the proper quantity
    2. engineering drawings or specifications that are inaccurate
    3. production personnel trying to produce before drawings or specifications are complete
    4. unknown customer demands.
    (Just-in-time philosophy, moderate)

83. EOQ models used several parameters in a formula to calculate a cost-minimizing order quantity. From that basis, explain how JIT and EOQ are related.
    Just-In-Time calls for small lot sizes and low setup times. Low setup times should produce low setup costs. In the EOQ formula, as setup cost falls, order size falls also. (Inventory, moderate)

84. List the broad categories through which JIT contributes to competitive advantage.
    Suppliers, layout, inventory, scheduling, preventive maintenance, quality production, employee empowerment, commitment of management, employees, and suppliers. (Just-in-time philosophy, moderate)

85. Differentiate between a push and a pull system.
    A push system pushes material into downstream workstations regardless of the resources available. A pull system uses signals to request delivery from upstream stations to the station that has production facilities available. In a pull system, materials or parts are pulled where they are needed when they are needed. (Just-in-time philosophy, moderate)

86. Which of the JIT techniques are unlikely to work in a services environment? (list them) Which JIT techniques are likely to be of value in either manufacturing or in services?
    Not in services: Maintenance, Quality production. In either environment: suppliers, layout, inventory, and scheduling. (JIT in services, moderate)

87. List the goals of JIT partnerships. Which do you think would be the hardest to accomplish? Explain, with examples.
    Elimination of unnecessary activities, elimination of in-plant inventory, elimination of in-transit inventory, and elimination of poor suppliers. (Just-in-time philosophy, moderate)

88. JIT attempts to remove delays, which do not add value. How then does JIT cope with weather, and its impact on crop harvest and transportation times?
    Suggestion: JIT allows for safety stock and in-transit inventory (but no more than necessary). Where external, unpredictable issues such as weather arise, more safety stock is necessary. Consignment inventory is also useful. Beyond that, JIT is at risk for events such as weather and work stoppages. (Just-in-time philosophy, difficult)

89. JIT uses the word "moment" with reference to added value. Explain.
    Moment refers to time material is held. (Suppliers, moderate)

90. List the benefits of JIT.
Queue and delay reduction, quality improvement, cost reduction, variability reduction, rework reduction. (Just-in-time philosophy, moderate)

91. What is the ultimate benefit of JIT to the customer?
Faster response to the customer at lower cost and higher quality. (Just-in-time philosophy, moderate)

92. Define manufacturing cycle time within the context of JIT systems.
Manufacturing cycle time is the time between receipt of raw materials and shipment of the finished product. (Just-in-time philosophy, moderate)

93. State six reasons given by suppliers for their reluctance to enter into JIT systems. Elaborate on one of these, of your choosing.
The six reasons are desire for diversification, poor customer scheduling, engineering changes, quality assurance, small lot sizes, and proximity. (Suppliers, moderate)

94. List the layout tactics appropriate for a JIT environment.
Work cells for families of products, distance minimized, little space for inventory, facilitation of employee communication, poka-yoke devices, flexible/movable equipment, and cross-trained workers and flexibility. (JIT layouts, moderate)

95. How was the analogy of lake, water, and rocks applied to JIT? Which of these terms is analogous to "inventory"?
Lowering the water (inventory) exposed rocks (inefficiencies, problems). (Inventory, moderate)

96. List the inventory tactics appropriate for a JIT environment.
A pull system to move inventory, ever smaller lots, just-in-time deliveries from suppliers, deliveries directly to point of use, performance to schedule, setup reduction, and group technology. (Inventory, moderate)

97. What are the potential benefits of effective scheduling?
Support JIT, improve the ability to meet customer orders, drive inventory down by allowing smaller production lot sizes, and reduce work-in-process. (Scheduling, moderate)

98. Describe level schedules? What purpose do they serve?
Level schedules act on frequent small batches rather than a few large batches; the small batches are always changing. Matching one day's demand to one day's work. (Scheduling, moderate)

99. List the JIT scheduling tactics.
Communicate the schedule to suppliers; level schedules; freeze part of the schedules; performance to schedule; seek one piece make and one piece move; elimination of waste; small lots; kanban; and make each operation produce a perfect part. (Scheduling, moderate)

100. Discuss how the Japanese word for "card" has application in the study of JIT.
The word is kanban, and is closely associated with JIT. It relies on visual or other simple signals to indicate when items need to be "pulled." It is symbolic of the waste reduction, distance reduction, and small lot size that characterize JIT. (Scheduling, moderate)

101. Standardized, reusable containers have fairly obvious benefits when shipping. (State them briefly) What is the purpose of these devices **within** the plant?
In shipping: protect the specific quantities to be moved; reduce weight and disposal costs; generate less wasted space in trailers; and require less labor to pack, unpack, and prepare items. Inside the plant: to convey the quantity of the kanban, and to protect the items. (Scheduling, moderate)

102. State the three ways in which JIT and quality are related.
JIT cuts the cost of obtaining good quality; JIT improves quality; and better quality means fewer buffers and therefore a better, easier-to-use JIT system. (Quality, moderate)

103. State the JIT quality tactics.
Statistical process control; empowered employees; poka yoke or fail-safe methods; and immediate feedback. (Quality, moderate)

104. What are the characteristics of Just-In-Time partnerships with respect to suppliers?
Few suppliers; nearby suppliers; repeat business with the same suppliers; analysis to enable desirable suppliers to become/stay price competitive; competitive bidding mostly limited to new purchases; buyer resists vertical integration and subsequent wipeout of supplier business; and suppliers are encouraged to extend JIT buying to their suppliers. (Just-in-time philosophy, moderate)

105. What are the characteristics of Just-in-time partnerships with respect to quantities?
Steady output rate; frequent deliveries in small lot quantities; long-term contract agreements; minimal release paperwork; delivery quantities fixed for whole contract term; little or no permissible overage or underage; package in exact quantities; and reduce production lot sizes. (Just-in-time philosophy, moderate)

106. State the characteristics of Just-in-Time partnership with respect to shipping.
Scheduling of inbound freight; gaining control by use of company-owned or contract shipping and warehouses. (Just-in-time philosophy, moderate)

107. Explain how JIT works in services. After all, how does "small lot size" and "reduce setup cost" make sense in services? Supply examples to support your work.
In services, JIT works more on scheduling than on inventory, but is otherwise quite applicable. Furthermore, many services, such as restaurants, have significant inventories to deal with. (JIT in services, moderate)

PROBLEMS

108. Weekly usage of a product is 8 units. Since the plant operates 50 weeks per year, this leads to annual usage of 400 units. Setup cost is $40 and annualized carrying cost is $80. Lead time is four weeks, and safety stock is one week's production. Instantaneous receipt applies. What is optimal kanban size? What is the optimal number of kanbans?
    20; 2 (Scheduling, moderate)

109. Daily usage of a product is 10; daily production rate for this product is 20 when production is occurring. Setup cost is $30 and annualized carrying cost is $120. Lead time is 16 days; safety stock is 4 days usage. Assume 250 working days per year. What is the optimum kanban size, and number of kanbans?
    50; 4 (Scheduling, moderate)

110. Daily usage of a product is 10 in a facility that operates every day of the year. Setup cost is $73 and annualized carrying cost is $100. Instantaneous receipt applies. Lead time is 14 days; safety stock is 1 days usage. What is the optimum kanban size, and number of kanbans?
    73; approximately 2 (Scheduling, moderate)

111. Daily usage of an assembly is 100 in a facility that operates 300 days of the year. Setup cost is $5 and annualized carrying cost is $160. Production of this assembly occurs at the rate of 400 per day when production of the assembly is underway. Lead time is 3 days; safety stock is 1/2 days usage. What is the optimum kanban size, and number of kanbans?
    50; 7 (Scheduling, moderate)

CHAPTER 13: AGGREGATE PLANNING

TRUE/FALSE

1. Minimizing cost may not be the most important strategic issue in aggregate planning.
    True (Introduction, easy)

2. The only objective of aggregate planning is to minimize the cost of matching capacity to demand over the planning period.
    False (Introduction, easy)

3. Aggregate planning in manufacturing ties organizational strategic goals to a production plan; in services, the tie is to a work force schedule.
    True (Introduction, moderate)

4. Plans for new products and investment do not generally fall within the scope of aggregate planning.
    True (The planning process, moderate)

5. The aggregate planning process usually includes expediting and dispatching of individual products.
    False (The planning process, moderate)

6. Aggregate production planning occurs over the medium or intermediate range of 3 to 18 months.
    True (Introduction, easy)

7. Aggregate planning occurs before the long-term capacity decision is made.
    False (The planning process, moderate)

8. In the context of aggregate planning, "aggregate" means combining resources in general, or overall, terms.
    True (The nature of aggregate planning, easy)

9. Aggregate planning is an activity carried out by operations personnel, with little interaction with other departments in the organization.
    False (The nature of aggregate planning, moderate)

10. The strategies of aggregate planning are broadly divided into demand options and capacity options.
    True (Aggregate planning strategies, easy)

11. The strategy of varying workforce size by hiring is a demand option.
    False (Aggregate planning strategies, moderate)

12. In aggregate planning, one of the adjustable elements of capacity is the size of the work force.
    True (Aggregate planning strategies, moderate)

13. In aggregate planning, one of the adjustable elements of capacity is the amount of overtime.
    True (Aggregate planning strategies, moderate)

14. In aggregate planning, one of the adjustable elements of capacity is the extent of subcontracting.
    True (Aggregate planning strategies, moderate)

15. Advertising and promotion are some of the ways of manipulating product or service supply in aggregate planning.
False (Aggregate planning strategies, moderate)

16. In aggregate planning, the strategy of back ordering for many consumer goods leads to lost sales.
True (Aggregate planning strategies, moderate)

17. One motive for using demand-influencing aggregate planning options is to create uses for excess capacity within an organization.
True (Aggregate planning strategies, moderate)

18. The level scheduling strategy seeks to keep inventory level or constant throughout the planning period.
False (Aggregate planning strategies, moderate)

19. Because service firms do not inventory their output, pure chase strategy is not appropriate.
False (Aggregate planning strategies, moderate)

20. The pure chase strategy allows lower inventories than pure level and mixed strategies.
True (Aggregate planning strategies, moderate)

21. The pure chase strategy maintains constant production rates or work force levels, while inventory levels are adjusted to match demand over the planning horizon.
False (Aggregate planning strategies, moderate)

22. Mixed strategies in aggregate planning utilize both inventory changes and work force and production rate changes over the planning horizon.
True (aggregate planning strategies, moderate)

23. Graphical and charting techniques for aggregate planning are easy to understand and use.
True (Methods for aggregate planning, easy)

24. Charting and graphing techniques are trial-and-error devices not well-suited for generating optimal strategies.
True (Methods for aggregate planning, moderate)

25. The transportation method of linear programming is a trial-and-error approach to constructing an aggregate plan.
False (Methods for aggregate planning, easy)

26. The management coefficients model assumes that the manager's past performance was pretty good, then uses historical data and regression analysis to prepare the aggregate plan.
True (Methods for aggregate planning, moderate)

27. For some service firms, aggregate planning is simpler than in manufacturing.
True (Aggregate planning in services, moderate)

28. Service firms, because of the intangible nature of their product, all use the same strategy for aggregate planning.
False (Aggregate planning in services, moderate)

MULTIPLE CHOICE

29. Aggregate planning is capacity planning for
    a. the long range
    b. the intermediate range
    c. the short range
    d. typically one to three months
    e. typically one or more years
    b (Introduction, easy)

30. Which of the following is the term used for medium range capacity planning with a time horizon of three to eighteen months?
    a. material requirements planning
    b. short range planning
    c. aggregate planning
    d. strategic planning
    e. none of the above
    c (Introduction, easy)

31. Planning tasks associated with job scheduling, machine loading, and dispatching typically fall under
    a. long-range plans
    b. intermediate-range plans
    c. short-range plans
    d. mission-related planning
    e. strategic planning
    c (The planning process, moderate)

32. The typical time horizon for aggregate planning is
    a. less than a month
    b. up to 3 months
    c. 3 to 18 months
    d. over one year
    e. over 5 years
    c (Introduction, easy)

33. The planning tasks associated with staffing, production, inventory, and sub-contracting levels typically fall under
    a. long-range plans
    b. intermediate-range plans
    c. short-range plans
    d. demand options
    e. strategic planning
    b (The planning process, easy)

34. Dependence on an external source of supply is found in which of the following aggregate planning strategies?
   a. varying production rates through overtime or idle time
   b. using part-time workers
   c. backordering during high demand periods
   d. subcontracting
   e. hiring and laying off
   d (Aggregate planning strategies, moderate)

35. Which of the following aggregate planning strategies might direct your client to a competitor?
   a. using part-time workers
   b. subcontracting
   c. changing inventory level
   d. varying production rates through overtime or idle time
   e. varying workforce size by hiring or layoffs
   b (Aggregate planning strategies, moderate)

36. An option for altering the availability of capacity is
   a. pricing
   b. promotion
   c. backorders
   d. inventory levels
   e. none of the above
   d (Aggregate planning strategies, moderate)

37. Which of these aggregate planning strategies adjusts capacity to match demand?
   a. backordering
   b. counter-seasonal product mixing
   c. changing price
   d. using part-time workers
   e. none of the above is a capacity option
   d (Aggregate planning strategies, moderate)

38. Which of the following aggregate planning strategies may lower employee morale?
   a. varying production rates through overtime or idle time
   b. using part-time workers
   c. back-ordering during high demand periods
   d. sub-contracting
   e. varying workforce size by hiring or layoffs
   e (Aggregate planning strategies, moderate)

39. Which of the following aggregate planning strategies is a "capacity option"?
   a. influencing demand by changing price
   b. influencing demand by extending lead times
   c. changing inventory levels
   d. influencing demand by back ordering
   e. counter-seasonal product mixing
   c (Aggregate planning strategies, moderate)

40. Which of the following attempts to manipulate product or service demand?
    a. inventories
    b. part-time workers
    c. subcontracting
    d. price cuts
    e. overtime/idle time
    d (Aggregate planning strategies, moderate)

41. Which of the following aggregate planning strategies is a "demand option"?
    a. sub-contracting
    b. varying production levels
    c. changing inventory levels
    d. changing price
    e. using part-time workers
    d (Aggregate planning strategies, moderate)

42. In aggregate planning, which one of the following is **not** a basic option for altering demand?
    a. promotion
    b. backordering
    c. pricing
    d. subcontracting
    e. all are demand options
    d (Aggregate planning strategies, moderate)

43. Which of the following is **not** associated with manipulation of product or service demand?
    a. price cuts or discounts
    b. promotion
    c. counter-seasonal products or services
    d. advertising
    e. subcontracting
    e (Aggregate planning strategies, moderate)

44. Which of the following statements about aggregate planning is **true**?
    a. Advertising/promotion is a way of manipulating product or service supply.
    b. Work station loading and job assignments are examples of aggregate production planning.
    c. Overtime/idle time is a way of manipulating product or service demand.
    d. Aggregate planning uses the adjustable part of capacity to meet production requirements.
    e. All of the above are true.
    d (The planning process, moderate)

45. Which of the following statements about aggregate planning is **true**?
    a. In aggregate planning, backorders are a means of manipulating demand while part-time workers are a way of manipulating product or service supply.
    b. A pure chase strategy allows lower inventories when compared to pure level and hybrid strategies.
    c. In spite of the research into mathematical models, aggregate production planners continue to use trial and error methods when developing their plans.
    d. All of the above are true.
    e. None of the above are true.
    d (Aggregate planning strategies, moderate)

46. Which of the following statements regarding aggregate planning is **true**?
    a. In a pure level strategy, production rates or work force levels are adjusted to match demand requirements over the planning horizon.
    b. In a mixed strategy, there are changes in both inventory and in work force and production rate over the planning horizon.
    c. A pure level strategy allows lower inventories when compared to pure chase and hybrid strategies.
    d. Because service firms have no inventory, the pure chase strategy does not apply.
    e. All of the above are true.
    b (Aggregate planning strategies, moderate)

47. Which of the following is **not** consistent with a pure level strategy?
    a. variable work force levels
    b. little or no use of inventory to meet demand requirements
    c. varying production levels and/or work force to meet demand requirements
    d. varying the use of subcontracting
    e. all of the above are inconsistent with the pure level strategy
    e (Aggregate planning strategies, moderate)

48. In level scheduling, what is kept uniform from month to month?
    a. product mix
    b. inventory levels
    c. demand levels
    d. production/workforce levels
    e. sub-contracting levels
    d (Aggregate planning strategies, moderate)

49. Which of the following is not an advantage of level scheduling?
    a. stable employment
    b. lower absenteeism
    c. lower turnover
    d. matching production exactly with sales
    e. more employee commitment
    d (Aggregate planning strategies, moderate)

50. Which of the following actions is consistent with use of pure level strategy?
   a. vary the amount of subcontracting to meet demand requirements
   b. vary production levels to meet demand requirements
   c. vary production levels work force to meet demand requirements
   d. use of inventory to meet demand requirements
   e. none of the above
   d (Aggregate planning strategies, moderate)

51. Which of the following is consistent with a pure chase strategy?
   a. vary production levels to meet demand requirements
   b. vary work force to meet demand requirements
   c. vary production levels and work force to meet demand requirements
   d. little or no use of inventory to meet demand requirements
   e. all of the above.
   e (Aggregate planning strategies, moderate)

52. Graphical and charting methods of aggregate planning have the disadvantage that
   a. they are difficult to use
   b. they require a large number of computations
   c. they require expensive, sophisticated software
   d. they often yield poor results
   e. only a few variables can be considered in the plan
   e (Methods for aggregate planning, moderate)

53. "An optimal plan for minimizing the cost of allocating capacity to meet demand over several planning periods" best describes
   a. the linear decision rule
   b. the transportation method
   c. simulation
   d. the management coefficients model
   e. graphical or charting methods
   b (Methods for aggregate planning, moderate)

54. Which of the following aggregate planning methods does not work if hiring and layoffs are possible?
   a. linear decision rule
   b. management coefficients model
   c. transportation method
   d. simulation
   e. charting method
   c (Methods for aggregate planning, moderate)

55. Which of the following aggregate planning models is based primarily upon a manager's past experience?
    a. search decision rule
    b. simulation
    c. linear decision rule
    d. management coefficients model
    e. linear programming
    d (Methods for aggregate planning, moderate)

56. Which of the following uses regression to incorporate historical managerial performance into aggregate planning?
    a. parametric production planning
    b. simulation
    c. linear decision rule
    d. management coefficients model
    e. keiretsu
    d (Methods for aggregate planning, moderate)

57. An aggregate planning method that mimics the scheduling situation and uses a search procedure to look for the minimum-cost values for workforce and production rate is
    a. the search decision rule
    b. linear programming
    c. linear decision rule
    d. transportation model
    e. simulation
    e (Methods for aggregate planning, moderate)

58. Yield management is most likely to be used in which one of the following industries?
    a. higher education
    b. healthcare
    c. airlines
    d. trucking
    e. construction
    c (Aggregate planning in services, moderate)

59. Which of the following is **not** an ingredient for controlling labor cost in services?
    a. close control of labor hours to assure quick customer response
    b. some form of on-call labor resource that can be added or deleted to meet unexpected demand
    c. contract overseas labor for lower wage scale
    d. flexibility of individual worker skills that permits reallocation of available labor time
    e. individual worker flexibility in rate of output or hours of work to meet expanded demand
    c (Aggregate planning in services, moderate)

60. Aggregate planning for service firms with high-volume tangible output is directed toward
    a. yield management
    b. centralized purchasing
    c. decreasing the demand rate during peak periods
    d. planning for human resource requirements and managing demand
    e. smoothing the production rate
    e (Aggregate planning in services, moderate)

61. "Yield management" is best described as
    a. a situation where management yields to labor demands
    b. capacity allocation to different classes of customers in order to maximize profits
    c. a situation where the labor union yields to management demands
    d. process designed to increase the rate of output
    e. management's selection of a product mix yielding maximum profits
    b (Aggregate planning in services, moderate)

FILL-IN-THE BLANK

62. _____ is an approach to determine the quantity and timing of production for the intermediate future.
    Aggregate planning (Introduction, easy)

63. _____ is the process of breaking the aggregate plan into greater detail.
    Disaggregation (The nature of aggregate planning, moderate)

64. A _____ is a timetable that specifies what is to be made and when.
    master production schedule (The nature of aggregate planning, moderate)

65. The _____ strategy sets production equal to forecasted demand.
    chase (Aggregate planning strategies, easy)

66. The _____ strategy maintains a constant output rate, or workforce level, over the planning horizon.
    level (Aggregate planning strategies, easy)

67. The _____ is a formal planning model built around a manager's experience and performance.
    management coefficients model (Methods for aggregate planning, moderate)

SHORT ANSWERS

68. List the strategic objectives of aggregate planning. Which one of these is most often addressed by the quantitative techniques of aggregate planning? Which one of these is generally the most important?
    Minimize cost over the planning period, smooth fluctuations in work force, drive down inventory levels for time-sensitive stock, and meet a high level of service regardless of cost. Cost minimization is the most often treated quantitatively, and is generally the most important. (Introduction, moderate)

69. Define aggregate planning.
It is concerned with the quantity and timing of production for the immediate future, typically encompasses a time horizon of three to eighteen months. (Introduction, easy)

70. Explain what the term **aggregate** in "aggregate planning" means.
Combining the appropriate products and resources into general, or overall, terms. (The nature of aggregate planning, easy)

71. List (a) the demand options for aggregate planning; and (b) the capacity (supply) options for aggregate planning.
Capacity options are: changing inventory levels, varying work force size by hiring or layoffs, varying production rate through overtime or idle time, subcontracting, and using part-time workers. Demand options are: influencing demand (through price, promotion, advertising, selling), back-ordering during high demand periods, and counter-seasonal product mixing. (Aggregate planning strategies, moderate)

72. Explain the fundamental difference between the "capacity options" and the "demand options" of aggregate planning strategies.
Capacity options do not try to change the demand but attempt to absorb the demand fluctuations; capacity options deal with supply, not demand. Demand options try to smooth the demand pattern, but do not impact supply or capacity. (Aggregate planning strategies, moderate)

73. The textbook illustrates demand management in the form of price cuts or discounts. Can demand manipulation for aggregate planning involve price increases? Explain; provide an example.
The text did allude to price increases when it stated that air conditioners are "least expensive in winter"-they must be more expensive when demand is high. Lower prices for one circumstance implies higher prices (or lower discounts) in other circumstances. Student examples may build from text examples, or come from experience, such as: Energy companies can use peak load pricing. Transit systems have higher rush hour fares. (Aggregate planning strategies, moderate)

74. Define chase strategy.
Production rates or work force levels are adjusted to match demand requirements over the planning horizon. (Aggregate planning strategies, moderate)

75. What is level scheduling? What is the basic philosophy underlying it?
Level scheduling is an aggregate plan in which daily capacities are uniform from month to month. The underlying philosophy is that stable employment leads to better quality, less turnover, less absenteeism and more employee commitment. (Aggregate planning strategies, moderate)

76. Most people would argue that a service firm must follow chase or mixed strategies. On the other hand, most state agencies, which are clearly service-oriented, are not at all able to "chase" demand. Discuss how they manipulate demand to allow the level strategy to be used.

    This is a critical-thinking item for students. Most will recognize that state agencies (drivers' license, tax , etc.) are often level because of restrictions on their ability to hire and fire at will. Some students will liken these agencies as high-volume quasi-manufacturing organizations. Most students will uncover examples from personal experience, such as: demand is forced to meet level capacity by queues, waiting lines, processing delays (backorders), and ultimately by lost "sales". (Aggregate planning strategies, difficult)

77. Chase strategy ordinarily results in less inventory than level strategy. In a previous chapter, you studied Just-in-Time strategies. Would a JIT firm prefer chase to level strategy for its aggregate plan? Discuss.

    Suggestion: JIT attempts to reduce waste; one form of waste is inventory. Therefore a chase strategy seems to fit well within JIT. A level strategy keeps workforce level; inventory varies for production to meet demand. JIT would regard this inventory as covering up problems. (Aggregate planning strategies, moderate)

78. Define mixed strategy. Why would a firm use a mixed strategy instead of a simple pure strategy?

    Mixed strategy is a planning approach in which two or more options such as overtime, subcontracting, hiring and layoff, etc., are used. There are both inventory changes and work force and production rate changes over the planning horizon. Typically, mixed strategies are better (result in lower costs) than pure strategies. (Aggregate planning strategies, moderate)

79. If a service firm were to attempt a pure level strategy for aggregate planning, should its level of output be at average demand, peak demand, or minimum demand?

    Critical-thinking item. The answer depends on the ability of customers to reschedule or reserve service times, and upon the organization's view toward lost sales. Level = average if customers can reserve or reschedule. Level = maximum if the organization wishes to prevent lost sales. (Aggregate planning strategies, difficult)

80. Build a T-account to display the advantages and limitations of the graphical method of aggregate planning.

Advantages	Limitations
Easy to understand	**Trial-and-error approach**
Easy to use	**Does not guarantee to be optimal**
	Works with only a few variables at a time

(Methods for aggregate planning, moderate)

81. Normally, the transportation model is used to solve problems involving several physical sources of product and several physical uses of the product, as in factories and warehouses. How is it possible to use the transportation model where the "routes" are from one time period to another? Describe how this provides aggregate planners with a usable mathematical model.

Time travel is not involved. "From" regular time, March "To" demand, May simply describes when production took place to provide the units sold in May. "From" April production to "To" March demand simply describes backorders-demand in one month is met by production in a later period. The algorithm is optimizing-it minimizes cost over the planning period; the algorithm balances supply and demand by combinations of capacity options and demand options. (Methods for aggregate planning, moderate)

82. List, in order, the five steps of the graphical method of aggregate planning. Is it possible that these steps can be properly followed and the solution properly implemented without using a graph? Explain.

The steps are:
1. determine the demand in each period
2. determine what the capacity is for regular time, overtime, and sub-contracting each period
3. find the labor costs, hiring and layoff costs, and inventory holding costs
4. consider company policy that may apply to the workers or to stock levels.
5. develop alternative plans and examine their total costs.
The steps can be followed and the solution implemented with tables of values, not graphs.
(Methods for aggregate planning, moderate)

83. Build a T-account to display the advantages and limitations of the transportation method for aggregate planning.

Advantages	Limitations
Provides optimal solutions	**Doesn't work when more factors such as hiring and layoff are introduced**
Flexible, allows overtime, sub-contracting, extra shifts, inventory carryover options	
(Methods for aggregate planning, moderate)	

84. What are the elements of controlling the cost of labor involved in service firms?
1. close control of labor hours to assure quick customer response
2. some form of on-call labor resource that can be added or deleted to meet unexpected demand
3. flexibility of individual worker skills that permits reallocation of available labor
4. individual worker flexibility in rate of output or hours of work to meet expanded demand.
(Aggregate planning in services, moderate)

85. What are the primary aggregate planning concerns of services whose output is high-volume, tangible output?
Smoothing the production rate, and finding the size of the work force to be employed.
(Aggregate planning in services, moderate)

86. The text states that trial and error methods continue to be widely used, in spite of the development of various models. Using your knowledge from earlier in this course or from other quantitative courses you might have taken, speculate on why managers continue to use "primitive" devices when such sophistication is available.

Ease of use is preferred to sophistication; simpler models are superior in dynamic decision environments. (Methods for aggregate planning, moderate)

PROBLEMS

87. Eagle Fabrication has the following aggregate demand requirements and other data for the upcoming four quarters.

Quarter	Demand
1	1400
2	1200
3	1500
4	1300

Previous quarter's output	1500 units
Beginning inventory	200 units
Stockout cost	$50 per unit
Inventory holding cost	$10 per unit at end of quarter
Hiring workers	$4 per unit
Firing workers	$8 per unit
Unit cost	$30 per unit
Overtime	$10 extra per unit

Which of the following production plans is better: Plan A-chase demand by hiring and firing; or Plan B-produce at a constant rate of 1200 and obtain the remainder from overtime?

Plan A would cost $161,200, while Plan B would cost $162,400. In this case it is cheaper to vary workforce than to use overtime. POM for Windows outputs follow.

Plan A (chase)

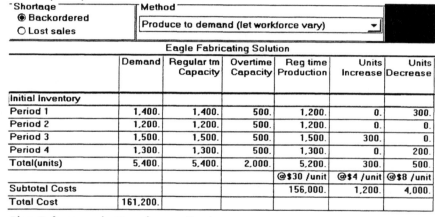

Shortage: ◉ Backordered ○ Lost sales
Method: Produce to demand (let workforce vary)

Eagle Fabricating Solution

	Demand	Regular tm Capacity	Overtime Capacity	Reg time Production	Units Increase	Units Decrease
Initial Inventory						
Period 1	1,400.	1,400.	500.	1,200.	0.	300.
Period 2	1,200.	1,200.	500.	1,200.	0.	0.
Period 3	1,500.	1,500.	500.	1,500.	300.	0.
Period 4	1,300.	1,300.	500.	1,300.	0.	200.
Total(units)	5,400.	5,400.	2,000.	5,200.	300.	500.
				@$30 /unit	@$4 /unit	@$8 /unit
Subtotal Costs				156,000.	1,200.	4,000.
Total Cost	161,200.					

Plan B (base production plus overtime)

Shortage: ◉ Backordered ○ Lost sales
Method: Produce to demand (let workforce vary)

Eagle Fabricating Solution

	Demand	Regular tm Capacity	Overtime Capacity	Reg time Production	Overtime Production	Units Decrease
Initial Inventory						
Period 1	1,400.	1,200.	500.	1,200.	0.	300.
Period 2	1,200.	1,200.	500.	1,200.	0.	0.
Period 3	1,500.	1,200.	500.	1,200.	300.	0.
Period 4	1,300.	1,200.	500.	1,200.	100.	0.
Total(units)	5,400.	4,800.	2,000.	4,800.	400.	300.
				@$30 /unit	@$40 /unit	@$8 /unit
Subtotal Costs				144,000.	16,000.	2,400.
Total Cost	162,400.					

(Methods for aggregate planning, moderate)

88. Falcon Fabrication has the following aggregate demand requirements and other data for the upcoming four quarters.

Quarter	Demand
1	1400
2	1200
3	1500
4	1300

Previous quarter's output	1500 units
Beginning inventory	0 units
Stockout cost	$50 per unit
Inventory holding cost	$10 per unit at end of quarter
Hiring workers	$40 per unit
Firing workers	$80 per unit
Unit cost	$30 per unit
Overtime	$15 extra per unit

Which of the following production plans is better: Plan A-chase demand by hiring and firing; or Plan B-pure level strategy?

Level will cost $180,000, while chase will cost $214,000. POM for Windows outputs follow.

Plan A (chase)

Shortage
- ◉ Backordered
- ○ Lost sales

Method: **Produce to demand (let workforce vary)** ▼

Falcon Fabrication Solution

	Demand	Regular tm Capacity	Reg time Production	Units Increase	Units Decrease
Initial Inventory					
Period 1	1,400.	1,500.	1,400.	0.	100.
Period 2	1,200.	1,500.	1,200.	0.	200.
Period 3	1,500.	1,500.	1,500.	300.	0.
Period 4	1,300.	1,500.	1,300.	0.	200.
Total(units)	5,400.	6,000.	5,400.	300.	500.
			@$30 /unit	@$40 /unit	@$80 /unit
Subtotal Costs			162,000.	12,000.	40,000.
Total Cost	214,000.				

Plan B (level)

Shortage
- ◉ Backordered
- ○ Lost sales

Method: **Smooth production (Average GROSS demand)** ▼

Falcon Fabrication Solution

	Demand	Regular tm Capacity	Reg time Production	Inventory (end PD)	Shortage (end PD)	Units Decrease
Initial Inventory				0.		
Period 1	1,400.	1,500.	1,350.	0.	50.	150.
Period 2	1,200.	1,500.	1,350.	100.	0.	0.
Period 3	1,500.	1,500.	1,350.	0.	50.	0.
Period 4	1,300.	1,500.	1,350.	0.	0.	0.
Total(units)	5,400.	6,000.	5,400.	100.	100.	150.
			@$30 /unit	@$10 /unit	@$50 /unit	@$80 /unit
Subtotal Costs			162,000.	1,000.	5,000.	12,000.
Total Cost	180,000.					

(Methods for aggregate planning, moderate)

89. Osprey Fabrication has the following aggregate demand requirements and other data for the upcoming four quarters.

Quarter	Demand
1	1400
2	1200
3	1500
4	1300

Previous quarter's output	1300 units
Beginning inventory	0 units
Stockout cost	$50 per unit
Inventory holding cost	$10 per unit at end of quarter
Hiring workers	$40 per unit
Firing workers	$80 per unit
Subcontracting cost	$60 per unit
Unit cost	$30 per unit
Overtime	$15 extra per unit

Which of the following production plans is better: Plan A-chase demand by hiring and firing; Plan B-pure level strategy, or Plan C-1300 level with the remainder by subcontracting?
Plan A will cost $210,000, Plan B will cost $170,000, and Plan C will cost $169,000. Plan C is the cheapest, by a small margin. (Methods for aggregate planning, moderate)

SEE NEXT PAGE, page 300

Plan A (chase)

Shortage: ◉ Backordered ○ Lost Sales

Method: Produce to demand (let workforce vary) ▼

Osprey Fabrication Solution

	Demand	Regular trn Capacity	Subcontractin Capacity	Reg time Production	Units Increase	Units Decrease
Initial Inventory						
Period 1	1,400.	1,500.	200.	1,400.	100.	0.
Period 2	1,200.	1,500.	200.	1,200.	0.	200.
Period 3	1,500.	1,550.	200.	1,500.	300.	0.
Period 4	1,300.	1,500.	200.	1,300.	0.	200.
Total(units)	5,400.	6,000.	800.	5,400.	400.	400.
				@$30 /unit	@$40 /unit	@$80 /unit
Subtotal Costs				162,000.	16,000.	32,000.
Total Cost	210,000.					

Plan B (level)

Shortage: ◉ Backordered ○ Lost Sales

Method: Smooth production (Average GROSS demand) ▼

Osprey Fabrication Solution

	Demand	Regular trn Capacity	Subcontract Capacity	Reg time Production	Inventory (end PD)	Shortage (end PD)	Units Increase
Initial Inventory					0.		
Period 1	1,400.	1,500.	200.	1,350.	0.	50.	50.
Period 2	1,200.	1,500.	200.	1,350.	100.	0.	0.
Period 3	1,500.	1,500.	200.	1,350.	0.	50.	0.
Period 4	1,300.	1,500.	200.	1,350.	0.	0.	0.
Total(units)	5,400.	6,000.	800.	5,400.	100.	100.	50.
				@$30 /unit	@$10 /unit	@$50 /unit	@$40 /unit
Subtotal Costs				162,000.	1,000.	5,000.	2,000.
Total Cost	170,000.						

Plan C (base plus subcontracting)

Shortage: ◉ Backordered ○ Lost Sales

Method: Constant Reg time, then OT and sub ▼

Osprey Fabrication Solution

	Demand	Regular trn Capacity	Subcontractin Capacity	Reg time Production	Subcontractin	Inventory (end PD)
Initial Inventory						0.
Period 1	1,400.	1,300.	200.	1,300.	100.	0.
Period 2	1,200.	1,300.	200.	1,300.	0.	100.
Period 3	1,500.	1,300.	200.	1,300.	100.	0.
Period 4	1,300.	1,300.	200.	1,300.	0.	0.
Total(units)	5,400.	5,200.	800.	5,200.	200.	100.
				@$30 /unit	@$60 /unit	@$10 /unit
Subtotal Costs				156,000.	12,000.	1,000.
Total Cost	169,000.					

90. Kite Fabrication has the following aggregate demand requirements and other data for the upcoming four quarters.

Quarter	Demand
1	1800
2	1100
3	1600
4	900

Previous quarter's output	1300 units
Beginning inventory	0 units
Stockout cost	$150 per unit
Inventory holding cost	$40 per unit at end of quarter
Hiring workers	$40 per unit
Firing workers	$80 per unit
Subcontracting cost	$60 per unit
Unit cost	$30 per unit
Overtime	$15 extra per unit

Which of the following production plans is better: Plan A-chase demand by hiring and firing; Plan B-pure level strategy, or Plan C-1200 level with the remainder by subcontracting? Explain how the relative costs of storage, shortage, overtime, subcontracting, layoffs, etc., influence the choice of strategy.

Chase costs $314,000; Level costs $329,000; Mixed costs $236,000. Mixed is by far the cheapest. In this problem, stockouts and storage are relatively expensive compared to subcontract cost and hiring/firing costs. This leads to the low-cost solution that avoids inventory-chase strategy. (Methods for aggregate planning, moderate)

SEE NEXT PAGE, page 302

Plan B (pure level strategy)

Shortage
- ● Backordered
- ○ Lost sales

Method
Smooth production (Average GROSS demand) ▾

Kite Fabrication Solution

	Demand	Regular tm Capacity	Reg time Production	Shortage (end PD)	Units Increase
Initial Inventory					
Period 1	1,800.	1,800.	1,350.	450.	50.
Period 2	1,100.	1,800.	1,350.	200.	0.
Period 3	1,600.	1,800.	1,350.	450.	0.
Period 4	900.	1,800.	1,350.	0.	0.
Total(units)	5,400.	7,200.	5,400.	1,100.	50.
			@$30 /unit	@$150 /unit	@$40 /unit
Subtotal Costs			162,000.	165,000.	2,000.
Total Cost	329,000.				

Plan A (pure chase strategy)

Shortage
- ● Backordered
- ○ Lost sales

Method
Produce to demand (let workforce vary) ▾

Kite Fabrication Solution

	Demand	Regular tm Capacity	Reg time Production	Shortage (end PD)	Units Increase
Initial Inventory					
Period 1	1,800.	1,800.	1,800.	500.	0.
Period 2	1,100.	1,800.	1,100.	0.	700.
Period 3	1,600.	1,800.	1,600.	500.	0.
Period 4	900.	1,800.	900.	0.	700.
Total(units)	5,400.	7,200.	5,400.	1,000.	1,400.
			@$30 /unit	@$40 /unit	@$80 /unit
Subtotal Costs			162,000.	40,000.	112,000.
Total Cost	314,000.				

Plan C (mixed strategy: base level plus subconracting)

Shortage
- ● Backordered
- ○ Lost sales

Method
Produce to demand (let workforce vary) ▾

Kite Fabrication Solution

	Demand	Regular tm Capacity	Subcontract Capacity	Reg time Production	Subcontract	Units Increase	Units Decrease
Initial Inventory							
Period 1	1,800.	1,200.	600.	1,200.	600.	0.	100.
Period 2	1,100.	1,200.	600.	1,100.	0.	0.	100.
Period 3	1,600.	1,200.	600.	1,200.	400.	100.	0.
Period 4	900.	1,200.	600.	900.	0.	0.	300.
Total(units)	5,400.	4,800.	2,400.	4,400.	1,000.	100.	500.
				@$30 /unit	@$60 /unit	@$40 /unit	@$80 /unit
Subtotal Costs				132,000.	60,000.	4,000.	40,000.
Total Cost	236,000.						

91. A manufacturer of industrial seafood processing equipment wants you to develop an aggregate plan for the four quarters of the upcoming year using the following data on demand and capacity.

Quarter	Units	Regular Time	Over- time	Sub- contract
1	200	400	80	100
2	750	400	80	100
3	1200	800	160	100
4	450	400	80	100

initial inventory : 250 units
regular time cost $1.00/unit
overtime cost $1.50/unit
sub-contracting cost 2.00/unit
carrying cost $0.20/unit/quarter
no back ordering is allowed

a. Find the optimal plan using the transportation method.
b. What is the cost of the plan?
c. Does any regular time capacity go unused? How much in what periods?
d. What capacity went unused in this solution (list in detail)?

The problem data are in the following panel. The optimal plan appears below the data. There are 13 sources (three for each period, plus beginning inventory) and five destinations (four periods plus ending inventory). In the data panel a cost of 100 is assigned to "impossible" cells (no backorders are allowed.) Cost increases 0.20 for each period past the current period (carrying cost). The minimum cost solution is $2,675. No regular time capacity went unused. Available production was not used in OT-1, 20; Sub-1, 100; Sub-2, 100, OT-4, 30; and Sub-4, 100 units. (Methods for aggregate planning, moderate)

SEE NEXT PAGE, page 304

Data

Seafood Processors

	Period 1	Period 2	Period 3	Period 4	Ending In	SUPPLY
Overtime 1	1.5	1.7	1.9	2.1	2.3	80
Subcontract 1	2.	2.2	2.4	2.6	2.8	100
Regular 2	100.	1.	1.2	1.4	1.6	400
Overtime 2	100.	1.5	1.7	1.9	2.1	80
Subcontract 2	100.	2.	2.2	2.4	2.6	100
Regular 3	100.	100.	1.	1.2	1.4	800
Overtime 3	100.	100.	1.5	1.7	1.9	160
Subcontract 3	100.	100.	2.	2.2	2.4	100
Regular 4	100.	100.	100.	1.	1.2	400
Overtime 4	100.	100.	100.	1.5	1.7	80
Subcontract 4	100.	100.	100.	2.	2.2	100
DEMAND	200.	750.	1,200.	450	0.	

Solution

▦ Transportation Shipments

Seafood Processors Solution

Optimal cost = $2,675	Period 1	Period 2	Period 3	Period 4	Ending Inventory	Dummy
Beginning Inventory	200.	50.				
Regular 1		220.	180.			
Overtime 1			60.			20.
Subcontract 1						100.
Regular 2		400.				
Overtime 2		80.				
Subcontract 2						100.
Regular 3			800.			
Overtime 3			160.			
Regular 4				400.		
Overtime 4				50.	0.	30.
Subcontract 4						100.

92. A manufacturer of industrial seafood processing equipment wants you to develop an aggregate plan for the four quarters of the upcoming year using the following data on demand and capacity.

Quarter	Units	Regular Time	Over- time	Sub- contract
1	200	400	80	100
2	750	400	80	100
3	1200	800	160	100
4	450	400	80	100

initial inventory : 250 units
regular time cost $1.00/unit
overtime cost $1.50/unit
sub-contracting cost 2.00/unit
carrying cost $0.20/unit/quarter
backorders 0.50/unit/quarter

a. Find the optimal plan using the transportation method.
b. What is the cost of the plan?
c. Does any regular time capacity go unused? How much in what periods?
d. What is the extent of backordering (units and dollars)?

The optimal plan will cost $2,591, by scheduling the quantities illustrated in the solution panel. All regular time capacity is used up. Forty units are produced in period 3 to satisfy demand from period 2. The cost of these backorders is $20. (Methods for aggregate planning, moderate)

SEE NEXT PAGE, page 306

Data, backorders allowed.

Seafood Processors

	Period 1	Period 2	Period 3	Period 4	Ending In	SUPPLY
Overtime 1	1.5	1.7	1.9	2.1	2.3	80
Subcontract 1	2.	2.2	2.4	2.6	2.8	100
Regular 2	1.5	1.	1.2	1.4	1.6	400
Overtime 2	2.	1.5	1.7	1.9	2.1	80
Subcontract 2	2.5	2.	2.2	2.4	2.6	100
Regular 3	2.	1.5	1.	1.2	1.4	800
Overtime 3	2.5	2.	1.5	1.7	1.9	160
Subcontract 3	3.	2.5	2.	2.2	2.4	100
Regular 4	2.5	2.	1.5	1.	1.2	400
Overtime 4	3.	2.5	2.	1.5	1.7	80
Subcontract 4	3.5	3.	2.5	2.	2.2	100
DEMAND	500.	750.	800	450.	0.	

Solution

Seafood Processors Solution

Optimal cost = $2,591	Period 1	Period 2	Period 3	Period 4	Ending Inventory	Dummy
Beginning Inventory	100.	150.				
Regular 1	400.					
Overtime 1		80.				
Subcontract 1						100.
Regular 2		400.				
Overtime 2		80.				
Subcontract 2						100.
Regular 3			800.			
Overtime 3		40.	100.			20.
Subcontract 3						100.
Regular 4				400.		
Overtime 4				50.	0.	30.
Subcontract 4						100.

93. Washington Laundry Products, Inc., makes commercial and industrial laundry machines (the kinds hotels use), and has these aggregate demand requirements for the next six months. The firm has regular capacity for 120 units, and overtime capacity for 40 more. Currently, subcontracting can supply up to 100 units per month, but the subcontracting firm may soon be unavailable.

Month	Demand
1	110
2	160
3	200
4	210
5	190
6	190

Costs and other data	
Previous output level	150 units
Beginning inventory	100 units
Stockout cost	$250 per unit
Inventory holding cost	$100 per unit at end of month
Unit Cost, regular time	$1,200 per unit
Subcontracting	$2,000 per unit
Unit Cost, overtime	$1,500 per unit
Hiring workers	$200 per unit
Firing workers	$500 per unit

Which is cheaper: to produce level, incurring backorders and inventory charges; to chase, incurring the costs of varying the labor force; or to produce a base quantity of 120, using overtime, then subcontracting, to meet demand?

The chase strategy is cheapest at $1,272,000. Excel OM solutions follow.

Chase Strategy
Data   RESULTS

Period	Demand	Reg Time Production	Overtime Production	Subcontract Production	Inventory	Holding	Shortage	Change	Increase	Decrease
Period 1	110	10	0	0	0	0	0	-140	0	140
Period 2	160	160	0	0	0	0	0	150	150	0
Period 3	200	200	0	0	0	0	0	40	40	0
Period 4	210	210	0	0	0	0	0	10	10	0
Period 5	190	190	0	0	0	0	0	-20	0	20
Period 6	190	190	0	0	0	0	0	0	0	0
Total	1060	960	0	0		0	0		200	160
Cost		$1,152,000	$	$ -		$ -	$ -		$40,000	$80,000

Total Cost $1,272,000

Level Strategy
Data   RESULTS

Period	Demand	Reg Time Production	Overtime Production	Subcontract Production	Inventory	Holding	Shortage	Change	Increase	Decrease
Period 1	110	177	0	0	167	167	0	27	27	0
Period 2	160	177	0	0	184	184	0	0	0	0
Period 3	200	177	0	0	161	161	0	0	0	0
Period 4	210	177	0	0	128	128	0	0	0	0
Period 5	190	176	0	0	114	114	0	-1	0	1
Period 6	190	176	0	0	100	100	0	0	0	0
Total	1060	1060	0	0		854	0		27	1
Cost		$1,272,000	$	$		$ 85,400	$ -		$ 5,400	$ 500

Total Cost $1,363,300

Base = 120 plus OT plus Sub.

Data

Period	Demand	Reg Time Production	Overtime Production	Subcontract Production	Inventory	Holding	Shortage	Change	Increase	Decrease
Period 1	110	120	0	0	110	110	0	-30	0	30
Period 2	160	120	0	0	70	70	0	0	0	0
Period 3	200	120	10	0	0	0	0	0	0	0
Period 4	210	120	40	50	0	0	0	0	0	0
Period 5	190	120	40	30	0	0	0	0	0	0
Period 6	190	120	40	30	0	0	0	0	0	0
Total	1060	720	130	110		180	0		0	30
Cost		$ 864,000	$195,000	$ 220,000		$18,000	$ -		$ -	$15,000

Total Cost $1,312,000

(Methods for aggregate planning, moderate)

94. Reddick's Specialty Electronics makes weatherproof surveillance systems for parking lots. Demand estimates for the next four quarters are 25, 9, 13, and 17 units. Prepare an aggregate plan that uses inventory, regular time and overtime and backorders. Subcontracting is not allowed. Regular time capacity is 15 units for quarters 1 and 2, 18 units for quarters 3 and 4. Overtime capacity is 3 units per quarter. Regular time cost is $2000 per unit, while overtime cost is $3000 per unit. Backorder cost is $300 per unit per quarter, inventory holding cost is $100 per unit per quarter. Beginning inventory is zero.

The data inputs for this problem, and the optimal solution, generated by microcomputer software, appear below. Answer the following questions based on the scenario and the solution.
a. How many total units will be produced in quarter 1 for delivery in quarter 1?
b. How many units in total will be used to fill backorders over the four quarters?
c. What is the cost to produce one unit in Quarter 4 using overtime to deliver in quarter 1 (filling a backorder)?
d. At the end of quarter 3, what is the ending inventory of finished systems?
e. What is the total demand over the four quarters?
f. What is the total supply over the four quarters?
g. What is the total cost of the solution?
h. What is the average cost per unit?

Reddick's Data

Objective	Starting method
O Maximize	
● Minimize	Any starting method ▼

Reddick's Specialty Electronics						
	Period 1	Period 2	Period 3	Period 4	Ending	SUPPLY
Regular 1	2,000	2,100	2,200	2,300	2,400	15
Overtime 1	3,000	3,100	3,200	3,300	3,400	3
Regular 2	2,300	2,000	2,100	2,200	2,300	15
Overtime 2	3,300	3,000	3,100	3,200	3,300	3
Regular 3	2,600	2,300	2,000	2,100	2,200	18
Overtime 3	3,600	3,300	3,000	3,100	3,200	3
Regular 4	2,900	2,600	2,300	3,000	3,100	18
Overtime 4	3,900	3,600	3,300	3,000	3,100	3
DEMAND	25	9	13	17	0	

Reddick's Solution

Objective	Starting method
O Maximize	
● Minimize	Any starting method ▼

Reddick's Specialty Electronics Solution						
Optimal cost = $138,700	Period 1	Period 2	Period 3	Period 4	Ending Inventory	Dummy
Regular 1	15.					
Overtime 1						3.
Regular 2	10.	5.				
Overtime 2						3.
Regular 3		1.		17.	0.	
Overtime 3						3.
Regular 4		3.	13.			2.
Overtime 4						3.

a. 15; b. 27; c. $3,900; d. 0; e. 64; f. 78; g. 138,700; h. 138700 / 64 = $2,167.
(Methods for aggregate planning, moderate)

95. Houma Containers, Inc., makes industrial fiberglass tanks that are used on offshore oil platforms. Demand for the next four months, and capacities of the plant are shown in the table below. Unit cost on regular time is $400. Overtime cost is 150% of regular time cost. Subcontracting is available in substantial quantity but at a very high cost, $1100 per unit. Holding costs are $200 per tank per month; backorders cost the firm $1000 per unit per month. Houma's management believes that the transportation algorithm can be used to optimize this scheduling problem. The firm has no beginning inventory and anticipates no ending inventory.

	March	April	May	June
Demand	250	500	200	350
Regular capacity	200	200	200	200
Overtime capacity	50	50	50	50
Subcontract cap.	0	150	50	150

a. How many units will be produced on regular time in June?
b. How many units will be produced by subcontracting over the four-month period?
c. What will be the inventory at the end of April?
d. What will be total production from all sources in April?
e. What will be the total cost of the optimum solution?
f. Does the firm utilize the expensive options of subcontracting and backordering? When; why?

(a) 200; (b) 300; (c) 0, and 100 units are backordered; (d) 400; (e) $870,000; (f) they use subcontracting in April, May, and June; there are backorders in April filled with May production. The firm has so little excess capacity, even with the short-term options, that it must utilize almost every unit available, which forces the use of the more expensive options.

(Methods for aggregate planning, moderate)

SEE NEXT PAGE, page 311

Houma Container Data

Objective		Starting method			
O Maximize		Any starting method ▼			
● Minimize					

Houma Containers

	March	April	May	June	SUPPLY
March Regular	400	600	800	1.000	200
March Overtime	600	800	1.000	1.200	50
March Subcontract	1.100	1.300	1.500	1.700	0
April Regular	1.400	400	600	800	200
April Overtime	1.600	600	800	1.000	50
April Subcontract	2.100	1.100	1.300	1.500	150
May regular	2.400	1.400	400	600	200
May Overtime	2.600	1.600	600	800	50
May Subcontract	3.100	2.100	1.100	1.300	50
June Regular	3.400	2.400	1.400	400	200
June Overtime	3.600	2.600	1.600	600	50
June Subcontract	4.100	3.100	2.100	1.100	150
DEMAND	250	500	200	350	

Houma Container Solution

Objective		Starting method			
O Maximize		Any starting method ▼			
● Minimize					

Houma Containers Solution

Optimal cost = $870.000	March	April	May	June	Dummy
March Regular	200.				
March Overtime	50.	0.			
March Subcontract	0.				
April Regular		200.			
April Overtime		50.			
April Subcontract		150.			
May regular			200.		
May Overtime		50.	0.		
May Subcontract		50.			0.
June Regular				200.	
June Overtime				50.	
June Subcontract				100.	50.

311

CHAPTER 14: MATERIAL REQUIREMENTS PLANNING (MRP)

TRUE/FALSE

1.   MRP is applicable only in product manufacturing operations, not in services.
     False (MRP in services, easy)

2.   The demand for dependent demand items is derived from the demand for some other item.
     True (Introduction, easy)

3.   MRP is generally practiced on items with independent demand.
     False (Introduction, easy)

4.   Since MRP is quite detailed in nature, it has no influence on the longer-range, less detailed aggregate production planning.
     False (Dependent inventory model requirements, moderate)

5.   A dependent demand item is so called because its demand is dependent on customer preferences.
     False (Introduction, moderate)

6.   The quantity required of a dependent demand item is computed from the demand for the final products in which the item is used.
     True (Introduction, moderate)

7.   The Aggregate Production Plan, derived from the Master Production Schedule, specifies in more detail how much of which products is to be made at what times.
     False (Dependent inventory model requirements, moderate)

8.   The bills of material for items that are still in the planning phase are called planning bills.
     False (Dependent inventory model requirements, moderate)

9.   A bill of materials lists all components, ingredients, and materials needed to produce one unit of an end item.
     True (Dependent inventory model requirements, moderate)

10. Planning bills of material are bills of material for "kits" of inexpensive items such as washers, nuts and bolts.
     True (Dependent inventory model requirements, moderate)

11. The time phased product structure, unlike the bill of materials, adds the concept of lead times.
     True (Dependent inventory model requirements, moderate)

12. Although the concepts behind MRP are complicated, its execution can be simple.
     False (MRP structure, easy)

13. Gross material requirements do not take into account the amount of inventory on hand.
     True (MRP structure, easy)

14. If X consists of one A and one B, and each A consists of one F and two Gs, then A is the "child" component of G.
False (Dependent inventory model requirements, moderate)

15. If 10 units of X are required, and each X consists of 2 of Y and 3 of Z, then 30 units is the gross requirement for Z.
True (Dependent inventory model requirements, moderate)

16. If 100 units of Q are needed and 10 are already in stock, then the gross requirement is 100 and the net requirement is 90.
True (MRP structure, easy)

17. In MRP, net requirements at one level generate the gross requirements at the next lower level.
False (MRP structure, easy)

18. Pegging is particularly helpful in reducing the MRP system nervousness.
True (MRP management, moderate)

19. In MRP, a "bucket" refers to a fixed order quantity, such as an EOQ.
False (MRP management, moderate)

20. One advantage of using MRP is that lot sizing need not be considered.
False (MRP management, moderate)

21. The lot-for-lot lot-sizing technique is particularly appropriate when demand is not very smooth and set-up cost is small compared to holding cost.
True (MRP management, moderate)

22. Part period balancing attempts to balance setup and holding costs.
True (MRP management, moderate)

23. The Wagner Whitin algorithm is the MRP lot sizing procedure of choice in industry.
False (MRP management, moderate)

24. Closed-loop MRP systems allow production planners to move work between time periods to smooth the load or to at least bring it within capacity.
True (Extensions to MRP, moderate)

25. Operations splitting involves sending pieces to the next operation before the entire lot is completed on the previous operation.
False (Extensions to MRP, moderate)

26. Enterprise Resource Planning extends MRP II into the areas of purchasing and order entry.
True (Extensions to MRP, moderate)

27. Distribution Resource Planning is the use of dependent techniques in distribution environments.
True (Distributions resource planning, moderate)

MULTIPLE CHOICE

28. The phrase "demand derived from the demand for other products" describes
    a. independent demand
    b. a dependent variable
    c. dependent demand
    d. recursive demand
    e. regression analysis
    c (Introduction, easy)

29. Demand for a given item is said to be dependent if
    a. it originates from the external customer
    b. there is a clearly identifiable parent
    c. there is a deep bill of materials
    d. the finished products are mostly services (rather than goods)
    e. the item has several children
    b (Introduction, easy)

30. Dependent demand and independent demand items differ in that
    a. the need for independent-demand items is forecast
    b. the need for dependent-demand items is calculated
    c. for any product, all components are dependent-demand items
    d. all of the above are true
    e. none of the above are true
    d (Introduction, moderate)

31. A master production schedule specifies
    a. the raw materials required to complete the product
    b. what product is to be made, and when
    c. the labor hours required for production
    d. the financial resources required for production
    e. what component is to be made, and when
    b (Dependent inventory model requirements, moderate)

32. _____ is the MRP input detailing which end items are to be produced, when they are needed, and in what quantities.
    a. Gross requirements
    b. Inventory records
    c. Master production schedule
    d. Assembly time chart
    e. Bill of materials
    c (Dependent inventory model requirements, moderate)

33. A master production schedule contains information about
    a. quantities and required delivery dates of final products
    b. quantities and required delivery dates of all sub-assemblies
    c. inventory on hand for each final product
    d. inventory on hand for each sub-assembly
    e. scheduled receipts for each final product
    a (Dependent inventory model requirements, moderate)

34. In continuous (make-to-stock) operations, the master production schedule is usually expressed in terms of
    a. end-items
    b. modules
    c. kits
    d. customer orders
    e. warehouse orders
    a (Dependent inventory model requirements, moderate)

35. In a job shop (made-to-order) operation the master production schedule is usually expressed in terms of
    a. end-items
    b. modules
    c. kits
    d. customer orders
    e. warehouse orders
    d (Dependent inventory model requirements, moderate)

36. The following table is an example of a(n)

	Week 1	Week 2	Week 3	Week 4	Week 5
Clothes Washer		200		100	
Clothes Dryer	300	100	100		100
Upright Freezer			200	500	

    a. aggregate plan
    b. master production schedule
    c. capacity plan
    d. load report
    e. inventory record
    b (Dependent inventory model requirements, moderate)

37. A bill of materials lists the
    a. production schedules for all products
    b. components, ingredients, and materials required to produce an item
    c. operations required to produce an item
    d. components, ingredients, materials and assembly operations required to produce an item
    e. times needed to perform all phases of production
    b (Dependent inventory model requirements, moderate)

38.   _____ is the input to Materials Requirements Planning which lists the assemblies, subassemblies, parts and raw materials needed to produce one unit of finished product.
   a.   Master production schedule
   b.   Inventory records
   c.   Assembly time chart
   d.   Net requirements chart
   e.   Bill of materials
   e (Dependent inventory model requirements, moderate)

39.   The bill of materials contains information necessary to
   a.   calculate quantities on hand and on order
   b.   convert net requirements into higher level gross requirements
   c.   convert gross requirements into net requirements
   d.   convert (explode) net requirements at one level into gross requirements at the next level
   e.   place an order to replenish the item
   d (Dependent inventory model requirements, moderate)

40.   One way to facilitate production scheduling and production in firms making a large number of different final products is to use
   a.   planning bills
   b.   phantom bills
   c.   overdue bills
   d.   modular bills
   e.   none of the above
   d (Dependent inventory model requirements, moderate)

41.   Which of the following statements best compares modular bills and phantom bills?
   a.   There is no difference between the two.
   b.   Both pertain to assemblies that are inventoried.
   c.   Both pertain to assemblies that are not inventoried.
   d.   Modular bills are used for assemblies that are not inventoried, unlike phantom bills.
   e.   Modular bills represent subassemblies that actually exist and are inventoried, while phantom bills represent subassemblies that exist only temporarily and are not inventoried.
   e (Dependent inventory model requirements, moderate)

42. Given the following bill-of-materials

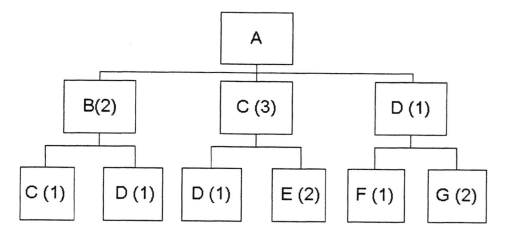

If the demand for product A is 50 units, what will be the gross requirement for component C?
a. 4
b. 150
c. 200
d. 250
e. 300
d (Dependent inventory model requirements, moderate)

43. Given the following bill of materials

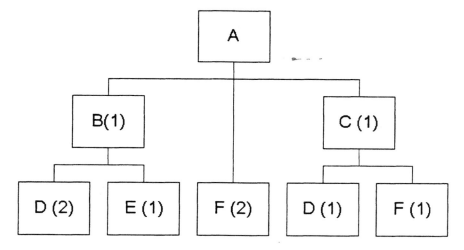

If the demand for product A is 50 units, what will be the gross requirement for component F?
a. 2
b. 3
c. 150
d. 200
e. 300
c (Dependent inventory model requirements, moderate)

44. Given the following bill of materials

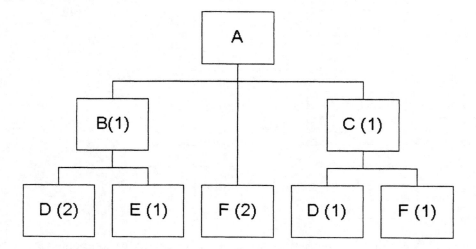

If the demand for product A is 30 units, and there are on hand 10 units of B and none of C, how many units of part D will be needed?
a. 3
b. 40
c. 70
d. 90
e. 110
c (Dependent inventory model requirements, moderate)

45. The minimum record accuracy required for successful MRP is approximately
a. 95%
b. 90%
c. 97%
d. 99%
e. lower than 90%
d (Dependent inventory model requirements, moderate)

46. Low level coding means that
a. a final item has only a few levels in the BOM structure
b. a component item is coded at the lowest level at which it appears in the BOM structure
c. the code for the lowest level in the BOM structure
d. the top level of the BOM is below level zero and that BOM's are not organized around the finished product
e. none of the above
b (Dependent inventory model requirements, moderate)

47. "Exploding" the bill of materials means
a. converting the bill of materials into components and raw material requirements
b. identifying the various components, ingredients, and materials that make a product
c. identifying the lead time of all the components
d. determining the various components' quantities that are already on hand
e. determining the net requirements for all the components
a (Dependent inventory model requirements, moderate)

48. Each X requires 2 of component Y; each Y requires 4 of part Z. The lead time for assembly of X is 1 week. The lead time for the manufacture of Y is 1 week. The lead time for the procurement of Z is 6 weeks. The cumulative lead time for X is _____ weeks.
   a. 6
   b. 7
   c. 8
   d. 10
   e. cannot be determined

   c (MRP structure, moderate)

49. Each R requires 4 of component S; each S requires 3 of part T. The lead time for assembly of R is 1 week. The lead time for the manufacture of S is 2 weeks. The lead time for the procurement of T is 6 weeks. The cumulative lead time for R is _____ weeks.
   a. 6
   b. 9
   c. 12
   d. 18
   e. 28

   b (MRP structure, moderate)

50. The MPS calls for 110 units of Product M. There are currently 30 of Product M on hand. Each M requires 4 of Component N. There are 20 units of N on hand. The gross requirements for N are
   a. 440
   b. 320
   c. 240
   d. 170
   e. 150

   b (MRP structure, moderate)

51. The MPS calls for 110 units of Product A, there are currently 60 of Product A on hand. Each A requires 4 of Part B, there are 20 units of B available. The net requirements for B are
   a. 20
   b. 120
   c. 180
   d. 260
   e. 300

   c (MRP structure, moderate)

52. The MPS calls for 50 units of Product A and 60 of B. There are currently 25 of Product B on hand. Each A requires 2 of Part C; each B requires 5 of C. There are 160 units of C available. The net requirements for C are
   a. 115
   b. 225
   c. 240
   d. 690
   e. 700

   a (MRP structure, moderate)

53. A material requirements plan contains information with regard to all of the following **except**
   a. quantities and required delivery dates of all sub-assemblies
   b. quantities and required delivery dates of final products
   c. inventory on hand for each final product
   d. the capacity needed to provide the projected output rate
   e. inventory on hand for each sub-assembly
   d (MRP structure, moderate)

54. The number of units projected to be available at the end of each time period refers to
   a. net requirements
   b. scheduled receipts
   c. the amount projected to be on hand
   d. the projected usage of the item
   e. the amount necessary to cover a shortage
   c (MRP structure, moderate)

55. In MRP record calculations, the appearance of a negative value for the gross requirements of an end item in a specific time bucket
   a. signals the need to purchase that end item in that period
   b. implies that value was scheduled by the MPS
   c. signals the need for a negative Planned Order Receipt in that period
   d. is impossible
   e. all of the above are true
   d (MRP structure, moderate)

56. Linking a part requirement with the parent component that caused the requirement is referred to as
   a. net requirements planning
   b. economic lot sizing
   c. pegging
   d. Kanban
   e. leveling
   c (MRP management, moderate)

57. In MRP, system nervousness is caused by
   a. the use of the lot-for-lot approach
   b. the use of phantom bills of materials
   c. management's attempt to continually respond to minor changes in production requirements
   d. management's marking part of the master production schedule as "not to be rescheduled"
   e. management's attempt to evaluate alternative plans before making a decision
   c (MRP management, moderate)

58. A major strength of MRP is its capability
   a. to minimize labor hours used in production
   b. to reduce lead times
   c. to maximize production throughput
   d. for timely and accurate replanning
   e. to minimize scrap
   d (MRP management, moderate)

59. One of the tools that is particularly useful in reducing the system nervousness in the MRP system is
   a. modular bills
   b. time fences
   c. time phasing
   d. lot sizing
   e. closed loop system
   b (MRP management, moderate)

60. Material requirements plans specify
   a. the quantities of the product families that need to be produced
   b. the capacity needed to provide the projected output rate
   c. the costs associated with alternative plans
   d. the quantity and timing of planned order releases
   e. whether one should use phantom bills of materials or not
   d (MRP structure, moderate)

61. Which of the following statements is **true** about the MRP plan when using lot-for-lot ordering?
   a. The quantity of gross requirements for a child item is always equal to the quantity of planned order releases for its parent.
   b. The quantity of gross requirements for a child item is always equal to the quantity of gross requirements for its parent.
   c. The quantity and gross requirements for a child item is always equal to the quantity of net requirements for its parent.
   d. The quantity of gross requirements for a child item is equal to the quantity of net requirements for its parent(s) multiplied by the number of child items used in the parent assembly.
   e. All of the above are both true.
   d (MRP structure, moderate)

62. For the lot-for-lot lot-sizing technique to be appropriate
   a. future demand should be known for several weeks
   b. annual volume should be rather low
   c. item unit cost should be relatively small
   d. set-up cost should be relatively small
   e. the independent demand rate should be very stable
   d (Lot-sizing techniques, moderate)

63. Which of the following lot-sizing-techniques results in the lowest holding costs?
    a. part-period-balancing
    b. lot-for-lot
    c. EOQ
    d. Wagner-Whitin
    e. the quantity discount model
    b (Lot-sizing techniques, moderate)

64. What lot sizing technique is generally preferred when inventory holding costs are extremely high?
    a. lot-for-lot
    b. EOQ
    c. part-period balancing
    d. the Wagner-Whiten algorithm
    e. all of the above are appropriate for the situation
    a (Lot-sizing techniques, moderate)

65. The holding cost for an item is 60 cents per week and each setup costs $120. Lead time is 2 weeks. Calculate the EPP.
    a. 40
    b. 60
    c. 72
    d. 100
    e. 200
    e (Lot-sizing techniques, moderate)

66. MRP II is accurately described as
    a. MRP with a new set of computer programs which execute on micro-computers
    b. MRP augmented by other resource variables
    c. usually employed to isolate manufacturing operations from other aspects of an organization
    d. a new generation of MRP software that extends MRP to planning and scheduling functions
    e. an MRP software designed for services
    b (Extensions of MRP, moderate)

67. The extension of MRP which extends to resources such as labor hours and machine hours, as well as to order entry, purchasing, and direct interface with customers and suppliers is
    a. MRP II
    b. the master production schedule
    c. closed-loop MRP
    d. Enterprise Resource Planning
    e. not yet technically possible
    d (Extensions of MRP, moderate)

68. Enterprise Resource Planning (ERP) is
   a. not related to MRP
   b. an advanced MRP II system that ties-in customers and suppliers
   c. not currently practical
   d. severely limited by current MRP computer systems
   e. do not provide any benefit over a simple MRP system
   b (Extensions of MRP, moderate)

69. In what way are Distribution Resource Planning (DRP) and Material Requirements Planning (MRP) similar?
   a. both are employed in a manufacturing organization
   b. both work most efficiently with largest lot sizes
   c. both are employed by retail organizations
   d. both employ similar logic and procedures
   e. both work best with lumpy demand
   d (Distribution resource planning (DRP), moderate)

70. Distribution Resource Planning (DRP) is
   a. a transportation plan to ship materials to warehouses
   b. a time-phased stock replenishment plan for all levels of a distribution network
   c. a shipping plan from a central warehouse to retail warehouses
   d. material requirements planning with feedback loop from distribution centers
   e. a material requirements planning package used exclusively by warehouses
   b (Distribution resource planning (DRP), moderate)

FILL-IN-THE BLANK

71. _____ is a dependent demand technique that uses bill-of-material, inventory, expected receipts, and a master production schedule to determine material requirements.
   Material Requirements Planning or MRP (Introduction, easy)

72. A _____ is a timetable that specifies what is to be made and when.
   Master Production Schedule or MPS (Dependent inventory model requirements, moderate)

73. A _____ is a listing of the components, their description, and the quantity of each required to make one unit of a product.
   Bill of material or BOM (Dependent inventory model requirements, moderate)

74. Bills of material organized by major subassemblies or by product options are called

   _____.
   Modular bills (Dependent inventory model requirements, moderate)

75. _____ are material groupings created in order to assign an artificial parent to the bill or material.
   Planning bills or kits (Dependent inventory model requirements, moderate)

76. _____ are a bill of materials for components, usually assemblies, that exist only temporarily; they are never inventoried.
   Phantom bill of materials (Dependent inventory model requirements, moderate)

77. _____ are the result of adjusting gross requirements for inventory on hand and scheduled receipts.
   Net material requirements (MRP structure, moderate)

78. The scheduled date for an order to be released is called the _____.
   planned order release (MRP structure, moderate)

79. _____ refers to frequent changes in the MRP system.
   System nervousness (MRP management, moderate)

80. _____ are a way of allowing a segment of the master schedule to be designated as "not to be rescheduled."
   Time fences (MRP management, moderate)

81. _____ in materials requirements planning systems traces upward in the bill of materials from the component to the parent item.
   Pegging (MRP management, moderate)

82. _____ refers to the time units in a material requirements planning (MRP) system.
   Buckets (MRP management, easy)

83. _____ is a lot-sizing technique that generate exactly what was required to meet the plan.
   Lot-for-lot (Lot-sizing techniques, moderate)

84. A _____ provides feedback to the capacity plan, master production schedule, and production plan so planning can be kept valid at all times.
   Closed-loop MRP system (Extensions of MRP, moderate)

85. _____ is a system that allows, with MRP in place, inventory data to be augmented by other resource variables.
   Material Requirements Planning II or Material Resource Planning or MRP II (Extensions of MRP, moderate)

86. _____ is an MRP II system that ties customers and orders to enterprise-wide resources and ultimately to suppliers.
   Enterprise Resource Planning or ERP (Extensions of MRP, moderate)

87. _____ is a time-phased stock-replenishment plan for all levels of a distribution network.
   Distribution Resource Planning or DRP (Distributions resources planning (DRP), easy)

SHORT ANSWERS

88. List and describe briefly the information requirements of basic and extended MRP systems. Comment on the challenge of maintaining timely, accurate information for a large manufacturing operation based on MRP.

    MRP requires very high accuracy of inventory data file. MRP needs inputs from the master production schedule, bills of material, inventory records, and expected receipts. As MRP is extended to MRP II and ERP, the information needs are intensified. (MRP structure, moderate)

89. What information is necessary for an operations manager to make effective use of a dependent inventory demand model?

    The master production schedule (what is to be made, and when); specifications or bills-of-material (how to make the product); inventory availability (what is in stock); purchase orders outstanding (what is on order); and lead times (how long does it take to get or make each component). (MRP structure, moderate)

90. List the typical benefits of MRP.

    Better response to customers orders as the result of improved adherence to schedules, faster response to market changes, improved utilization of facilities and labor, and reduced inventory levels. (Introduction, moderate)

91. What are the three "styles" in which the master schedule can be expressed?

    End items in a continuous (make-to-stock) company; customer orders in a job shop (make-to-order) company; and modules in a repetitive (assemble-to-stock) company. (Dependent inventory model requirements, moderate)

92. What are modular bills? Why are they used?

    Modular bills are bills-of-material organized around product modules or product options. They are used by firms that make a large number of different final products using combinations of relatively fewer modules. (Dependent inventory model requirements, moderate)

93. Explain what is meant by the "explosion" of the bill of materials.

    The explosion reveals the requirements for each component underneath the parent. Drawn graphically, the "explosion" may look like the product has been disassembled. (Dependent inventory model requirements, moderate)

94. Explain the use of the terms "child" and "parent" in bills of materials.

    In a bill-of-materials, items below any level are called children; items above any level are called parents. (Dependent inventory model requirements, moderate)

95. Compare planning bills to phantom bills. Why are they used?

Planning bills are bills-of-material created to assign an artificial parent to the bill-of-materials. They are used (1) to group sub-assemblies together to reduce the number of items to be scheduled and (2) to issue "kits" to the production department. Phantom bills are bills-of-material for components, usually sub-assemblies, which exist only temporarily. These are used for components that go into another assembly directly without being inventoried so that these components can be handled as an integral part of their parent item. (Dependent inventory model requirements, moderate)

96. What is low-level coding? Why is it important?

Low-level coding means the item is coded at the lowest level at which it occurs. It is necessary when identical items exist at various levels in the bill-of-material structure. It allows easy computing of the requirements of an item. (Dependent inventory model requirements, moderate)

97. If the explosion of the bill if materials tells MRP **how much** of each part is needed, how does MRP learn **when** each of these parts is needed?

Timing is established with the time-phased product structure, which factors item quantities with item lead times. The lead times are cumulative, in the sense that the lead time for a child part is the sum of its lead time and that of all of its parent components. (Dependent inventory model requirements, moderate)

98. Explain the difference between a gross requirements plan and a net requirements plan.

A gross requirements plan multiplies each part quantity in the bill of materials by the number of top level parents needed. This ignores any inventory on hand, whether of parents or children. A net requirements plan starts with the top level requirements from the bill of materials, then subtracts inventory of that item on hand. This net requirement becomes the gross requirement to the next level of the product structure. (MRP structure, easy)

99. A working MRP system allows a firm to react to even minor changes in production requirements. Discuss both the advantages and disadvantages of having such an ability.

**Advantage: It allows the firm to react quickly, and, conceivably, to minimize costs.
Disadvantage: The reaction to a large number of minor changes may introduce an instability (nervousness) into the purchasing and production departments. (MRP structure, moderate)**

100. Explain what is meant by "nervousness" of the MRP schedule. Provide an example. Name two tools that are particularly useful in reducing system nervousness in MRP systems.

Nervousness is the reaction to a large number of minor changes that may introduce an instability into the purchasing and production departments. Two tools for reducing system nervousness are time fences and pegging. (MRP management, moderate)

101. How can MRP and JIT be effectively integrated?
One approach is the small bucket approach that involves the following steps:
1. reduce the MRP buckets from weekly to daily to perhaps hourly
2. the planned receipts that are part of firm planned orders in an MRP system are communicated to the assembly areas and are used to sequence production
3. inventory is moved through the plant using kanbans
4. as products are completed, they are moved into inventory in the normal way
5. a back flush is used to reduce inventory balances.
Another approach is the balance flow. In this system, execution is achieved by maintaining a carefully balanced flow of materials to assembly areas with small lot sizes.
(MRP management, difficult)

102. List the several lot-sizing algorithms used in MRP. Provide at least one advantage and one disadvantage of each.

Algorithm	Advantage	Disadvantage
Lot for lot	**no inventory; use whenever economical**	**expensive when setup costs are significant**
Wagner-Whitin	**good results**	**complexity**
Part period balancing	**lot size varies with needs; good when setup cost is significant**	**none found**
Economic order quantity (EOQ)	**use when the demand is constant and set up costs are high**	**lot size fixed; incurs holding costs; works best with independent demand**

(Lot-sizing techniques, moderate)

103. What does the part-period balancing lot-sizing technique attempt to do in deciding the lot sizes?
It balances the setup and holding costs. PPB uses additional information by changing the lot size to reflect requirements of the next lot size in the future. (Lot-sizing techniques, moderate)

104. Describe how MRP II differs from MRP.
MRP II is MRP in which inventory data are augmented by labor hours, material cost, capital cost, or by virtually any resource. (Extensions to MRP, moderate)

105. Describe the tactics for load smoothing and for minimizing the impact of changed lead time in MRP.
Overlapping - send pieces to the second operation before the entire lot is completed on the first operation; operations splitting - send the lot to two different machines for the same operation; and lot splitting - break up the order and run part of it ahead of schedule. (Extensions to MRP, moderate)

106. Describe how Enterprise Resource Planning is a major extension of MRP II. Discuss the importance of organizational information systems in support of ERP.
MRP II adds resource bills (machine time, labor hours, material cost, etc.) to material bills; ERP integrates MRP II with order entry, purchasing, and creates direct interfaces with customers and suppliers. The integration requires enterprise-wide information systems. The added interfaces are fully dependent on electronic means-EDI and ASN cannot function without high-quality, powerful information systems. The major ERP systems are software systems. (Extensions to MRP, moderate)

107. What is DRP? What are the four inputs required for DRP?

DRP is a time-phased stock replenishment plan for all levels of a distribution network. Gross requirements; minimum levels of inventory to meet customer service levels; alternate lead time; and distribution structure. (Distribution resource planning (DRP), moderate)

PROBLEMS

108. The large parts of a Playground A-frame (from which to hang a swing or glider) consist of a ridge pole, 4 legs, and two side braces. Each pair of legs fastens to the ridge with two fastener sets. Each side brace requires two fastener sets for attachment to the legs. Each fastener set includes one zinc-plated bolt, one lock-washer, and one nut.

There is one order outstanding, to make 100 frame kits. There are 260 legs in inventory. There are no other large items in inventory, and no scheduled receipts. Fasteners are available from the small parts area.

a. Draw the product structure tree
b. Calculate the net requirements to fulfill the outstanding order.

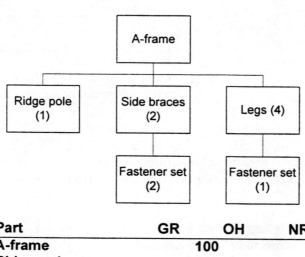

Part	GR	OH	NR
A-frame	100		100
Ridge pole	100		100
Side braces	200		200
Legs	400	260	140
Fastener set	540		540

(MRP structure, easy)

109. A very simple product (A) consists of a base (B) and a casting (C). The base consists of a plate (P) and three fasteners (F). There are currently 30 castings and 100 bases on hand. Final assembly takes one week. The casting has a lead time of three weeks. All other parts have one week lead times. There are no scheduled receipts. All components are lot for lot. The MPS requires 100 units of product A in week 5 and 150 in week 8. Produce the MRP for the upcoming eight weeks. Produce a list of all planned order releases.

A has releases of 100 in 4, 150 in 7; B has a release of 150 in 6, but on hand inventory accounted for all other needs; C has releases of 150 in 4, 70 in 1; P has a release of 150 in 5 and F has a release of 450 in 5 (the beginning inventory of B leads to no other gross requirements of P or F).

			A very simple product Solution					
Item name (low level)	pd1	pd2	pd3	pd4	pd5	pd6	pd7	pd8
A (0)								
TOT. REG.	0.	0.	0.	0.	100.	0.	0.	150.
ON HAND	0.	0.	0.	0.	0.	0.	0.	0.
SchdREC.	0.	0.	0.	0.	0.	0.	0.	0.
NET REQ.	0.	0.	0.	0.	100.	0.	0.	150.
ORD REL.	0.	0.	0.	100.	0.	0.	150.	0.
B (1)								
TOT. REG.	0.	0.	0.	100.	0.	0.	150.	0.
ON HAND	100.	100.	100.	100.	0.	0.	0.	0.
SchdREC.	0.	0.	0.	0.	0.	0.	0.	0.
NET REQ.	0.	0.	0.	0.	0.	0.	150.	0.
ORD REL.	0.	0.	0.	0.	0.	150.	0.	0.
C (1)								
TOT. REG.	0.	0.	0.	100.	0.	0.	150.	0.
ON HAND	30.	30.	30.	30.	0.	0.	0.	0.
SchdREC.	0.	0.	0.	0.	0.	0.	0.	0.
NET REQ.	0.	0.	0.	70.	0.	0.	150.	0.
ORD REL.	70.	0.	0.	150.	0.	0.	0.	0.
P (2)								
TOT. REG.	0.	0.	0.	0.	0.	150.	0.	0.
ON HAND	0.	0.	0.	0.	0.	0.	0.	0.
SchdREC.	0.	0.	0.	0.	0.	0.	0.	0.
NET REQ.	0.	0.	0.	0.	0.	150.	0.	0.
ORD REL.	0.	0.	0.	0.	150.	0.	0.	0.
F (2)								
TOT. REG.	0.	0.	0.	0.	0.	450.	0.	0.
ON HAND	0.	0.	0.	0.	0.	0.	0.	0.
SchdREC.	0.	0.	0.	0.	0.	0.	0.	0.
NET REQ.	0.	0.	0.	0.	0.	450.	0.	0.
ORD REL.	0.	0.	0.	0.	450.	0.	0.	0.

(MRP structure, moderate)

110. A Bill of Materials is desired for a bracket (1.000) that is made up of a base (1.011), two springs (1.021) and four clamps (1.022). The base is assembled from one clamp (1.022) and two housings (1.032). Each clamp has one handle (1.013) and one casting (1.023). Each housing has two bearings (1.033) and one shaft (1.043).

a. Design a product structure tree that includes the level coding information.

b. Determine the gross quantities of all parts required to assemble 50 Z100 brackets.

The appropriate diagram appears below. Level coding is the last digit of each part number. The clamp is a level 2, not level 1 because it appears lower in the base than in the bracket.

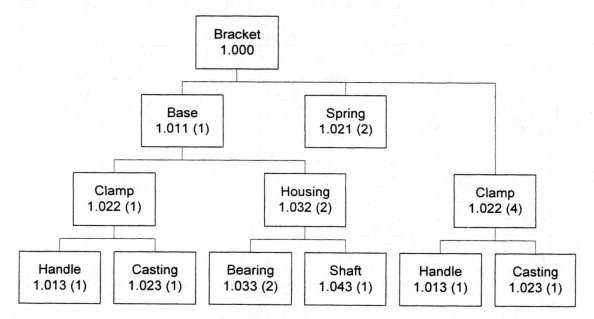

For 50 brackets, the gross requirements are for 50 bases, 100 springs, 250 clamps, 250 handles, 250 castings, 100 housings, 200 bearings, and 100 shafts. (MRP structure, moderate)

111. Consider the following requirements for a certain product.

Period	1	2	3	4	5	6	7	8
Gross requirements		400	300	500		400		200

Beginning inventory = 500 units
Setup cost = $600 per setup
Lead time = 1 week
Holding cost = $3 per unit per week
a. Develop the lot-for-lot MRP table.
b. Calculate the total relevant cost.
The POM for Windows data inputs and solution screen appear below. There are four setups at $600 each, totaling $2,400. There are 500 units held in period 1 and 2, and 100 in period 3. The holding costs are 1100 units x $3 per unit, for a total of $3,300. Total relevant costs are $5,700.

Lot size costing

Item name	Lead time	# per parent	Onhand inv	Lot size	pd1	pd2	pd3	pd4	pd5	pd6	pd7	pd8
Product	1	0	500	0	0	400	300	500	0	400	0	200
BOM line 2	1	0	0	0	0	0	0	0	0	0	0	0

Lot size costing Solution

Item name (low level)	pd1	pd2	pd3	pd4	pd5	pd6	pd7	pd8
Product (0)								
TOT.REQ.	0.	400.	300.	500.	0.	400.	0.	200.
ON HAND	500.	500.	100.	0.	0.	0.	0.	0.
SchdREC.	0.	0.	0.	0.	0.	0.	0.	0.
NET REQ	0.	0.	200.	500.	0.	400.	0.	200.
ORD REL.	0.	200.	500.	0.	400.	0.	200.	0.

(Lot-sizing techniques, easy)

112. Consider the following bill of materials. Fifty units of Product A are needed. Assuming no on-hand inventory, explode the bill of materials.

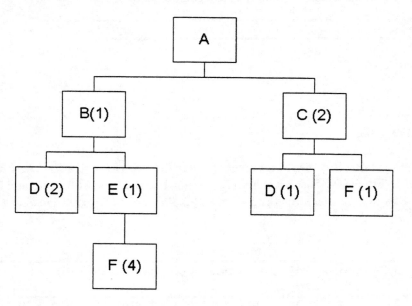

Item A: 50 units; Item B: 50 * 1 = 50 units; Item C: (50 * 2) = 100 units; Item D: (50 * 2 * 1) + (100 * 1) = 200 units; Item E: (50 * 1 * 1) = 50 units; Item F: (50 * 1 * 1 * 4) + (50 * 2 * 1) = 300 units. (MRP structure, moderate)

113. Consider the following bill of materials. Two hundred units of Product J are needed. Assume that there is no inventory on hand. Explode the bill of materials.

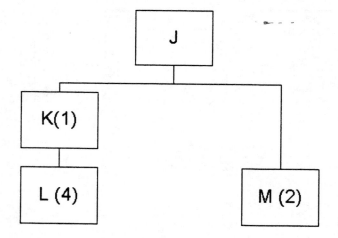

Item J: 200 units; Item K: 200 * 1 = 200 units; Item L: 200 * 4 = 800 units; Item M: 200 * 2 =400 units. (MRP structure, easy)

114. Clancy's Motors has the following demand to meet for custom manufactured fuel injector parts. The holding cost for that item is $.40 per month and each setup costs $100. Calculate the order quantity by use of the part-period algorithm. Lead time is 2 months.

Month	1	2	3	4	5	6	7
Requirement	100	150	200	150	100	150	250

$$\text{EPP} = \frac{\text{Setup cost}}{\text{Holding cost}} = \frac{\$100}{\$0.40} = 250 \text{ units}$$

In Period 1, an order for 250 units should be received; in Period 3, an order for 450 units should be received; and in Period 6, an order for 400 units should be received, as per the table below.

Period	Order size	# of Units	# period	PP	CumPP
1	100	0			
1, 2	250	150	1	150	150*
1, 2, 3	450	200	2	400	550
3	200	0			
3, 4	350	150	1	150	150
3, 4, 5	450	100	2	200	350*
6	150	0			
6, 7	400	250	1	250	250*

(Lot-sizing techniques, moderate)

115. Consider the bill of materials for Product J and the data given in the following table. The gross requirements for J are 100 units in week 6 and 200 units in week 8. Develop the MRP tables for each item for an 8-week planning period. Use the lot-for-lot lot-sizing rule.

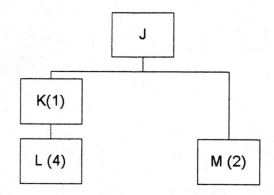

Item	Lead Time	Quantity on Hand	Scheduled receipts
J	1	0	
K	2	10	30 in week 3
L	2	0	
M	1	20	10 in week 4

POM for Windows solution follows (MRP structure, moderate)

SEE NEXT PAGE, page 335

Product J

Item name	Level	Lead time	# per parent	Onhand inv	Lot size	pd1	pd2	pd3	pd4	pd5	pd6	pd7	pd8
Product J	0	1	0	0	0	0	0	0	0	0	100	0	200
Component K	1	2	1	10	0	0	0	30	0	0	0	0	0
Part L	2	2	4	0	0	0	0	0	0	0	0	0	0
Part M	1	1	2	20	0	0	0	0	10	0	0	0	0

Product J Soluction

Item name (low level)	pd1	pd2	pd3	pd4	pd5	pd6	pd7	pd8
Product J (0)								
TOT. REQ.	0.	0.	0.	0.	0.	100.	0.	200.
ON HAND	0.	0.	0.	0.	0.	0.	0.	0.
SchdREC.	0.	0.	0.	0.	0.	0.	0.	0.
NET REQ.	0.	0.	0.	0.	0.	100.	0.	200.
ORD REL.	0.	0.	0.	0.	100.	0.	200.	0.
Component K (1)								
TOT. REQ.	0.	0.	0.	0.	100.	0.	200.	0.
ON HAND	10.	10.	10.	40.	40.	0.	0.	0.
SchdREC.	0.	0.	30.	0.	0.	0.	0.	0.
NET REQ.	0.	0.	0.	0.	60.	0.	200.	0.
ORD REL.	0.	0.	60.	0.	200.	0.	0.	0.
Part M (1)								
TOT. REQ.	0.	0.	0.	0.	200.	0.	400.	0.
ON HAND	20.	20.	20.	20.	30.	0.	0.	0.
SchdREC.	0.	0.	0.	10.	0.	0.	0.	0.
NET REQ.	0.	0.	0.	0.	170.	0.	400.	0.
ORD REL.	0.	0.	0.	170.	0.	400.	0.	0.
Part L (2)								
TOT. REQ.	0.	0.	240.	0.	800.	0.	0.	0.
ON HAND	0.	0.	0.	0.	0.	0.	0.	0.
SchdREC.	0.	0.	0.	0.	0.	0.	0.	0.
NET REQ.	0.	0.	240.	0.	800.	0.	0.	0.
ORD REL.	240.	0.	800.	0.	0.	0.	0.	0.

116. Each R requires 4 of component S and 2 of material A; each S requires 3 of part T. The lead time for assembly of R is 1 week. The lead time for the manufacture of S is 2 weeks. The lead time for material A is 1 week. The lead time for the procurement of T is 4 weeks.

a. Construct the time-phased product structure.

b. Construct the bill of materials

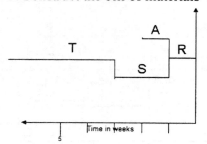

Bill of Materials			
Item			Quantity
R			1
	S(4)		4
		T(3)	12
	A(2)		2

(MRP structure, moderate)

117. Each X requires 3 of component Y and 1 of part W. Each Y requires 10 of Z. Each W requires 3 of Q and 1 of R. Lead times are X = 1 week, Y = 1 week, W = 2 weeks, R = 1 week, Z = 3 weeks, and Q = 3 weeks.

a. Construct the time-phased product structure.

b. Construct the bill of materials

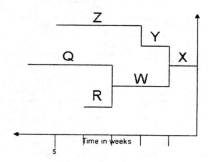

Bill of Materials			
Item			Quantity
X			1
	Y(3)		3
		Z(10)	30
	W(1)		1
		Q(3)	3
		R(1)	1

(MRP structure, moderate)

336

118. The MPS calls for 110 units of Product M. There are currently 30 of Product M on hand. Each M requires 4 of Component N. There are 20 units of N on hand.
a. Calculate the net requirements for M
b. Calculate the gross requirements for N
c. Calculate the net requirements for N
(a) 110 - 30 = 80; (b) 80 x 4 = 320; 320 - 20 = 300
(MRP structure, easy)

119. The MPS calls for 110 units of Product A. There are currently 60 of Product A on hand. Each A requires 4 of Part B. There are 20 units of B available.
a. Calculate the net requirements for A
b. Calculate the gross requirements for B
c. Calculate the net requirements for B.
(a) 110 - 60 = 50; (b) 50 x 4 = 200; (c) 200 - 20 = 180
(MRP structure, easy)

120. The MPS calls for 50 units of Product A and 60 of B. There are currently 25 of Product B on hand. Each A requires 2 of Part C; each B requires 5 of C. There are 160 units of C available.
a. Calculate the net requirements for B
b. Calculate the gross requirements for C
c. Calculate the net requirements for C
(a) 35; (b) 50 x 2 + 35 x 5 = 275; (c) 275 - 160 = 115
(MRP structure, easy)

121. A product has the following gross requirements. Which is cheaper-lot for lot, part period balance, or EOQ lot sizing?

Week	1	2	3	4	5	6
Requirements	50	80	90	50	30	60

Other data for this scenario include: setup cost = $250, inventory holding cost $2 per week. There is no beginning inventory, there are no scheduled receipts.

Lot for lot will cost $250 x 6 = $1,500 for the six periods.

EOQ is based on 60 units per week demand: $\sqrt{\dfrac{2 \cdot 60 \cdot 250}{2}} = 122.47$

Annual setup costs = $\dfrac{60 \cdot 52}{122.47} \cdot 250 = 6369$;

Annual holding costs = $\dfrac{122.47}{2} \cdot 2 \cdot 52 = 6369$

Total annual costs = 12,738; Cost for six weeks = $12738 \cdot \dfrac{6}{52} = 1470$

For part period balancing, the EPP=250/2 = 125. Total cost for PPB over the six periods is $1,130.

Period	Order size	# of Units	CumPP	Setup cost	Holding cost
1	50	0	0		
1, 2	130	80	80*	250	160
1, 2, 3	220	90 * 2	260		
3	90	0	0		
3, 4	140	50	50		
3, 4, 5	170	30 * 2	110 *	250	220
3, 4, 5, 6	230	60 * 3	290		
6	60	0	0	250	0
			Total	750	380

Summary of costs: LFL = $1,500; EOQ = $1,470; PPB = $1,130. PPB is cheapest lot sizing model for this problem. (Lot-sizing techniques, moderate)

CHAPTER 15: SHORT-TERM SCHEDULING

TRUE/FALSE

1. Two of the criteria for effective scheduling are minimizing completion time and utilization.
   False (Scheduling issues, easy)

2. A good production planning and control system does not provide feedback on plant and production activities.
   False (Scheduling process-focused work center, moderate)

3. In forward scheduling, jobs are scheduled as late as possible within the time allowed by the customer due dates.
   False (Scheduling issues, moderate)

4. Scheduling is more complex in a job shop than in a repetitive manufacturing environment.
   True (Scheduling process-focused work center, moderate)

5. The Work Center Master File contains data such as capacity and efficiency.
   True (Scheduling process-focused work center, moderate)

6. Loading involves assigning jobs to work centers.
   True (Loading jobs in work centers, easy)

7. Gantt charts are useful for both loading and for scheduling tasks.
   True (Loading jobs in work centers, easy)

8. A Gantt load chart shows the loading and idle time of several departments, machines, or facilities.
   True (Loading jobs in work centers, moderate)

9. The assignment method provides an optimum, one-to-one assignment of jobs to resources.
   True (Loading jobs in work centers, easy)

10. The assignment method works for minimizing problems, but not for maximizing problems.
    False (Loading jobs in work centers, moderate)

11. Earliest Due Date is a shop floor dispatching (sequencing) rule that relates the time available to complete a job to the amount of work left to be completed.
    False (Sequencing jobs in work centers, moderate)

12. Dispatching rules are typically judged by four effectiveness criteria: average completion time, utilization, average number of jobs in the system, and average job lateness.
    True (Sequencing jobs in work centers, moderate)

13. The critical ratio sequencing rule prioritizes the jobs based on the importance or value of the customers who have placed the orders.
    False (Sequencing jobs in work centers, moderate)

14. The advantage of the First Come, First Serve rule is that it is dynamic and easily updated.
False (Sequencing jobs in work centers, moderate)

15. Johnson's rule (and its extensions) sequences a set of jobs through a set of operations where the operations must be performed in a specific order.
True (Sequencing jobs in work centers, moderate)

16. The Theory of Constraints is based on the desire to increase throughput.
True (Theory of constraints, moderate)

17. Work centers that limit the output of the entire production process are known as bottlenecks.
True (Theory of constraints, moderate)

18. Reduced floor-space requirements is one of the advantages of level material use.
True (Repetitive manufacturing, easy)

19. In services, the scheduling emphasis is usually on staffing.
True (Scheduling in services, easy)

20. Two elements that make service scheduling different from manufacturing scheduling are the absence of inventories in services, and the variable demand for labor in services.
True (Scheduling in services, moderate)

MULTIPLE CHOICE

21. Which of the following best describes how short-term schedules are prepared? Short-term schedules are prepared
    a. directly from the aggregate plans
    b. directly from the capacity plans
    c. from master schedules which are derived from aggregate plans
    d. from inventory records for items that have been used up
    e. from the purchasing plans
    c (Scheduling issues, moderate)

22. Which of the following is **true** regarding forward scheduling? Forward scheduling is the scheduling of
    a. the end items or finished products
    b. the start items or component parts
    c. the final operation first beginning with the due date
    d. jobs as soon as the requirements are known
    e. jobs according to their profit contributions
    d (Scheduling issues, moderate)

23. The scheduling activity
    a. assigns jobs to work centers
    b. specifies the order in which jobs should be done at each center
    c. is best handled with the assignment algorithm
    d. assigns due dates to specific jobs or operations steps
    e. occurs before aggregate planning
    d (Scheduling issues, moderate)

24. Which scheduling technique should be employed when due dates are important for a job order?
    a. forward scheduling
    b. backward scheduling
    c. loading
    d. dispatching
    e. master scheduling
    b (Scheduling issues, moderate)

25. Forward scheduling
    a. begins with a delivery date, then each operation is offset one at a time, in reverse order
    b. assumes that procurement of material and operations start as soon as requirements are known
    c. is well suited where the supplier is usually able to meet precise delivery dates
    d. tends to minimize in-process inventory
    e. produces a schedule only if it meets the due date
    b (Scheduling issues, moderate)

26. Which of the following is **not** an effectiveness criterion for scheduling?
    a. minimizing customer waiting time
    b. minimizing completion time
    c. maximizing flow time
    d. minimizing WIP inventory
    e. maximizing utilization
    c (Scheduling issues, moderate)

27. Which of these is **not** part of the planning files of a production planning and control system?
    a. a work center master file
    b. an item master file
    c. a routing file
    d. a progress file
    e. they are all part of the planning files
    d (Scheduling issues, moderate)

28. Which of the following files tracks work order progress?
    a. control files
    b. work center master files
    c. routing files
    d. item master files
    e. none of the above track work order progress
    a (Scheduling issues, moderate)

29. Which file contains important information regarding an item's flow through the shop?
    a. item master file
    b. routing file
    c. work center master file
    d. control files
    e. none of the above provide information regarding an item's flow through the shop
    b (Scheduling issues, moderate)

30. The production database containing information about each of the components that a firm produces or purchases is the
    a. item master file
    b. routing file
    c. work center master file
    d. control file
    e. none of the above
    a (Scheduling issues, moderate)

31. The short-term scheduling activity called **loading**
    a. assigns dates to specific jobs or operations steps
    b. assigns jobs to work centers
    c. specifies the order in which jobs should be done at each center
    d. assigns workers to jobs
    e. assigns workers to machines
    b (Loading jobs in work centers, easy)

32. The usual application of Gantt load charts is to show
    a. all the operations to be performed by a specific machine or work center
    b. loading and idle time of several departments, machines, or facilities
    c. all the operations to be performed on a specific product
    d. a time phased schedule of operations to be performed on a specific product
    e. which dispatching rule is more appropriate for a particular work center
    b (Loading jobs in work centers, moderate)

33. The assignment method is
    a. a computerized method of determining appropriate tasks for an operation
    b. a form of linear programming for optimally assigning tasks or jobs to resources
    c. the same thing as the Gantt schedule chart
    d. a method for achieving a balance between forward and backward scheduling
    e. a method to highlight overloads in a given work center
    b (Loading jobs in work centers, moderate)

34. Which of the following is an aid used to monitor jobs in process?
    a. a Gantt load chart
    b. a Gantt schedule chart
    c. the assignment method
    d. Johnson's Rule
    e. none of the above
    b (Loading jobs in work centers, moderate)

35. A scheduling technique used to achieve optimum, one-to-one matching of tasks and resources is
    a. the assignment method
    b. Johnson's rule
    c. the CDS Algorithm
    d. the appointment method
    e. the reservation method
    a (Loading jobs in work centers, moderate)

36. Orders are processed in the sequence in which they arrive if (the) _____ rule sequences the jobs.
    a. earliest due date
    b. first come, first serve
    c. slack time remaining
    d. critical ratio
    e. Johnson's
    b (Scheduling jobs in work centers, moderate)

37. Which of the following dispatching rules ordinarily tends to give the best results when the criterion is lowest time for completion of the full sequence of jobs?
    a. shortest processing time (SPT)
    b. first in, still here (FISH)
    c. first in, first out (FIFO)
    d. first come, first serve (FCFS)
    e. longest processing time
    a (Scheduling jobs in work centers, moderate)

38. If an assignment problem consists of 6 workers and 7 projects,
    a. one worker will not get a project assignment
    b. one project will not get a worker assigned
    c. one worker will be assigned two projects
    d. each worker will contribute work toward the seventh project
    e. the problem cannot be solved by assignment method
    b (Loading jobs in work centers, moderate)

39. Sequencing (or dispatching)
    a. assigns dates to specific jobs or operations steps
    b. assigns jobs to work centers
    c. specifies the order in which jobs should be done at each center
    d. assigns workers to jobs
    e. assigns workers to machines
    c (Scheduling jobs in work centers, moderate)

40. Five jobs (A, B, C, D, E) are waiting to be processed. Their processing times and due dates are given below. Using the **shortest processing time** dispatching rule, in which order should the jobs be processed?

Job	Processing Time (days)	Job due date (days)
A	4	7
B	2	4
C	8	11
D	3	5
E	5	8

    a.   A, B, C, D, E
    b.   C, E, A, D, B
    c.   B, D, A, E, C
    d.   B, D, E, A, C
    e.   C, E, A, D, B

c (Scheduling jobs in work centers, moderate)

41. Five jobs are waiting to be processed. Their processing times and due dates are given below. Using the **earliest due date** dispatching rule, in which order should the jobs be processed?

Job	Processing Time (days)	Job due date (days)
A	4	8
B	2	4
C	8	11
D	3	5
E	5	7

    a.   C, E, A, D, B
    b.   A, B, C, D, E
    c.   B, D, A, E, C
    d.   C, B, A, E, D
    e.   none of the above

e (Scheduling jobs in work centers, moderate)

42. Flowtime represents the time
    a. an order spends waiting for processing at a workcenter
    b. an order spends being processed at a workcenter
    c. to complete an order, including time spent in processing and in waiting
    d. an order spends moving from one workcenter to another
    e. None of the above

c (Scheduling jobs in work centers, moderate)

43. Average completion time for a schedule sequence at a work center is total
    a. processing time divided by the number of jobs
    b. flow time divided by the number of jobs
    c. flow time divided by total processing time
    d. processing time plus total late time divided by number of jobs
    e. flow time plus total late time divided by number of jobs
    b (Scheduling jobs in work centers, moderate)

44. Which of the following dispatching rules tends to minimize job flowtime?
    a. FCFS: first come, first served
    b. EDD: earliest due date
    c. SPT: shortest processing time
    d. LPT: longest processing time
    e. FCLS: first come, last served
    c (Scheduling jobs in work centers, moderate)

45. Five welding jobs are waiting to be processed. Their processing times and due dates are given below. Using the **critical ratio** dispatching rule, in which order should the jobs be processed?

Job	Processing Time (days)	Job due date (days)
A	4	7
B	2	4
C	8	11
D	3	5
E	5	8

    a. B, D, A, E, C
    b. A, E, C, D, B
    c. C, E, A, D, B
    d. C, E, D, A, B
    e. none of the above
    d (Scheduling jobs in work centers, moderate)

46. The priority rule which processes jobs according to the smallest ratio of due date to processing time is:
    a. critical ratio
    b. earliest due date
    c. first come, first serve
    d. longest processing time
    e. shortest processing time
    a (Scheduling jobs in work centers, moderate)

47. Which of the following dispatching rules allows easy updates?
    a. FCFS: first come, first served
    b. CR: critical ratio
    c. SPT: shortest processing time
    d. EDD: earliest due date
    e. LPT: longest processing time
    b (Scheduling jobs in work centers, moderate)

48. Which of the following is an advantage of the FCFS dispatching rule when used in services?
    a. FCFS is easy to update
    b. FCFS minimizes the average number of jobs in the system
    c. FCFS minimizes the average lateness of all jobs
    d. FCFS maximizes the number of jobs completed on time
    e. FCFS seems fair to customers
    e (Scheduling jobs in work centers, moderate)

49. The most appropriate sequencing rule to use if the goal is to dynamically track the progress of jobs and establish relative priority on a common basis is
    a. shortest processing time
    b. earliest due date
    c. longest processing time
    d. critical ratio
    e. Johnson's rule
    d (Scheduling jobs in work centers, moderate)

50. Which of the following dispatching rules is typically the best technique for taking first those jobs with the most urgent needs?
    a. shortest processing time
    b. critical ratio
    c. earliest due date
    d. longest processing time
    e. none of the above
    e (Scheduling jobs in work centers, moderate)

51. Use of the sequencing rule Shortest Processing Time generally results in
    a. minimum average flowtime
    b. minimum average lateness
    c. maximum utilization
    d. maximum effectiveness
    e. none of the above
    a (Scheduling jobs in work centers, moderate)

52. When a set of jobs must pass through two workstations whose sequence is fixed, _____ is the rule most commonly applied.
    a. earliest due date rule
    b. first come, first serve rule
    c. slack time remaining
    d. critical ratio
    e. Johnson's Rule
    e (Scheduling jobs in work centers, moderate)

53. A recent advance in short term scheduling that makes use of expert systems and simulation in solving dynamic scheduling problems is
    a. forward scheduling
    b. finite scheduling
    c. backward scheduling
    d. infinite scheduling
    e. progressive scheduling
    b (Finite scheudling, moderate)

54. Which of the following techniques does **not** contribute to increasing throughput at a bottleneck?
    a. increase capacity of constraint
    b. have cross-trained employees available to operate the constraint
    c. develop alternate routings
    d. move inspections and tests to a position immediately after the bottleneck
    e. schedule throughput to match capacity of the bottleneck
    d (Theory of constraints, moderate)

55. An appliance manufacturer assembles icemakers in large batches. The operations manager would like to significantly reduce the batch size. What would you suggest?
    a. use the SPT rule
    b. use forward scheduling
    c. use Gantt charts
    d. develop level material use schedules
    e. use finite scheduling
    d (Repetitive manufacturing, moderate)

56. A firm wants to develop a level material use schedule based on the following data. What should be the set-up cost?

desired lot size:	60
annual demand:	40,000
holding cost:	$20 per unit per year
daily production rate:	320
# of work days per year:	250

    a. $0.45
    b. $4.50
    c. $45
    d. $450
    e. $500
    a (Repetitive manufacturing, moderate)

57. Factory X is trying to use level use scheduling. If their first target were to cut the current lot size in half, by what proportion must setup cost change?
   a. setup cost must also be cut in half from its current value
   b. setup cost must double from its current value
   c. setup cost must be cut to one fourth its current value
   d. cannot be determined
   e. none of the above
   c (Repetitive manufacturing, moderate)

58. Which of the following is **true** regarding services scheduling?
   a. the emphasis is on staffing levels, not materials
   b. reservation systems are often used a means of manipulating the supply of services
   c. labor use can be intensive, and labor demand is usually stable
   d. the Critical Ratio sequencing rule is widely used for fairness to customers
   e. all of the above are true
   a (Scheduling in services, moderate)

Fill-In-The Blank

59. _____ scheduling begins as soon as the requirements are known.
   Forward (Scheduling issues, moderate)

60. _____ scheduling begins with the due date and schedules the final operation first and the other job steps in reverse order.
   Backward (Scheduling issues, moderate)

61. _____ is a system that allow operations personnel to manage facility work flows by tracking work added to a work center and its work completed.
   Input-output control (Loading jobs in work centers, moderate)

62. _____ is the assignment of jobs to work or processing centers.
   Loading (Loading jobs in work centers, easy)

63. _____ are used to schedule resources and allocate time.
   Gantt charts (Loading jobs in work centers, moderate)

64. The _____ is a special class of linear programming models that involves assigning tasks or jobs to resources.
   assignment method (Loading jobs in work centers, moderate)

65. _____ determines the order in which jobs should be done at each work center.
   Sequencing (Sequencing jobs in work centers, easy)

66. _____ determine the sequence of jobs in process-oriented facilities.
   Priority rules (Sequencing jobs in work centers, easy)

67. _____ uses computerized short-term scheduling to overcome the disadvantages of rule-based systems by providing the user with graphical interactive computing.
   Finite scheduling (Finite scheduling, moderate)

68. The _____ is a body of knowledge that deals with anything that limits an organization's ability to achieve its goals.
theory of constraints (Theory of constraints, moderate)

69. A _____ is an operation that limits output in the production sequence.
bottleneck (Theory of constraints, moderate)

70. _____ means frequent, high-quality, small lot sizes that contribute to just-in-time production.
Level material use (Repetitive manufacturing, moderate)

SHORT ANSWERS

71. List the benefits of good scheduling.
Lower costs, faster delivery, and dependable delivery. (The strategic importance of short-term scheduling, easy)

72. List those factors that complicate scheduling.
Machine breakdowns, absenteeism, quality problems, and shortages. (Scheduling issues, moderate)

73. Explain, in your own words, how backward scheduling and forward scheduling differ.
Forward scheduling starts the schedule as soon as the requirements are known. Backward scheduling begins with the due date, scheduling the final operation first and proceeding in the reverse order. (Scheduling issues, moderate)

74. What is the overall objective of scheduling?
To optimize the use of resources so that production objectives are met. (Scheduling issues, moderate)

75. List the four criteria presented in the text for determining the effectiveness of a **scheduling** decision. How do these criteria relate to the four criteria for **sequencing** decisions?
Minimizing completion time, maximizing utilization, minimizing work-in-process inventory, and minimizing customer waiting time. There is a one-to-one correspondence minimizing completion time = minimizing flowtime, etc. (Scheduling issues, moderate)

76. What factors makes a job shop different from an assembly line factory?
They differ in materials used, order of processing, processing requirements, time of processing, and in setup requirements. (Scheduling issues, moderate)

77. List the types of planning files used in scheduling decisions. Which are used in manual systems, and which are used in automated systems?
The three types are item master files, routing files, and work center master files. All three are used in both systems. (Scheduling issues, moderate)

78. Describe what is meant by "loading" work centers? What are the two ways work centers can be loaded? What are two techniques used in loading?

Loading is the assignment of jobs to work processing centers. Work centers can be loaded by capacity or by assigning specific jobs to specific work centers. Gantt charts and assignment method are loading techniques. (Loading jobs in work centers, moderate)

79. List the disadvantages of the Gantt load chart.

It does not account for production variability such as unexpected breakdowns or human errors that require reworking a job, and it must be updated regularly to account for new jobs and revised time estimates. (Loading jobs in work centers, moderate)

80. List five dispatching rules (sequencing rules) found in your text.

FCFS-first come, first served; EDD-earliest due date; SPT-shortest processing time; LPT-longest processing time; and CR-critical ratio. (Sequencing jobs in work centers, moderate)

81. Which shop floor scheduling rule would you prefer to apply if you are the leader of the only team of experts charged with the defusing of several time bombs which are scattered throughout your building. You can see the bombs; they are of different types. You can tell how long each one will take to defuse. Discuss.

Most students will go for EDD, to gain minimum lateness. Others will go for SPT, on the grounds that the team can't afford to tackle a job with an early due date and a long processing time. Interesting to see student assumptions about sequence, damage, etc. (Sequencing jobs in work centers, difficult)

82. Utilization, in some views, might be taken to mean that percentage of the time that a facility, a resource, a worker, etc., was effectively occupied. Is that the case with utilization as a measure of the effectiveness of job sequencing? Explain.

No, it is not the same concept. Rather, it is a measure of what percent of jobs in the system are being worked on-some jobs are being "utilized," others are not. In sequencing, the assumption is that the machinery is busy and that the jobs may not be. (Sequencing jobs in work centers, moderate)

83. State the four effectiveness measures for dispatching rules.

Average completion time, average number of jobs in the system, average job lateness, and utilization. (Sequencing jobs in work centers, moderate)

84. In retail outlets, customers are usually processed on a first come, first served basis. Why? Is the express lane in the supermarket an exception? Craft a sequencing rule to explain express lane behavior.

Because all customers are considered equally important, and none should be given a higher priority. Most students will write a rule like "FCFS, except for very short processing times." "8 items or less" is a proxy for processing time. (Sequencing jobs in work centers, moderate)

85. What is the primary disadvantage of the shortest processing time dispatch rule? Is this a problem if there can be no new jobs arriving after the sequence is set?

As new jobs arrive, new short-duration jobs will push back existing long-duration jobs in priority in favor of short-duration jobs. If newly arriving jobs must wait for a new sequence to be built, this is less problematic. (Sequencing jobs in work centers, moderate)

86. What are some limitations of Rule-Based Scheduling systems? What alternatives are there to Rules-Based Scheduling Systems?

Three limitations are (1) Rules need to be revised to adjust to changes in process, equipment, product mix, etc.; (2) Rules do not look at upstream or downstream, and (3) Rules do not look beyond due dates. Finite scheduling is one recently-developed option. (Limitations of rule-based dispatching systems, easy)

87. Can the reading of the sections of a daily paper be analyzed as a shop floor scheduling problem? Consider the case of n readers of m sections, where the ith reader spends time t_{ij} reading section j. Is Johnson's rule appropriate? Is the work flow unidirectional? What is the objective of the system? What dispatch rule would you suggest for this problem? A simple example may help.

The problem does not fit Johnson's Rule, because there is no sequence to the sections. The problem is an interesting one, because there seems to be considerable conflict over timely access to sections of the newspaper (or some other multi-part report or object). Students will offer various objectives, including those based on flowtime, utilization, and lateness. Students will craft various rules, including those that favor faster readers, those that pay attention to popular sections, etc. (Sequencing jobs in work centers, difficult)

88. State the five-step process that serves as the basis of the Theory of Constraints.

1. identify the constraints.
2. develop a plan for overcoming the identified constraints.
3. focus resources on accomplishing step 2.
4. reduce the effects of the constraints by off loading work or by expanding capacity. Make sure that the constraints are recognized by all those who can have impact upon them.
5. once a set of constraints is overcome, go back to step 1 and identify new constraints.
(Theory of constraints, moderate)

89. What are the techniques available to operations managers to deal with a bottleneck operation? Which of these does not increase throughput?

1. increasing capacity of the constraint
2. ensuring that well-trained and cross-trained employees are available to operate and maintain the work center causing the constraint
3. developing alternate routings, processing procedures, or subcontractor
4. moving inspections and tests to a position just before the constraint
5. scheduling throughput to match the capacity of the bottleneck
The last technique may involve off-loading work from the bottleneck, scheduling less, meaning that the bottleneck itself gained no capacity, and no more throughput was accomplished through the bottleneck. (Theory of constraints, moderate)

90. In repetitive manufacturing, what are the advantages of level material use? Does level material use have any role in intermittent process facilities?

The five advantages are
1. lower inventory levels, which release capital for other uses
2. faster product throughput
3. improved component quality and hence improved product quality
4. reduced floor-space requirements
5. improved communication among employees because they are closer together
6. smoother production process because large lots have not "hidden" the problems
Intermittent (job shop) facilities have so many additional sources of variation (materials, requirements, workcenter order, etc.) that there is little role for level material use. (Repetitive manufacturing, moderate)

91. Explain, in your own words, what is meant by "level material use." In what types of facilities is it appropriate? Explain.

It means frequent, high quality, small lot sizes that contribute to just-in-time production. It is appropriate in repetitive processing, not in intermittent processing, because repetitive processing has much more predictable material and processing needs. (Repetitive manufacturing, moderate)

92. In what three ways does the problem of scheduling service systems differ from that of scheduling manufacturing systems?

1. In manufacturing, emphasis is on materials, whereas in services it is on staffing levels
2. service systems do not store inventories of services
3. services are very labor intensive, and demand for this labor can be highly variable
(Scheduling for services, moderate)

PROBLEMS

93. Jack's Refrigeration Repair Service is under contract to repair, recondition, and/or refurbish commercial and industrial icemakers from restaurants, seafood processors, and similar organizations. Jack currently has five jobs to be scheduled, shown in the order in which they arrived.

Job	Processing Time (hours)	Due (hours)
V	30	50
W	10	35
X	40	90
Y	15	35
Z	50	75

a. Complete the following table. (Show your supporting calculations below).
b. Which dispatching rule has the best score for flow time?
c. Which dispatching rule has the best score for work-in-process (jobs in the system)?
d. Which dispatching rule has the best score for lateness?
e. What dispatching rule would **you** select? Support your decision.

Dispatching Rule	Job sequence	Flow time	Average Time per Job	Average number of jobs	Average lateness
FCFS					
SPT					
EDD					
CR					

SPT best on all three criteria: flowtime, work-in-process, and lateness. Most students will select SPT as quite obvious; note that EDD is a close second in all criteria. See POM for Windows solution below for supporting work.

Dispatching Rule	Job sequence	Flow time	Average Time per Job	Average number of jobs	Average lateness
FCFS	V, W, X, Y, Z	390	78	2.69	27
SPT	W, Y, V, X, Z	330	66	2.28	16
EDD	W, Y, V, Z, X	340	68	2.34	18
CR	Z, V, X, Y, W	530	106	3.66	54

Method: SPT - Shortest Processing Time
Starting Day Number: 0

	Machine1	Due Date	Order	Flow time	Late
V	30	50	3	55	5
W	10	35	1	10	0
X	40	90	4	95	5
Y	15	35	2	25	0
Z	50	75	5	145	70
Total				330	80
Average				66	16

Sequence of jobs: W,Y,V,X,Z Average # jobs in system = 2.275862

Method: FCFS - First Come First Serve

	Machine1	Due Date	Order	Flow time	Late
V	30	50	1	30	0
W	10	35	2	40	5
X	40	90	3	80	0
Y	15	35	4	95	60
Z	50	75	5	145	70
Total				390	135
Average				78	27

Sequence of jobs: V,W,X,Y,Z Average # jobs in system = 2.689655

Method: Due Date - Due date; earliest to latest date

	Machine1	Due Date	Slack	Order	Flow time	Late
V	30	50	0	3	55	5
W	10	35	0	1	10	0
X	40	90	0	5	145	55
Y	15	35	0	2	25	0
Z	50	75	0	4	105	30
Total					340	90
Average					68	18

Sequence of jobs: W,Y,V,Z,X Average # jobs in system = 2.344828

Method: Critical ratio - (due date-today)/processing time

	Machine1	Due Date	CR	Order	Flow time	Late
V	30	50	1.6667	2	80	30
W	10	35	3.5	5	145	110
X	40	90	2.25	3	120	30
Y	15	35	2.3333	4	135	100
Z	50	75	1.5	1	50	0
Total					530	270
Average					106	54

Sequence of jobs: Z,V,X,Y,W Average # jobs in system = 3.655172
(Sequencing jobs in work centers, moderate)

94. The operations manager of a body and paint shop has five cars to schedule for repair. He would like to minimize the throughput time (makespan) to compete all work on these cars. Each car requires body work prior to painting. The estimates of the times required to do the body and paint work on each are as follows:

Car	Body Work (Hours)	Paint (Hours)
A	8	2
B	6	4
C	7	5
D	3	4
E	2	7

Chart the progress of these five jobs through the two centers on the basis of the arbitrary order A ⇒ B ⇒ C ⇒ D ⇒ E. After how many hours will all jobs be completed?

Body Work										
Paint										
	5	10	15	20	25	30	35	40	45	50

a. Use Johnson's Rule to sequence these five jobs for minimum total duration. Show your work in determining job sequence.
b. The optimal sequence is _____.
c. Chart the progress of the five jobs in this optimal sequence.
d. After how many hours will all jobs be completed?

Body Work	A	B	C	D	E					
Paint		A	B		C	D	E	37		
	5	10	15	20	25	30	35	40	45	50

POM for Windows printout:

	Body Work	Paint		Done 1	Done 2 (flow time)
Car A	8	2	fifth	26	28
Car B	6	4	fourth	18	22
Car C	7	5	third	12	18
Car D	3	4	second	5	13
Car E	2	7	first	2	9

Sequence of jobs: Car E, Car D, Car C, Car B, Car A Makespan = 28

Johnson's Method Steps

Step	Task added	Position
1	Car A	5
2	Car E	1
3	Car D	2
4	Car B	4
5	Car C	3

Chart of optimum solution:

Body and Paint Shop
Gantt Chart

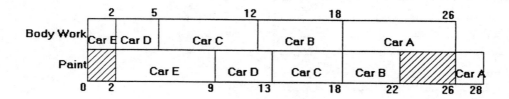

(Sequencing jobs in work centers, moderate)

95. The president of a consulting firm wants to minimize the total number of hours it will take to complete four projects for a new client. Accordingly, she has estimated the time it should take for each of her top consultants -- Charlie, Gerald, Johnny, and Rick -- to complete any of the four projects, as follows:

Consultant	Project (hours)			
	A	B	C	D
Charlie	13	16	11	13
Gerald	11	15	10	12
Johnny	15	22	12	15
Rick	17	17	12	22

a. In how many different ways can she assign these consultants to these projects?
b. What is the total number of hours required by the following arbitrary assignment?
Charlie $\Rightarrow$ A; Gerald $\Rightarrow$ D; Johnny $\Rightarrow$ B; Rick $\Rightarrow$ C
c. What is the optimal assignment of consultants to projects? (Use the assignment method; **SHOW YOUR WORK!**)
d. For the optimal schedule, what is the total number of hours it will take these consultants to complete these projects?
e. What is the significance, if any, of the fact that Gerald is the best performer at all four projects?
(a) 4! Or 24 ways. (b) 13+12+22+12=59 hours. (c) POM for Windows printout (d) 53 hours. (e) Each person must get exactly one assignment. Note that Gerald does not get one assignment at which he is absolutely most productive (C). Optimum assignment is about opportunity cost, not absolute high or low values.

Objective: Minimize

	Project A	**Project B**	**Project C**	**Project D**
Charlie			1	ASSIGN
Gerald	ASSIGN	1	2	1
Johnny	0	4	ASSIGN	
Rick	3	ASSIGN	1	8

(Loading jobs in work centers, moderate)

356

96. The following jobs are waiting to be processed at your work center, which cleans valve body castings. Job numbers are assigned sequentially upon arrival in the facility (a missing number means that job does not require your workcenter). All dates are specified as days from present.

Job	Due Date	Duration (days)
101	34	10
102	43	7
104	37	11
107	39	5
108	37	15

a. In what sequence should the jobs be processed according to the FCFS scheduling rule?
b. In what sequence should the jobs be processed according to the EDD scheduling rule?
c. In what sequence should the jobs be processed according to the SPT scheduling rule?
d. In what sequence should the jobs be processed according to the LPT scheduling rule?
e. In what sequence should the jobs be processed according to the Critical Ratio scheduling rule?
FCFS: 101, 102, 104, 107, 108
EDD: 101, 104 and 108 (tie), 107, 102
SPT: 107, 102, 101, 104, 108
LPT: 108, 104, 101, 102, 107
CR: 108 (2.47), 104 (3.36), 101 (3.4), 102 (6.14), 107 (7.8)
(Sequencing jobs in work centers, moderate)

97. The following jobs are waiting to be processed at a machine center. This machine center has relatively long backlog and sets fresh schedules every two weeks, which do not disturb earlier schedules. Below are the jobs received during the previous two weeks. They are ready to be scheduled today, which is day 241. Job names refer to names of clients and contract numbers.

Job	Date Job Received	Production Days Needed	Date Job Due
CX-01	225	25	270
BR-02	228	15	300
DE-06	230	35	320
SY-11	231	30	310
RG-05	235	40	360

a. Complete the following table. (Show your supporting calculations below).
b. Which dispatching rule has the best score for flow time?
c. Which dispatching rule has the best score for utilization?
d. Which dispatching rule has the best score for lateness?
e. What dispatching rule would you select? Support your decision.

Dispatching Rule	Job sequence	Flow time	Utilization	Average number of jobs	Average lateness
EDD					
SPT					
LPT					

The best flowtime is EDD; best utilization is SPT; best lateness is EDD. Student could support either of these choices. LPT scores poorly on all three criteria. POM for Windows solution below.

Dispatching Rule	Job sequence	Flow time	Utilization	Average number of jobs	Average lateness
EDD	BX-BR-SY-DE-RG	385	37.6%	2.66	10
SPT	BR-CX-SY-DE-RG	375	38.6%	2.59	12
LPT	RG-DE-SY-CX-BR	495	29.3%	3.41	44

Method: SPT - Shortest Processing Time
Starting Day Number: 241

	Machine1	Due Date	Order	Flow time	Completion Time	Late
CX-01	25	270	2	40	180	10
BR-02	15	300	1	15	255	0
DE-06	35	320	4	105	345	25
SY-11	30	310	3	70	310	0
RG-05	40	360	5	145	385	25
Total				375	4,710	60
Average				75	942	12

Sequence:BR-02,CX-01,SY-11,DE-06,RG-05 Average # in system = 2.586207

Method: LPT - Longest processing time

	Machine1	Due Date	Order	Flow time	Completion Time	Late
CX-01	25	270	4	130	370	100
BR-02	15	300	5	145	385	85
DE-06	35	320	2	75	315	0
SY-11	30	310	3	105	345	35
RG-05	40	360	1	40	280	0
Total				495	1,695	220
Average				99	339	44

Sequence: RG-05,DE-06,SY-11,CX-01,BR-02 Average # in system = 3.413793

Method: Due Date - Due date; earliest to latest date

	Machine1	Due Date	Slack	Order	Flow time	Late
CX-01	25	270	0	1	25	0
BR-02	15	300	0	2	40	0
DE-06	35	320	0	4	105	25
SY-11	30	310	0	3	70	0
RG-05	40	360	0	5	145	25
Total					385	50
Average					77	10

Sequence: CX-01,BR-02,SY-11,DE-06,RG-05 Average # in system = 2.655172
(Sequencing jobs in work centers, moderate)

98. The following set of jobs is to be processed through two work centers, in sequence (Operation 1 before Operation 2). Processing time at each of the work centers is shown below.

Job	Operation 1 hours	Operation 2 hours
T	15	3
U	7	9
V	4	10
W	7	6
X	10	9
Y	4	5
Z	7	8

a. What is the optimal sequence for these jobs be scheduled?
b. Chart these jobs through the two workcenters.
c. What is the makespan of this optimal solution?

The jobs should be processed in the sequence V-Y-U-Z-X-W-T for a makespan of 57.

Job Shop Scheduling Results					
		Job Shop Scheduling			
	Machine1	Machine2		Done 1	Done 2 (flow time)
T	15.	3.	seventh	54.	57.
U	7.	9.	third	15.	28.
V	4.	10.	first	4.	14.
W	7.	6.	sixth	39.	51.
X	10.	9.	fifth	32.	45.
Y	4.	5.	second	8.	19.
Z	7.	8.	fourth	22.	36.
Makespan					57.

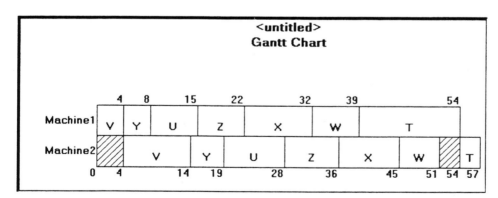

<untitled>
Gantt Chart

(Sequencing jobs in work centers, moderate)

99. Use the following data to prepare for level material use. The firm uses a work-year of 305 days.

Annual demand	30500
Daily demand	100
Daily production	800
Desired lot size (2 hours of production)	200
Holding cost per unit per year	$10

a. What is the setup cost, based on the desired lot size?
b. What is the setup time, based on $40 per hour setup labor?

Using the model $S = \dfrac{Q^2 * H * (1 - d/p)}{2D}$

$$= \frac{200^2 * 10 * (1 - 100/800)}{2 * 30500}$$

S =   **$5.74**
Setup time = 8.61 min
(Repetitive manufacturing, moderate)

100. Lockport Marine Services, Inc., wishes to assign a set of jobs to a set of machines. The following table provides data on the value of production of each job when performed on a specific machine.
 a. Determine the set of assignments that maximizes production value.
 b. What is the total production value of your assignments?

	Machine			
Job	**A**	**B**	**C**	**D**
1	27	29	28	30
2	30	29	27	26
3	31	25	29	26
4	29	31	25	28

POM for Windows solution below.

Assignments				_ □ ✕
Lockport Marine Solution				
Optimal profit = **$120**	Machine1	Machine2	Machine3	Machine4
Job 1	27.	29.	28.	Assign 30
Job 2	Assign 30	29.	27.	26.
Job 3	31.	25.	Assign 29	26.
Job 4	29.	Assign 31	25.	28.

(Loading jobs in work centers, moderate)

101. At Morgan's Transformer Rebuilding, a set of five jobs is ready now for dispatching to a machine center. The processing times and due dates for the jobs are given in the table below.

Job	Work Time (days)	Due Date (days)
A	15	38
B	13	30
C	12	20
D	18	52
E	9	15

Determine, using the SPT priority rule
a. the sequence in which the jobs should be dispatched
b. the average completion time
c. the average job lateness
d. the average number of jobs in the machine center
e. the utilization of the machine center
POM for Windows solution below.

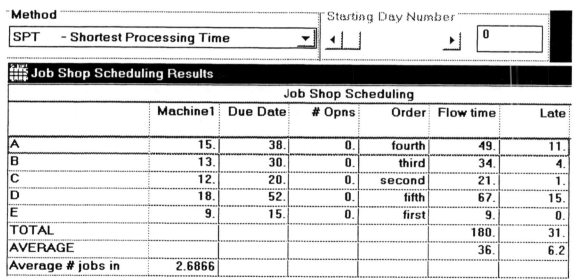

Method

SPT   - Shortest Processing Time

Starting Day Number   0

Job Shop Scheduling Results

	Machine1	Due Date	# Opns	Order	Flow time	Late
A	15.	38.	0.	fourth	49.	11.
B	13.	30.	0.	third	34.	4.
C	12.	20.	0.	second	21.	1.
D	18.	52.	0.	fifth	67.	15.
E	9.	15.	0.	first	9.	0.
TOTAL					180.	31.
AVERAGE					36.	6.2
Average # jobs in	2.6866					

(Sequencing jobs in work centers, moderate)

102. At Morgan's Transformer Rebuilding, a set of five jobs is ready now for dispatching to a machine center. The processing times and due dates for the jobs are given in the table below.

Job	Work Time (days)	Due Date (days)
A	15	38
B	13	30
C	12	20
D	18	52
E	9	15

Determine, using the EDD priority rule
a. the sequence in which the jobs should be dispatched
b. the average completion time
c. the average job lateness
d. the average number of jobs in the machine center
e. the utilization of the machine center
POM for Windows solution below.

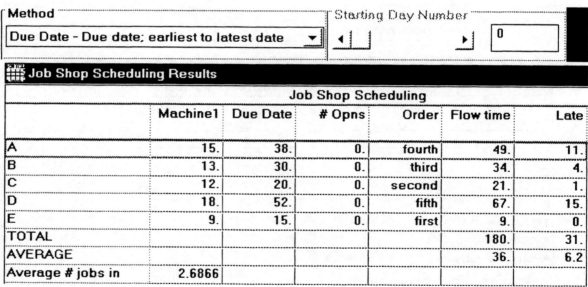

Method
Due Date – Due date: earliest to latest date ▼

Starting Day Number ◄ | ► | 0 |

Job Shop Scheduling Results

	Machine1	Due Date	# Opns	Order	Flow time	Late
A	15.	38.	0.	fourth	49.	11.
B	13.	30.	0.	third	34.	4.
C	12.	20.	0.	second	21.	1.
D	18.	52.	0.	fifth	67.	15.
E	9.	15.	0.	first	9.	0.
TOTAL					180.	31.
AVERAGE					36.	6.2
Average # jobs in	2.6866					

(**Sequencing jobs in work centers, moderate**)

103. Use Johnson's rule to determine the optimal sequencing for the five jobs to be processed on two machines in a fixed order (Machine 1 before Machine 2). The processing times are given in the table below.
a. What is the optimal sequence?
b. What is the makespan for this sequence?

Job	Machine 1	Machine 2
L	5	11
M	7	12
N	13	9
O	12	6
P	10	8

POM for Windows solution below.

Job Shop Scheduling Results

	Machine1	Machine2		Done 1	Done 2 (flow time)
			Job Shop Scheduling		
A	5.	11.	first	5.	16.
B	7.	12.	second	12.	28.
C	13.	9.	third	25.	37.
D	12.	6.	fifth	47.	53.
E	10.	8.	fourth	35.	45.
Makespan					53.

(Sequencing jobs in work centers, moderate)

363

104. A firm that specializes in desktop publishing for local charities has agreed to take on the following jobs. The firm has not decided which dispatching rule to apply in order to prioritize the jobs and fix them into the schedule.

Job name	A	B	C	D	E	F
Time required	5	4	3	1	3	2
Due date (days from now)	17	10	16	2	6	3

a. Complete the following table. Show your supporting calculations below.
b. Which dispatching rule has the best score for flow time?
c. Which dispatching rule has the best score for work-in-process (jobs in the system)?
d. Which dispatching rule has the best score for lateness?
e. Is there ANY sequence that can avoid all lateness? Explain or provide an example.

Dispatching Rule	Job sequence	Flow time	Utilization	Average number of jobs	Average lateness
EDD					
SPT					
LPT					

POM for Windows solution below. SPT is best for flowtime, and for average jobs in system; EDD is best for lateness. There is no solution that can avoid some lateness, since there are only 17 days to do 18 days work.

Dispatching Rule	Job sequence	Flow time	Utilization	Average number of jobs	Average lateness
EDD	D-F-E-B-C-A	51	8.5	2.83	0.17
SPT	D-F-C-E-B-A	50	8.33	2.78	1.17
LPT	F-D-E-B-A-C	54	9.0	3.00	0.5

Method: SPT - Shortest Processing Time

	Machine1	Due Date	Order	Flow time	Late
A	5	17	6	18	1
B	4	10	5	13	3
C	3	16	3	6	0
D	1	2	1	1	0
E	3	6	4	9	3
F	2	3	2	3	0
Total				50	7
Average				8.3333	1.1667

Average # jobs in system = 2.777778
Sequence of jobs D,F,C,E,B,A

Method: Due Date - Due date; earliest to latest date

	Machine1	Due Date	Order	Flow time	Late
A	5	17	6	18	1
B	4	10	4	10	0
C	3	16	5	13	0
D	1	2	1	1	0
E	3	6	3	6	0
F	2	3	2	3	0

Total   51   1
Average   8.5   1.1667
Average # jobs in system = 2.833333
Sequence of jobs: D,F,E,B,C,A

Method: Crit rat - (due date-today)/processing time
Starting Day Number: 0

	Machine1	Due Date	CR	Order	Flow time	Late
A	5	17	3.4	5	15	0
B	4	10	2.5	4	10	0
C	3	16	5.3333	6	18	2
D	1	2	2	2	3	1
E	3	6	2	3	6	0
F	2	3	1.5	1	2	0

Total   54   3
Average   9   0.5
Average # jobs in system = 3
Sequence of jobs: F,D,E,B,A,C
(Sequencing jobs in work centers, moderate)

105. Bob Dresser operates a major appliance warranty service center. His operation has two check stations that are required at the end of every repair task performed by his appliance repair staff. These are the Functionality Review (FR) and the Overall Scan (OS). The FR must be performed successfully before the OS is begun. On Friday morning, six repair jobs are completed, awaiting these two inspection activities. Processing times are given in minutes.

	Job					
	A	B	C	D	E	F
FR	50	35	25	20	15	10
OS	30	60	20	40	20	25

a. What is the optimal sequence of jobs for the objective of minimizing the makespan?
b. Show your work, and document the sequence.
c. Chart the solution to this problem.
d. What jobs are being processed at time period 90?
e. What is the makespan of this problem?

FR	
OS	

| | 20 | 40 | 60 | 80 | 100 | 120 | 140 | 160 | 180 | 200 |

POM for Windows solution below.

Job Shop Scheduling Results

Job Shop Scheduling					
	FR	OS		Done 1	Done 2 (flow time)
A	50.	30.	fifth	130.	185.
B	35.	60.	fourth	80.	155.
C	25.	20.	sixth	155.	205.
D	20.	40.	third	45.	95.
E	15.	20.	second	25.	55.
F	10.	25.	first	10.	35.
Makespan					205.

Bob Dresser
Gantt Chart

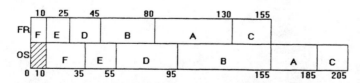

Johnson's Method Steps

Bob Dresser Solution		
Step	JOB	Position
1	F	1.
2	E	2.
3	C	6.
4	D	3.
5	A	5.
6	B	4.

d) Job A is being processed at FR, while Job D is being processed at OS C) the makespan is 205. (Sequencing jobs in work centers, moderate)

106. Machines A, B, C, and D have been in use for several years, while machine E is new. The following table provides data on the value of production of each job when performed on a specific machine.

a. Determine the set of assignments that maximizes production value.

b. What is the total production value of your assignments?

c. Which machine should be retired (i.e., gets no assignment)?

d. If they do retire one machine, will they be as profitable without it as with it? Explain.

Job	Machine				
	A	B	C	D	E
1	27	29	28	30	40
2	30	29	27	26	46
3	31	25	29	26	37
4	29	31	25	28	28

C gets no assignment, and should be the machine retired. POM for Windows solution below.

Taking away what was arguably the least productive machine still reduces the options available to the firm, and alters the opportunity costs. They cannot be better off without the machine, and, as this case, shows, they become worse off. (However, they are better off with four machines ABDE than with four machines BCDE).

Assignments					
Lockport Marine–B Solution					
Optimal profit = $138	MachineA	MachineB	MachineC	MachineD	MachineE
Job 1	27.	29.	28.	Assign 30	40.
Job 2	30.	29.	27.	26.	Assign 46
Job 3	Assign 31	25.	29.	26.	37.
Job 4	29.	Assign 31	25.	28.	28.
Job 5 (nonexistent)	0.	0.	Assign 0	0.	0.

Assignments				
Lockport Marine–B Solution				
Optimal profit = $136	MachineB	MachineC	MachineD	MachineE
Job 1	29.	28.	Assign 30	40.
Job 2	29.	27.	26.	Assign 46
Job 3	25.	Assign 29	26.	37.
Job 4	Assign 31	25.	28.	28.

(Loading jobs in work centers, moderate)

CHAPTER 16: PROJECT MANAGEMENT

TRUE/FALSE

1. Work Breakdown Structures is a useful tool in project management because it addresses the timing of individual work elements.
   False (Project planning, moderate)

2. A project is a set of tasks or activities directed toward a major output.
   True (Project planning, easy)

3. The limited lifetime of projects sets project management apart from the management of more traditional activities.
   True (Project planning, moderate)

4. Gantt charts give a timeline for each of a project's activities, but do not adequately show the interrelationships of activities.
   True (Project scheduling, moderate)

5. Gantt charts are not sophisticated enough to have any real value in project management.
   False (Project scheduling, moderate)

6. Networks are analyzed by Pareto methods, by isolating the "vital few" (activities that will account for a large majority of the project's problems) from the "trivial many."
   False (Project controlling, moderate)

7. In project management, an activity takes only an instant of time.
   False (Project management techniques: PERT and CPM, easy)

8. In project management an event has a measured duration.
   False (Project management techniques: PERT and CPM, easy)

9. The fundamental difference between PERT and CPM is that PERT uses the beta distribution for crashing projects while CPM uses cost estimates.
   False (Project management techniques: PERT and CPM, moderate)

10. The Activity on Arrow convention for drawing networks works for PERT, while the Activity on Node convention works for CPM.
    False (Project management techniques: PERT and CPM, moderate)

11. Dummy activities are required in order to make all paths of equal length, like adding slack variables in linear programming.
    False (Project management techniques: PERT and CPM, moderate)

12. The PERT optimistic time estimate is an estimate of the minimum time an activity will require.
    True (Project management techniques: PERT and CPM, moderate)

13. Slack is the amount of time an activity can be delayed without delaying the entire project.
    True (Project management techniques: PERT and CPM, moderate)

14. A given project can have multiple critical paths, all of which may have different duration.
False (Project management techniques: PERT and CPM, moderate)

15. The Beta distribution, when used in project management, weights the pessimistic time, probable time, and optimistic time equally.
False (Project management techniques: PERT and CPM, moderate)

16. The shortest of all paths through the network is the critical path.
False (Project management techniques: PERT and CPM, moderate)

17. The critical path is the set of activities that form the longest path through a network.
True (Project management techniques: PERT and CPM, moderate)

18. Every network has at least one critical path.
True (Project management techniques: PERT and CPM, moderate)

19. The "forward pass" technique for identifying the critical path in project management was illegal until the 1920s.
False (Project management techniques: PERT and CPM, moderate)

20. In PERT analysis, the identification of the critical path can be mistaken if a non-critical activity takes substantially longer than its probable time.
True (Project management techniques: PERT and CPM, difficult)

21. The standard deviation of project duration is the average of the standard deviation of all critical activities.
False (Project management techniques: PERT and CPM, moderate)

22. Because it does not deal with event completion probabilities, project crashing is a PERT technique, not a CPM technique.
False (Cost-time trade-offs and project crashing, moderate)

23. Shortening the project by deleting unnecessary activities is called "project crashing."
False (Cost-time trade-offs and project crashing, moderate)

24. In project management, crashing an activity must consider the impact on all paths in the network.
True Cost-time trade-offs and project crashing, moderate)

MULTIPLE CHOICE

25. Which of the following statements regarding project management is **false**?
    a. Project organization works well when the work contains simple, independent tasks.
    b. Gantt charts give a timeline for each of a project's activities, but do not adequately show the interrelationships of activities.
    c. Project organization is most suitable for projects that are temporary but critical to the organization.
    d. All of the above are true.
    e. None of the above are true.
    a (Project planning, moderate)

26. Which of the following statements regarding Gantt charts is **true**?
    a. Gantt charts are visual devices that show the duration of activities in a project.
    b. Gantt charts give a timeline and precedence relationships for each activity of a project.
    c. Gantt charts use the four standard spines of Methods, Materials, Manpower, and Machinery.
    d. Gantt charts are expensive.
    e. All of the above are true.
    a (Project scheduling, moderate)

27. Why are dummy activities used in PERT/CPM?
    a. to indicate a zero-length activity duration
    b. because no two activities can have the same starting and ending nodes
    c. to ensure that the network properly reflects the project under consideration
    d. all of the above are valid reasons
    e. none of the above are valid reasons
    d (Project management techniques: PERT and CPM, moderate)

28. Which of the following statements regarding PERT times is **true**?
    a. Optimistic time estimate is an estimate of the minimum time an activity will require.
    b. Optimistic time estimate is an estimate of the maximum time an activity will require.
    c. The probable time estimate is calculated as $t = (a + 4m + b)/6$.
    d. Pessimistic time estimate is an estimate of the minimum time an activity will require.
    e. Most likely time estimate is an estimate of the maximum time an activity will require.
    a (Project management techniques: PERT and CPM, moderate)

29. Which of the following statements regarding critical paths is **true**?
    a. The shortest of all paths through the network is the critical path.
    b. Some activities on the critical path may have slack.
    c. Every network has exactly one critical path.
    d. On a specific project, there can be multiple critical paths, all with exactly the same duration.
    e. The duration of the critical path is the average duration of all paths in the project network.
    d (Project management techniques: PERT and CPM, moderate)

30. Which of the following statements regarding CPM is **false**?
    a. The critical path is the shortest of all paths through the network.
    b. The critical path is that set of activities that has positive slack.
    c. Some networks have no critical path.
    d. All activities on the critical path have their LS equal EF.
    e. All of the above are false.

    e (Project management techniques: PERT and CPM, moderate)

31. Activity D on a CPM network has predecessors B and C, and has successor F. D has duration 6. B's late finish is 18, while C's is 20. F's late start is 26. Which of the following is **true**?
    a. B is a critical activity.
    b. C is completed before B.
    c. D has no slack but is not critical.
    d. D is critical, and has zero slack.
    e. All of the above are true.

    d (Project management techniques: PERT and CPM, moderate)

32. Which of the following statements regarding CPM networks is **true**?
    a. The early finish of an activity is the latest early start of all preceding activities.
    b. The late start of an activity is its late finish plus its duration.
    c. If a specific project has multiple critical paths, all of them will have the same duration.
    d. There can be multiple critical paths on the same project, all with different durations.
    e. All of the above are true.

    c (Project management techniques: PERT and CPM, moderate)

33. Which of the following statements concerning CPM activities is **false**?
    a. The late finish of an activity is the earliest late start of all preceding activities.
    b. The early finish of an activity is the early start of that activity plus its duration.
    c. The late finish is the earliest of the late start times of all successor activities.
    d. The late start of an activity is its late finish less its duration.
    e. The early start of an activity is the latest early finish of all preceding activities.

    a (Project management techniques: PERT and CPM, difficult)

34. Activity M on a CPM network has predecessors N and R, and has successor S. M has duration 5. N's late finish is 18, while R's is 20. S's late start is 12. Which of the following is **true**?
    a. M is critical, and has zero slack.
    b. M has no slack but is not critical.
    c. N is a critical activity.
    d. S is a critical activity.
    e. The last start time of S is impossible.

    e (Project management techniques: PERT and CPM, moderate)

35. Which of the following statements regarding CPM networks is **true**?
    a. The early finish of an activity is the latest early start of all preceding activities.
    b. The late finish of an activity is the earliest late start of all preceding activities.
    c. On a specific project, there can be multiple critical paths, all of which will have exactly the same duration.
    d. A project does not have to have a critical path.
    e. All of the above are true.
    c (Project management techniques: PERT and CPM, moderate)

36. The critical path for the network activities shown below is _____ with duration _____.

Activity	Nodes	Duration
A	1-2	10
B	1-3	8
C	2-4	2
D	2-3	3
E	3-4	5

    a. A-C; 12
    b. A-D-E; 18
    c. B-E; 13
    d. A-B-C-D-E; 28
    e. none of the above
    b (Project management techniques: PERT and CPM, moderate)

37. Activities that are not on a PERT critical path but have little slack need to be monitored closely because
    a. PERT treats all activities as equally important
    b. near-critical paths could become critical paths with small delays in these activities
    c. they are causing the entire project to be delayed
    d. slack is undesirable and needs to be eliminated
    e. they have a high risk of not being completed
    b (Project management techniques: PERT and CPM, moderate)

38. A local project being analyzed by PERT has 42 activities, 13 of which are on the critical path. If the estimated time along the critical path is 105 days with a variance of 25 days, the probability that the project will be completed in 95 days or less is
    a. 0.0228
    b. 0.3444
    c. 4.2
    d. 0.9772
    e. -0.4
    a (Project management techniques: PERT and CPM, moderate)

39. A project being analyzed by PERT has 60 activities, 13 of which are on the critical path. If the estimated time along the critical path is 214 days with a variance of 100 days, the probability that the project will take 224 days or more to complete is
   a. 0.0126
   b. 0.8413
   c. 0.1587
   d. 2.14
   e. near zero

   c (Project management techniques: PERT and CPM, moderate)

40. A contractor's project being analyzed by PERT has an estimated time for the critical path of 120 days. The sum of all activity variances is 81; the sum of variances along the critical path is 64. The probability that the project will take 130 or more days to complete is
   a. 0.1335
   b. 1.29
   c. 0.1056
   d. 0.8512
   e. 0.8943

   c (Project management techniques: PERT and CPM, moderate)

41. A project being analyzed by PERT has 38 activities, 16 of which are on the critical path. If the estimated time along the critical path is 90 days with a variance of 25 days, the probability that the project will be completed in 80 days or less is
   a. 0.0228
   b. 0.6554
   c. 0.3446
   d. 0.9772
   e. 18

   a (Project management techniques: PERT and CPM, moderate)

42. A PERT project has 45 activities, 19 on the critical path. The estimated time for the critical path is 120 days. The sum of all activity variances is 64, while the sum of variances along the critical path is 36. The probability that the project can be completed between days 110 and 120 is
   a. 0.0475
   b. 0.4525
   c. 0.1058
   d. 0.9525
   e. -1.67

   b (Project management techniques: PERT and CPM, difficult)

43. Analysis of a PERT problem shows the estimated time for the critical path to be 108 days with a variance of 64 days. There is a .75 probability that the project will be completed before approximately day _____.
   a. 116
   b. 102.6
   c. 113.4
   d. 172
   e. 112.2

   c (Project management techniques: PERT and CPM, difficult)

44. A project whose critical path has an estimated time of 120 days with a variance of 100 days has a 10% chance that the project will be completed before day _____.
   a. 130
   b. 107.2
   c. 132.8
   d. 127.5
   e. 100
   b (Project management techniques: PERT and CPM, difficult)

45. Which of the following statements regarding project management is **true**?
   a. Both PERT and CPM require that network tasks have unchanging durations.
   b. Shortening the project by assigning more resources to one or more of the critical tasks is called "project crashing."
   c. Crashing need not consider the impact of crashing an activity on other paths in the network.
   d. Project crashing is an optimizing technique.
   e. Crash cost depends upon the variance of the activity to be crashed.
   b (Project management techniques: PERT and CPM, moderate)

46. Which of these statements regarding time-cost tradeoffs in CPM networks is **true**?
   a. Crashing is not possible unless there are multiple critical paths.
   b. Crashing a project often reduces the length of long-duration, but non-critical, activities.
   c. Activities not on the critical path can never be on the critical path, even after crashing.
   d. Crashing shortens the project duration by assigning more resources to one or more of the critical tasks.
   e. None of the above.
   d (Cost-time trade-offs and project crashing, moderate)

47. Which of the following statements regarding time-cost tradeoffs in CPM networks is **false**?
   a. Shortening the project duration by assigning more resources to one or more of the critical tasks is called "project crashing."
   b. Crashing procedures must consider the impact of crashing an activity on all paths in the network.
   c. Crashing sometimes has the reverse result of lengthening the project duration.
   d. Activities not on the critical path can become critical after crashing takes place.
   e. All of the above are true.
   c (Cost-time trade-offs and project crashing, moderate)

48. If an activity whose normal duration is 12 days can be shortened to 10 days for an added cost of $1500, the crash cost per unit time K_i is
   a. $750
   b. $1500
   c. $3000
   d. $15,000
   e. $18,000
   a (Cost-time trade-offs and project crashing, moderate)

49. Two activities are candidates for crashing on a CPM network. Activity details are in the table below. To cut one day from the project's duration, activity _____ should be crashed first, adding _____ to project cost.

Activity	Normal Time	Normal Cost	Crash Duration	Crash Cost
One	8 days	$6,000	6 days	$6,600
Two	10 days	$4,000	9 days	$6,000

    a. One; $6,600
    b. One; $300
    c. Two; $1,000
    d. Two; $6,000
    e. One; $600
    b (Cost-time trade-offs and project crashing, moderate)

50. If an activity whose normal duration is 15 days can be shortened to 10 days for an added cost of $1500, the crash cost per unit time is
    a. $300
    b. $1500
    c. $6000
    d. $15,000
    e. $22,500
    a (Cost-time trade-offs and project crashing, moderate)

51. Two activities are candidates for crashing on a CPM network. Activity details are in the table below. To cut one day from the project's duration, activity _____ should be crashed first, adding _____ to project cost.

Activity	Normal Time	Normal Cost	Crash Duration	Crash Cost
B	4 days	$6,000	3 days	$6,600
C	6 days	$4,000	4 days	$6,000

    a. B; $6,600
    b. B; $600
    c. C; $1,000
    d. C; $2,000
    e. B; $12,600
    b (Cost-time trade-offs and project crashing, moderate)

52. Which of the following statements regarding project management is **false**?
    a. Project management differs from the management of more traditional activities due to the limited lifetime of projects.
    b. Dummy activities are added to paths to make all paths of equal length, analogous to adding slack variables in linear programming.
    c. A Gantt chart contains no precedence relationships, but may be useful for simple projects.
    d. Dummy activities consume no time.
    e. Slack is the amount of time an activity can be delayed without delaying the entire project, assuming its preceding activities are completed as early as possible.
    b (Project management techniques: PERT and CPM, moderate)

53. Which of the following statements regarding time-cost tradeoffs in CPM networks is **true**?
    a. Crashing shortens the critical path by assigning more resources to one or more non-critical tasks.
    b. Crashing is not possible unless there are multiple critical paths.
    c. Crashing a project reduces the length of critical activities only.
    d. Project crashing is not effective when applied to tasks with zero slack.
    e. All of the above are false.
    c (Project management techniques: PERT and CPM, moderate)

FILL-IN-THE BLANK

54. _____ is an organization formed to ensure that programs (projects) receive the proper management and attention.
    Project organization (Project planning, moderate)

55. _____ divides a project into more and more detailed components.
    Work breakdown structure or WBS (Project planning, moderate)

56. _____ are used to schedule resources and allocate time for projects.
    Gantt charts (Project scheduling, moderate)

57. _____ is a technique to enable managers to schedule, monitor, and control large and complex projects by employing three time estimates for each activity.
    Program evaluation and review technique or PERT (Project management techniques: PERT and CPM, easy)

58. _____ is a network technique using only one time factor per activity that enables managers to schedule, monitor, and control large and complex projects.
    Critical path method or CPM (Project management techniques: PERT and CPM, easy)

59. The _____ is the computed longest time path(s) through a network.
    critical path (Project management techniques: PERT and CPM, easy)

60. An _____ is/are an instant that marks the start or completion of a task or activity in a network.
    event (Project management techniques: PERT and CPM, moderate)

61. An _____ is a task or subproject in a CPM or PERT network that occurs between two events.
    activity (Project management techniques: PERT and CPM, moderate)

62. A _____ is a sequence of activities defined by starting and ending events and the activities that occur between them.
    network (Project management techniques: PERT and CPM, moderate)

63. _____ are activities having no time, inserted into the network to maintain the logic of the network.
    Dummy activities (Project management techniques: PERT and CPM, moderate)

64. The _____ time is the "worst" activity time that could be expected in a PERT network.
pessimistic (Project management techniques: PERT and CPM, moderate)

65. _____ is the amount of times an individual activity in a network can be delayed without delaying the entire project.
Slack time (Project management techniques: PERT and CPM, moderate)

66. _____ is shortening activity time in a network to reduce time on the critical path so total completion time is reduced.
Crashing (Cost-time trade-offs and project crashing, easy)

SHORT ANSWER

67. Explain the purpose of project organization.
To make sure existing programs continue to run smoothly while new projects are successfully completed. (Project planning, moderate)

68. Define Work Breakdown Structure. How is it used?
WBS is a family tree subdivision of effort required to achieve an objective. It defines a project by breaking it down into manageable parts and even finer subdivisions. (Project planning, moderate)

69. List the responsibilities of project managers.
Project managers are directly responsible for making sure that (1) all necessary activities are finished in proper sequence and on time; (2) the project comes in within budget; (3) the project meets its quality goals; and (4) the people assigned to the project receive the motivation, direction, and information needed to do their jobs. (Project planning, moderate)

70. What is a project, in the context of project management?
A project is a set of tasks or activities all directed toward a specific purpose. (Project planning, easy)

71. What is the use of Gantt charts in project management?
A Gantt chart is a visual device that shows the duration of tasks in a project. They represent a low cost means of ensuring that (1) all activities are planned for, (2) their order of performance is planned for, (3) the activity times are recorded, and (4) the overall project time is developed. (Project scheduling, moderate)

72. It has been said that WBS and Gantt are each useful tools, but neither is "complete" for managing projects. What is missing from one that is present in the other so that the two tools are complementary? Discuss.
WBS deals with activity details, while Gantt charts deal more with activity timing. The former answers questions about what is to be done, and the latter answers questions about when tasks are done. Neither does an adequate job with task interrelationships. (Project planning and Project scheduling, moderate)

73. List, in order, the six steps basic to both PERT and CPM.
   1. Define the project and prepare the WBS
   2. Develop the relationships among the activities
   3. Draw the network connecting all of the activities
   4. Assign the time and/or cost estimates to each activity
   5. Compute the critical path-the longest time path through the network
   6. Use the network to help plan, schedule, monitor and control the project.
   (Project management techniques: PERT and CPM, moderate)

74. What are dummy activities? Why are they used in project management?
   Dummy activities have no time duration. They are inserted into a network to maintain the logic of the network, such as when two activities have exactly the same beginning and ending events. A dummy activity is inserted with one of them so that the computer software can handle the problem. (Project management techniques: PERT and CPM, moderate)

75. What are the three time estimates used with PERT?
   They are (1) Optimistic time estimate (a), an estimate of the minimum time an activity will require; (2) Most likely time estimate (m), an estimate of the normal time an activity will require; and (3) Pessimistic time estimate (b), an estimate of the maximum time an activity will require. (Project management techniques: PERT and CPM, moderate)

76. What is the objective of critical path analysis?
   To find the shortest possible schedule for a series of activities, and identify those activities so they can receive management focus. (Project management techniques: PERT and CPM, moderate)

77. Define early start, early finish, late finish, and late start.
   Early start (ES) of an activity is the latest of the early finish times of all its predecessors. Early finish (EF) is the early start of an activity plus its duration. Late finish (LF) of an activity is the earliest of the late start times of all successor activities. Late start (LS) of an activity is its late finish less its duration. (Project management techniques: PERT and CPM, moderate)

78. Define slack.
   Slack is the amount of time an activity can be delayed without delaying the entire project, assuming its preceding activities are completed as early as possible. (Project management techniques: PERT and CPM, moderate)

79. Define the term **critical path**.
   Critical path is that set of activities in a project network that controls the duration of the entire project. (Project management techniques: PERT and CPM, moderate)

80. Students are sometimes confused by the concept of critical path, and want to believe that it is the **shortest** path through a network. Convincingly explain why this is not so.
   The critical path is the shortest time possible for the completion of a series of activities, but that shortest time is the longest path through the network. Only the longest path allows time for all activities in the series; any smaller amount will leave activities unfinished. (Project management techniques: PERT and CPM, moderate)

81. PERT calculations typically include the duration variance of each activity. What is the purpose of this calculation-what's the role of variances in PERT analysis?
The activity variances influence the probability of project completion. Specifically, the sum of the variances of the critical tasks equals the variance of the project. Further, large variances on non-critical tasks need to be monitored. Such an activity might have an actual completion time so large that the task becomes a critical task. (Project management techniques: PERT and CPM, moderate)

82. Describe the process of "crashing" a CPM project. Explain the purpose of crashing analysis.
Project crashing is shortening the project by assigning more resources to one or more of the critical tasks. Crashing is not an optimizing technique, but a trade-off technique-managers can decide whether to finish later but cheaper, or earlier but more expensively. Once a decision is made to crash a project, the technique points to the cheapest way to save a unit of time on the project. (Cost-time trade-offs and project crashing, moderate)

83. Would a project manager ever consider crashing a non-critical activity in a CPM project network? Explain convincingly.
No! In CPM, there is no possibility that crashing a non-critical task can reduce the project duration. Only critical tasks offer the possibility of reducing path length. (Cost-time trade-offs and project crashing, moderate)

PROBLEMS

84. Three activities are candidates for crashing on a CPM network (all are of course critical). Activity details are in the table below.

Activity	Normal Time	Normal Cost	Crash Duration	Crash Cost
A	7 days	$6,000	6 days	$6,600
B	4 days	$1,200	2 days	$3,000
C	11 days	$4,000	9 days	$6,000

a. What action would you take to reduce the critical path by one day?
b. Assuming no other paths become critical, what action would you take to reduce the critical path one additional day?
c. What is the total cost of the two day reduction?
Crash costs per unit time are $600 for A, $900 for B, and $1,000 for C. A offers the cheapest path to a single day reduction. A cannot supply a second reduction, so the next best choice is B, which adds $900. The total for both days is $1,500. (Cost-time trade-offs and project crashing, moderate)

85. Consider the tasks, durations, and predecessor relationships in the following network. Draw the network and answer the questions that follow.

Activity Description	Preceding	Optimistic	Most Likely	Pessimistic
A	none	4	8	10
B	A	2	8	24
C	A	8	12	16
D	A	4	6	10
E	B	1	2	3
F	E, C	6	8	20
G	E, C	2	3	4
H	F	2	2	2
I	F	6	6	6
J	D, G, H	4	6	12
K	I, J	2	2	3

a. What is the expected time for activity C?
b. What is the variance for activity C?
c. Based on the calculation of estimated times, what is the critical path?
d. What is the estimated time of the critical path?
e. What is the activity variance along the critical path?
f. What is the probability of completion of the project before week 36?
The network appears in the sketch below.
(a) estimated time for C is (8 + 4*12 + 16)/6 = 72/6 = 12; (b) variance for C is ((16-8)/6)² = 16/9
or 1.78; (c) A-C-F-I-K (see POM for Windows solution); (d) 7.667+12+9.667+6+3.167 = 37.5;
(e) 1+1.778+5.444+0+0.028 = 8.25; (f) Using the POM for Windows normal calculator, the
probability of completion before week 36 is based on z=(36-37.5)/sqrt(8.25) = -.522 or about
30%.

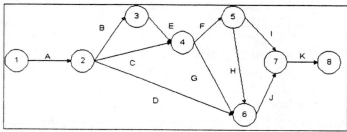

	Activity time	Early Start	Early Finish	Late Start	Late Finish	Slack	Standard Deviation
Project	37.5						2.8723
A	7.6667	0.	7.6667	0.	7.6667	0.	1.
B	9.6667	7.6667	17.3333	8.	17.6667	0.3333	3.6667
C	12.	7.6667	19.6667	7.6667	19.6667	0.	1.3333
D	6.3333	7.6667	14.	22.3333	28.6667	14.6667	1.
E	2.	17.3333	19.3333	17.6667	19.6667	0.3333	0.3333
F	9.6667	19.6667	29.3333	19.6667	29.3333	0.	2.3333
G	3.	19.6667	22.6667	25.6667	28.6667	6.	0.3333
H	2.	29.3333	31.3333	35.5	37.5	6.1667	0.
I	6.	29.3333	35.3333	29.3333	35.3333	0.	0.
J	6.6667	22.6667	29.3333	28.6667	35.3333	6.	1.3333
K	2.1667	35.3333	37.5	35.3333	37.5	0.	0.1667

(Project management techniques: PERT and CPM, moderate)

86. The network below represents a project being analyzed by Critical Path Methods. Activity durations are:

A 4	B 2	C 12
D 3	E 5	F 1
G 7	H 2	I 10
J 4		

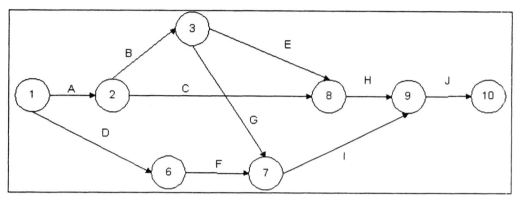

a. What task that must be on the critical path, regardless of activity durations?
b. What is the duration of path A-B-E-H-J?
c. What is the critical path of this network?
d. What is the length of the critical path?
e. What is slack time at activity H?
f. What is the Late Finish of activity H?
g. If activity C were delayed by two time units, what would happen to the project duration?
(a) J; (b) 21; (c) A-B-G-I-J; (d) 27; (e) 10; (f) 23; (g) no impact. See POM for Windows solution below.

	CPM Problem Solution					
	Activity time	Early Start	Early Finish	Late Start	Late Finish	Slack
Project	27.					
A	4.	0.	4.	0.	4.	0.
B	2.	4.	6.	4.	6.	0.
C	12.	4.	16.	9.	21.	5.
D	3.	0.	3.	9.	12.	9.
E	5.	6.	11.	16.	21.	10.
F	1.	3.	4.	12.	13.	9.
G	7.	6.	13.	6.	13.	0.
H	2.	16.	18.	21.	23.	5.
I	10.	13.	23.	13.	23.	0.
J	4.	23.	27.	23.	27.	0.

(Project management techniques: PERT and CPM, moderate)

87. A network consists of the following list. Times are given in weeks.

Activity	Preceding	Optimistic	Probable	Pessimistic
A	--	7	9	14
B	A	2	2	8
C	A	8	12	16
D	A	4	5	10
E	B	3	6	8
F	B	6	8	10
G	C, F	2	3	4
H	D	2	2	6
I	H	6	8	16
J	F, G, I	4	6	12
K	E, J	2	2	3

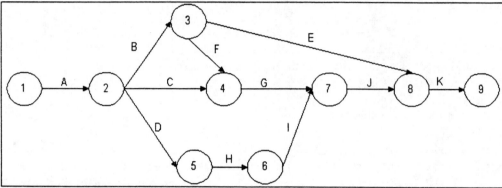

a. What is the expected time for activity D?
b. What is the standard deviation for activity C?
c. Based on the calculation of estimated times, which activities form the critical path?
d. What is the estimated time of the critical path?
e. What is the variance along the critical path?
f. What is the probability of completion of the project after week 40?
(a) 5.67; (b) 1.33; (c) A-D-H-I-J-K; (d) 35.7; (e) 7.3889; (f) 0.0559. See POM for Windows solution.

PERT Problem Solution						
	Activity time	Early Start	Early Finish	Late Start	Late Finish	Slack	Standard Deviation
Project	35.6667						2.7183
A	9.5	0.	9.5	0.	9.5	0.	1.1667
B	3.	9.5	12.5	12.8333	15.8333	3.3333	1.
C	12.	9.5	21.5	11.8333	23.8333	2.3333	1.3333
D	5.6667	9.5	15.1667	9.5	15.1667	0.	1.
E	5.8333	12.5	18.3333	27.6667	33.5	15.1667	0.8333
F	8.	12.5	20.5	15.8333	23.8333	3.3333	0.6667
G	3.	21.5	24.5	23.8333	26.8333	2.3333	0.3333
H	2.6667	15.1667	17.8333	15.1667	17.8333	0.	0.6667
I	9.	17.8333	26.8333	17.8333	26.8333	0.	1.6667
J	6.6667	26.8333	33.5	26.8333	33.5	0.	1.3333
K	2.1667	33.5	35.6667	33.5	35.6667	0.	0.1667

PERT Problem Solution						
	Optimistic time	Most Likely	Pessimisti time	Activity time	Standard Deviation	Variance
A	7.	9.	14.	9.5	1.1667	1.3611
B	2.	2.	8.	3.	1.	1.
C	0.	12.	16.	12.	1.3333	1.7770
D	4.	5.	10.	5.6667	1.	1.
E	3.	6.	8.	5.8333	0.8333	0.6944
F	6.	8.	10.	8.	0.6667	0.4444
G	2.	3.	4.	3.	0.3333	0.1111
H	2.	2.	6.	2.6667	0.6667	0.4444
I	6.	8.	16.	9.	1.6667	2.7778
J	4.	6.	12.	6.6667	1.3333	1.7778
K	2.	2.	3.	2.1667	0.1667	0.0278
Project results						
Total of critical						7.3889
Square root of total					2.7183	

(Project management techniques: PERT and CPM, moderate)

88. Three activities are candidates for crashing on a CPM network. Activity details are in the table below.

Activity	Normal Time	Normal Cost	Crash Duration	Crash Cost
Delta	8 days	$6,000	6 days	$10,000
Omicron	3 days	$1,800	2 days	$3,000
Alpha	12 days	$5,000	11 days	$6,500

a. What is the crash cost per unit time for activity Delta?
b. What is the crash cost per unit time for activity Alpha?
c. Which activity should be crashed first to cut one day from the project's duration; how much is added to project cost?
d. Which activity should be the next activity crashed to cut a second day from the project's duration; how much is added to project cost?
e. Assuming no other paths become critical, how much can this project be shortened at what total added cost?
(a) $2,000; (b) $1500; (c) Omicron, $1,200; (d) Alpha, $1,500; (e) 4, $6,700
(Cost-time trade-offs and project crashing, moderate)

89. Diagram the network described below. Calculate its critical path. How long is the minimum duration of this network?

Activity	Nodes	Duration	Activity	Nodes	Duration
J	1-2	10	N	3-4	2
K	1-3	8	O	4-5	7
L	2-4	6	P	3-5	5
M	2-3	3			

The diagram is shown below.
The paths through this network are: J-L-O, J-M-P, J-M-N-O, K-P, and K-N-O. Their path durations are 23, 18, 22, 13, and 17. J-L-O, is the critical path; its duration is 23.

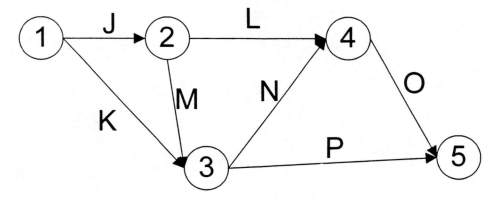

(Project management techniques: PERT and CPM, moderate)

384

90. Consider the network described in the table below.

Activity	Nodes	Pessimistic	Probable	Optimistic
J	1-2	14	10	8
K	1-3	9	8	7
L	2-4	10	6	5
M	2-3	3	3	3
N	3-4	6	2	1
O	3-5	8	7	4
P	4-5	10	5	3

a. Calculate the expected duration of each activity.
b. Calculate the expected duration and variance of the critical path.
c. Calculate the probability that the project will be completed in under 20 time units

(a) is detailed in the table below. (b) Tasks J-L-P are critical. The sum of their expected durations is 22.33; the sum of their variances is 3.056. (c) The standard deviation along the path is sqrt(3.056) = 1.748; the probability that Duration < 20 is the probability that z < (20 - 22.33)/1.748 = -1.33. The associated normal curve area is 0.0918.

PERT Problem Solution

	Start node	End node	Activity time	Early Start	Early Finish	Late Start	Late Finish	Slack	Standard Deviation
Project			22.3333						1.748
J	1.	2.	10.3333	0.	10.3333	0.	10.3333	0.	1.
K	1.	3.	8.	0.	8.	6.3333	14.3333	6.3333	0.3333
L	2.	4.	6.5	10.3333	16.8333	10.3333	16.8333	0.	0.8333
M	2.	3.	3.	10.3333	13.3333	11.3333	14.3333	1.	0.
N	3.	4.	2.5	13.3333	15.8333	14.3333	16.8333	1.	0.8333
O	3.	5.	6.6667	13.3333	20.	15.6667	22.3333	2.3333	0.6667
P	4.	5.	5.5	16.8333	22.3333	16.8333	22.3333	0.	1.1667

PERT Problem Solution

	Start node	End node	Optimistic time	Most Likely	Pessimistic time	Activity time	Standard Deviation	Variance
J	1.	2.	8.	10.	14.	10.3333	1.	1.
K	1.	3.	7.	8.	9.	8.	0.3333	0.1111
L	2.	4.	5.	6.	10.	6.5	0.8333	0.6944
M	2.	3.	3.	3.	3.	3.	0.	0.
N	3.	4.	1.	2.	6.	2.5	0.8333	0.6944
O	3.	5.	4.	7.	8.	6.6667	0.6667	0.4444
P	4.	5.	3.	5.	10.	5.5	1.1667	1.3611
Project results								
Total of critical								3.0556
Square root of total							1.748	

(Project management techniques: PERT and CPM, moderate)

91. Consider the network pictured below.
   a. Enumerate all paths through this network.
   b. Calculate the critical path for the network.
   c. What is the minimum duration of the project?
   d. How much slack exists at each activity?

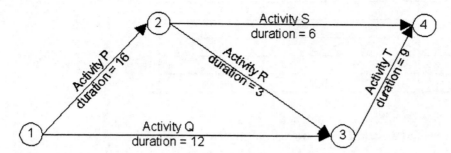

(a) Possible paths are P-S (length 22), P-R-T (length 28), and Q-T (length 21). (b) The longest of these, P-R-T, is the critical path, at 28 time units. (c) There is no slack at P, R, or T since these are critical tasks. S has 6 units slack, since the path it is on totals only 22 units, compared to the critical path length of 28. Q has 7 units of slack since it is on a 21 length path, 7 less than the maximum. (Project management techniques: PERT and CPM, moderate)

92. The network below represents a project being analyzed by Critical Path Methods. Activity durations are

A	4	B	3	C	12
D	3	E	6	F	8
G	4	H	2	I	2
J	7	K	5		

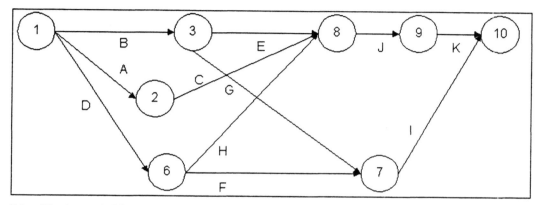

a. Identify the activities on the critical path.
b. What is the duration of the critical path?
c. Calculate the amount of slack time at activity H.
d. If activity I were delayed by ten time units, what would be the impact on the project duration?
(a) Critical activities are A-C-J-K; (b) The critical path is 28 time units; (c) Slack at H is 11 units, based on its EF = 28 and its ES = 5; (d) I has 15 units slack--a ten unit delay would have no impact on the project. POM for Windows solution follows.

CPM Problem Solution

	Start node	End node	Activity time	Early Start	Early Finish	Late Start	Late Finish	Slack
Project			28.					
A	1.	2.	4.	0.	4.	0.	4.	0.
B	1.	3.	3.	0.	3.	7.	10.	7.
C	2.	8.	12.	4.	16.	4.	16.	0.
D	1.	6.	3.	0.	3.	11.	14.	11.
E	3.	8.	6.	3.	9.	10.	16.	7.
F	6.	7.	8.	3.	11.	18.	26.	15.
G	3.	7.	4.	3.	7.	22.	26.	19.
H	6.	8.	2.	3.	5.	14.	16.	11.
I	7.	10.	2.	11.	13.	26.	28.	15.
J	8.	9.	7.	16.	23.	16.	23.	0.
K	9.	10.	5.	23.	28.	23.	28.	0.

(Project management techniques: PERT and CPM, moderate)

CHAPTER 17: MAINTENANCE AND RELIABILITY

TRUE/FALSE

1. Reliability is the probability that a machine part or product will function properly for a specified time regardless of conditions.
    False (The strategic importance of maintenance and reliability, easy)

2. The reliability of a system in which each individual component must function in order for the entire system to function, and in which each component has its own unique reliability, independent of other components, is the product of the probabilities of each of those components.
    True (Reliability, moderate)

3. The product failure rate is the percentage of failures among the total number of products tested, and is calculated without regard to amounts of operating time.
    True (Reliability, moderate)

4. The MTBF (mean time between failure) is calculated as the reciprocal of the product failure rate.
    False (Reliability, moderate)

5. Adding an additional part to a component or product ordinarily reduces reliability by introducing an additional source of failure.
    True (Reliability, moderate)

6. A redundant part or component increases reliability because it is connected in parallel, not in series.
    True (Reliability, moderate)

7. Preventive maintenance is reactive.
    False (Maintenance, moderate)

8. Many infant mortality failures may be due to improper use.
    True (Maintenance, moderate)

9. Preventive maintenance is nothing more than keeping the equipment and machinery running.
    False (Maintenance, moderate)

10. Preventive maintenance implies that we can determine when a system needs service or will need repair.
    True (Maintenance, moderate)

11. Infant mortality refers to the high failure rate often encountered in the very early stages of the lifetime of a product.
    True (Maintenance, moderate)

12. Failures occur at a relatively constant rate over the lifetime of a typical product.
    False (Maintenance, moderate)

13. Failures are tolerable as long as their results are not catastrophic.
    False (Maintenance, moderate)

14. Small standard deviations in the MTBF distribution indicate a candidate for preventive maintenance.
True (Maintenance, moderate)

15. The more expensive the maintenance, the wider (more dispersed) must be the MTBF distribution.
False (Maintenance, moderate)

16. In identifying the optimal maintenance policy, the full costs of breakdowns are rarely considered.
True (Maintenance, moderate)

17. When identifying the optimal maintenance policy, the cost of inventory maintained to compensate for the downtime is a cost often ignored.
True (Maintenance, moderate)

18. An optimal maintenance policy strikes a balance between the costs of breakdown and preventive maintenance so that the total cost of maintenance is at a minimum.
True (Maintenance, moderate)

19. While breakdowns occur randomly, their frequency is somewhat predictable through such tools as the product failure rate, MTBF, and the breakdown costs model.
True (Maintenance, moderate)

20. Employee involvement is an important aspect of a maintenance program.
True (Increasing repair capabilities, moderate)

21. TPM (Total Productive Maintenance) is an application of TQM (Total Quality Management) principles to the area of maintenance.
True (Increasing repair capabilities, moderate)

22. Simulation models and expert systems are useful tools for determining maintenance policies.
True (Increasing repair capabilities, moderate)

MULTIPLE CHOICE

23. The objective of maintenance is to
    a. ensure that no breakdowns will ever occur
    b. ensure that preventive maintenance costs are kept as low as possible
    c. maintain the capability of the system while controlling costs
    d. ensure that maintenance employees are fully utilized
    e. ensure that breakdowns do not affect the quality of the products
    c (The strategic importance of maintenance and reliability, moderate)

24. The probability that a product will function properly for a specified time under stated conditions is
    a. reliability
    b. functionality
    c. ruggedness
    d. durability
    ι fitness for use.
    a (The strategic importance of maintenance and reliability, moderate)

25. Which of the following is a tactic for improving reliability?
    a. improve individual components
    b. improve preventive maintenance procedures
    c. remove redundancy
    d. improve production processes
    e. all of the above are reliability tactics
    a (Reliability, moderate)

26. A system is composed of three components A, B, and C. All three must function for the system to function. There are currently no backups in place. The system has a reliability of 0.966. If a backup is installed for component A, the new system reliability will be
    a. unchanged
    b. less than 0.966
    c. less than 0.998
    d. cannot be determined from the information given
    e. none of the above
    d (Reliability, moderate)

27. What is the reliability of a four-component product with component reliabilities of .90, .95, .98, and .99?
    a. no less than .99
    b. under 0.83
    c. 0.955
    d. at most 0.90
    e. none of the above
    d (Reliability, moderate)

28. A system has three components in series with reliabilities 0.9, 0.8, and 0.8. System reliability is
    a. 2.500
    b. 0.576
    c. 0.988
    d. 0.800
    e. 0.050
    b (Reliability, moderate)

29. A job consists of a series of three tasks. Task 1 is performed correctly 98% of the time, task 2 is performed correctly 99% of the time, and task 3 is performed correctly 96% of the time. The reliability of this job is
    a. 97.66%
    b. 96.37%
    c. 93.14%
    d. 95.45%
    e. 98.00%
    c (Reliability, moderate)

30. A product has three components, A, B, and C, with reliabilities of 0.90, 0.98, and 0.995. Engineers intend to put a redundant component A that has reliability 0.60. With this change, system reliability will
    a. fall by 20%
    b. fall by 10% or less
    c. rise
    d. cannot determine from the information provided
    e. none of the above
    c (Reliability, moderate)

31. As the number of non-redundant components in a system decreases, all other things being equal, the reliability of the system usually
    a. increases
    b. stays the same
    c. decreases
    d. increases, then decreases
    e. decreases, then increases
    a (Reliability, moderate)

32. What is the reliability of the system shown below?

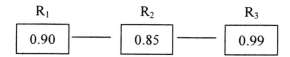

    a. 2.74
    b. 0.90000
    c. 0.75735
    d. 0.91333
    e. at least 0.85
    c (Reliability, moderate)

33. For the system shown below, the reliability is

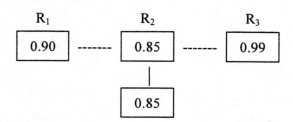

R₁: 0.90 ------- R₂: 0.85 ------- R₃: 0.99
0.85

a. 0.9775
b. 1.6073
c. 0.87095
d. 0.8989
e. 0.8000
c (Reliability, moderate)

34. Ten high-technology batteries are tested for 200 hours each. One failed at 50 hours; all others completed the test. FR(%) is _____ and FR(N) is _____.
a. 10%; 1/1850
b. 10%; 1/2000
c. 25%; 1850 hours
d. 90%; 1/2000
e. indeterminate; no standard deviation is given
a (Reliability, moderate)

35. Ten high-technology batteries are tested for 200 hours each. One failed at 20 hours; all others completed the test. FR(%) is _____ and MTBF is _____.
a. 10%; 1/1820
b. 90%; 1/1820
c. 10%; 1980 hours
d. 10%; 1820 hours
e. cannot calculate from information provided
d (Reliability, moderate)

36. Ten high-technology batteries are tested for 200 hours each. One failed at 20 hours; another failed at 140 hours; all others completed the test. FR(%) is _____ and MTBF is _____.
a. 80%; 920 hours
b. 20%; 880 hours
c. 10%; 1980 hours
d. 20%; 1760 hours
e. cannot calculate from information provided
b (Reliability, moderate)

37. MTBF measures the average
   a. calendar time between failures
   b. number of failures per unit time
   c. number of operations between failures
   d. operating time between failures
   e. downtime per failure
   d (Reliability, moderate)

38. A system is composed of four parts, J, K, L, and M. All four must function for the system to function. The four component reliabilities are .99, .98, .992, and .998. The designers are considering putting a .80 reliable backup at K. This backup will change the system reliability from _____ to _____.
   a. 0.99 to 0.952
   b. 0.9605 to 0.9752
   c. 0.9605 to some smaller value
   d. cannot be determined
   e. none of the above
   b (Reliability, moderate)

39. Infant mortality refers to which one of the following examples?
   a. failure of items used in the nursery ward of a hospital
   b. failure of products with a very short life cycle
   c. market failure of brand new products
   d. high failure rate often encountered in the very early stages of the lifetime of a product
   e. high frequency on the left side of the MTBF distribution
   d (maintenance, moderate)

40. The process that involves repair on an emergency or priority basis is known as
   a. breakdown maintenance
   b. failure maintenance
   c. preventive maintenance
   d. emergency maintenance
   e. priority maintenance
   a (maintenance, moderate)

41. Which one of the following statements about maintenance is **true**?
   a. Breakdown maintenance is proactive.
   b. Preventive maintenance is reactive.
   c. Preventive maintenance is limited to keeping machinery and equipment running.
   d. Human resources are a major component of effective maintenance management.
   e. The optimal degree of preventive maintenance is associated with zero breakdowns.
   d (maintenance, moderate)

42. As a firm's maintenance commitment increases,
    a. the breakdown maintenance costs increase and the preventive maintenance costs decrease
    b. both the breakdown maintenance costs and the preventive maintenance costs decrease
    c. the breakdown maintenance costs decrease and the preventive maintenance costs increase
    d. both the breakdown maintenance costs and the preventive maintenance costs increase
    e. none of the above is true
    c (maintenance, moderate)

43. For a machine to be a good candidate for preventive maintenance
    a. the consequences of failure must exceed the cost of preventive maintenance and the MTBF distribution must have a large standard deviation
    b. the consequences of failure must exceed the cost of preventive maintenance and the MTBF must be relatively low
    c. the consequences of failure must exceed the cost of preventive maintenance and the MTBF distribution must have a relatively low standard deviation
    d. the consequences of failure must exceed the cost of preventive maintenance and the MTBF must be relatively high
    e. the consequences of failure must be relatively unknown, and therefore risky
    c (maintenance, moderate)

44. As far as maintenance costs are concerned,
    a. preventive maintenance is always more economical than breakdown maintenance
    b. for low levels of maintenance commitment, breakdown maintenance costs exceed preventive maintenance costs
    c. for low levels of maintenance commitment, preventive maintenance costs exceed breakdown maintenance costs
    d. for high levels of maintenance commitment, breakdown maintenance costs exceed preventive maintenance costs
    e. all of the above are true
    b (maintenance, moderate)

45. Which one of the following is **not** necessary to identify the optimal maintenance policy?
    a. historical data on maintenance costs
    b. breakdown probabilities
    c. breakdown occurrences
    d. cost of performing the analysis
    e. repair times
    d (maintenance, moderate)

46. Which of the following costs tend to be ignored in determining the optimal maintenance policy?
    a. cost of low morale
    b. expected breakdown costs
    c. preventive maintenance costs
    d. the costs associated with various levels of commitment to maintenance
    e. all of the above
    a (maintenance, moderate)

47. DuLarge Marine manufactures diesel engines for shrimp trawlers and other small commercial boats. One of their CNC machines has caused several problems. Over the past 30 weeks, the machine has broken down as indicated below.

Number of breakdowns	0	1	2	3	4
Number of weeks that breakdowns occurred	8	2	6	10	4

What is the expected number of breakdowns per week?
a. 1
b. 2
c. 6
d. 10
e. 30
b (maintenance, moderate)

48. DuLarge Marine manufactures diesel engines for shrimp trawlers and other small commercial boats. One of their CNC machines has caused several problems. Over the past 30 weeks, the machine has broken down as indicated below. Each time the machine breaks down, the firm loses an average of $1,000 in time and repair expenses.

Number of breakdowns	0	1	2	3	4
Number of weeks that breakdowns occurred	8	2	6	10	4

What is the expected breakdown cost per week?
a. $1,000
b. $2,000
c. $6,000
d. $10,000
e. $60,000
b (maintenance, moderate)

49. DuLarge Marine manufactures diesel engines for shrimp trawlers and other small commercial boats. One of their CNC machines has caused several problems. Over the past 30 weeks, the machine has broken down as indicated below. Each time the machine breaks down, the firm loses an average of $1,000 in time and repair expenses. If preventive maintenance was implemented, it is estimated that an average of only one breakdown per week would occur. The cost of preventive maintenance is $500 per week.

Number of breakdowns	0	1	2	3	4
Number of weeks that breakdowns occurred	8	2	6	10	4

What is the weekly maintenance cost of this program?
a. $1,000
b. $1,500
c. $2,000
d. $2,500
e. $3,000
b (maintenance, moderate)

FILL-IN-THE BLANK

50. _____ consists of all activities involved in keeping a system's equipment in working order.
Maintenance (The strategic importance of maintenance and reliability, easy)

51. _____ is the probability that a machine part or product will function properly for a specified time under stated conditions.
Reliability (The strategic importance of maintenance and reliability, easy)

52. _____ is the expected time between a repair and the next failure of a component, machine, process, or product.
Mean time between failures or MTBF (Reliability, moderate)

53. _____ is the use of a component in parallel to raise reliabilities.
Redundancy (Reliability, moderate)

54. _____ is a plan that involves routine inspections, servicing, and keeping facilities in good repair to prevent failure.
Preventive maintenance (Maintenance, moderate)

55. _____ is remedial maintenance that occurs when equipment fails and must be repaired on an emergency or priority basis.
Breakdown mainenance (Maintenance, moderate)

56. _____ is the failure rate early in the life of a product or process.
Infant mortality (Maintenance, moderate)

57. _____ combines total quality management with a strategic view of maintenance from process equipment design to preventative maintenance.
Total preventative maintenance or TPM (Increasing repair capabilities, moderate)

SHORT ANSWERS

58. State the objective of maintenance and reliability.
To maintain the capability of the system while controlling costs. (The strategic importance of maintenance and reliability, moderate)

59. Define reliability; define maintenance.
Reliability is the probability that a machine part or product will function properly for a specified time under stated conditions. Maintenance is all activities involved in keeping a system's equipment in working order. (The strategic importance of maintenance and reliability, moderate)

60. What are the reliability tactics?
Improving individual components and providing redundancy. (The strategic importance of maintenance and reliability, moderate)

61. What is the impact on product reliability of increasing the number of items in series? Explain. **More items in series decreases reliability, because each item added has a reliability less than one which is then multiplied by the reliability before the item was added. (Reliability, moderate)**

62. "High reliability can be achieved in a product without having high reliability in the component parts. In fact, any reliability target, no matter how high, can be achieved with only mediocre parts, so long as enough of them are present." Discuss; an example may help. **This carries the redundancy concept one step beyond textbook, to having multiple redundancies on the same component. If only one part in a parallel system needs to work to provide reliability of that part of the system, then several parts in parallel should offer very high reliability. Example: four parts in parallel, each with only 0.50 reliability, provides reliability of .50+.25+.125+.0625=.9375. Additional parts in parallel continue to improve reliability. (Reliability, moderate)**

63. What is FR(N)? How is it calculated? How are FR(N) and MTBF related? **FR(N) is the product failure number; it is the ratio of failed units to total operating hours; MTBF is the reciprocal of FR(N). (Reliability, moderate)**

64. Increasing the number of parts or components in a product tends to reduce its reliability. Why is this true only when adding components in series? **Adding parts in series involves an additional multiplication by a value less than one, so that reliability must fall. Adding parts in parallel (the redundancy concept) increases reliability because only one part of the parallel system must function. (Reliability, moderate)**

65. Explain carefully how redundancy improves product reliability. **A redundant part or component is connected in parallel with the primary part or component. "In parallel" means that either the original part or its backup needs to work, not that both must work at the same time. Redundancy increases reliability by providing an additional path (through the redundant part) to provide system reliability. (Reliability, moderate)**

66. List the two types of maintenance. **Preventive maintenance and breakdown maintenance. (Maintenance, moderate)**

67. Explain the notion of "infant mortality" in the context of product reliability. **Infant mortality refers to the high rate of failures that exists for many products when they are relatively new. (Maintenance, moderate)**

68. Explain how it is possible to have too much or too little preventive maintenance, and that there is an optimal amount of preventive maintenance. **Too little PM causes breakdown costs to rise sharply, adding more to cost than is saved by less PM; too much PM reduces breakdowns, but by an amount insufficient to offset the added cost of PM. (Maintenance, moderate)**

69. How does one identify a candidate for preventive maintenance? **By looking at the distributions for MTBF (mean time between failure). If the distributions have a small standard deviation, there is usually a candidate for preventive maintenance. (Maintenance, moderate)**

70. How do many electronic firms deal with infant mortality in their products?
They "burn in" their products prior to shipment; they execute a variety of tests to detect start-up problems prior to shipment. (Maintenance, moderate)

71. What are the limitations of the approach to seeking an optimal point of maintenance commitment through balancing the preventive and the breakdown maintenance costs?
The cost curves seldom consider the full costs of a breakdown. Many costs are ignored because they are not directly related to the immediate breakdown (e.g., inventory costs, costs associated with loss of morale). (Maintenance, moderate)

72. What are the elements of Total Productive Maintenance?
1. Reducing variability through employee involvement and excellent maintenance records
2. Designing machines that are reliable, easy to operate, and easy to maintain
3. Emphasizing total cost of ownership when purchasing machines
4. Developing preventive maintenance plans that utilize best practices of operators, maintenance departments, and depot service
5. Training workers to operate and maintain their own machines
(Increasing repair capabilities, moderate)

PROBLEMS

73. Ten high-intensity bulbs are tested for 100 hours each. One failed at 80 hours; all others completed the test. Calculate FR(%) and FR(N).
10%; 1/980 or 0.00102 (Reliability, moderate)

74. Ten high-intensity bulbs are tested for 100 hours each. One failed at 20 hours; all others completed the test. Calculate FR(%) and MTBF.
10%; 920 hours (Reliability, moderate)

75. Ten high-intensity bulbs are tested for 100 hours each. One failed at 20 hours; another failed at 70 hours; all others completed the test. Calculate FR(%) and MTBF.
20%; 445 hours (Reliability, moderate)

76. Given the following data, find the expected breakdown cost. The cost per breakdown is $100.

Number of breakdowns	0	1	2	3	4
Weekly frequency	5	10	20	10	5

Number of breakdowns	0	1	2	3	4	Total
Weekly frequency	.10	.20	.40	.20	.10	1.00

Expected number of breakdowns = (0 * .10) + (1 * .20) + (2 * .40) + (3 * .20) + (4 * .10) = 2
Expected cost of breakdowns = 2 * $100 = $200 (Maintenance, moderate)

77. Given the following data, find the expected breakdown cost. The cost per breakdown is $50.

Number of breakdowns	0	1	2	3
Monthly frequency	5	10	13	2

Number of breakdowns	0	1	2	3	Total
Monthly frequency	.1667	.3333	.4333	.0667	1.000

Expected number of breakdowns per month = (0 * .1667) + (1 * .3333) + (2 * .4333) + (3 * .0667) = 1.4; Expected cost of breakdowns = 1.4 * $50 = $70 (Maintenance, moderate)

78. Great Southern Consultants Group's computer system has been down several times over the past few months, as shown below.

Number of breakdowns	0	1	2	3	4
Monthly frequency	1	2	4	4	1

Each time the system is down, the firm loses an average of $400 in time and service expenses. They are considering signing a contract for preventive maintenance. With preventive maintenance, the system would be down only once a month. The monthly cost of preventive maintenance would be $200 a month. Which is cheaper, breakdown or preventive maintenance?

Number of breakdowns	0	1	2	3	4	Total
Monthly frequency	0.0833	0.1667	0.3333	0.3333	0.0833	1.0000

Expected number of breakdowns per month = (1 * .1667) + (2 * .3333) + (3 * .3333) + (4 * .0833) = 2.166; Expected cost of breakdowns per month = 2.166 * $400 = $866.67 Preventive maintenance cost per month = (1 * $400) + $200 = $600; Preventive maintenance is more cost-effective. (Maintenance, moderate)

79. Tiger Island Fabricators, which builds offshore oil platforms, has been experiencing problems with their profiling machine, which cuts the ends of pipe so that it can be welded to another pipe, as shown in the data below.

Number of breakdowns	0	1	2	3	4	5
Breakdown frequency	2	2	2	6	7	1

Each time a press breaks down, the company loses an average of $300. If they implement preventive maintenance, they will be able to reduce the number of breakdowns to 2 per month. Preventive maintenance costs would be $500 a month. Is preventive maintenance a cost-effective option?

Number of breakdowns	0	1	2	3	4	5	Total
Breakdown frequency	.10	.10	.10	.30	.35	.05	1.00

Expected number of breakdowns per month = (0 * .10) + (1 * .10) + (2 * .10) + (3 * .30) + (4 * .35) + (5 * .05) = 2.85; Expected cost of breakdowns per month = 2.85 * $300 = $855; Cost of preventive maintenance = (2 * $300) + $500 = $1,100. It is less expensive to suffer the breakdowns without preventive maintenance. (Maintenance, moderate)

80. A system consists of four components in series. The reliability of each component is 0.95. What is the reliability of the system?
The reliability of the system is R = $(0.95)^4$ = 0.8145 (Reliability, moderate)

81. A product is composed of a series connection of four components with the following reliabilities. What is the reliability of the system?

Component	1	2	3	4
Reliability	.90	.95	.95	.85

The reliability of the system is R = 0.90 * 0.95 * 0.80 * 0.85 = 0.69 (Reliability, moderate)

82. A system has five components in series. Each component has a reliability of 0.99. What is the reliability of the system?
$(0.99)^5$ = 0.9510 (Reliability, moderate)

83. A system has four components in a series. What is the reliability of the system?

Component	1	2	3	4
Reliability	.85	.95	.90	.99

0.85 * 0.95 * 0.90 * 0.99 = .7195 (Reliability, moderate)

84. Which product design below, A or B, has the higher reliability?

A

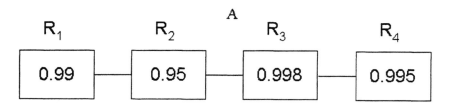

B

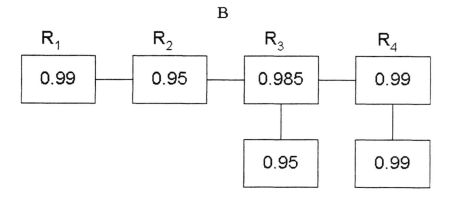

The reliability of A is .99 * .95 * .998 * .995=.9339. The reliability of B is .99 * .95 * (.985 + .015 * .95) *(.99 + .01 * .99) = .9397. System B has the higher reliability. (Reliability, difficult)

85. The diagram below identifies the elements of service as provided by a soft drink vending machine. Each element has an estimate of its own reliability, independent of the others. What is the reliability of the "system"?

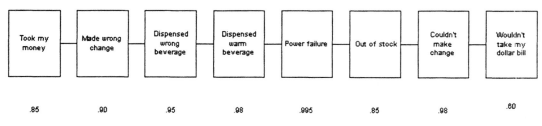

.85 * .90 * .95 * .98 * .995 * .85 * .98 * .60=0.3542 (Reliability, moderate)

86. Century Digital Phone advertises phone battery life (on standby) of up to three days. The standard deviation is thought to be five hours. Tina Talbot, an employee at CDP, tested 10 of these batteries for 72 hours. One failed at 40 hours; one failed at 54 hours; one failed at 60 hours. All others completed the test. Calculate FR(%), FR(N), and MTBF.
FR(%) = 3/10 or 30%. FR(N) = 3/(72*10-32-18-12) = 3/658 = .00456. MTBF is 1/FR(N) = 219 hours. (Reliability, moderate)

87. The Everstart is a battery with an intended design life of 72 months. Stephanie Bradley recently put 5 of these batteries through accelerated testing (the company couldn't wait six years) to simulate failure patterns. The test results had one failure at 24 months, one failure at 30 months, one failure at 48 months, and one failure at 60 months. Calculate FR(%), FR(N), and MTBF.
FR(%) = 4/5 or 80%. FR(N) = 4/(5*72-48-42-24-12) =4/234 = .017. The MTBF is 1/FR(N) = 58.5. (Reliability, moderate)

88. A portable telephone manufacturer claims that its BTE-700 Detachable Battery Pack offers approximately 140 minutes of talk time. If the battery is actually manufactured to meet this claim, what percent of these batteries will wear out within the first 60 minutes of use? It is believed that the standard deviation is approximately 20 minutes.
(This model is not contained within the chapter, but should be within students' grasp, as it uses the normal distribution covered earlier in the course. and available through the Normal Calculator in POM for Windows.) z = (60-140)/20 = 4, P(X < 60) = 0.00003 (Reliability, moderate)

89. Walt Specialty Tools manufactures a 12 volt floodlight whose bulb has a life of 65 hours thought to be normally distributed. The standard deviation is estimated to be 10 hours. If Walt offers a full-replacement warranty for bulbs that burn out before 50 hours of use, what percent of all bulbs will require replacement? If the standard deviation can be reduced to 8 hours, what is the new, smaller fraction of bulbs needing replacement under warranty?
(This model is not contained in the chapter, but should be within students' grasp, as it uses the normal distribution covered earlier in the course, and available through POM for Windows.) P(x < = 50, 65, 10) = 0.066807; P(x < = 50, 65, 8) = 0.030396 (Reliability, moderate)

90. The academic service commonly referred to as "registration" consists of several smaller components: advising, registration for courses, fee assessment, financial aid calculations, and fee payment. Each of these modules operates independently and has some probability of failure for each student. If the five probabilities which accompany these services are 80%, 90%, 98%, 95%, and 99%, what is the "reliability" of the entire product from the student's perspective-the probability that all five will work according to plan?
Reliability is .80 * .90 * .98 * .95 * .99 = .6636 (Reliability, moderate)

91. A simple electrical motor has three components: windings, armature, and housing. These three components have reliabilities of .97, .992, .999. There is no possibility of redundant parts. What is the reliability of the motor?
097 * 0.992 * 0.999 = 0.961278 (Reliability, moderate)

92. A simple electrical motor has three components: windings, armature, and housing. These three components have reliabilities .97, .992, .999. There is no possibility of redundant parts. The motor must have an overall reliability of 0.985, according to the manager of the product line manager who will use the motor as an input. What would you do to redesign the motor to meet this specification. Discuss, including a recalculation to meet the standard.
Since no backup is possible, individual components must be redesigned. The windings represent the weak link, and are the obvious choice. The windings must be at least 0.985 / (0.992* 0.999) = 0.993937 (Reliability, moderate)

93. A product has four components a, b, c, and d. The finished product must have a reliability of .96. The first three components come from a supplier, and have reliabilities .99, .98, and .995. The fourth component is being designed now. What must the reliability of component d be in order to meet the product reliability condition?

0.96 /(0.99 * 0.98 * 0.995) = 0.994459 (Reliability, moderate)

94. A product has three components X, Y, and Z. X has reliability 0.992; Y has reliability 0.995. If Z has reliability 0.991, what is the reliability of the entire product? Can Z be redesigned to be reliable enough for the entire product to have reliability of 0.99? Explain.

The product has reliability 0.992 * 0.995 * 0.991 = 0.978157; No: the required component reliability is impossible. 0.99 / (0.992 * 0.995) = 1.003 (Reliability, moderate)

95. A typical retail transaction consists of several smaller parts, which can be considered components subject to failure. A list of such components might include

Component	Description	Definition of Failure
1.	Find product in proper size, color, etc.	can't find product
2.	Enter cashier line	no lines open, lines too long, lane experiencing difficulty
3.	Scan product UPS for name, price, etc.	won't scan, item not on file, scans incorrect name or price
4.	Calculate purchase total	wrong weight, wrong extension, wrong data entry, wrong tax
5.	Make payment	customer lacks cash, check not acceptable, credit card refused
6.	Make change	makes change incorrectly
7.	Bag merchandise	damages mecahandise while bagging, bag splits
8.	Conclude transaction and exit	no receipt, unfriendly, rude, or aloof clerk

Let these eight probabilities be .92, .94, .99, .998, .98, .97, .95, and .96. What is the reliability of the system-the probability that there will be a satisfied customer? If you were the store manager, what do you think should be an acceptable value for this probability? Which components would be good candidates for backup, which for redesign?

Reliability is 0.74075. Students will probably argue that reliability should be higher, perhaps over 90%. Suggested candidates for backup include fuller inventory, more cashier lanes and overrides for faulty scanning. Suggested candidates for redesign include bagging and exit. (Reliability, difficult)

96. A component must have reliability .9925. Two technologies are available for this component: one produces a component with .999 reliability at a cost of $2000. Another produces a component with .73 reliability at a cost of $450. Which is cheaper: one high quality component or a parallel set of inferior components?

First determine how many of the 0.73 reliable component are needed: 2: 0.9271   3: 0.980317 4: 0.994686   Four are needed, which will cost $1800. This is cheaper than the $2000 single high-quality component. (Reliability, difficult)

97. General Grant must send orders to General Butler. Carrier pigeons are the medium of choice. A single pigeon has a .8 probability of arriving at the proper destination in a timely fashion. How many pigeons, each carrying an identical set of orders, must Grant send in order for him to have 98% confidence that the orders reached General Butler?

2: 0.96   3: 0.992   4: 0.9984 One or two is not enough; three is sufficient; four is wasteful. (Reliability, difficult)

98. A product design team is preparing to build a new doohickey. A doohickey consists of one A module, one B module, and one C module. There are different versions of these modules available in the company's design library. For example, there are two choices for A: A1 is .99 reliable, while A2 is .975 reliable. The table below details the choices available, along with the cost of each choice.

Module variation	Reliability	Cost, each
A1	.99	$17
A2	.975	$10
B1	.995	$4
B2	.992	$3
C1	.98	$2
C2	.90	$0.50
C3	.60	$0.25

Help the design team by selecting the least costly version of a doohickey that has system reliability of at least .96.

Trial and error. $A2_{0.975} * B2_{0.992} * C1_{0.98} = 0.947856$ costs $15 but does not meet the reliability specification.

The reliability of A2 + B2 is $0.975 * 0.992 = 0.9672$, which means that multiple redundancies at C are an option. Student may consider backing up C1 with C3. There are a dozen design alternatives which have no redundant parts. There are many more choices with one or more redundancies built in.

$A2_{0.975} * B2_{0.992} * C2+C2_{0.99} = 0.957528$ costs $16 but still does not meet the test.

(Reliability, difficult)

Module A: Decision-Making Tools

TRUE/FALSE

1. Practically speaking, three states of nature is the upper limit in a decision table.
    False (Decision tables, moderate)

2. An alternative is a course of action that may be chosen by a decision maker.
    True (Fundamentals of decision making, easy)

3. In a decision tree, a square symbol represents a state of nature node.
    False (Fundamentals of decision making, moderate)

4. The sequence in which decisions are made is unimportant when constructing a decision tree.
    False (Fundamentals of decision making, moderate)

5. If a decision maker can assign probabilities of occurrence to the states of nature, then the decision is being made under conditions of risk.
    True (Decision tables, moderate)

6. An example of a conditional value would be the payoff from selecting a particular alternative when a particular state of nature occurs.
    True (Decision tables, moderate)

7. An example of expected monetary value would be the payoff from selecting a particular alternative when a particular state of nature occurs.
    False (Decision tables, moderate)

8. If a decision maker knows for sure which state of nature will occur, he/she is making a decision under certainty.
    True (Decision tables, moderate)

9. If a decision maker has to make a certain decision only once, expected monetary value is a good indication of the payoff associated with the decision.
    False (Decision tables, moderate)

10. The expected value of perfect information is the same as the expected value under certainty.
    False (Decision tables, moderate)

11. The probability of a certain state of nature occurring given a particular prior result is an example of a conditional probability.
    True (Decision tables, moderate)

12. In a decision tree, the expected monetary values are computed by working from right to left.
    True (Decision tables, moderate)

MULTIPLE CHOICE

13. Which of the following is **not** considered a step in the decision making process?
    a. clearly identify the problem
    b. select the best alternative
    c. develop objectives
    d. evaluate alternatives
    e. minimize costs when possible

    e (The decision process in operations, moderate)

14. In terms of decision theory, an occurrence or situation over which the decision maker has no control is called a(n)
    a. decision tree
    b. state of nature
    c. alternative
    d. decision under uncertainty
    e. none of the above

    b (Fundamentals of decision making, easy)

15. The first step, and a key element, in the decision making process is to
    a. clearly define the problem
    b. develop objectives
    c. monitor the results
    d. consult a specialist
    e. select the best alternative

    a (The decision process in operations, easy)

16. A tabular presentation that shows the outcome for each decision alternative under the various possible states of nature is called a(n)
    a. payoff table
    b. isoquant table
    c. payback period matrix.
    d. feasible region.
    e. decision tree.

    a (Decision tables, easy)

17. The difference between the expected payoff under certainty and the maximum expected payoff under risk is
    a. expected monetary value
    b. economic order quantity
    c. PERT
    d. expected value of perfect information
    e. expected monetary payoff

    d (Decision tables, moderate)

18. The outcome of an alternative/state of nature combination is a(n)
    a. conditional value
    b. expected value
    c. conditional probability
    d. price
    e. all of the above are correct
    a (Decision tables, moderate)

19. The expected value of perfect information (EVPI) is the
    a. payoff for a decision made under perfect information
    b. payoff under minimum risk
    c. difference between the payoff under certainty and the payoff under risk
    d. average expected payoff
    e. none of the above
    c (Decision tables, moderate)

20. A decision tree is a(n)
    a. algebraic representation of alternatives and states of nature
    b. schematic representation of alternatives and states of nature
    c. behavioral representation of alternatives and states of nature
    d. matrix representation of alternatives and states of nature
    e. tabular representation of alternatives and states of nature
    b (Decision trees, moderate)

21. The likelihood that a decision maker will ever receive a payoff precisely equal to the EMV when making any one decision is
    a. high (near 100%)
    b. low (near 0%)
    c. dependent upon the number of alternatives
    d. dependent upon the number of states of nature
    e. none of the above
    b (Decision tables, moderate)

22. What is the EMV for Option 1 in the following decision table?

States of nature

Alternatives	S_1	S_2
p	.3	.7
Option 1	20,000	10,000
Option 2	5,000	30,000

    a. 10,000
    b. 12,500
    c. 13,000
    d. 15,000
    e. 30,000
    c (Decision tables, easy)

23. What is the EMV for Option 2 in the following decision table?

States of nature

Alternatives	S_1	S_2
p	.3	.7
Option 1	20,000	10,000
Option 2	5,000	30,000

a. 5,000
b. 17,500
c. 21,000
d. 22,500
e. 30,000
d (Decision tables, moderate)

24. The expected value under certainty is
a. the maximum EMV for a set of alternatives
b. the same as the expected value of perfect information
c. valuable in situations involving risk
d. the average return obtained when the decision maker knows which state of nature is going to occur before the decision is made
e. obtained using conditional probabilities
d (Decision tables, moderate)

25. Decision trees
a. give more accurate solutions than decision tables
b. give less accurate solutions than decision tables
c. are rarely used because one needs specialized software to graph them
d. are especially powerful when a sequence of decisions must be made
e. are too complex to be used by decision makers
d (Decision trees, moderate)

26. All of the following steps are taken to analyze problems with decision trees **except**
a. define the problem
b. structure or draw a decision tree
c. assign probabilities to the alternatives
d. estimate payoffs for each possible alternative/state of nature combination
e. solve the problem by computing expected monetary values for each state of nature node
c (Decision treees, moderate)

27. What is the EMV for Option 1 in the following decision table?

States of nature

Alternatives	S_1	S_2
p	.4	.6
Option 1	10,000	30,000
Option 2	40,000	5,000
Option 3	-2,000	50,000

a. 10,000
b. 20,000
c. 22,000
d. 40,000
e. 48,000
c (Decision tables, moderate)

28. What is the EMV for Option 2 in the following decision table?

States of nature

Alternatives	S_1	S_2
p	.4	.6
Option 1	10,000	30,000
Option 2	40,000	5,000
Option 3	-2,000	50,000

a. 19,000
b. 26,000
c. 22,500
d. 40,000
e. 83,000
a (Decision tables, moderate)

29. What is the expected value under certainty of the following decision table?

States of nature

Alternatives	S_1	S_2
p	.4	.6
Option 1	10,000	30,000
Option 2	40,000	15,000
Option 3	-2,000	50,000

a. 30,000
b. 40,000
c. 34,000
d. 46,000
e. 90,000
d (Decision tables, moderate)

30. What is the EMV for Option 1 in the following decision table?

States of nature

Alternatives	S_1	S_2
p	.6	.4
Option 1	200	100
Option 2	50	250

a. 100
b. 150
c. 160
d. 200
e. 300
c (Decision tables, moderate)

31. What is the EMV for Option 2 in the following decision table?

States of nature

Alternatives	S_1	S_2
p	.6	.4
Option 1	200	100
Option 2	50	250

a. 50
b. 100
c. 130
d. 150
e. 250
c (Decision tables, moderate)

32. What is the expected value under certainty in the following decision table?

States of nature

Alternatives	S_1	S_2
p	.6	.4
Option 1	200	100
Option 2	50	250

a. 200
b. 220
c. 250
d. 300
e. 450
b (Decision tables, moderate)

33. What is the expected value of perfect information of the following decision table?

States of nature

Alternatives	S_1	S_2
p	.6	.4
Option 1	200	100
Option 2	50	250

a. 20
b. 40
c. 50
d. 60
e. 90
d (Decision tables, moderate)

FILL-IN-THE BLANK

34. A _____ is a tabular means of analyzing decision alternatives and states of nature.
decision table (Decision tables, easy)

35. _____ is the criterion for decision making under uncertainty that finds an alternative that maximizes the maximum outcome or consequences.
Maximax (Decision tables, moderate)

36. _____ is the criterion for decision making under uncertainty that finds an alternative that maximizes the minimum outcome or consequences.
Maximin (Decision tables, moderate)

37. _____ is the criterion for decision making under certainty that assigns equal probability to each state of nature.
Equally likely (Decision tables, moderate)

38. _____ is the expected payout or value of a variable that has different possible states of nature, each with an associated probability.
Expected monetary value or EMV (Decision tables, moderate)

39. _____ is the difference between the payoff under certainty and the payoff under risk.
Expected value of perfect information or EVPI (Decision tables, moderate)

40. _____ is the expected return if perfect information is available.
Expected value under certainty (Decision tables, moderate)

41. A _____ is a graphical means of analyzing decision alternatives and states of nature.
decision tree (Decision trees, easy)

SHORT ANSWER

42. List, in order, the six steps in the decision process.
1. Clearly define the problem and the factors that influence it.
2. Develop specific and measurable objectives.
3. Develop a model.
4. Evaluate each alternative solution.
5. Select the best alternative.
6. Implement the solution.
(The decision process in operations, moderate)

43. In the context of decision-making, define **state of nature.**
An occurrence or situation over which the decision maker has little or no control.
(Fundamentals of decision making, moderate)

44. In the context of decision-making, define **alternative.**
A course of action or a strategy that may be chosen by a decision maker. (Fundamentals of decision making, moderate)

45. Explain the graphical shapes used in decision tree analysis.
A decision node from which one or several alternatives may be selected is represented by a square; a state of nature node out of which states of nature will occur is represented by a circle. (Fundamentals of decision making, moderate)

46. Define Expected Monetary Value (EMV).
EMV is the expected value or return for an alternative if we were to repeat the decision a large number of times, each time choosing that alternative. (Decision tables, moderate)

47. List, in order the five steps in analyzing a problem using a decision tree.
1. Define the problem
2. Structure or draw the decision tree
3. Assign probabilities to the states of nature
4. Estimate payoffs for each possible combination of alternatives and states of nature
5. Solve the problem by computing the EMV for each state of nature node.
(Decision tress, moderate)

48. What is a conditional value?
It is an outcome of a particular alternative/state of nature combination. (Decision trees, moderate)

49. What is the expected value of perfect information?
It is the difference between payoff under certainty and maximum EMV under risk. (Decision trees, moderate)

50. What is the expected value under certainty?
The expected or average return if we have perfect information about the states of nature before a decision has to be made. (Decision trees, moderate)

51.   What is a decision tree?

A decision tree is a graphic display of the decision process that indicates decision alternatives, states of nature and their respective probabilities, and payoffs for each combination of alternative and states of nature. (Decision trees, moderate)

PROBLEMS

52.   Steve Gentry, the operations manager of Baja Fabricators, wants to purchase a new profiling machine (it cuts compound angles on the ends of large structural pipes used in the fabrication yard). However, because the price of crude oil is depressed, the market for such equipment is down. Steve believes that the market will improve in the near future and that the company should expand its capacity. The table below displays the three equipment options he is currently considering, and the profit he expects each one to yield over a two-year period. The consensus forecast at Baja is that there is about a 30 percent probability that the market will pick up "soon" (within 3 to 6 months) and a 70 percent probability that the improvement will come "later" (in 9 to 12 months, perhaps longer).

Profit from Capacity Investment (in Dollars)

Equipment Option	Market picks up "soon" $p = 0.30$	Market picks up "later" $p = 0.70$
Manual Machine	-100000	250000
NC Machine	120000	150000
CNC Machine	150000	-300000

a. Calculate the expected monetary value of each decision alternative.
b. Which equipment option should Steve take?

Based upon the EMV criterion, Baja should purchase a manually operated machine.

Profit from Capacity Investment (in Dollars)

Equipment Option	**Market picks up "soon"** $p = 0.30$	**Market picks up "later"** $p = 0.70$	**Expected Monetary Value**
Manual Machine	**-100000**	**250000**	**145000**
NC Machine	**120000**	**150000**	**141000**
CNC Machine	**150000**	**-300000**	**-165000**

(Decision tables, easy)

53. Miles is considering buying a new pickup truck for his lawn service firm. The economy in town seems to be growing, and he is wondering whether he should opt for a sub-compact, compact, or full-size pickup truck. The smaller truck would have better fuel economy, but would sacrifice capacity and some durability. A friend at the Bureau of Economic Research told him that there is a 30 percent chance of lower gas prices in his area this year, a 20 percent chance of higher gas prices, and a 50 percent chance that gas prices will stay roughly unchanged. Based on this information, Miles has developed a decision table that indicates the profit amount he would end up with after a year for each combination of truck and gas prices.

States of nature

Alternatives	Lower gas prices	Gas prices unchanged	Higher gas prices
probability	.3	.5	.2
Sub-compact	16,000	19,000	21,000
Compact	15,000	20,000	22,000
Full-size	24,000	19,000	6,000

Calculate the expected monetary value for each decision alternative. Which decision yields the highest EMV?

The expected monetary values appear in the table below. The highest EMV (18,900) is that of the compact truck.

States of nature

Alternatives	Lower gas prices	Gas prices unchanged	Higher gas prices	EMV
probability	.3	.5	.2	
Sub-compact	16,000	19,000	21,000	18,500
Compact	15,000	20,000	22,000	18,900
Full-size	24,000	19,000	6,000	17,900

(Decision tables, moderate)

54. Miles is considering buying a new pickup truck for his lawn service firm. The economy in town seems to be growing, and he is wondering whether he should opt for a sub-compact, compact, or full-size pickup truck. The smaller truck would have better fuel economy, but would sacrifice capacity and some durability. A friend at the Bureau of Economic Research told him that there is a 30 percent chance of lower gas prices in his area this year, a 20 percent chance of higher gas prices, and a 50 percent chance that gas prices will stay roughly unchanged. Based on this information, Miles has developed a decision table that indicates the profit amount he would end up with after a year for each combination of truck and gas prices. Develop a decision tree for this situation and indicate which type of truck he should select.

<table>
<tr><td></td><td colspan="3">States of nature</td></tr>
<tr><td>Alternatives</td><td>Lower gas prices</td><td>Gas prices unchanged</td><td>Higher gas prices</td></tr>
<tr><td>probability</td><td>.3</td><td>.5</td><td>.2</td></tr>
<tr><td>Sub-compact</td><td>16,000</td><td>19,000</td><td>21,000</td></tr>
<tr><td>Compact</td><td>15,000</td><td>20,000</td><td>22,000</td></tr>
<tr><td>Full-size</td><td>24,000</td><td>19,000</td><td>6,000</td></tr>
</table>

The tree appears in the drawing below. The highest expected value decision alternative is the compact truck, at $18,900, as shown in the POM for Windows solution.

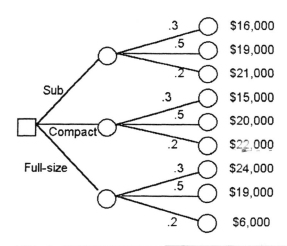

Objective
- ● Profits (maximize)
- ○ Costs (minimize)

Truck Decision Solution

	Start Node	End Node	Branch Probabili	Profit	Use Branch?	End node	Node Type	Node Value
Start	0.	1.	0.	0.		1.	Decision	18,900.
Branch 1	1.	2.	0.	0.		2.	Chance	18,500.
Branch 2	1.	3.	0.	0.	Yes	3.	Chance	18,900.
Branch 3	1.	4.	0.	0.		4.	Chance	17,900.
Branch 4	2.	5.	0.3	16,000.		5.	Final	16,000.
Branch 5	2.	6.	0.5	19,000.		6.	Final	19,000.
Branch 6	2.	7.	0.2	21,000.		7.	Final	21,000.
Branch 7	3.	8.	0.3	15,000.		8.	Final	15,000.
Branch 9	3.	10.	0.2	22,000.		10.	Final	22,000.
Branch 10	4.	11.	0.3	24,000.		11.	Final	24,000.
Branch 11	4.	12.	0.5	19,000.		12.	Final	19,000.
Branch 12	4.	13.	0.2	6,000.		13.	Final	6,000.

(Decision tree, easy)

55. A toy manufacturer has three different mechanisms that can be installed in a doll that it sells. The different mechanisms have three different setup costs (overheads) and variable costs, and therefore the profit from the dolls is dependent on the volume of sales. The anticipated payoffs are as follows.

	Light Demand	Moderate Demand	Heavy Demand
Wind-up action	$300,000	$180,000	$160,000
Pneumatic action	$280,000	$440,000	$400,000
Electrical action	$-350,000	$240,000	$780,000
probability	.25	.45	.30

a. What is the EMV of each decision alternative?
b. Which action should be selected?
c. What is the expected value under certainty?
d. What is the expected value of perfect information?
(a) Wind-up=$160,000; Pneumatic = $388,000; and Electrical = $254,500. (b) Pneumatic has the best EMV, at $388,000. (c) Expected value under certainty is $507,000; (d) EVPI = $507,000 - $388,000 = $119,000. POM for Windows solution follows.

Decision Table Results

<untitled> Solut

	Light	Moderate	Heavy	EMV
Probabilities	0.25	0.45	0.3	
Wind-up	300,000.	180,000.	160,000.	204,000.
Pneumatic	280,000.	440,000.	400,000.	388,000.
Electrical	-350,000.	240,000.	780,000.	254,500.
			maximum	388,000.
				Best EV

Summary

The maximum expected monetary value is 388,000 given by Pneumatic
The maximin is 280,000 given by Pneumatic
The maximax is 780,000 given by Electrical

<untitled> Solution

	Light	Moderate	Heavy	Maximum
Probabilities	0.25	0.45	0.3	
Wind-up	300,000.	180,000.	160,000.	
Pneumatic	280,000.	440,000.	400,000.	
Electrical	-350,000.	240,000.	780,000.	
Perfect Information	300,000.	440,000.	780,000.	
Perfect*probability	75,000.	198,000.	234,000.	507,000.
Best Expected Value				388,000.
Exp Value of Perfect Info				119,000.

(Decision table, moderate)

56. Daily sales of bread by Salvador Monella's Baking Company follow the historical pattern shown in the table below. It costs the bakery 50 cents to produce a loaf of bread which sells for 95 cents. Any bread unsold at the end of the day is sold to the parish jail for 25 cents per loaf. Construct the decision table of conditional payoffs. How many loaves should Sal bake each day in order to maximize contribution?

Demand	400	500	600	700	800
Probability	.10	.15	.45	.25	.05

The POM for Windows decision table and solution appear below. The best expected value is $245.5, which occurs with the decision to bake 600 loaves.

Objective
◉ Profits (maximize)
○ Costs (minimize)

Sal Monella

	Sell 400	Sell 500	Sell 600	Sell 700	Sell 800
Probabilities	0	0	0	0	0
Bake 400	180	180	180	180	180
Bake 500	155	225	225	225	225
Bake 600	130	200	270	270	270
Bake 700	105	175	245	315	315
Bake 800	80	150	220	290	360

Sal Monella Solution

	Sell 400	Sell 500	Sell 600	Sell 700	Sell 800	EMV
Probabilities	0.1	0.15	0.45	0.25	0.05	
Bake 400	180.	180.	180.	180.	180.	180.
Bake 500	155.	225.	225.	225.	225.	218.
Bake 600	130.	200.	270.	270.	270.	245.5
Bake 700	105.	175.	245.	315.	315.	241.5
Bake 800	80.	150.	220.	290.	360.	220.
					maximum	245.5
						Best EV

(Decision tables, moderate)

57. Earl Shell owns his own Sno-Cone business and lives 30 miles from a beach resort. The sale of Sno-Cones is highly dependent upon his location and upon the weather. At the resort, he will profit $120 per day in fair weather, $10 per day in foul weather. At home, he will profit $70 in fair weather, $55 in foul weather. Assume that on any particular day, the weather service suggests a 60 percent chance of fair weather.

a. Construct Earl's payoff table.

b. What decision is recommended by the expected value criterion?

c. What is the EVPI?

Objective
- ◉ Profits (maximize)
- ○ Costs (minimize)

Earl's Sno-Cone Truck

	Fair Weather	Foul weather
Probabilities	0.6	0.4
Resort	120.	10.
Home	70.	55

▦ Decision Table Results

Earl's Sno-Cone Truck Solution

	Fair Weather	Foul weather	EMV	Row Min	Row Max
Probabilities	0.6	0.4			
Resort	120.	10.	76.	10.	120.
Home	70.	55.	64.	55.	70.
		maximum	76.	55.	120.
			Best EV	maximin	maximax

Summary

The maximum expected monetary value is 76 given by Resort

◆ Perfect Information

Earl's Sno-Cone Truck Solution

	Fair Weather	Foul weather	Maximum
Probabilities	0.6	0.4	
Resort	120.	10.	
Home	70.	55.	
Perfect Information	120.	55.	
Perfect probability	72.	22.	94.
Best Expected Value			76.
Exp Value of Perfect Info			18.

(Decision tables, moderate)

58. Earl Shell owns his own Sno-Cone business and lives 30 miles from a beach resort. The sale of Sno-Cones is highly dependent upon his location and upon the weather. At the resort, he will profit $120 per day in fair weather, $10 per day in bad weather. At home, he will profit $60 in fair weather, $35 in bad weather. Assume that on any particular day, the weather service suggests a 40 percent chance of foul weather.

a. Construct Earl's decision tree.

b. What decision is recommended by the expected value criterion?

Analysis of the decision tree with POM for Windows finds that Resort has a higher EMV ($76) than Home

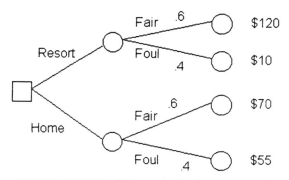

Decision Tree Results							
Earl's Truck Solution							
	Start Node	End Node	Branch Probabili	Profit	Use Branch?	End node	Node Type	Node Value
Start	0.	1.	0.	0.		1.	Decision	76.
Resort	1.	2.	0.	0.	Yes	2.	Chance	76.
Home	1.	3.	0.	0.		3.	Chance	64.
Fair/Resort	2.	4.	0.6	120.		4.	Final	120.
Foul/Resort	2.	5.	0.4	10.		5.	Final	10.
Fair/Home	3.	6.	0.6	70.		6.	Final	70.
Fair/Home	3.	7.	0.4	55.		7.	Final	55.

(Decision tress, moderate)

59. The campus bookstore sells highlighters that it purchases by the case. Cost per case, including shipping and handling, is $200. Revenue per case is $350. Any cases unsold will be discounted and sold at $175. The bookstore has estimated that demand will follow the pattern below

Demand level	Probability
10 cases	35 percent
11 cases	25 percent
12 cases	20 percent
13 cases	15 percent
14 cases	5 percent

a. Construct the bookstore's payoff table.
b. How many cases should the bookstore stock in order to maximize profit?
c. How would your answer differ if the clearance price were not $175 per case but $225 per case? (It is not necessary to re-solve the problem to answer this.)

(a) The POM for Windows table of conditional payoffs appears below. (b) The highest EMV is 1643.75, from stocking 13 cases. (c) If the clearance price exceeds the case cost, there will be no disincentive to stocking the maximum demand level, 14 cases.

Highlighter Sale

	Demand 10	Demand 11	Demand 12	Demand 13	Demand 14
Probabilities	0.35	0.25	0.2	0.15	0.05
Stock 10	1,500.	1,500.	1,500.	1,500.	1,500.
Stock 11	1,475.	1,650.	1,650.	1,650.	1,650.
Stock 12	1,450.	1,625.	1,800.	1,800.	1,800.
Stock 13	1,425.	1,600.	1,775.	1,950.	1,950.
Stock 14	1,400.	1,575.	1,750.	1925	2,100.

Decision Table Results

Highlighter Sale Solution

	Demand 10	Demand 11	Demand 12	Demand 13	Demand 14	EMV
Probabilities	0.35	0.25	0.2	0.15	0.05	
Stock 10	1,500.	1,500.	1,500.	1,500.	1,500.	1,500.
Stock 11	1,475.	1,650.	1,650.	1,650.	1,650.	1,588.75
Stock 12	1,450.	1,625.	1,800.	1,800.	1,800.	1,633.75
Stock 13	1,425.	1,600.	1,775.	1,950.	1,950.	1,643.75
Stock 14	1,400.	1,575.	1,750.	1,925.	2,100.	1,627.5
					maximum	1,643.75
						Best EV

(Decision tables, moderate)

60. The campus bookstore sells stadium blankets embroidered with the university crest. The blankets must be purchased in bundles of one dozen each. Each blanket in the bundle costs $65, and will sell for $90. Blankets unsold by homecoming will be clearance priced at $20. The bookstore estimates that demand patterns will follow the table below.

a. Build the decision table.

b. What is the maximum expected value?

c. How many bundles should be purchased?

Demand level	Probability
1 bundle	20 percent
2 bundles	40 percent
3 bundles	30 percent
4 bundles	10 percent

In the POM for Windows decision table below, the cell "Order 3, Demand 1" generates revenues of $90 * 12 + $20 * 24 = 1080 + 480 = 1560, and costs of $65 * 36 = $2340, for a conditional loss of $780. Order 2 has the highest expected value, $432.

	Blankets			
	Demand 1	Demand 2	Demand 3	Demand 4
Probabilities	0.2	0.4	0.3	0.1
Order 1	300.	300.	300.	300.
Order 2	-240.	600.	600.	600.
Order 3	-780.	60.	900.	900.
Order 4	-1,320.	-480.	360.	1200

Decision Table Results

	Blankets Solution				
	Demand 1	Demand 2	Demand 3	Demand 4	EMV
Probabilities	0.2	0.4	0.3	0.1	
Order 1	300.	300.	300.	300.	300.
Order 2	-240.	600.	600.	600.	432.
Order 3	-780.	60.	900.	900.	228.
Order 4	-1,320.	-480.	360.	1,200.	-228.
				maximum	432.
					Best EV

(Decision tables, moderate)

61. Bratt's Bed and Breakfast, in a small historic New England town, must decide how to subdivide (remodel) the large old home that will become their inn. There are three alternatives: Option A would modernize all baths and combine rooms, leaving the inn with four suites, each suitable for two to four adults each. Option B would modernize only the second floor; the results would be six suites, four for two to four adults, two for two adults only. Option C (the status quo option) leaves all walls intact. In this case, there are eight rooms available, but only two are suitable for four adults, and four rooms will not have private baths. Below are the details of profit and demand patterns that will accompany each option. Which option has the highest expected value?

Annual profit under various
demand patterns

	Capacity	p	Average	p
A (Modernize all)	$90,000	.5	$25,000	.5
B (Modernize 2nd)	$80,000	.4	$70,000	.6
C (Status Quo)	$60,000	.3	$55,000	.7

Branch 2, which represents Option B-Modernize 2nd floor, has the highest expected value, $74,000. This cannot be done as a decision table. POM for Windows solution follows.

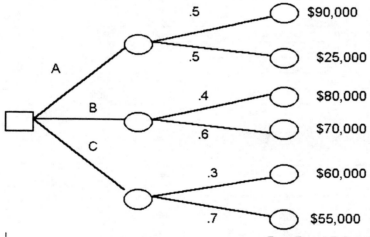

	Start Node	End Node	Branch Probabili	Profit	Use Branch?	End node	Node Type	Node Value
Start	0.	1.	0.	0.		1.	Decision	74,000.
Branch 1	1.	2.	0.	0.		2.	Chance	57,500.
Branch 2	1.	3.	0.	0.	Yes	3.	Chance	74,000.
Branch 3	1.	4.	0.	0.		4.	Chance	56,500.
Branch 4	2.	5.	0.5	90,000.		5.	Final	90,000.
Branch 5	2.	6.	0.5	25,000.		6.	Final	25,000.
Branch 6	3.	7.	0.4	80,000.		7.	Final	80,000.
Branch 7	3.	8.	0.6	70,000.		8.	Final	70,000.
Branch 8	4.	9.	0.3	60,000.		9.	Final	60,000.
Branch 9	4.	10.	0.7	55,000.		10.	Final	55,000.

Bratt B and B Solution

(Decision trees, moderate)

MODULE B: LINEAR PROGRAMMING

TRUE/FALSE

1. Linear programming helps operations managers make decisions necessary to allocate resources.
   True (Introduction, easy)

2. The graphical method of solving linear programming can handle only maximizing problems.
   False (Solving minimization problems, moderate)

3. In linear programming, a statement such as "Maximize contribution" becomes an objective function when the problem is formulated.
   True (Formulating linear programming problems, moderate)

4. The graphic solution method of linear programming uses constraints.
   True (Graphical solution to a linear programming problem, easy)

5. In linear programming, a statement such as "the blend must consist of at least 10% of ingredient A, at least 30% of ingredient B, and no more than 50% of ingredient C" cannot be made into valid constraints because it fails to specify a quantity.
   False (Linear programming applications, difficult)

6. In linear programming, the unit profit or unit contribution associated with one decision variable can be affected by the quantity made of that variable or of any other variable in the problem.
   False (requirements of a linear programming problem, difficult)

7. A common form of the product-mix linear programming seeks to find the quantities of items in the product mix that maximizes profit in the presence of limited resources.
   True (Formulating linear programming problems, moderate)

8. The graphical solution method of linear programming works only when there are two dimensions (two decision variables).
   True (Graphical solution to a linear programming problem, moderate)

9. In terms of linear programming, the fact that the solution is infeasible implies that the "profit" can increase without limit.
   False (Graphical solution to a linear programming problem, moderate)

10. The optimum solution to a linear programming problem is within the feasible region.
    True (Graphical solution to a linear programming problem, moderate)

11. The region that satisfies all of the constraints in graphical linear programming is called the region of optimality.
    False (Graphical solution to a linear programming problem, moderate)

12. The corner point solution method requires that we move the iso-profit line up until it no longer intersects with any constraint equation.
    False (Graphical solution to a linear programming problem, moderate)

13. In sensitivity analysis, a zero shadow price (or reduced cost) for a resource ordinarily means that the resource has not been used up.
True (Sensitivity analysis, difficult)

14. In linear programming, if there are three constraints, each representing a resource that can be used up, the optimal solution must use up all of each of the three resources.
False (Graphical solution to a linear programming problem, moderate)

15. The optimal solution of a linear programming problem which consists of two variables and six constraints will probably not satisfy all six constraints precisely.
True (Graphical solution to a linear programming problem, difficult)

MULTIPLE CHOICE

16. Which of the following represent valid constraints in linear programming?
   a. $2X \geq 7X*Y$
   b. $2X + 7Y \geq 100$
   c. $2X * 7Y \geq 500$
   d. $2X^2 + 7Y \geq 50$
   e. all of the above are valid linear programming constraints
   b (Requirements of a linear programming problem, moderate)

17. In sensitivity analysis, a zero shadow price (or reduced cost, or dual value) for a resource ordinarily means that
   a. the resource has not been used up
   b. the resource is scarce
   c. the resource constraint was redundant
   d. something is wrong with the problem formulation
   e. none of the above
   a (Sensitivity analysis, difficult)

18. The graphical method of linear programming can only handle _____ decision variable(s).
   a. one
   b. two
   c. three
   d. none of the above
   b (Graphical solution to a linear programming problem, moderate)

19. The feasible region plotted on the diagram below is consistent with which one of the following constraints?

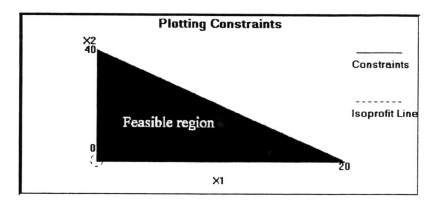

a. $8X1 + 4X2 \geq 160$
b. $8X1 + 4X2 \leq 160$
c. $4X1 + 8X2 \leq 160$
d. $8X1 - 4X2 \leq 160$
e. $4X1 - 8X2 \leq 160$

b (Graphical solution to a linear programming problem, moderate)

20. The feasible region plotted on the diagram below is consistent with which one of the following constraints?

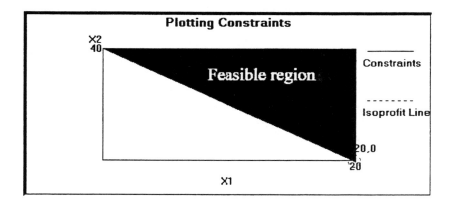

a. $8X1 + 4X2 \geq 160$
b. $8X1 + 4X2 \leq 160$
c. $4X1 + 8X2 \leq 160$
d. $8X1 - 4X2 \leq 160$
e. $4X1 - 8X2 \leq 160$

a (Graphical solution to a linear programming problem, difficult)

21. Which of the following is **not** a requirement of a linear programming problem?
    a. An objective function, expressed in terms of linear equations.
    b. Constraint equations, expressed as linear equations.
    c. An objective function, to be maximized or minimized.
    d. Alternative courses of action.
    e. For each decision variable, there must be one constraint or resource limit.
    e (Requirements of a linear programming problem, moderate)

22. The iso-profit line is
    a. a method for solving a linear programming problem
    b. a line with the same profit at all points
    c. parallel to all other iso-profit lines in the same problem
    d. generally going to have a greater value as it is moved further from the origin
    e. all of the above
    e (Graphical solution to a linear programming problem, moderate)

23. In linear programming, a statement such as "Maximize contribution" becomes a(n)
    a. constraint
    b. slack variable
    c. objective function
    d. violation of linearity
    e. decision variable
    c (Formulating linear programming problems, moderate)

24. Which of the following combinations of constraints has no feasible region?
    a. $X + Y \geq 15$ and $X - Y \leq 10$
    b. $X + Y \geq 5$ and $X \geq 10$
    c. $X + Y \geq 100$ and $X + Y \leq 50$
    d. $X \geq 10$ and $Y \geq 20$
    e. all of the above have a feasible region
    c (Graphical solution to a linear programming problem, moderate)

25. Which of the following sets of constraints results in an unbounded maximizing problem?
    a. $X + Y \geq 15$ and $X - Y \leq 10$
    b. $X + Y \leq 10$ and $X \geq 5$
    c. $X + Y \geq 100$ and $X + Y \leq 50$
    d. $X \leq 10$ and $Y \leq 20$
    e. all of the above have a bounded maximum
    a (Graphical solution to a linear programming problem, moderate)

26. The region which satisfies all of the constraints in graphical linear programming is called the
    a. optimum solution space
    b. profit maximization space
    c. feasible solution space
    d. region of optimality
    e. region of non-negativity
    c (Graphical solution to a linear programming problem, moderate)

27. The corner point solution method requires
    a. moving the iso-profit line to the highest level that still touches some part of the feasible region
    b. moving the iso-profit line to the lowest level that still touches some part of the feasible region
    c. finding the coordinates for each corner of the feasible solution space
    d. finding the value of the objective function at the origin
    e. none of the above
    c (Graphical solution to a linear programming problem, moderate)

28. Using the graphical solution method to solve a maximization problem requires that we
    a. move the iso-profit line to the highest level that still touches some part of the feasible region
    b. move the iso-cost line to the lowest level that still touches some part of the feasible region
    c. apply the method of simultaneous equations to solve for the intersections of constraints
    d. find the value of the objective function at the origin
    e. none of the above
    a (Graphical solution to a linear programming problem, moderate)

29. A shadow price (or dual value) reflects which of the following in a maximization problem?
    a. The market price that must be paid to obtain additional resources.
    b. The increase in profit that would accompany one added unit of a scarce resource.
    c. The reduction in cost that would accompany a one unit decrease in the resource.
    d. The marginal gain in the objective realized by subtracting one unit of a resource.
    e. None of the above.
    b (Sensitivity analysis, moderate)

30. For the two constraints given below, which point is in the feasible solution space of this maximization problem?   (1) $14x + 6y \leq 42$ (2) $x - y \leq 3$
    a. $x = 1, y = 5$
    b. $x = -1, y = 1$
    c. $x = 4, y = 4$
    d. $x = 2, y = 1$
    e. $x = 2, y = 8$
    d (Graphical solution to a linear programming problem, moderate)

31. For the two constraints given below, which point is in the feasible solution space of this minimization problem?   (1) $14x + 6y \geq 42$ (2) $x - y \geq 3$
    a. $x = 5, y = 1$
    b. $x = -1, y = 1$
    c. $x = 0, y = 4$
    d. $x = 2, y = 1$
    e. $x = 2, y = 0$
    a (Graphical solution to a linear programming problem, moderate)

32.   The graphical method of linear programming can handle _____ decision variables and _____ constraints.
       a. two; two
       b. one; three
       c. two; unlimited
       d. three; two
       e. none of the above
       c (Graphical solution to a linear programming problem, moderate)

33.   What combination of x and y will yield the optimum for this problem? Maximize $3x + $15y, subject to (1) $2x + 4y \leq 12$ and (2) $5x + 2y \leq 10$.
       a. x = 2, y = 0
       b. x = 0, y = 3
       c. x = 0, y = 0
       d. x = 1, y = 5
       e. none of the above
       b (Graphical solution to a linear programming problem, moderate)

34.   What combination of x and y will yield the optimum for this problem? Minimize $3x + $15y, subject to (1) $2x + 4y \leq 12$ and (2) $5x + 2y \leq 10$.
       a. x = 2, y = 0
       b. x = 0, y = 3
       c. x = 0, y = 0
       d. x = 1, y = 5
       e. none of the above
       c (Graphical solution to a linear programming problem, moderate)

35.   What combination of a and b will yield the optimum for this problem? Maximize $6a + $15b, subject to (1) $4a + 2b \leq 12$ and (2) $5a + 2b \leq 20$.
       a. a = 0, b = 0
       b. a = 3, b = 3
       c. a = 0, b = 6
       d. a = 6, b = 0
       e. cannot solve without values for a and b
       c (Graphical solution to a linear programming problem, moderate)

36.   A linear programming maximization problem has been solved. In the optimal solution, two resources are scarce. If an added amount could be found for only one of these resources, how would the optimal solution be changed?
       a. stays the same; the extra resource can't be used without more of the other scarce resource
       b. the extra resource will cause the value of the objective to fall
       c. the shadow price of the added resource will rise
       d. the optimal mix will be rearranged to use the added resource, and the value of the objective function will rise
       e. none of the above
       d (Sensitivity analysis, moderate)

FILL-IN-THE-BLANK

37. _____ is a mathematical technique designed to help operations managers plan and make decisions relative to the trade-offs necessary to allocate resources.
Linear programming (Introduction, easy)

38. The _____ is a mathematical expression in linear programming that maximizes or minimizes some quantity.
objective function (Requirements of a linear programming problem, easy)

39. _____ are restrictions that limit the degree to which a manager can pursue an objective.
Constraints (Requirements of a linear programming problem, moderate)

40. The _____ is the set of all feasible combinations of the decision variables.
feasible region (Graphical solution to a linear programming problem, moderate)

41. _____ is an analysis that projects how much a solution might change if there were changes in the variables or input data.
Sensitivity analysis (Sensitivity analysis, moderate)

42. The _____ is an algorithm developed by Danzig for solving linear programming problems of all sizes.
simplex method (The simplex method of LP, moderate)

SHORT ANSWERS

43. List at least four applications of linear programming problems.
Students may select from eight given in the introduction. These include school bus scheduling, police patrol allocation, scheduling bank tellers, selecting product mix, picking blends to minimize cost, minimizing shipping cost, developing production schedules, and allocating space. (Introduction, easy)

44. State the requirements of a linear programming problem.
An objective function to be minimized or maximized; constraints; alternative courses of action; and linear relationships. (Requirements of a linear programming problem, easy)

45. You have been exposed to three different solution methods for linear programming. Can all three techniques be used on all problems? Will the three techniques agree on the optimal solution? Explain.
The graphic method, whether corner point or iso-profit version, works only with two decision variables; the simplex method (and POM for Windows) works for two variables and more. Thus a three or more variable problem cannot be handled by graphic techniques. For two-dimensional problems, all methods reach the same solution. (Graphical solution to a linear programming problem, and The simplex method of LP, moderate)

46. What is a "corner point"? Explain why solutions to linear programming problems focus on "corner points."
LP theory states that the optimum lies on a corner. All three solution techniques make use of this feature. (Graphical solution to a linear programming problem, moderate)

47. Where a constraint crosses the vertical or horizontal axis, the quantity is fairly obvious. How does one go about finding the quantity coordinates where two constraints cross, not at an axis? **Simultaneous equations--there is only one point where two linear equations (constraints) cross. (Graphical solution to a linear programming problem, moderate)**

48. Define shadow price (or dual value).
The value of one additional unit of a resource, such as one more hour of a scarce labor resource or one more dollar to invest. (Sensitivity analysis, moderate)

PROBLEMS

49. A craftsman builds two kinds of birdhouses, one for wrens (X1), one for bluebirds (X2). Each wren birdhouse takes four hours of labor and four units of lumber. Each bluebird house requires two hours of labor and twelve units of lumber. The craftsman has available 60 hours of labor and 120 units of lumber. Wren houses profit $6 each and bluebird houses profit $15 each. Write out the objective and constraints. Solve graphically or by corner points.
The POM for Windows formulation appears below. The following panel contains the graphical solution and the corner points. The maximum value of the objective is $162, obtained by producing 12 wren houses and 6 bluebird houses.

	X1	X2		RHS
Maximize	6	15		
Constraint 1	4	2	<=	60
Constraint 2	4	12	<=	120

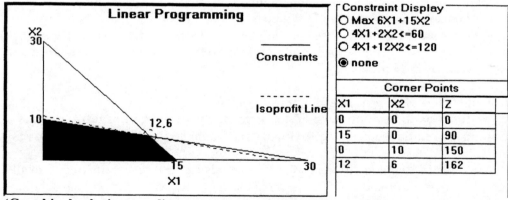

(Graphical solution to a linear programming problem, moderate)

50. A craftsman builds two kinds of birdhouses, one for wrens (X1), one for bluebirds (X2). Each wren birdhouse takes four hours of labor and four units of lumber. Each bluebird house requires two hours of labor and twelve units of lumber. The craftsman has available 60 hours of labor and 120 units of lumber. Wren houses profit $6 each and bluebird houses profit $15 each.

Use the software output that follows to interpret the problem solution. Include a statement of the solution quantities (how many of which product), a statement of the maximum profit achieved by your product mix, and a statement of "resources unused" and "shadow prices."

◆ Ranging

Bird Houses Solution					
Variable	Value	Reduced	Original Val	Lower Bound	Upper Bound
X1	12.	0.	6.	5.	30.
X2	6.	0.	15.	3.	18.
Constraint	Dual Value	Slack/Surplus	Original Val	Lower Bound	Upper Bound
Constraint 1	0.3	0.	60.	20.	120.
Constraint 2	1.2	0.	120.	60.	360.

The optimum solution is X1 = 12, X2 = 6, which earns a profit of 12 * 6 + 6 * 15 = $162. Both labor and lumber are used up, so there are no resources unused. Additional labor is worth $0.30 per hour, and additional lumber is worth $1.20 per unit. (Sensitivity analysis, moderate)

51. The Queen City Nursery manufactures bags of potting soil from compost and topsoil. Each cubic foot of compost costs 12 cents and contains 4 pounds of sand, 3 pounds of clay, and 5 pounds of humus. Each cubic foot of topsoil costs 20 cents and contains 3 pounds of sand, 6 pounds of clay, and 12 pounds of humus. Each bag of potting soil must contain at least 12 pounds of sand, 12 pounds of clay, and 10 pounds of humus. Explain how this problem meets the conditions of a linear programming problem. Plot the constraints and identify the feasible region. Graphically or with corner points find the best combination of compost and topsoil which meets the stated conditions at the lowest cost per bag. Identify the lowest cost possible.

The problem formulation appears in the POM for Windows panel below. The second panel contains the graphical and corner point solutions. The minimum cost per bag is $0.45, and is achieved by using 2.4 cubic feet of compost and 0.8 cubic feet of topsoil.

Queen City Nursery

	Compost	Topsoil		RHS
Minimize	0.12	0.2		
Sand	4.	3.	>=	12
Clay	3.	6.	>=	12
Humus	5.	12.	>=	10

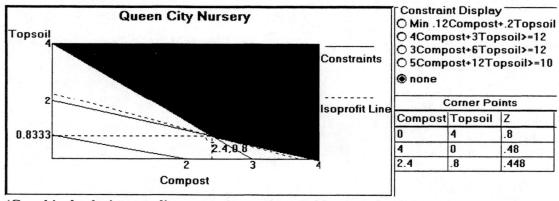

(Graphical solution to a linear programming problem, moderate)

52. A stereo mail order center has 8,000 cubic feet available for storage of its private label loudspeakers. The ZAR-3 speakers cost $295 each and require 4 cubic feet of space; the ZAR-2ax speakers cost $110 each and require 3 cubic feet of space; and the ZAR-4 model costs $58 and requires 1 cubic foot of space. The demand for the ZAR-3 is at most 20 units per month. The wholesaler has $100,000 to spend on loudspeakers this month. Each ZAR-3 contributes $105, each ZAR-2ax contributes $50, and each ZAR-4 contributes $28. The objective is to maximize total contribution. Write out the objective and the constraints.

The objective is to maximize 105 ZAR-3 + 50 ZAR-2ax + 28 ZAR-4. There are constraints on storage space, budget, and maximum sales. The space constraint is 4 ZAR-3 + 3 ZAR-2ax + 1 ZAR-4 < 8000. The budget constraint is 295 ZAR-3 + 110 ZAR-2ax + 58 ZAR-4 < $100,000. The marketing constraint is 1 ZAR-3 < 20. (Formulating linear programming problems, moderate)

53. Schriever Cabinet Specialties produces wall shelves, bookends, and shadow boxes. It is necessary to plan the production schedule for next week. The wall shelves, bookends, and shadow boxes are made of oak, of which the company currently has 600 board feet. A wall shelf requires 4 board feet, bookends require 2 board feet, and a shadow box requires 3 board feet. The company has a power saw for cutting the oak boards; a wall shelf requires 30 minutes, book ends require 15 minutes, and a shadow box requires 15 minutes. The power saw is available for 32 hours next week. After cutting, the pieces are hand finished in the finishing department, which consists of 4 skilled and experienced craftsmen, each of whom can complete any of the products. A wall shelf requires 30 minutes of finishing, bookends require 60 minutes, and a shadow box requires 90 minutes. The finishing department is expected to operate for 80 hours next week. Wall shelves sell for $29.95 and have a unit variable cost of $17.95; bookends sell for $11.95 and have a unit variable cost of $4.95; a shadow box sells for $16.95 and has a unit variable cost of $8.95. The company has a commitment to produce 10 wall shelf units for the Languages and Literature Department. The firm normally operates to achieve maximum contribution.

a. What are the decision variables of this problem (name them)?
b. What are the constraints of this problem (name them)?
c. Write out the objective and the constraints for this problem.
(a) The decision variables are X_1 = quantity of wall shelves, X_2 = quantity of bookends, and X_3 = quantity of shadow boxes. (b) The constraints are lumber: $4X_1 + 2X_2 + 3X_3 < 600$; saw: $30X_1 + 15X_2 + 15X_3 < 32 * 60$; finishing: $30X_1 + 60X_2 + 90X_3 < 80 * 60 * 4$; and commitment: $1X_1 > 10$. (c) The proper objective is to maximize contribution, which is $12X_1 + 7X_2 + 8X_3$. (Formulating linear programming problems, moderate)

54. Rienzi Farms grows sugar cane and soybeans on its 500 acres of land. An acre of soybeans brings a $1000 contribution to overhead and profit, an acre of sugar cane has a contribution of $2000. Because of a government program no more than 200 acres may be planted in soybeans. During the planting season 1200 hours of planting time will be available. Each acre of soybeans requires 2 hours, while each acre of sugar cane requires 6 hours. The company seeks maximum contribution (profit) from its planting decision.

a. algebraically state the decision variables, objective and constraints.

b. plot the constraints

c. solve graphically, using the corner point method.

The problem statement is contained in the POM for Windows first panel below. The graphical and corner point solutions are found in the second POM for Windows panel. The optimum solution is 200 acres in soybeans and 133.3 acres in sugar cane. There's not enough labor to plant all 500 acres when 200 acres is in soybeans.

Rienzi Farms

	Soybeans	Sugar cane		RHS
Maximize	1,000	2,000		
Acres	1	1	<=	500
Soybean restriction	1	0	<=	200
Planting labor	2	6	<=	1,200

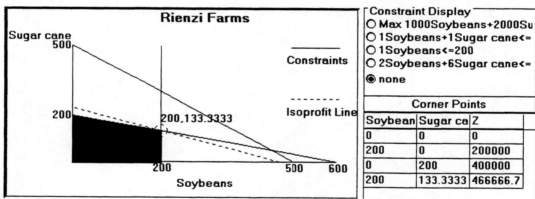

Constraint Display
- ○ Max 1000Soybeans+2000Su
- ○ 1Soybeans+1Sugar cane<=
- ○ 1Soybeans<=200
- ○ 2Soybeans+6Sugar cane<=
- ◉ none

Corner Points

Soybean	Sugar ca	Z	
0	0	0	
200	0	200000	
0	200	400000	
200	133.3333	466666.7	

(Graphical solution to a linear programming problem, moderate)

55. South Coast Papers wants to mix two lubricating oils (A and B) for its machines in order to minimize cost. It needs no less than 3,000 gallons in order to run its machines during the next month. It has a maximum oil storage capacity of 4,000 gallons. There are 2,000 gallons of oil A and 4,000 of oil B available. The mixed fuel must have a viscosity rating of no less than 40.

When mixing fuels, the amount of oil obtained is exactly equal to the sum of the amounts put in. The viscosity rating is the weighted average of the individual viscosities, weighted in proportion to their volumes. The following is known: oil A has an viscosity of 45 and costs 60 cents per gallon; oil B has an viscosity of 37.5 and costs 40 cents per gallon.

State the objective and the constraints of this problem. Plot all constraints and highlight the feasible region. Use your (by now, well-developed) intuition to suggest a feasible (but not necessarily optimal) solution. Be certain to show that your solution meets all constraints.

The problem formulation appears below. The only unusual constraint is the fifth one. This begins as the viscosity expression: viscosity = $(40A + 37.5B) / (A + B) > 40$, which becomes $5A > 2.5B$. It is not possible to meet the restrictions with only Oil A or only Oil B. Most students will discover that a combination is required. They need to show that their mix has a high enough viscosity by substituting their quantities into the viscosity inequality (as well as showing that their quantities are within the four volume constraints).

Linear Programming Results

South Coast Papers Solution	Oil A	Oil B		RHS	Dual
Minimize	0.6	0.4			
Constraint 1	1.	1.	>=	3,000.	-0.4667
Constraint 2	1.	1.	<=	4,000.	0.
Constraint 3	1.	0.	<=	2,000.	0.
Constraint 4	0.	1.	<=	4,000.	0.
Constraint 5	5.	-2.5	>=	0.	-0.0267
Solution->	1,000.	2,000.		1,400.	

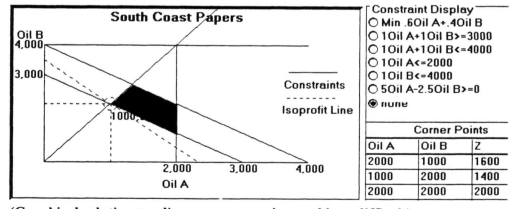

Constraint Display
- O Min .6Oil A+.4Oil B
- O 1Oil A+1Oil B>=3000
- O 1Oil A+1Oil B<=4000
- O 1Oil A<=2000
- O 1Oil B<=4000
- O 5Oil A-2.5Oil B>=0
- ● none

Corner Points		
Oil A	Oil B	Z
2000	1000	1600
1000	2000	1400
2000	2000	2000

(Graphical solution to a linear programming problem, difficult)

56. Lost Maples Winery makes three varieties of contemporary Texas Hill Country wines: Austin Formation (a fine Red), Ste. Genevieve (a Table White), and Los Alamos (a hearty Pink Zinfandel). The raw materials, labor, and contribution per case of each of these wines is summarized below.

	Grapes Variety A bushels	Grapes Variety B bushels	Sugar pounds	Labor (man-hours)	Contrib. per case
Austin Formation	4	0	1	3	$24
Ste. Genevieve	0	4	0	1	$28
Los Alamos	2	2	2	2	$20

The winery has 2800 bushels of Variety A grapes, 2040 bushels of Variety B grapes, 800 pounds of sugar, and 1060 man-hours of labor available during the next week. The firm operates to achieve maximum contribution. Refer to the POM for Windows panels showing the solution to this problem.

Linear Programming Results

Lost Maples Solution

	Austin	Ste. Genevieve	Los Alamos		RHS	Dual
Maximize	24.	28.	20.			
Variety A	4.	0.	2.	<=	2,800.	0.
Variety B	0.	4.	2.	<=	2,040.	5.
Sugar	1.	0.	2.	<=	800.	0.
Labor	3.	1.	2.	<=	1,060.	8.
Solution->	183.3333	510.	0.		18,680.	

Ranging

Lost Maples Solution

Variable	Value	Reduced	Original Val	Lower Bound	Upper Bound
Austin	183.3333	0.	24.	12.	84.
Ste. Genevieve	510.	0.	28.	16.	Infinity
Los Alamos	0.	6.	20.	-Infinity	26.
Constraint	Dual Value	Slack/Surplus	Original Val	Lower Bound	Upper Bound
Variety A	0.	2,066.667	2,800.	733.3333	Infinity
Variety B	5.	0.	2,040.	0.	4,240.
Sugar	0.	616.6667	800.	183.3333	Infinity
Labor	8.	0.	1,060.	510.0001	2,610.

Answer the following questions.

a. For maximum contribution, how much of each wine should be produced?

b. How much contribution will be made by selling the output?

c. Is there any sugar left over? If so, how much? If not, what is its shadow price (dual value)? Explain what this value means to Lost Maples' management.

d. Interpret the meaning of the lower bound to **Labor** in the Ranging analysis. That is, explain how the solution would change if the amount of labor fell below that lower value.

e. Interpret the meaning of the upper bound to Los Alamos wine in the Ranging analysis.

(a) 183 1/3 cases of Austin Formation, 510 cases of Ste. Genevieve; (b) maximum contribution is $18,680; (c) There are 617 pounds of sugar remaining; its dual value is zero, indication that management should not seek out any more sugar; (d) if the amount of labor fell below the 510 hour level, its dual value would rise; (e) Los Alamos is not currently included in the solution; it would enter the solution only if its contribution rose over the ranging limit of $26 per case. (Sensitivity analysis, moderate)

MODULE C: TRANSPORTATION MODELS

TRUE/FALSE

1. The transportation model, since it has a single source with multiple destinations, is like the center of gravity model used in location analysis.
    False (Transportation modeling, moderate)

2. The transportation model is a special type of linear programming model.
    True (Transportation modeling, easy)

3. The optimum solution to a transportation problem is referred to as the Northwest Passage.
    False (Developing an initial solution, easy)

4. The northwest corner rule does not consider shipping cost in making initial allocations.
    True (Developing an initial solution , moderate)

5. The added cost of shipping one unit through an unused cell XY in a transportation problem without changing the edge requirements, is the shipping cost associated with cell of the matrix.
    False (The stepping-stone method, moderate)

6. A feasible solution in transportation models is one in which all of the supply and demand constraints are satisfied.
    True (Developing an initial solution, moderate)

7. When using the stepping stone method, the closed path sometimes has the shape of a triangle as diagonal moves are permitted.
    False (The stepping-stone method, moderate)

8. In a transportation minimization problem, the negative improvement index associated with a square indicates that reallocating units to that cell would lower costs.
    True (The stepping-stone method, moderate)

9. Redundancy in a transportation problem is when multiple closed paths exist for evaluating an unused cell.
    False (The stepping-stone method, moderate)

10. When using the stepping stone method for a minimization problem, the number of units that reallocates corresponds to the smallest number found in the cells containing minus signs.
    True (The stepping-stone method, moderate)

11. A transportation problem cannot have more supply constraints than demand constraints.
    False (Special issues in modeling, moderate)

12. A transportation problem with a total supply of 500 and a total demand of 400 will have an optimal solution that leaves 100 units of supply unused.
    True (Special issues in modeling, moderate)

13. A transportation problem with 8 sources and 6 destinations will have an optimal solution that uses at least 15 of the 48 possible routes.
False (Special issues in modeling, moderate)

14. If demand exceeds supply in a transportation problem, the problem must be balanced by adding a dummy source with additional supply.
True (Special issues in modeling, moderate)

15. To handle degeneracy, a very small quantity is placed in one of the unused squares.
True (Special issues in modeling, moderate)

16. Degeneracy occurs when the number of used squares is less than the number of rows plus the number of columns.
False (Special issues in modeling, moderate)

MULTIPLE CHOICE

17. Which of the following is not needed in order to use the transportation model?
    a. the source points and their capacity
    b. the destination points and their demand
    c. the cost of shipping one unit from each source to each destination
    d. fixed costs of source points
    e. all of the above are needed
    d (Transportation modeling, easy)

18. The purpose of the transportation approach for locational analysis is to minimize
    a. total costs
    b. total shipping costs
    c. total variable costs
    d. total fixed costs
    e. the number of shipments
    b (Transportation modeling, moderate)

19. A transportation problem consists of 8 points of origin and 6 destinations. The number of possible routes for this problem is
    a. 2
    b. 14
    c. 48
    d. 64
    e. unknown
    c (Transportation modeling, moderate)

20. The transportation method is a special case of the family of problems known as
    a. regression problems
    b. linear programming problems
    c. decision tree problems
    d. simulation problems
    e. statistical problems
    b (Transportation modeling, easy)

21. The initial solution to a transportation problem can be generated in any manner, so long as
    a. it minimizes cost
    b. it ignores cost
    c. all supply and demand are satisfied
    d. degeneracy does not exist
    e. all cells are filled
    c (Developing an initial solution, moderate)

22. Which of the following statements about the northwest corner rule is false?
    a. One must exhaust the supply for each row before moving down to the next row.
    b. One must exhaust the demand requirements of each column before moving to the next column.
    c. When moving to a new row or column, one must select the cell with the lowest cost.
    d. One must check that all supply and demand constraints are met.
    e. All of the above are false.
    c (Developing an initial solution, moderate)

23. For the problem data set below, what is the northwest corner allocation to the cell Source 1-
    Destination 1?

Data				
COSTS	Dest. 1	Dest. 2	Dest. 3	Supply
Source 1	2	1	3	30
Source 2	4	2	1	40
Source 3	3	8	6	20
Demand	15	50	25	90 \ 90

    a. 0
    b. 2
    c. 15
    d. 30
    e. 90
    c (Developing an initial solution, easy)

24. In transportation model analysis the stepping-stone method is used to
    a. obtain an initial optimum solution
    b. obtain an initial feasible solution
    c. evaluate empty cells for potential solution improvements
    d. evaluate empty cells for possible degeneracy
    e. balance supply and demand
    c (The stepping-stone method, easy)

25. For the problem data set below, what is the northwest corner allocation to the cell Source 1 - Destination 2?

Data				
COSTS	Dest. 1	Dest. 2	Dest. 3	Supply
Source 1	2	1	3	30
Source 2	4	2	1	40
Origin 3	3	8	6	20
Demand	15	50	25	90 \ 90

a. 0
b. 15
c. 25
d. 35
e. 45
b (Developing an initial solution, moderate)

26. For the problem data set below, what is the northwest corner allocation to the cell Source 3- Destination 3?

Data				
COSTS	Dest. 1	Dest. 2	Dest. 3	Supply
Source 1	2	1	3	30
Source 2	4	2	1	40
Source 3	3	8	6	20
Demand	15	50	25	90 \ 90

a. 0
b. 15
c. 20
d. 35
e. 45
c (Developing an initial solution, moderate)

27. A transportation problem has a feasible solution when
    a. all of the improvement indexes are positive
    b. the number of filled cells is one less than the number of rows plus the number of columns
    c. all the squares are used
    d. the solution yields the lowest possible cost
    e. all demand and supply constraints are satisfied
    e (The stepping-stone method, moderate)

28. When the number of shipments in a feasible solution is less than the number of rows plus the number of columns minus one
   a. the solution is optimal
   b. there is degeneracy, and an artificial allocation must be created
   c. a dummy source must be created
   d. a dummy destination must be created
   e. the closed path has a triangular shape
   b (Special issues in modeling, moderate)

29. The total cost of the optimal solution to a transportation problem
   a. is calculated by multiplying the total supply (including any dummy values) by the average cost of the cells
   b. cannot be calculated from the information given
   c. can be calculated from the original non-optimal cost, by adding the savings made at each improvement
   d. is found by multiplying the amounts in each cell by the cost for that cell for each row and then subtract the products of the amounts in each cell times the cost of each cell for the columns
   e. can be calculated based only on the entries in the filled cells of the solution
   e (The stepping-stone method, moderate)

30. The stepping-stone method
   a. is an alternative to using the northwest corner rule
   b. often involves tracing closed paths with a triangular shape
   c. is used to evaluate the cost effectiveness of shipping goods via transportation routes not currently in the solution
   d. is used to identify the relevant costs in a transportation problem
   e. helps determine whether a solution is feasible or not
   c (The stepping-stone method, moderate)

31. In a minimization problem, a negative improvement index in a cell indicates that the
   a. solution is optimal
   b. total cost will increase if units are reallocated to that cell
   c. total cost will decrease if units are reallocated to that cell
   d. current iteration is worse than the previous one
   e. problem has no feasible solution
   c (The stepping-stone method, moderate)

32. In a minimization problem, a positive improvement index in a cell indicates that
   a. the solution is optimal
   b. the total cost will increase if units are reallocated to that cell
   c. the total cost will decrease if units are reallocated to that cell
   d. there is degeneracy
   e. the problem has no feasible solution
   b (The stepping-stone method, moderate)

33. An improvement index indicates
    a. whether a method other than the stepping stone should be used
    b. whether a method other that the northwest corner rule should be used
    c. whether the transportation cost in the upper left-hand corner of a cell is optimal
    d. how much total cost would increase or decrease if the largest possible quantity were reallocated to that cell
    e. how much total cost would increase or decrease if a single unit was reallocated to that cell
    e (The stepping-stone method, moderate)

FILL-IN-THE-BLANK

34. The _____ finds the least-cost means of shipping supplies from several origins to several destinations.
    transportation model (Transportation modeling, easy)

35. The _____ is a procedure in the transportation model where one starts at the upper left-hand cell of a table and systematically allocates units to shipping points.
    northwest-corner rule (Developing an initial solution, moderate)

36. The _____ is an iterative technique for moving from an initial feasible solution to an optimal solution in the transportation method.
    stepping-stone method (The stepping-stone method, moderate)

37. _____ is an occurrence in transportation problems when too few shipping routes are being used.
    Degeneracy (Special issues in modeling, moderate)

SHORT ANSWERS

38. State the three information needs of the transportation model.
    The origin points and the capacity or supply per period at each; the destination points and the demand per period at each; and the cost of shipping one unit from each origin to each destination. (Transportation modeling, moderate)

39. All of the transportation examples appear to apply to long distances. Is it possible for the transportation model to apply on a much smaller scale, for example, within the departments of a store or the offices of a building? Discuss; create an example or prove the application impossible.
    Nothing prohibits the model from applying over short distances. The three assumptions do not address issues of scale. An office could easily offer several sources of shipments, as well as several destinations for shipments. A job shop could easily use this model. (Transportation model, difficult)

40. The transportation model is said to be a special case of linear programming. If so, then there must be a way to show a transportation problem as a system of decision variables and constraints. Demonstrate this relationship, using the following simple problem.
    Critical thinking exercise. Students should recognize that each source-destination combination is a variable, and that there are S + D of them (6 here). Students should recognize that each source and each destination represents a constraint (5 here). (Transportation model, difficult) SEE TOP OF NEXT PAGE, page 437

	Destination 1	Destination 2	Destination 3	SUPPLY
Source 1	5	9	4	20
Source 2	2	1	8	30
DEMAND	15	10	25	

Objective
○ Maximize
◉ Minimize

Starting method
Any starting method ▼

<untitled>

c40.JPG

41. State, in order, the three steps in making an initial allocation with the northwest corner rule.
Exhaust the supply of each row before moving down to the next row; exhaust the demand requirements of each column before moving to the next column on the right, and check that all supply and demand constraints are met. (Developing an initial solution, moderate)

42. Explain the significance of a negative improvement index in a transportation-minimizing problem.
It represents the amount by which total transportation costs could be decreased if one unit of product were shipped by the source-destination combination. (The stepping-stone method, moderate)

43. Explain what is meant by the term "degeneracy" within the context of transportation modeling.
You are unable to trace a closed path from any unused square back to the original unused square via squares that are currently being used; special techniques are needed to complete the improvement indexes. (Special issues in modeling, moderate)

44. What action must be taken in a transportation problem where total demand exceeds total supply?
Supply and demand must be balanced. In this case, by creating a dummy source with a supply equal to the excess of demand over supply. (Special issues in modeling, moderate)

45. The more sources and destinations there are for a transportation problem, the smaller the percentage of all routes that will be used in the optimal solution. Explain.
The number of routes used is S + D - 1; the number of routes available is S x D. Example: for a 2 x 3 problem, 4 of 6 routes will be used, for a 5 x 6 problem, 10 of 30 routes will be used. (Special issues in modeling, difficult)

PROBLEMS

46. Consider the transportation problem in the Excel OM data set and optimal solution below. Verify by hand or by calculator (show your work) the value of the objective function.

Data					
COSTS	Dest 1	Dest 2	Dest 3	Dest 4	Supply
Source 1	12	18	9	11	100
Source 2	21	7	30	15	150
Source 3	8	10	14	16	50

Demand		80	60	70	90	300 \ 300
Shipments						
Shipments	Dest 1	Dest 2	Dest 3	Dest 4	Row Total	
Source 1	30	0	70	0	100	
Source 2	0	60	0	90	150	
Source 3	50	0	0	0	50	
Column Total	80	60	70	90 300 \ 300		

The objective is $12 *30 + $9*70 + $ 7*60 + $15*90 +$8*50 = $3,160 (The stepping-stone method, easy)

47. Consider the transportation problem in the Excel OM data set and optimal solution below. Calculate improvement indexes on each empty cell. Is this solution optimal?

Data					
COSTS	Dest 1	Dest 2	Dest 3	Dest 4	Supply
Source 1	12	18	9	11	100
Source 2	21	7	30	15	150
Source 3	8	10	14	16	50
Demand	80	60	70	90 300 \ 300	

Shipments					
Shipments	Dest 1	Dest 2	Dest 3	Dest 4	Row Total
Source 1	30	0	70	0	100
Source 2	0	60	0	90	150
Source 3	50	0	0	0	50
Column Total	80	60	70	90 300 \ 300	

The solution is optimal. (The stepping-stone mehod, moderate)

48. Consider the transportation problem data set in the Excel OM panel below.

Data			
COSTS	Dest 1	Dest 2	Supply
Source 1	5	9	20
Source 2	8	2	30
Source 3	4	5	15
Source 4	12	11	20
Source 5	7	7	25
Demand	70	40	110 \ 110

   a. Find the optimal solution.
   b. What is the cost of the optimal solution?

(a) The optimal solution is depicted in the Excel OM solutions below. (b) The minimum cost is $625. (The stepping-stone method, moderate)

Shipments			
Shipments	Dest 1	Dest 2	Row Total
Source 1	20	0	20
Source 2	0	30	30
Source 3	15	0	15
Source 4	10	10	20
Source 5	25	0	25
Column Total	70	40 110 \ 110	

Total Cost   625

49. Consider the transportation data set for a minimization problem below.

Data				
COSTS	Dest 1	Dest 2	Dest 3	Supply
Origin 1	2	1	3	30
Origin 2	4	2	1	40
Origin 3	3	8	6	20
Demand	15	50	25 90 \ 90	

a. Calculate the initial solution using the northwest corner rule.
b. Calculate improvement indexes, iterate, and solve for the optimal shipping pattern.
The optimal solution appears in the Excel OM panel below.

Shipments				
Shipments	Dest 1	Dest 2	Dest 3	Row Total
Origin 1	0	30	0	30
Origin 2	0	20	20	40
Origin 3	15	0	5	20
Column Total	15	50	25 90 \ 90	

Total Cost $165
(The stepping-stone method, moderate)

50. The following table presents data for a transportation problem. Set up the appropriate transportation table and find the optimal solution. Explain carefully the meaning of any quantity in a "dummy" row or column.

Data				
COSTS	Dest 1	Dest 2	Dest 3	Supply
Source 1	30	10	5	20
Source 2	10	10	10	30
Source 3	20	10	25	75
Dummy	0	0	0	30
Demand	40	60	55	155 \ 155

The optimum solution, which costs $1300, appears in the Excel OM solution below. A dummy row was added since total supply was less than total demand. Thirty units are shipped from Dummy to Destination 3. This means that Destination 3 does not receive 30 units that it demanded. The dummy row can be interpreted as unfilled demand, or shortfall.

Shipments				
Shipments	Dest 1	Dest 2	Dest 3	Row Total
Source 1	0	0	20	20
Source 2	25	0	5	30
Source 3	15	60	0	75
Dummy	0	0	30	30
Column Total	40	60	55	155 \ 155

Total Cost $1300

(The stepping-stone method, moderate)

51. The Shamrock Transportation Company has four terminals: A, B, C, and D. At the start of a particular day, there are 8, 8, 6 and 3 tractors available at those terminals, respectively. During the previous night, trailers were loaded at plants R, 5, T, and U. The number of trailers at each plant is 2, 12, 5, and 6, respectively. The company dispatcher has determined the distances between each terminal and each plant, as follows. How many tractors should be dispatched from each terminal to each plant in order to minimize the total number of miles traveled?

Data					
COSTS	Dest 1	Dest 2	Dest 3	Dest 4	Supply
Origin 1	22	46	16	40	8
Origin 2	42	15	50	18	8
Origin 3	82	32	48	60	6
Origin 4	40	40	36	30	3
Demand	2	12	5	6	25 \ 25

The optimal solution from Excel OM is in the table below.

Shipments					
Shipments	Dest 1	Dest 2	Dest 3	Dest 4	Row Total
Origin 1	2	0	5	1	8
Origin 2	0	6	0	2	8
Origin 3	0	6	0	0	6
Origin 4	0	0	0	3	3
Column Total	2	12	5	6 25 \ 25	

Total Cost 572

(The stepping-stone method, difficult)

MODULE D: WAITING-LINE MODELS

TRUE/FALSE

1. Objects wait for service in a waiting line; but when people wait, the process is called a queue.
    False (Introduction, easy)

2. The three parts of a waiting-line system are the arrivals (or inputs), the waiting line itself, and the service facility.
    True (Characteristics of a waiting-line system, moderate)

3. The study of waiting lines calculates the cost of providing good service but does not value the cost of customers' waiting time.
    False (Queuing costs, moderate)

4. The cost of waiting decreases as the service level increases.
    True (Queuing costs, moderate)

5. A technician responsible for the university's personal computers is dealing with a finite population.
    True (Characteristics of a waiting-line system, moderate)

6. A medical emergency room always follows a first-in, first-served queue discipline in the interest of fairness.
    False (Characteristics of a waiting-line system, moderate)

7. In queuing problems, arrival rates are always described by the Poisson probability distribution.
    False (Characteristics of a waiting-line system, moderate)

8. In queuing problems, the terms "balk" and "renege" mean the same thing.
    False (Characteristics of a waiting-line system, moderate)

9. In queuing problems, the term "balk" refers to the fact that some customers find the service performed to be unsatisfactory.
    False (Characteristics of a waiting-line system, moderate)

10. In queuing problems, the term "renege" refers to the fact that some customers leave the queue before service is completed.
    True (Characteristics of a waiting-line system, moderate)

11. All queuing systems exhibit first-in, first-out queue discipline.
    False (Characteristics of a waiting-line system, moderate)

12. A bank office with five tellers, each with a separate line of customers, exhibits the characteristics of a multi-phase queuing system.
    False (Characteristics of a waiting-line system, moderate)

13. If the service time within a queuing system is constant, the service rate can be easily described by a negative exponential distribution.
    False (Characteristics of a waiting-line system, moderate)

14. In queuing systems, service rates may be either constant or random.
   True (Characteristics of a waiting-line system, moderate)

15. One of the disadvantages of analytical queuing models is that the models do not contain any information about extreme values or outliers (maximum wait time, etc.).
   True (Characteristics of a waiting-line system, moderate)

16. In the analysis of queuing models, arrival rates are often described by the Poisson distribution.
   True (Characteristics of a waiting-line system, moderate)

17. In the analysis of queuing models, service times are often described by the negative exponential distribution.
   True (Characteristics of a waiting-line system, moderate)

18. In a queuing system with random arrivals and random service times, the performance will be best if the arrival rate is equal to the service rate.
   False (Characteristics of a waiting-line system, difficult)

19. In a queuing system with random arrivals and random service times, a low utilization factor suggests that the system is providing good service.
   True (Characteristics of a waiting-line system, difficult)

MULTIPLE CHOICE

20. In queuing problems, which of the following probability distributions is typically used to describe the number of arrivals per unit of time?
   a. normal
   b. Poisson
   c. exponential
   d. binomial
   e. lognormal
   b (Characteristics of a waiting-line system, easy)

21. In queuing problems, which of the following probability distributions is typically used to describe the time to perform the service?
   a. normal
   b. Poisson
   c. exponential
   d. binomial
   e. lognormal
   c (Characteristics of a waiting-line system, easy)

22. The parameters of a waiting line system include all of the following **except**
    a. arrival rates
    b. queue discipline
    c. service time
    d. cost of capacity
    e. all of the above are parameters of the waiting line
    d (Characteristics of a waiting-line system, moderate)

23. The source population is considered to be either _____ in its size.
    a. fixed or variable
    b. known or unknown
    c. finite or infinite
    d. random or scheduled
    e. small or large
    c (Characteristics of a waiting-line system, moderate)

24. The two most important characteristics of the waiting line in typical queuing problems are the
    a. length of the line and the queue discipline
    b. length of the line and the probability distribution of arrival rates
    c. queue discipline and the service rate
    d. arrival rate and the service rate
    e. arrival rate and the number of channels
    a (Characteristics of a waiting-line system, moderate)

25. The common measures of a queuing system's performance include
    a. average time each customer spends in the system, probability that the service system will be idle, average time each customer spends in the queue
    b. average queue length, maximum time a customer may spend in the queue, the utilization factor for the system
    c. average time each customer spends in the system, maximum queue length, probability of a specific number of customers in the system
    d. probability that the service facility will be idle, average queue length, probability that the waiting time will exceed a specified duration
    a (Characteristics of a waiting-line system, moderate)

26. The shopper who says to himself "I've waited too long in this line. I don't really need to buy this product today" and leaves the store is an illustration of which element of queue discipline?
    a. balking
    b. reneging
    c. random departure
    d. random arrival
    e. none of the above
    b (Characteristics of a waiting-line system, moderate)

27. The potential restaurant customer who says to her husband "the line looks too long; let's eat somewhere else" is an illustration of which element of queue discipline?
   a. balk
   b. renege
   c. random departure
   d. first-in, first-out
   e. none of the above
   a (Characteristics of a waiting-line system, moderate)

28. The sign at the bank that reads "Wait here for the first available teller" suggests the use of a _____ waiting line system.
   a. single phase
   b. multi-phase
   c. single channel
   d. multi-channel
   e. multiple line
   d (Characteristics of a waiting-line system, moderate)

29. An airline ticket counter, with several agents for one line of customers is an example of a
   a. single channel, single phase system
   b. single channel, multi-phase system
   c. multi-channel, single phase system
   d. multi-channel, multi-phase system
   c (Characteristics of a waiting-line system, moderate)

30. If the food service for the university operates a cafeteria with a single serving line, that system behaves most like a
   a. single channel, single phase system
   b. single channel, multi-phase system
   c. multi-channel, single phase system
   d. multi-channel, multi-phase system
   b (Characteristics of a waiting-line system, moderate)

31. A theater, employing both ticket takers and ushers to seat patrons, behaves typically as a
   a. single channel, single phase system
   b. single channel, multi-phase system
   c. multi-channel, single phase system
   d. multi-channel, multi-phase system
   d (Characteristics of a waiting-line system, moderate)

32. A beauty shop, with several operators, typically provides an example of a
   a. single channel, limited queue system
   b. single channel, limited population system
   c. multi-channel, limited queue system
   d. multi-channel, limited population system
   e. none of the above
   c (Characteristics of a waiting-line system, moderate)

33. A university has only one technician in the repair station to care for the computers in the student labs. This system is most likely
    a. a single channel, limited queue system
    b. a single channel, limited population system
    c. a multi-channel, limited queue system
    d. a multi-channel, limited population system
    b (Characteristics of a waiting-line system, moderate)

34. "Women and children first!" declares the captain of a sinking ship. His directive employs which of the following queue disciplines in disembarking passengers?
    a. random
    b. FIFO
    c. LIFO
    d. priority
    d (Characteristics of a waiting-line system, moderate)

35. A university has several technicians in the repair station to care for the computers in the student labs. This system is most likely
    a. single channel, limited queue system
    b. single channel, limited population system
    c. multi-channel, limited queue system
    d. multi-channel, limited population system
    d (Characteristics of a waiting-line system, moderate)

36. A system in which the customer receives service from only one station and then exits the system is
    a. a multiple-channel system
    b. a multiple-phase system
    c. a single-phase system
    d. a single channel system
    c (Characteristics of a waiting-line system, easy)

37. In a repetitive focus factory, the number of channels available for the processing of a certain part would likely refer to
    a. the number of successive operations that have to be performed on that part
    b. the number of machines doing the same necessary operations
    c. the number of parts waiting to be processed
    d. all of the above depending on the layout
    e. none of the above
    b (Characteristics of a waiting-line system, moderate)

38. In a repetitive focus factory, the number of phases found in the system might refer to
    a. the number of successive operations that have to be performed on a part
    b. the number of machines doing the same necessary operations
    c. the number of parts waiting to be processed
    d. a or b depending on the layout
    e. none of the above
    a (Characteristics of a waiting-line system, moderate)

39. Which of the following are measures of queue performance?
   a. average queue length
   b. probability of a specific number of customers in the system
   c. average waiting time in the line
   d. utilization factor
   e. all of the above
   e (Characteristics of a waiting-line system, moderate)

40. Which of the following are measures of queue performance?
   a. maximum queue length
   b. probability of no customers in the system
   c. minimum waiting time in the line
   d. efficiency factor
   e. none of the above
   b (Characteristics of a waiting-line system, moderate)

41. Which one of the following is **not** a characteristic of a Model A or M/M/1 system?
   a. single number of channels
   b. single number of phases
   c. Poisson arrival rate pattern
   d. limited population size
   e. exponential service time pattern
   d (The variety of queuing models, moderate)

42. Which one of the following is **not** a characteristic of a Model B or M/M/S system?
   a. single channel
   b. single queue
   c. single phase
   d. Poisson arrival rate pattern
   e. unlimited population size
   a (The variety of queuing models, moderate)

43. Which one of the following is **not** a characteristic of a Model C or M/D/1 system?
   a. single channel
   b. single phase
   c. Poisson arrival rate pattern
   d. exponential service time pattern
   e. unlimited population size
   d (The variety of queuing models, moderate)

44. In the basic queuing model (M/M/1), arrival rates are distributed by
   a. continuous probability distributions
   b. Poisson distributions
   c. normal probability distributions
   d. negative exponential probability distributions
   e. lognormal distributions
   b (The variety of queuing models, moderate)

45. In the basic queuing model (M/M/1), service times are described by
    a. continuous probability distributions
    b. Poisson probability distributions
    c. normal probability distributions
    d. negative exponential probability distributions
    e. lognormal distributions
    d (Characteristics of a waiting-line system, moderate)

46. A queuing model which follows the M/M/1 assumptions has $\lambda = 2$ and $\mu = 3$. The average number in the system is
    a. 2/3
    b. 1.5
    c. 2
    d. 1
    e. 6
    c (The variety of queuing models, moderate)

47. Which of the following is **not** an assumption of the M/M/1 model?
    a. The first customers to arrive are the first customers served.
    b. Each arrival comes independently of the arrival immediately before and after that arrival.
    c. The population from which the arrivals come is very large or infinite in size.
    d. Service times occur according to a normal curve.
    e. Customers do not renege.
    d (The variety of queuing models, moderate)

48. A queuing model which follows the M/M/1 assumptions has $\lambda = 2$ and $\mu = 3$. The average waiting time in the system is
    a. 2/3
    b. 1.5
    c. 2
    d. 1
    e. 6
    d (The variety of queuing models, moderate)

49. The assumptions of the basic queuing model (M/M/1) hold if
    a. the service time is constant
    b. the population of potential customers is limited
    c. the customer has to visit several different phases or servers
    d. the service times do not follow a negative exponential probability distribution
    e. there is only one channel
    e (Characteristics of a waiting-line system, moderate)

50. Students arrive randomly at the help desk of the computer lab. There is only one service agent, and the time required for inquiry varies from student to student. Arrival rates have been found to follow the Poisson distribution, and the service times follow the negative exponential distribution. The average arrival rate is 12 students per hour, and the average service rate is 20 students per hour. What is the average service time for this problem?
   a. 1 minute
   b. 2 minutes
   c. 3 minutes
   d. 5 minutes
   e. 20 minutes
   c (The variety of queuing models, moderate)

51. Students arrive randomly at the help desk of the computer lab. There is only one service agent, and the time required for inquiry varies from student to student. Arrival rates have been found to follow the Poisson distribution, and the service times follow the negative exponential distribution. The average arrival rate is 12 students per hour, and the average service rate is 20 students per hour. What is the utilization factor?
   a. 20%
   b. 30%
   c. 40%
   d. 50%
   e. 60%
   e (The variety of queuing models, moderate)

52. Students arrive randomly at the help desk of the computer lab. There is only one service agent, and the time required for inquiry varies from student to student. Arrival rates have been found to follow the Poisson distribution, and the service times follow the negative exponential distribution. The average arrival rate is 12 students per hour, and the average service rate is 20 students per hour. A student has just entered the system. How long is she expected to stay in the system?
   a. 1.5 minutes
   b. 0.9 minute
   c. 0.125 minute
   d. 7.5 minutes
   e. 0.075 hour
   d (The variety of queuing models, moderate)

53. Students arrive randomly at the help desk of the computer lab. There is only one service agent, and the time required for inquiry varies from student to student. Arrival rates have been found to follow the Poisson distribution, and the service times follow the negative exponential distribution. The average arrival rate is 12 students per hour, and the average service rate is 20 students per hour. How many students, on the average, will be waiting in line at any one time?
   a. 0.9 student
   b. 1.5 students
   c. 3 students
   d. 4 students
   e. 36 students
   a (The variety of queuing models, moderate)

FILL-IN-THE-BLANK

54. _____ is a body of knowledge about waiting lines.
    Queuing theory (Introduction, easy)

55. A _____ is where items or people are in a line awaiting service.
    waiting line or queue (Introduction, easy)

56. A _____ is a discrete probability distribution that often describes the arrival rate in queuing theory.
    Poisson distribution (Characteristics of a waiting-line system, moderate)

57. _____ is a queuing discipline where the first customers in line receive the first service.
    First-in, first-out (FIFO) or first-in, first-served (FIFS) (Characteristics of a waiting-line system, moderate)

58. A _____ queuing system has one line and one server.
    single-channel (Characteristics of a waiting-line system, moderate)

59. A _____ queuing system has one waiting line, but several servers.
    multiple-channel (Characteristics of a waiting-line system, moderate)

60. A _____ queuing system is one in which the customer receives service from only one station and then exits the system.
    single-phase (Characteristics of a waiting-line system, moderate)

61. A _____ queuing system is one in which the customer receives services from several stations before exiting the system.
    multiple-phase (Characteristics of a waiting-line system, moderate)

62. The _____ probability distribution is a continuous probability distribution often used to describe the service time in a queuing system.
    negative exponential (Characteristics of a waiting-line system, moderate)

SHORT ANSWERS

63. Name the three parts of a typical queuing system.
    Arrivals or inputs to the system; the queue discipline, or the waiting line itself; and the service facility. (Characteristics of a waiting-line system, moderate)

64. Define queue discipline. State at least three rules for queue discipline.
    Queue discipline is the order in which customers in the queue are served. Choices include FIFO, LIFO, and priority. (Characteristics of a waiting-line system, moderate)

65. List the three factors that govern the structure of "arrivals" in a queuing system.
    The size of the source population (finite or infinite); the pattern of arrivals at the system (on a schedule or randomly); and the behavior of the arrivals (joining the queue, balking, or reneging). (Characteristics of a waiting-line system, moderate)

66. Describe what is meant by the waiting-line terms "balk" and "renege." Provide an example of each.
"Balk" is to refuse to enter the queue; "renege" is to leave the queue (without being served) after entering. Examples of balk come from observing "the line is too long" or "the line isn't moving very fast." Renege examples may come from "the other line is moving faster" or "I can't wait any longer." (Characteristics of a waiting-line system, moderate)

67. Describe the difference between FIFO and LIFO queue disciplines.
FIFO (first-in, first-out) serves first the customer who entered earliest and who has been in line longest; LIFO serves first the customer who entered most recently. FIFO exhibits a fairness to people waiting; LIFO is something like an in-basket on a desk, where the top piece of paper was the last entered, but the first to be serviced. (Characteristics of a waiting-line system, moderate)

68. State the seven common measures of queuing system performance.
The average time each customer or object spends in the queue; the average queue length; the average time each customer or object spends in the system; the average number of customers in the system; the probability that the service facility is idle; the utilization factor for the system; and the probability of a specific number of customers or objects in the system. (Characteristics of a waiting-line system, moderate)

69. Which is larger, W_s or W_q? Explain using prose.
W_s is the time spent waiting plus being serviced; W_q is the time spent waiting for service. W_s is therefore larger than W_q by the amount of time spent on the service itself. (Characteristics of a waiting-line system, moderate)

70. Customers take a number as they join the waiting line of the customer service counter at a discount store. There are two customer service agents. Provide the most likely characteristics of this system.
   a. name of model
   b. number of channels
   c. number of phases
   d. arrival rate distribution
   e. service time distribution
   f. population size
   g. queue discipline
Multi-channel system (M/M/S); two; single; Poisson; exponential; unlimited; and FIFO. (Characteristics of a waiting-line system, moderate)

71. State the assumptions of the "basic" queuing model (Model A or M/M/1).
1. Arrivals are served on a first-come, first-served (FIFO) basis, and every arrival waits to be served, regardless of the length of the line or queue.
2. Arrivals are independent of preceding arrivals, but the arrival rate does not change over time.
3. Arrivals are described by a Poisson probability distribution and come from an infinite population.
4. Service times vary from one customer to the next and are independent of one another, but their average rate is known.
5. Service times occur according to the negative exponential distribution.
6. The service rate is faster then the arrival rate.
(The variety of queuing models, moderate)

72. Students arrive randomly at the help desk of a computer lab. There is only one service agent, and the service time varies from one student to the other. Provide the most likely characteristics for this system.
   a. name of model
   b. number of channels
   c. number of phases
   d. arrival rate distribution
   e. service time distribution
   f. population size
   g. queue discipline
   Single channel system (M/M/1); single; single; Poisson; exponential; unlimited; and FIFO. (Characteristics of a waiting-line system, moderate)

73. There is only one bay and one type of service at an automatic car wash. Provide the most likely characteristics of this system.
   a. name of model
   b. number of channels
   c. number of phases
   d. arrival rate distribution
   e. service time distribution
   f. population size
   g. queue discipline
   Constant service (M/D/1); single; single; Poisson; constant; unlimited; and FIFO. (Characteristics of a waiting-line system, moderate)

74. Discuss the likely outcome of a waiting line system where $\mu > \lambda$, but only by a tiny amount. (For example, $\mu = 4.1$, $\lambda = 4$).
   The denominator of the performance measures all include ($\mu - \lambda$). This value is now very small, making the performance measures large. Average number of objects in the system grows large, as does the average time spent waiting. (The variety of queuing models, moderate)

75. Describe the behavior of a waiting line where $\lambda > \mu$. Analysis and intuition are both welcome here.
   Intuitively, the queue will grow progressively longer, because the arrival rate is larger than the service rate. Analytically, the performance measures take on negative signs, which have no meaning, except as indicators of a queue with a serious problem. (The variety of queuing models, moderate)

PROBLEMS

76. A crew of mechanics at the Highway Department garage repair vehicles that break down at an average of $\lambda = 5$ vehicles per day (approximately Poisson in nature). The mechanic crew can service an average of $\mu = 10$ vehicles per day with a repair time distribution that approximates an exponential distribution.

   a. What is the utilization rate for this service system?
   b. What is the average time before the facility can return a breakdown to service?
   c. How much of that time is spent waiting for service?
   d. How many vehicles are likely to be in the system at any one time?

   (a) 50 percent; (b) 0.2 days; (c) 0.1 days; (d) 1. POM for Windows solution follows.

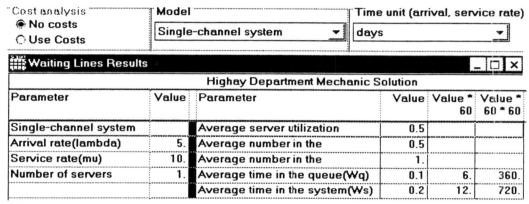

Parameter	Value	Parameter	Value	Value * 60	Value * 60 * 60
Single-channel system		Average server utilization	0.5		
Arrival rate(lambda)	5.	Average number in the	0.5		
Service rate(mu)	10.	Average number in the	1.		
Number of servers	1.	Average time in the queue(Wq)	0.1	6.	360.
		Average time in the system(Ws)	0.2	12.	720.

(The variety of queuing models, easy)

77. A crew of mechanics at the Highway Department garage repair vehicles that break down at an average of $\lambda = 8$ vehicles per day (approximately Poisson in nature). The mechanic crew can service an average of $\mu = 10$ vehicles per day with a repair time distribution that approximates an exponential distribution.

   a. What is the utilization rate for this service system?
   b. What is the average time before the facility can return a breakdown to service?
   c. How much of that time is spent waiting for service?
   d. How many vehicles are likely to be in the system at any one time?

   (a) 80 percent; (b) 0.5 days; (c) 0.4 days; (d) 4. POM for Windows solution follows.

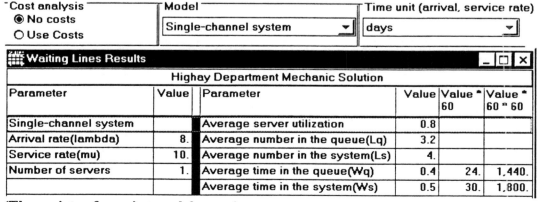

Parameter	Value	Parameter	Value	Value * 60	Value * 60 * 60
Single-channel system		Average server utilization	0.8		
Arrival rate(lambda)	8.	Average number in the queue(Lq)	3.2		
Service rate(mu)	10.	Average number in the system(Ls)	4.		
Number of servers	1.	Average time in the queue(Wq)	0.4	24.	1,440.
		Average time in the system(Ws)	0.5	30.	1,800.

(The variety of queuing models, easy)

78. A crew of mechanics at the Highway Department garage repair vehicles which break down at an average of $\lambda = 5$ vehicles per day (approximately Poisson in nature). The mechanic crew can service an average of $\mu = 10$ vehicles per day with a repair time distribution that approximates an exponential distribution.
a. What is the probability that the system is empty?
b. What is the probability that there is precisely one vehicle in the system?
c. What is the probability that there is more than one vehicle in the system?
d. What is the probability of 5 or more vehicles in the system?
(a) 0.50; (b) 0.25; (c) 0.25; (d) 0.313. POM for Windows solution follows.

Table of Probabilities

	Highay Department Mechanic Solution		
k	Prob (num in sys = k)	Prob (num in sys <= k)	Prob (num in sys >k)
0	0.5	0.5	0.5
1	0.25	0.75	0.25
2	0.125	0.875	0.125
3	0.0625	0.9375	0.0625
4	0.0313	0.9688	0.0313
5	0.0156	0.9844	0.0156

(The variety of queuing models, moderate)

79. A crew of mechanics at the Highway Department garage repair vehicles that break down at an average of $\lambda = 8$ vehicles per day (approximately Poisson in nature). The mechanic crew can service an average of $\mu = 10$ vehicles per day with a repair time distribution that approximates an exponential distribution.
a. What is the probability that the system is empty?
b. What is the probability that there is precisely one vehicle in the system?
c. What is the probability that there is more than one vehicle in the system?
d. What is the probability of 5 or more vehicles in the system?
(a) 0.20; (b) 0.16; (c) 0.64; (d) 0.3277. POM for Windows solution follows.

Table of Probabilities

	Highay Department Mechanic Solution		
k	Prob (num in sys = k)	Prob (num in sys <= k)	Prob (num in sys >k)
0	0.2	0.2	0.8
1	0.16	0.36	0.64
2	0.128	0.488	0.512
3	0.1024	0.5904	0.4096
4	0.0819	0.6723	0.3277
5	0.0655	0.7379	0.2621
6	0.0524	0.7903	0.2097

(The variety of queuing models, moderate)

80. A crew of mechanics at the Highway Department garage repair vehicles that break down at an average of λ = 8 vehicles per day (approximately Poisson in nature). The mechanic crew can service an average of μ = 10 vehicles per day with a repair time distribution that approximates an exponential distribution. The crew cost is approximately $300 per day. The cost associated with lost productivity from the breakdown is estimated at $150 per vehicle per day (or any fraction thereof).

a. What is the expected cost of this system?

Server cost is $300 per day; wait cost is $150 x 4 = $600, for a total of $900 POM for Windows solution follows.

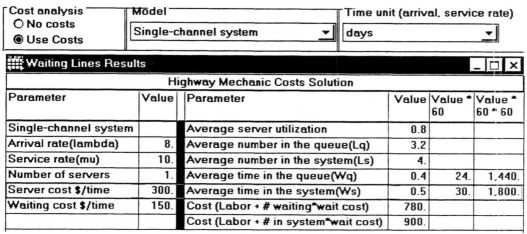

Cost analysis	Model	Time unit (arrival, service rate)
O No costs / ⊚ Use Costs	Single-channel system ▼	days ▼

Waiting Lines Results _ □ ✕

Highway Mechanic Costs Solution					
Parameter	Value	Parameter	Value	Value * 60	Value * 60 * 60
Single-channel system		Average server utilization	0.8		
Arrival rate(lambda)	8.	Average number in the queue(Lq)	3.2		
Service rate(mu)	10.	Average number in the system(Ls)	4.		
Number of servers	1.	Average time in the queue(Wq)	0.4	24.	1,440.
Server cost $/time	300.	Average time in the system(Ws)	0.5	30.	1,800.
Waiting cost $/time	150.	Cost (Labor + # waiting*wait cost)	780.		
		Cost (Labor + # in system*wait cost)	900.		

(The variety of queuing models, difficult)

81. A crew of mechanics at the Highway Department garage repair vehicles that break down at an average of $\lambda = 8$ vehicles per day (approximately Poisson in nature). The mechanic crew can service an average of $\mu = 10$ vehicles per day with a repair time distribution that approximates an exponential distribution. The crew cost is approximately $300 per day. The cost associated with lost productivity from the breakdown is estimated at $150 per vehicle per day (or any fraction thereof).

a. Which is cheaper, the existing system with one service crew, or a revised system with two service crews?

The single-server system server cost is $300 per day; wait cost is $150 x 4 = $600, for a total of $900. The two-server system will double the server cost to $600, but reduce the wait cost to $142, for a total of $742. The two-server system is cheaper. POM for Windows solution follows.

Single server system

Cost analysis	Model	Time unit (arrival, service rate)
○ No costs ◉ Use Costs	Single-channel system ▼	days ▼

Waiting Lines Results _ □ ✕

Highway Mechanic Costs Solution

Parameter	Value	Parameter	Value	Value * 60	Value * 60 * 60
Single-channel system		Average server utilization	0.8		
Arrival rate(lambda)	8.	Average number in the queue(Lq)	3.2		
Service rate(mu)	10.	Average number in the system(Ls)	4.		
Number of servers	1.	Average time in the queue(Wq)	0.4	24.	1,440.
Server cost $/time	300.	Average time in the system(Ws)	0.5	30.	1,800.
Waiting cost $/time	150.	Cost (Labor + # waiting*wait cost)	780.		
		Cost (Labor + # in system*wait cost)	900.		

Two-server system

Cost analysis	Model	Time unit (arrival, service rate)
○ No costs ◉ Use Costs	Multichannel system ▼	hours ▼

Waiting Lines Results _ □ ✕

Highway Mechanic Costs Solution

Parameter	Value	Parameter	Value	Value * 60	Value * 60 * 60
M/M/s		Average server utilization	0.4		
Arrival rate(lambda)	8.	Average number in the queue(Lq)	0.1524		
Service rate(mu)	10.	Average number in the system(Ls)	0.9524		
Number of servers	2.	Average time in the queue(Wq)	0.019	1.1429	68.5714
Server cost $/time	300.	Average time in the system(Ws)	0.119	7.1429	428.5714
Waiting cost $/time	150.	Cost (Labor + # waiting*wait cost)	622.8571		
		Cost (Labor + # in system*wait cost)	742.8571		

(The variety of queuing models, difficult)

82. A dental clinic at which only one dentist works is open only two days a week. During those two days, the traffic is uniformly busy with patients arriving at the rate of 2 per hour. The doctor serves patients at the rate of one every 20 minutes.
a. What is the probability that the clinic is empty (except for the dentist)?
b. What percentage of the time is the dentist busy?
c. What is the average number of patients waiting in the office?
d. What is the average time a patient spends in the office (wait plus service)?
e. What is the average time a patient waits for service?
(a) 0.333; (b) 0.667; (c)1.333; (d) 1.000 hours; (e) 0.667 hours. POM for Windows solution follows.

Cost analysis	Model	Time unit (arrival, service rate)
● No costs	Single-channel system ▼	hours ▼
○ Use Costs		

Dental Clinic

Parameter	Value	Parameter	Value	Value * 60	Value * 60 * 60
Single-channel system		Average server utilization	0.6667		
Arrival rate(lambda)	2.	Average number in the queue(Lq)	1.3333		
Service rate(mu)	3.	Average number in the system(Ls)	2.		
Number of servers	1.	Average time in the queue(Wq)	0.6667	40.	2,400.
		Average time in the system(Ws)	1.	60.	3,600.

(The variety of queuing models, easy)

83. A dental clinic at which only one dentist works is open only two days a week. During those two days, the traffic is uniformly busy with patients arriving at the rate of 2 per hour. The doctor serves patients at the rate of one every 20 minutes.
a. What is the probability that the clinic is empty (except for the dentist)?
b. What is the probability that there is one or more patients in the system?
c. What is the probability that there are four patients in the system?
d. What is the probability that there are four or more patients in the system?
(a) 0.3333; (b) 0.6667; (c) 0.0658; (d) 0.1975. POM for Windows solution follows.

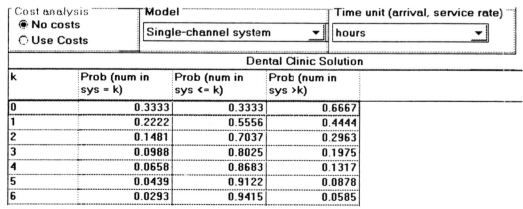

Cost analysis	Model	Time unit (arrival, service rate)
● No costs	Single-channel system ▼	hours ▼
○ Use Costs		

Dental Clinic Solution

k	Prob (num in sys = k)	Prob (num in sys <= k)	Prob (num in sys >k)
0	0.3333	0.3333	0.6667
1	0.2222	0.5556	0.4444
2	0.1481	0.7037	0.2963
3	0.0988	0.8025	0.1975
4	0.0658	0.8683	0.1317
5	0.0439	0.9122	0.0878
6	0.0293	0.9415	0.0585

(The variety of queuing models, easy)

84. At the order fulfillment center of a major mail-order firm, customer orders, already packaged for shipment, arrive at the sorting machines to be sorted for loading onto the appropriate truck for the parcel's address. The arrival rate at the sorting machines is at the rate of 120 per hour following a Poisson distribution. The machine sorts at the constant rate of 160 per hour.
a. What is the utilization rate of the system?
b. What is the average number of packages waiting to be sorted?
c. What is the average number of packages in the sorting system?
d. How long must the average package wait until it get sorted?
(a) 0.75 or 75 percent; (b) 1.125; (c) 1.875; (d) 0.0094 hours, or less than 0.6 minutes. POM for Windows solution follows.

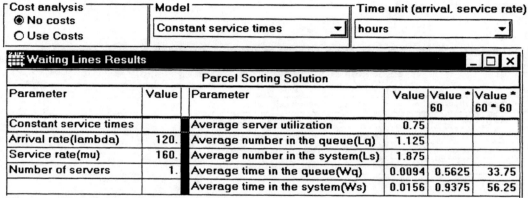

Parameter	Value	Parameter	Value	Value * 60	Value * 60 * 60
Constant service times		Average server utilization	0.75		
Arrival rate(lambda)	120.	Average number in the queue(Lq)	1.125		
Service rate(mu)	160.	Average number in the system(Ls)	1.875		
Number of servers	1.	Average time in the queue(Wq)	0.0094	0.5625	33.75
		Average time in the system(Ws)	0.0156	0.9375	56.25

(The variety of queuing models, easy)

85. At the order fulfillment center of a major mail-order firm, customer orders, already packaged for shipment, arrive at the sorting machines to be sorted for loading onto the appropriate truck for the parcel's address. The arrival rate at the sorting machines is at the rate of 150 per hour following a Poisson distribution. The machine sorts at the constant rate of 160 per hour.
a. What is the utilization rate of the system?
b. What is the average number of packages waiting to be sorted?
c. What is the average number of packages in the sorting system?
d. How long must the average package wait until it get sorted?
(a) 0.9375 or 94 percent; (b) 7.0313; (c) 7.969; (d) 0.0469 hours, or less than 3 minutes. POM for Windows solution follows.

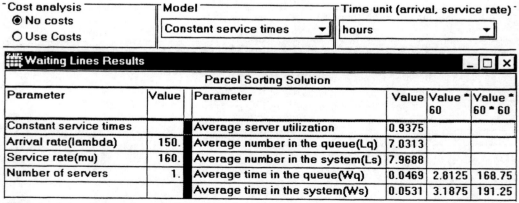

Parameter	Value	Parameter	Value	Value * 60	Value * 60 * 60
Constant service times		Average server utilization	0.9375		
Arrival rate(lambda)	150.	Average number in the queue(Lq)	7.0313		
Service rate(mu)	160.	Average number in the system(Ls)	7.9688		
Number of servers	1.	Average time in the queue(Wq)	0.0469	2.8125	168.75
		Average time in the system(Ws)	0.0531	3.1875	191.25

(The variety of queuing models, easy)

86. A cabinet-making shop has five tools that automate the drilling of holes for the installation of hinges. These machines need setting up for each order of cabinets. These orders appear to follow the Poisson distribution, averaging 3 per day. There is a single technician for setting these machines. His service times are exponential, averaging 2 hours each.

a. What is the service factor for this system?

b. What is the average number of these machines in service?

c. What impact on machines in service would there be if a second technician were available?

(a) The service factor is 1/4/(1/3 + 1/4) = .429 (closer to .420). (b) The average number of machines in service (using table D-7) is 5 * .471 * (1-.420) = 1.37 (c) With two servers, F rises to .826. The average number of machines in service grows to 5 * .826 * (1-.420) = 2.39. (The variety of queuing models, difficult)

MODULE E: LEARNING CURVES

TRUE/FALSE

1. If the first unit in a series of units takes 200 days to complete, and the learning rate is 80%, then the second unit will take 160 days.
    True (Introduction, easy)

2. If the first unit in a series of units takes 200 days to complete, and the learning rate is 80%, then the third will take 128 days.
    False (Introduction, moderate)

3. An 80% learning curve means that with each unit increase in production, labor requirements fall by 20%.
    False (Introduction, moderate)

4. A 90% learning curve implies that each time the production volume is doubled the direct time per unit is reduced to 90% of its previous value.
    True (Introduction, easy)

5. Changes in labor can disrupt the learning curve.
    True (Learning curves in services and manufacturing, moderate)

6. Changes in product do not disrupt the learning curve.
    False (Learning curves in services and manufacturing, moderate)

7. A 70% learning curve is steeper than an 80% learning curve.
    True (Learning curves in services and manufacturing, moderate)

8. Learning curve analysis holds only with respect to labor costs in industrial settings and not in service environments.
    False (Learning curves in services and manufacturing, moderate)

9. Learning curves can be used to establish budgets.
    True (Learning curves in services and manufacturing, moderate)

10. If the learning curve goes from 75% to 80%, it means that efficiency is increasing.
    False (Learning curves in services and manufacturing, moderate)

11. The arithmetic approach to learning curve calculations allows us to determine the hours required for any unit.
    False (Applying the learning curve, moderate)

12. The logarithmic approach to learning curve calculations allows us to determine the hours required for any unit.
    True (Applying the learning curve, moderate)

13. The learning curve coefficient approach is simpler to use than the logarithmic approach.
    True (Applying the learning curve, moderate)

14. In an operation with an 90% learning curve, if the second unit took 27 hours, the first unit would have taken 30 hours.
True (Introduction, moderate)

15. A project manager bases his time and labor estimates on a learning rate of 86%. The actual learning rate turns out to be 89%. The manager, because of the increased learning, will complete his project in less time and with less labor use.
False (Learning curves in manufacturing and services, moderate)

16. In the formula $T_N = T_1 N^b$ for the learning curve, the exponent b is the learning rate, expressed as a decimal.
False (Applying the learning curve, moderate)

17. A learning rate of 100% means that each unit in a series of units will have the same labor requirements.
True (Introduction, moderate)

18. Learning curves differ from industry to industry.
True (Limitations of learning curves, moderate)

19. Reevaluation of learning curves is inapproriate.
False (Limitations of learning curves, moderate)

MULTIPLE CHOICE

20. In order for a learning curve to exist
   a. costs must drop
   b. volume must increase
   c. costs must depend upon volume produced
   d. cost and volume must both increase; cost at a slower rate than volume
   e. the labor force must remain constant
   b (Strategic implications of learning curves, moderate)

21. The fundamental premise underlying learning curve analysis is that
   a. tasks can be easily learned in organizations
   b. learning takes place when people in organizations change
   c. organizations and people become better at their tasks as the tasks are repeated
   d. total labor costs decrease as the number of production units increases
   e. doubling output cuts labor requirements per unit in half
   c (Introduction, moderate)

22. Which of the following best conveys the essence of learning curves?
   a. As the number of repetitions increase, time per unit increases.
   b. As the number of repetitions decrease, time per unit increases.
   c. As the number of repetitions increase, time per unit remains constant.
   d. As the number of repetitions increase, time per unit doubles.
   e. As the number of repetitions increase, time per unit decreases.
   e (Introduction, moderate)

23. A job with a 70% learning curve required 20 hours for the initial unit. The fourth unit should require approximately how many hours?
    a. 6
    b. 9.8
    c. 14
    d. 20
    e. 34
    b (Introduction, easy)

24. A learning curve
    a. is based on the premise that organizations learn from experience
    b. plots man-hours per dollar versus time
    c. is mathematically described by a parabola
    d. should be plotted on polar coordinate graph paper
    e. follows a normal distribution
    a (Introduction, easy)

25. The fact that human activities typically improve when they are done on a repetitive basis is described by a
    a. normal distribution curve
    b. binomial distribution curve
    c. Poisson distribution curve
    d. learning curve
    e. exponential curve
    d (Introduction, easy)

26. Which of the following statements is most appropriate with respect to a 70% learning curve?
    a. There will be a 70% decrease in direct labor per unit each time the production volume doubles.
    b. There will be a 30% decrease in direct labor per unit each time production volume doubles.
    c. Each successive unit of production will take 70% of the direct labor of the previous unit.
    d. Thirty percent of the production will be defective until full learning takes place.
    e. None of the above is true.
    b (Introduction, moderate)

27. A 100% learning curve implies that
    a. learning is taking place for all products and workers
    b. learning is taking place at the best possible level
    c. no learning is taking place
    d. a 100% reduction in the direct labor time takes place each time the production is doubled
    e. none of the above is true
    c (Introduction, moderate)

28. The learning curve rate is
    a. the percentage of time it will take to make each unit when the production rate doubles
    b. the log-log of the annual rate change divided by the average unit cost
    c. always based on constant value dollars
    d. only considered valid after one year of data is accumulated
    e. always based on a constant work force

    a (Introduction, easy)

29. The learning rate depends on the characteristics of a company. Which one of the following companies usually has the lowest learning rate?
    a. a labor intensive company
    b. a product-focused company which produces high-volume products to stock
    c. a process-focused company which accepts orders from different customers with different specifications
    d. a company with a newly-installed flexible manufacturing system (FMS)
    e. a continuous process company

    a (Learning curves in services and manufacturing, difficult)

30. Which one of the following statements about learning curves is **true**?
    a. A learning curve assumes that the direct labor requirements per unit will DECREASE at an INCREASING rate as cumulative production increases.
    b. Learning at a capital intensive operation will usually be LESS than it is for a labor intensive operation.
    c. Learning for simple products will usually be MORE than it is for complex products.
    d. Learning curves can be used only for individuals, not for the whole organization
    e. None of the above are true.

    b (Learning curves in services and manufacturing, moderate)

31. Learning curves are
    a. the same for all products but different for different organizations
    b. the same for all organizations but different for different products
    c. different for different organizations and different products
    d. the same for all organizations and all products
    e. appropriate in services but not in manufacturing

    c (Learning curves in services and manufacturing, moderate

32. The first unit of a product took 832 hours to build, and the learning rate is 90%. How long will it take to make the 20th unit? (Use at least three decimals in the exponent if you use the logarithmic approach)
    a. time ≤ 500 hours
    b. 501 ≤ time ≤ 525
    c. 526 ≤ time ≤ 530
    d. 531 ≤ time ≤ 549
    e. time ≥ 550

    c (Applying the learning curve, moderate)

33. The first unit of a product took 832 hours to build, and the learning rate is 80%. How long will it take to make the 30th unit? (Use at least three decimals in the exponent if you use the logarithmic approach)
   a. less than 200 hours
   b. between 200 and 225 hours
   c. between 226 and 250 hours
   d. between 251 and 275 hours
   e. more than 275 hours
   e (Applying the learning curve, moderate)

34. The first unit of a product took 50 hours to build, and the learning rate is 80%. How long will it take to make the 10th unit? (Use at least three decimals in the exponent if you use the logarithmic approach)
   a. less than 24 hours
   b. between 25 and 30 hours
   c. between 31 and 35 hours
   d. between 36 and 40 hours
   e. more than 40 hours
   a (Applying the learning curve, moderate)

35. The first unit of a product took 1,000 hours to build and the learning curve is 85%. How long will it take to make the first 5 units? (Use Table E.3)
   a. less than 4,005 hours
   b. between 4,006 and 4,015 hours
   c. between 4,016 and 4,025 hours
   d. between 4,026 and 4,035 hours
   e. between 4,036 and 4,045 hours
   d (Applying the learning curve, moderate)

36. The first unit of a product took 900 hours to build and the learning curve is 90%. How long will it take to make the first 3 units? (Use Table E.3)
   a. less than or equal to 2,470 hours
   b. between 2,470 and 2,472 hours
   c. between 2,473 and 2,475 hours
   d. between 2,476 and 2,478 hours
   e. between 2,479 and 2,481 hours
   b (Applying the learning curve, moderate)

37. The first unit of a product took 80 work days. The learning rate is estimated to be 80%. The time for the fourth unit will be about _____ work days and the time for the first four units will be about _____ work days.
   a. 51; 250
   b. 250; 51
   c. 65; 285
   d. 51; cannot be determined
   e. 65; cannot be determined
   a (Applying the learning curve, moderate)

38. A defense contractor has just started producing turbines for a new government contract. The first turbine took 600 hours to produce. If the learning curve is 90%, how long will it take to produce the 10th turbine? (Use at least three decimals in the exponent if you use the logarithmic approach)
    a. less than 450 hours
    b. between 451 and 500 hours
    c. between 501 and 550 hours
    d. between 551 and 600 hours
    e. over 600 hours
    a (Applying the learning curve, moderate)

39. A defense contractor has just started producing engines for a new government contract. The first engine took 700 hours to produce. If the learning rate is 85%, how long will it take to produce the first 20 engines? (Use at least three decimals in the exponent if you use the logarithmic approach)
    a. less than or equal to 1000 hours
    b. between 1001 and 8000 hours
    c. between 8001 and 8500 hours
    d. between 8501 and 10000 hours
    e. more than 10,000 hours
    d (Applying the learning curve, moderate)

40. It took 60 hours to make the first unit of a product. After the second and third units were made, the learning rate was estimated to be 85%. At $10 per hour, estimate the labor bill for the fourth unit? (Use at least three decimals in the exponent if you use the logarithmic approach)
    a. $400 or less
    b. between $400 and $420
    c. between $420 and $440
    d. between $1800 and $2000
    e. over $2000
    c (Applying the learning curve, moderate)

41. A manager is trying to estimate the appropriate learning curve for a certain job. The manager notes that the first four units had a total time of 30 minutes. Which learning curve would yield approximately this result if the first unit took 10 minutes?
    a. 0.70
    b. 0.75
    c. 0.80
    d. 0.85
    e. 0.90
    b (Applying the learning curve, difficult)

42. Which one of the following courses of actions would **not** be taken by a firm wanting to pursue a learning curve steeper than the industry average?
    a. following an aggressive pricing policy
    b. focusing on continuing cost reduction.
    c. focusing on productivity improvement
    d. building on shared experience
    e. keeping capacity equal to demand to control costs
    e (Strategic implications of learning curves, moderate)

43. Which of the following is false regarding learning curves?
    a. Learning curves differ from company to company.
    b. Changes in personnel can change the learning cure.
    c. The learning curve may spike for a short time even if it is going to drop in the long run.
    d. Learning curves can always be used for indirect labor.
    e. All of the above are true.
    d (Limitations of learning curves, moderate)

FILL-IN-THE-BLANK

44. _____ are based on the premise that people and organizations get better at their tasks as the tasks are repeated.
    Learning curves (Introduction, easy)

45. Learning curves are defined in terms of the _____ of their improvement rates.
    complements (Learning curves in services and manufacturing, moderate)

46. Failure to consider the effects of learning can lead to _____ of labor needs.
    overestimates (Learning curves in services and manufacturing, moderate)

47. The _____ is the simplest approach to learning curve problems.
    arithmetic approach (Applying the learning curve, moderate)

48. The learning curve coefficient, C, depends on both the _____, and the unit of interest.
    learning rate (Applying the Learning curve, moderate)

SHORT ANSWERS

49. What is the basic premise underlying the learning curve?
    Organizations, like people, become better at their tasks as the tasks are repeated. (Introduction, easy)

50. "By tradition, learning rates are defined in terms of the complements of their improvement rates." Explain.
    The improvement in labor usage might be expressed as a 10% reduction. The complement of the 10% is 90%. We refer to learning not by the 10% improvement, but by improvement to 90% of the old value. The latter number, not the former, expresses learning rates. (Learning curves in services and manufacturing, moderate)

51. In your own words, explain what is meant by the steepness of the learning curve.
    A steeper curve has more (or faster) learning. An 80% curve is steeper than a 90% curve. The reduction in labor requirements is more rapid at 80% than at 90%. (Learning curves in services and manufacturing, moderate)

52. What problems in scheduling can arise if adjustments for learning curve effects in operations are not made?
Labor and productive facilities being idle a portion of the time; and firms may refuse additional work because improvements that result from learning are not considered. (Learning curves in services and manufacturing, moderate)

53. List three applications of the learning curve.
Internal manpower forecasting, scheduling, establishing costs and budgets; external purchasing and subcontracting of items; and strategic evaluation of company and industry performance, including costs and pricing. (Learning curves in services and manufacturing, moderate)

54. Two manufacturers have very different learning rates; one is under 70% while the other is over 80%. What factors might lead to such a gap?
The two firms might not have the same labor content in their output: learning is generally associated with high labor content output. The two firms might not have equally standardized outputs; if the product keeps changing, there is no basis for learning to occur. One firm might be engaged in high-volume, standardized production where no learning remains. (Learning curves in services and manufacturing, moderate)

55. What are the elements that can disrupt the learning curve?
Any change in process, product, or personnel. (Learning curves in services and manufacturing, moderate)

56. List one advantage and one disadvantage of the arithmetic approach over the logarithmic approach to learning curve calculations?
Advantage: simplest approach to learning curve problems. Disadvantage: can't find values for every value of n, only for exact doublings. (Applying learning curves, moderate)

57. List one advantage and one disadvantage of the logarithmic approach over the arithmetic approach to learning curve calculations.
Advantage: the logarithmic approach allows the determination of the hours required for any unit. Disadvantage: somewhat more complex. (Applying learning curves, moderate)

58. What cautions are in order when using learning curves?
**1. Estimates for each organization should be developed rather than applying someone else's.
2. When current information becomes available, reevaluation is appropriate.
3. Any change in personnel, design, or procedure can be expected to alter the learning curve.
4. Learning curves do not always apply to indirect labor and materials.
5. The culture of the work place, as well as resource availability and changes in the process, may alter the learning curve. (Limitations of learning curves, moderate)**

PROBLEMS

59. Your firm has a contract to make 20 specialty lenses for night vision equipment. The first one took 40 hours. Learning is expected at the 80% rate. How long will it take to finish all 20 units?
40 * 10.485 = 419.4 hours. (Applying the learning curve, moderate)

60. The first unit took 79 hours; the tenth took 56 hours. What learning rate is implied by the data? **The improvement is 56/79 = 0.709 at 10 units; this closely matches the learning rate of 90%. (Applying the learning curve, moderate)**

61. Your firm has expertise with a special type of hand-finished furniture. The learning rate is known to be 82%. If the first piece of furniture took 6 hours, how long will it take to do the second? How long will it take to do the fourth? **Use the successive doubling (arithmetic) approach. The second will take 0.82 * 6 = 4.92 hours; the fourth will take 0.82 * 0.82 * 6 = 4.03 hours. (Applying the learning curve, moderate)**

62. Your firm has expertise with a special type of hand-finished furniture. The learning rate is known to be 82%. If the first piece of furniture took 6 hours, estimate how long will it take to do the third unit? **Using the arithmetic approach, the second will take 0.82 * 6 = 4.92 hours and the fourth will take 0.82 * 0.82 * 6 = 4.03 hours. The third unit must take an amount of labor between these two values, but not exactly halfway. There is more absolute improvement from unit 2 to 3 than from unit 3 to 4. A reasonable estimate would be about 4.4 or 4.5 hours (the answer from Excel OM is 4.38 hours). (Applying the learning curve, moderate)**

63. Your firm has expertise with a special type of hand-finished furniture. The learning rate is known to be 82%. If the first piece of furniture took 6 hours, use the logarithmic approach to determine how long will it take to do the third unit? **For 82% learning, the factor b = log(.82)/log(2) = -0.2863. $T_3 = T_1 N^b = 6(3)^{-0.2863} = 6 * 0.7301 = 4.38$ hours. (Applying the learning curve, moderate)**

64. You are about to undertake manufacture of a labor-intensive electronics component. The first unit took 300 hours. You are not sure whether the learning rate is 75% or 80%. The initial phase of the contract calls for 6 of these components.
a. How much time will it take to complete all six at 75% learning?
b. How much time will it take to complete all six at 80% learning?
(a) 300 * 3.934 = 1180.2 hours; (b) 300 * 4.299 = 1289.7 hours. (Applying the learning curve, moderate)

65. A builder of government-contracted small ships has a steady work force of ten very skilled craftspeople. These workers can supply 2,500 labor hours each per year. They are about to undertake a new contract, building a new style of boat. The first boat is expected to take 6,000 hours to complete. The firm thinks that 90% is the expected learning rate.
a. What is the firm's "capacity" to make these boats--that is, how many units can the firm make in one year?
b. If the learning rate were found to be 85% instead of 90%, how many more units can the firm make?
(a) The firm can offer 25,000 hours of labor. From Table E.3, five boats would require 6000 * 4.339 = 26,034 hours, while four boats would require 6000 * 3.556 = 21,336 hours. Thus four boats can be completed, but five cannot. (b) At the improved learning rate, five boats requires 6000 * 4.031 = 24,186, now within the stated labor limits. (Applying the learning curve, moderate)

66. A firm is about to bid on a defense contract. The product uses new technology, so the firm believes that a learning rate of 75% is appropriate. The first unit is expected to take 700 hours, and the contract is for 40 units.

a. What is the total amount of hours to build the 40 units?

b. What is the average time to build each of the 40 units?

c. Assume that a worker works 2200 hours per year. How many workers should be assigned to this contract to complete it in a year?

From Table E.3, the 40 units will require 700 * 13.723 = 9,606.1 hours. The average time per unit is 9,606.1 / 40 = 240.2 hours. It will take 9,606.1 / 2200 = 4.37 workers to complete the contract within one year. (Applying the learning curve, moderate)

67. A certain product under development took 200 hours for the production of its 2nd unit and 160 hours for its 4th unit.

a. What is the learning rate?

b. How much time did the first unit take?

c. How much time would the production of the 10th unit take? (Use both the logarithmic and the Table E.3 approach. Do the two versions agree?)

(a) 160/200 = 80%; (b) 200/0.8 = 250 hours; (c) $T_{10} = T_1 N^b = 250(10)^{-0.322} = 119.25$ hours; from Table E.3, 250 * 0.477 = 119.25 hours. They generate the same result. (Applying the learning curve, moderate)

68. Your company is making experimental turbochargers for a new design of high-powered farm tractors. The production schedule for these new components is contained in the table below.

Month	Turbochargers
1	7
2	6
3	7
4	10
5	5

The first turbocharger, a trial unit, took 1,000 hours to produce. Based on your experience with similar products, the learning factor is 85%. You have 20 employees, and each employee works 160 hours per month. How many hours will be required in each month? In which month(s) will overtime be required to meet the production schedule?

Use the Total time column of the 85% section of Table E.3. The first seven turbochargers require 1000 * 5.322 = 5322 hours. The first 13 turbochargers require 1000 * 8.792 = 8792 hours. From this deduce that units 8 through 13 take 8792 - 5322 = 3470 hours. The 20 employees contribute 3200 hours per month. Therefore, overtime is needed in every month except the last. (Applying the learning curve, difficult)

Month	Number of Turbochargers	Cumulative hours	Hours this month
1	7	5,322	5,322
2	6	8,792	3,470
3	7	12,402	3,610
4	10	17,091	4,689
5	5	19,294	2,203

69. Tony and Steve are teammates at a discount store; their new job is assembling swing sets for customers. Assembly of a swing set has a learning rate of 90%. They forgot to time their effort on the first swing set, but spent 4.0 hours on the second set. They have six more sets to do. Determine approximately how much time will be (was) required for

a. the first unit

b. the eighth unit

c. all eight units

(a) 4.0 is 90% of 4.44 hours; (b) 4.44 * .729 = 3.24 hours; (c) 4.44 * 6.574 = 29.2 hours. (Applying the learning curve, moderate)

70. Sally suspects strongly that there is a learning curve associated with solving problems assigned for operations management. She notes that it took her approximately 33 minutes to solve the first problem and 17 minutes to solve the fifth problem.

a. Estimate Sally's learning percentage.

b. Using your answer from part a, estimate how much longer it will take Sally to finish the three problems which remain.

(a) Her improvement from the first to fifth unit is 17/33 = 0.515. This value is close to the entry 0.513 for the fifth unit under the 75% learning rate column of Table E.3. Thus her learning rate is 75%. (b) The total for eight problems is 33 * 4.802 = 158 minutes. She has already spent 33 * 3.459 = 114 minutes on the first five problems. She has 44 minutes remaining. (Applying the learning curve, moderate)

71. A company is preparing a bid on a government contract for 40 units of a certain product. The operations manager estimates the assembly time required for the first two units to be 10.4 hours and 8.8 hours respectively.

a. What is the appropriate learning curve?

b. What is the average time per unit for the 40 units?

c. Which unit, if any, will require approximately one-half the time of the first unit?

(a) The learning rate is 8.8/10.4 = 0.846 or approximately 85%. (b) The group of 40 units will take 10.4 * 21.425 = 222.82 hours total, for an average of 5.57 hours each. (c) The 19th unit has a unit time factor of 0.501, meaning that it requires 50% of the labor of the first unit. (Applying the learning curve, moderate)

72. You are a cost accountant for a firm that specializes in "small" (under 10 billion dollars) defense contracts for specialty electronics products, such as fully portable, miniaturized CD-ROM imaging stations and Global Positioning transmitters/transponders. Your company is well respected in this field. One project up for competitive bids is a Field Service, Hands-Free, Individual Multi-Protocol Secure Communicator (a battlefield version of a cellular telephone, but built into each soldier's helmet, and containing necessary encryption technology). The Department of Defense wants 8 of these experimental devices to test their practicality. You have reviewed the contract specifications, and estimated that the first FSHFIMPSC should require 2350 hours, and that the product is subject to a 75% learning rate. All costs of the project (machine purchase, machine time, direct and indirect labor and materials) have been bundled (allocated) into an hourly labor rate of $172 per hour. Determine the total project cost using the provided data.

From Table E.3, 2350 * 4.802 = 11,284.7 hours will be needed. At $172 per hour, the total cost is $1,940,968.4. (Applying the learning curve, moderate)

MODULE F: SIMULATION

TRUE/FALSE

1. Simulation is a useful tool, but its application is typically limited to queuing and inventory problems.
    False (Introduction, easy)

2. Simulation is a technique usually reserved for studying only the simplest and most straightforward of models.
    False (Advantages and disadvantages of simulation, moderate)

3. While most simulations take place on computerized models, small simulations can be conducted by hand.
    True (What is simulation? easy)

4. Simulation is usually capable of producing a more appropriate answer to a complex problem than can be obtained from an analytical model.
    True (What is simulation? moderate

5. A simulation is "Monte Carlo" when the elements of a system being simulated exhibit chance in their behavior.
    True (Monte Carlo simulation, moderate)

6. Simulation allows managers to test the effects of major policy decisions on real-life systems without disturbing the real system.
    True (Advantages and disadvantages of simulation, moderate)

7. Like mathematical and analytical models, simulation is restricted to using the standard probability distributions.
    False (Advantages and disadvantages of simulation, moderate)

8. Because simulations are generally run on computers, they are cheap to design and use.
    False (Advantages and disadvantages of simulation, moderate)

9. Simulation provides optimal solutions to problems.
    False (Advantages and disadvantages of simulation, moderate)

10. Since simulation makes use of numerical models, it will give the same solution in repeated use to any particular problem.
    False (Advantages and disadvantages of simulation, moderate)

11. A simulation model is designed to arrive at a single specific numerical answer to a given problem.
    False (Advantages and disadvantages of simulation, moderate)

12. In random numbers, the digits 0 and 9 have a higher chance of being drawn.
    False (Monte Carlo simulation, moderate)

13. Random number intervals are based on cumulative distributions.
True (Monte Carlo simulation, moderate)

14. By starting random number intervals at 01, not 00, the top of each range is the cumulative probability.
True (Monte Carlo simulation, moderate)

15. One reason for using simulation rather than an analytical model in an inventory problem is that the simulation is able to handle probabilistic demand and lead times.
True (Simulation and inventory analysis, moderate)

16. Results of simulation experiments with large numbers of trials or long experimental runs will generally be better than those with fewer trials or shorter experimental runs.
True (Monte Carlo simulation, moderate)

17. Specialized computer languages have been developed which allow one to readily simulate specific types of problems.
True (The role of computers in simulation, moderate)

18. Programming large simulations is more time-consuming with GPSS than with PASCAL.
False (The role of computers in simulation, moderate)

19. SIMSCRIPT is a general-purpose programming language that can be used in simulation work.
False (The role of computers in simulation, moderate)

MULTIPLE CHOICE

20. Which of the following is **true** regarding the use of simulation?
    a. It is always very easy to build a simulation model.
    b. It is very inexpensive to use a simulation model.
    c. It always yields optimum solutions.
    d. It allows time-compression in testing major policy decisions.
    e. Few constraints, if any, have to be considered.
    d (Advantages and disadvantages of simulation, moderate)

21. Simulation is used for several reasons, including
    a. MODEL development is a fast process.
    b. It can handle large and complex real-world problems.
    c. It is inexpensive.
    d. The models are usually simple.
    e. It always generates optimal solutions.
    b (Advantages and disadvantages of simulation, moderate)

22. One of the advantages of simulation is that
    a. it is much less expensive than a mathematical solution
    b. it always generates a more accurate solution than a mathematical solution
    c. model development is less time consuming than for mathematical models
    d. the policy changes may be tried out without disturbing the real-life system
    e. model solutions are transferable to a wide variety of problems
    d (Advantages and disadvantages of simulation, moderate)

23. One of the disadvantages of simulation is that it
    a. does not allow for very complex problem solutions
    b. is not very flexible
    c. is very limited in the type of probability distribution that can be used
    d. is a trial and error approach that may produce different solutions in different runs
    e. interferes with the production systems while the program is being run
    d (Advantages and disadvantages of simulation, moderate)

24. Elements of chance
    a. are present in all forms of simulation
    b. are present in Monte Carlo simulation
    c. are present only in physical simulations
    d. play little role in simulation
    e. cannot be modeled
    b (Advantages and disadvantages of simulation, moderate)

25. A simulation is said to be Monte Carlo if
    a. it is computerized
    b. it involves chance
    c. it simulates an element of gambling
    d. it saves a lot of money
    e. it uses the MONTECARLO language
    b (Advantages and disadvantages of simulation, moderate)

26. From a portion of a probability distribution, you read that P(demand=0) is 0.05 and P(demand=1) is 0.10. The **cumulative** probability for demand=1 would be
    a. 0.05
    b. 0.075
    c. 0.10
    d. 0.15
    e. cannot be determined
    d (Monte Carlo simulation, moderate)

27. From a portion of a probability distribution, you read that P(demand=0) is 0.05, P(demand=1) is 0.10, and P(demand=2) is 0.20. The random number intervals for this distribution beginning with 01 are
   a. 01 through 05, 06 through 15, and 16 through 35
   b. 01 through 05, 01 through 10, and 01 through 20
   c. 00 through 04, 05 through 14, and 15 through 34
   d. 00 through 04, 00 through 09, and 00 through 19
   e. 01 through 06, 07 through 16, and 17 through 36
   a (Monte Carlo simulation, moderate)

28. From a portion of a probability distribution, you read that P(demand=1) is 0.05, P(demand=2) is 0.15, and P(demand=3) is .20. The **cumulative** probability for demand=3 would be
   a. 0.133
   b. 0.200
   c. 0.400
   d. 0.600
   e. cannot be determined
   e (Monte Carlo simulation, moderate)

29. From a portion of a probability distribution, you read that P(demand=0) is 0.25, and P(demand=1) is 0.30. The random number intervals for this distribution beginning with 01 are
   a. 01 through 25, and 26 through 30
   b. 01 through 25, and 01 through 30
   c. 01 through 25, and 26 through 55
   d. 00 through 25, and 26 through 55
   e. 00 through 25, and 26 through 30
   c (Monte Carlo simulation, moderate)

30. Which of the following is **true** regarding simulation?
   a. Small problems can be done by hand.
   b. Most simulations are computerized.
   c. Some simulations are physical, not mathematical.
   d. Simulation is most suitable where standard analytical models are too complex.
   e. All of the above are true.
   e (Advantages and disadvantages of simulation, moderate)

31. Which of the following is **false** regarding simulation?
   a. If an analytical model can't solve a problem, neither can a simulation.
   b. Simulation can only be done by computer.
   c. Monte Carlo simulation requires the use of random numbers.
   d. Physical simulations involve elements of chance, and are called Monte Carlo simulations.
   e. All of the above are false.
   c (Advantages and disadvantages of simulation, moderate)

32.　Which of these is a general purpose computer language useful in developing a simulation model?
　　a.　PASCAL
　　b.　GPSS
　　c.　SimFactory
　　d.　DYNAMO
　　e.　SimCity
　　a (The role of computers in simulation, moderate)

33.　SimFactory is a
　　a.　general-purpose simulation language
　　b.　special-purpose simulation language
　　c.　commercial, easy-to-use, pre-written simulation program
　　d.　child's computer game
　　e.　none of the above
　　c (The role of computers in simulation, moderate)

34.　SIMSCRIPT is
　　a.　a general purpose simulation language
　　b.　a special-purpose simulation language
　　c.　an obsolete programming language
　　d.　the multi-lingual stone tablets that allowed the translation of Egyptian hieroglyphics
　　e.　none of the above
　　b (The role of computers in simulation, moderate)

35.　Which one of the following is **not** an advantage of special purpose simulation languages? They
　　a.　require less programming time for large simulations
　　b.　are so easy to use that clerical staff can program the simulations
　　c.　have random number generators already built-in as subroutines
　　d.　are easier to check for errors than general purpose-languages
　　e.　are more efficient than general purpose-languages
　　b (The role of computers in simulation, moderate)

36.　Which of these is a special purpose computer language useful in developing a simulation model?
　　a.　PASCAL
　　b.　COBOL
　　c.　SIMCSRIPT
　　d.　C++
　　e.　BASIC
　　c (The role of computers in simulation, moderate)

FILL-IN-THE-BLANK

37.　_____ is the attempt to duplicate the features, appearance, and characteristics of a real system, usually via a computerized model.
　　Simulation (What is simulation? easy)

38.　The _____ method is a simulation technique that uses random elements when chance exists in their behavior.
　　Monte Carlo (What is simulation? moderate)

39. A _____ is the accumulation of individual probabilities of a distribution. **cumulative probability distribution (Monte Carlo simulation, moderate)**

40. A _____ is a series of digits that have been selected by a totally random process. **random number (Monte Carlo simulation, moderate)**

SHORT ANSWERS

41. List five applications of simulation.
The five can be picked from a list in Table F.1. Some highlights are traffic-light timing, bus scheduling, plant layout, production scheduling, inventory planning, and waiting line analysis. (Introduction, easy)

42. State, in order, the seven steps an operations manager should perform when using simulation to analyze a problem.
Define the problem; introduce the important variables associated with the problem; construct a numerical model; set up possible courses of action for testing; run the experiment; consider the results; and decide what course of action to take. (What is simulation? moderate)

43. State the three-fold idea behind simulation.
To imitate a real-world situation mathematically; then to study its properties and operating characteristics; and finally to draw conclusions and make action decisions based on the results of the simulation. (What is simulation? moderate)

44. List the advantages of simulation.
1. It is relatively straightforward and flexible.
2. It can be used to analyze large and complex real-world situations that cannot be solved by conventional operations management models.
3. It allows for the inclusion of real-world complications that most models cannot permit.
4. It allows "time compression".
5. It allows the user to ask "what if" questions and experiment with various representations of the problem.
6. It does not interfere with the real world system.
7. It allows us to study interactive effects of individual components or variables.
(Advantages and disadvantages of simulation, moderate)

45. List the disadvantages of simulation.
1. It can be very expensive and complex.
2. It does not generate optimal solutions to problems.
3. Managers must generate all of the conditions and constraints for solutions that they want to examine.
4. Each solution model is unique. Its solutions and inferences are usually not transferable to other problems.
(Advantages and disadvantages of simulation, moderate)

46. List, in order, the five steps required to implement the Monte Carlo simulation technique.
Set up a probability distribution for important variables; build a cumulative probability distribution for each of these variables; establish an interval of random numbers for each variable; generate sets of random numbers; and actually simulate a set of trials. (Monte Carlo simulation, moderate)

47. Explain what is meant by "simulation is not limited to using the standard probability distributions."
"Standard models" include normal, binomial, beta, uniform, Poisson, exponential, and other probability distributions. Each has a specific set of assumptions and parameters. Real-world (empirical) systems can have any distribution imaginable. Simulation can mimic these real-world distributions by use of random number intervals based on real-world behavior, and can therefore generate more realistic models than would occur if a standard model were used in place of a system-specific one. (Monte Carlo simulation, moderate)

48. Explain how Monte Carlo simulation uses random numbers.
First, a cumulative probability distribution is set up for the element being modeled. From this, a set of random number intervals is established. A random number is generated, and matched against the set of intervals. The random number will fall into only one interval, and that determines the value for the element being modeled. (Monte Carlo simulation, moderate)

49. A waiting line problem that cannot be modeled by standard distributions has been simulated. The table below shows the result of a Monte Carlo simulation. (Assume that the simulation began at 8:00 a.m. and there is only one server)

Why do you think this problem does not fit the standard distribution for waiting lines? Explain briefly how a Monte Carlo simulation might work where analytical models cannot.

Customer number	Arrival Time	Service Time	Service Ends
1	8:05	2	8:07
2	8:06	10	8:17
3	8:10	15	8:32
4	8:20	12	8:44
5	8:30	4	8:48

(Requires a bit of memory from the waiting line chapter) Service times do not appear to be exponential. Rather, they seem to be extreme-very short or very long. Simulation can handle this with a cumulative probability distribution and a set of random number intervals. The Monte Carlo simulation will, with a large enough number of trials, mimic the reality of this system. (Monte Carlo simulation, difficult)

50. Explain the difference between **simulated** average demand and **expected** average demand.
Simulated average demand is based on the simulation model constructed, and is affected by the number of trials or repetitions, and is affected by the random numbers selected. For small numbers of repetitions, simulated average demand can be quite variable. Expected average demand is based on the mathematical model of demand, and is a precise and unchanging value, the weighted average or expectation of the values of the variable being modeled. Simulated average demand approaches expected average demand as the number of simulation repetitions increases. (Monte Carlo simulation, moderate)

51.   List the two classes of computer programming languages available for simulation.
General-purpose and special-purpose. (The role of computers in simulation, moderate)

52.   State three examples of general-purpose languages than can be used for simulation.
BASIC, C++, and PASCAL. (The role of computers in simulation, moderate)

53.   Explain how random numbers are used in Monte Carlo simulation. Provide a small example.
First, a cumulative probability distribution is set up for the element being modeled. From this, a set of random number intervals is established. A random number is generated, and matched against the set of intervals. The random number will fall into only one interval, and that determines the value for the element being modeled. For example, demand can be 0, 40 percent of the time, or 1, 60 percent of the time. The cumulative distribution is demand = 0, 0.40, and demand = 1, 1.00. The random number intervals are 01 through 40 for demand = 0 and 41 through 00 for demand = 1. A random number of 36 indicates demand = 0. (Monte Carlo simulation, moderate)

54.   State three examples of special-purpose languages than can be used for simulation.
GPSS, SIMSCRIPT, and DYNAMO. (The role of computers in simulation, moderate)

55.   What are the advantages of special-purpose simulation languages?
1. They require less programming time for large simulations.
2. They are usually more efficient and easier to check for errors.
3. They have random number generators already built-in as subroutines.
(The role of computers in simulation, moderate)

PROBLEMS

56.   A waiting line problem that cannot be modeled by standard distributions has been simulated. The table below shows the result of a Monte Carlo simulation. (Assume that the simulation began at 8:00 a.m. and there is only one server)

Customer number	Arrival Time	Service Time	Service Ends
1	8:05	2	8:07
2	8:06	10	8:17
3	8:10	15	8:32
4	8:20	11	8:43
5	8:30	5	8:48

a. What is the average waiting time in line?
b. What is the average time in the system?
(a) Waiting time is 0 + 1 + 7 + 12 + 13 = 33. Average waiting time is 33/5 = 6.6 min; (b) Total time in system is 2 + 11 + 22 + 23 + 18 = 76. Average time in system is 76/5 = 15.2 min. (Simulation of a queuing problem, moderate)

57. A manager needs to simulate a single-phase, single-server waiting line system for which the standard Poisson and exponential distributions are inadequate. The manager has a well-detailed history of arrivals and service times. These data are summarized in the table below. Use these data to construct cumulative probability distributions for arrival intervals and for service times.

Arrival intervals

minutes between arrivals	Probability
1	.1
2	.1
3	.2
4	.3
8	.2
12	.1

Service times

minutes	probability
2	.2
3	.3
4	.5

a. Calculate the cumulative probability distribution for arrivals and for service times.
b. Assign random number intervals for these cumulative distributions.

Arrivals

minutes between arrivals	probability	cumulative probability	Interval
1	0.1	0.1	01-10
2	0.1	0.2	11-20
3	0.2	0.4	21-40
4	0.3	0.7	41-70
8	0.2	0.9	71-90
12	0.1	1	91-00

Service times

minutes	probability	cumulative probability	random number intervals
2	0.2	0.2	01-20
3	0.3	0.5	21-50
4	0.5	1	51-00

(Simulation of a queuing problem, moderate)

58. A warehouse manager needs to simulate the demand placed on a product that does not fit standard models. The concept being measured is "demand during lead time," where both lead time and daily demand are variable. The historical record for this product suggests the following probability distribution. Convert this distribution into random number intervals.

Demand during lead time	Probability
100	.01
120	.15
140	.30
160	.15
180	.04
200	.10
220	.25

Demand during lead time	Probability	Cumulative probability	Random number intervals
100	.01	.01	01-01
120	.15	.16	02-16
140	.30	.46	17-46
160	.15	.61	47-61
180	.04	.65	62-65
200	.10	.75	66-75
220	.25	1.00	76-00

(Simulation and inventory analysis, moderate)

59. A warehouse manager needs to simulate the demand placed on a product which does not fit standard models. The concept being measured is "demand during lead time," where both lead time and daily demand are variable. The historical record for this product, along with the cumulative distribution and random number intervals, appear below. Random numbers have been generated to simulate the next 5 order cycles; they are 91, 45, 37. 65, and 51. What are the five demand values? What is their average?

Demand during lead time	Probability	Cumulative probability	Random number intervals
100	.01	.01	01-01
120	.15	.16	02-16
140	.30	.46	17-46
160	.15	.61	47-61
180	.04	.65	62-65
200	.10	.75	66-75
220	.25	1.00	76-00

91 generates demand of 220; 45 and 37 each generate demand of 140; 65 generates 180; and 51 generates 160. Their sum is 840, and their average is 168. (Simulation and inventory analysis, moderate)

60. The table below shows the partial results of a Monte Carlo simulation. Assume that the simulation began at 8:00 a.m. and there is only one server.

Customer number	Arrival Time	Service Time
1	8:01	6
2	8:06	7
3	8:09	8
4	8:15	6
5	8:20	6

a. When does service begin for customer #3?
b. When will customer #5 leave?
c. What is the average waiting time in line?
d. What is the average time in the system?

Customer Number	Arrival Time	Service Time	Service Begins	Service Ends	Time in Line	Time in System
1	8:01	6	8:01	8:07	0	6
2	8:06	7	8:07	8:14	1	8
3	8:09	8	8:14	8:22	5	13
4	8:15	6	8:22	8:28	7	13
5	8:20	6	8:28	8:34	8	14

(a) 8:14 (b) 8:34 (c) 4.2 min (d) 10.8 min. (Simulation of a queuing problem, moderate)

61. A local newsstand owner uses naive forecasting to order tomorrow's papers. The number of newspapers ordered corresponds to the previous day's demand. Today's demand for papers was 22. The owner buys the newspapers for $0.20 and sells them for $0.50. Whenever there is unsatisfied demand, the owner estimates the lost goodwill cost at $0.10. Complete the table below, and answer the questions that follow.

Demand	p
21	.25
22	.15
23	.10
24	.20
25	.30

Day	Papers ordered	Random number	Demand	Revenue	Cost	Goodwill cost	Net profit
1	22	37					
2		19					
3		52					
4		8					
5		61					
6		22					

a. What is the demand on day 3?
b. What is the total net profit at the end of the 6 days?
c. What is the lost goodwill on day 6?
d. What is the net profit on day 2?
e. How many papers has he ordered for day 5?
(a) 24 (b) $36.70 (c) $0.30 (d) $6.10 (e) 21

Demand	p	Cp	RNI
21	.25	.25	01-25
22	.15	.40	26-40
23	.10	.50	41-50
24	.20	.70	51-70
25	.30	1.00	71-100

Day	Papers ordered	Random number	Demand	Revenue	Cost	Goodwill cost	Net profit
1	22	37	22	$11.00	$4.40	$0.00	$6.60
2	22	19	21	$10.50	$4.40	$0.00	$6.10
3	21	52	24	$10.50	$4.20	$0.30	$6.00
4	24	8	21	$10.50	$4.80	$0.00	$5.70
5	21	22	21	$10.50	$4.20	$0.00	$6.30
6	21	61	24	$10.50	$4.20	$0.30	$6.00

(Simulation and inventory analysis, moderate)

62. Historical records on a certain product indicate the following behavior for demand. The data represent the 300 days that the business was open during 1998. Convert these data into random number intervals.

Demand in cases	number of occurrences
7	54
8	6
9	12
10	39
11	81
12	108

Demand in cases	number of occurrences	Cumulative probability	Random number intervals
7	54	.18	01-18
8	6	.20	19-20
9	12	.24	21-24
10	39	.37	25-37
11	81	.64	38-64
12	108	1.00	65-00

(Simulation and inventory analysis, moderate)

CD TUTORIAL 1: STATISTICAL TOOLS FOR MANAGERS

TRUE/FALSE

1. Discrete probability distributions require that events be mutually exclusive.
   True (Discrete probability distributions, easy)

2. Discrete probability distributions require that the probability values sum to 1.
   True (Discrete probability distributions, moderate)

3. In a continuous probability distribution, the sum of the probability values is 1.
   True (Continuous probability distributions, moderate)

4. In a continuous probability distribution, the individual probability values are 0.
   True (Continuous probability distribution, moderate)

5. A "standard normal" distribution is a normal distribution that has a $\mu = 1$ and $\sigma = 0$.
   False (Continuous probability distribution, moderate)

6. In all probability distributions, the total of the probability values sums to 1.
   True (Discrete probability distribution, moderate)

7. Expected value is a measure of dispersion.
   False (Discrete probability distribution, moderate)

MULTIPLE CHOICE

8. The expected value is a measure of
   a. variance
   b. central tendency
   c. standard deviation
   d. range
   e. none of the above
   b (Continuous probability distribution, moderate)

9. Variance is the measure of
   a. central tendency
   b. spread or dispersion
   c. maximum possible value
   d. minimum possible value
   e. none of the above
   b (Continuous probability distribution, moderate)

10. The normal distribution can be completely specified when which of the following values is/are specified
    a. mean (μ), and standard deviation (σ)
    b. mean (μ)
    c. standard deviation (σ)
    d. variance (σ^2)
    e. none of the above
    a (Continuous probability distribution, moderate)

11. The square root of variance is the
    a. expected value
    b. area under the normal curve
    c. standard deviation
    d. probability of a given value of the variable
    e. all of the above
    c (Discrete probability distribution, easy)

12. To find the area under a portion of a normal curve requires the
    a. mean
    b. standard deviation
    c. upper and lower values of the area to be found
    d. all of the above
    e. none of the above
    d (Continuous probability distribution, moderate)

FILL-IN-THE-BLANK

13. A _____ probability distribution has outcomes that are not continuous, and there is a probability value assigned to each event.
    discrete (Discrete probability distribution, easy)

14. The _____ of a probability distribution is a number that reveals the overall spread or dispersion of the distribution.
    variance (Discrete probability distribution, moderate)

15. The _____ is a measure of the central tendency, and is calculated as the weighted average of the values of the variable.
    expected value (Discrete probability distribution, moderate)

16. One of the most popular and useful continuous probability distributions is the _____, which is characterized by a bell-shaped curve.
    normal distribution (Continuous probability distribution, moderate)

SHORT ANSWER

17. The three rules required of all probability distributions are
    1. The events are mutually exclusive and collectively exhaustive.
    2. The individual probability values are between 0 and 1.
    3. The total of the probability values sums to 1.
    (Discrete probability distribution, moderate)

18. What is the difference between a **discrete** probability distribution and a **continuous** probability distribution?
    In discrete probability distribution, the random variable can take on any one of a limited set of values. In a continuous probability distribution, the random variable takes on any of an unlimited set of values. (Continuous probability distribution, moderate)

PROBLEMS

19. D&D Distributing stocks 8 cases of popsicles for each baseball game. The probability distribution for sales of popsicles is given below.
    a. On the average, how many cases of popsicles are sold each game?
    b. What is the variance of popsicles sales?

Cases of popsicles sold	Probability
1	.05
2	.05
3	.20
4	.10
5	.10
6	.20
7	.20
8	.10

    a. 5.05 cases b. 4.05 cases^2.
    (Discrete probability distribution, moderate)

20. On a certain assembly line, the average number of defects per day is normally distributed with a mean of 110 defects, and a standard deviation of 25 defects. What is the probability of getting more than 130 defects on a given day?
    Z = .8, P(Z≤ .8) = .788. Therefore, the probability of having more than 130 defects on a given day is 1 - .788 = .212. (Continuous probability distribution, moderate)

21. Given that the number of rainy days per year is normally distributed with a mean of 95 days and a standard deviation of 30 days. What is the probability of having more than 120 days of rain in a given year? What is the probability of having more than 130 days of rain in a given year?
    Z = (120-95)/30 = .83, P(Z≤.83) = .7967. Therefore, the probability of having more than 120 days of rain per year is 1 - .7967 = .2033. Z = (130-95)/30 = 1.17, P(Z≤ 1.17) = .8790. Therefore, the probability of having more than 120 days of rain per year is 1 - .8790 = .1210.

CD TUTORIAL 2: ACCEPTANCE SAMPLING

TRUE/FALSE

1. In acceptance sampling, as the sample size is increased, the sampling plan will be better able to discriminate between good and bad lots.
   True (Sampling plans, moderate)

2. Producer's risk is the risk of rejecting a bad lot.
   False (Producer's and consumer's risk, moderate)

3. Consumer's risk is the risk of rejecting a bad lot.
   False (Producer's and consumer's risk, moderate)

4. Double sampling is when units are randomly selected from a lot and tested one by one, with the cumulative number of inspected pieces and defects recorded.
   False (Sampling plan, moderate)

5. An operating characteristics curve describes how well an SPC chart discriminates between good and bad parts.
   False (Operating characteristics curves, moderate)

MULTIPLE CHOICE

6. Double sampling
   a. implies the sampling of two units from each batch of product
   b. implies the sampling of units from two different batches of the product
   c. is based upon the premise that a sample of two units from any batch is sufficient to determine the quality of the batch
   d. is based upon the premise that a decision to accept or reject is often clear cut and can be made with a relatively small sample; at other times, a larger sample is necessary
   e. none of the above
   d (Sampling plans, moderate)

7. An OC curve describes
   a. the sample size necessary to distinguish between good and bad
      lots
   b. the most appropriate sampling plan for a given incoming product quality level
   c. how well an acceptance sampling plan discriminates between good and bad lots
   d. the number of defective items required to reject a lot
   e. none of the above
   c (Operating characteristics curves, moderate)

8. When units are randomly selected from a lot and tested one by one, with the cumulative number of inspected pieces and defects recorded, the process is called
    a. single sampling
    b. sequential sampling
    c. double sampling
    d. simple sampling
    e. none of the above
    b (Sampling plans, moderate)

9. Producer's risk is the probability of
    a. accepting a good lot
    b. rejecting a bad lot
    c. accepting a bad lot
    d. rejecting a good lot
    e. none of the above
    d (Operating characteristics curves, moderate)

10. Consumer's risk is the probability of
    a. accepting a good lot
    b. rejecting a bad lot
    c. accepting a bad lot
    d. rejecting a good lot
    e. none of the above
    c (Operating characteristics curves, moderate)

11. In attribute sampling, a binomial probability distribution is usually used to build the OC curve. However, the Poisson probability distribution can be used as an approximation for the binomial distribution when the sample size is
    a. large and the percent defective is large
    b. small and the percent defective is large
    c. small and the percent defective is small
    d. large and the percent defective is small
    e. none of the above
    d (Operating characteristics curves, moderate)

12. The relationship between acceptable quality level (AQL) and the lot tolerance percent defective (LTPD) is usually such that

    a. $AQL \leq LTPD$
    b. $AQL = LTPD$
    c. $AQL \geq LTPD$
    d. these two parameters are completely unrelated
    e. none of the above
    a (Operating characteristics curves, moderate)

13. In most sampling plans, when a lot is rejected, the entire lot is inspected and defective items are replaced. Using this technique
    a. hurts the AOQ
    b. improves the AOQ
    c. may either reduce or increase the AOQ depending upon other factors
    d. has no effect on AOQ
    e. none of the above
    b (Operating characteristics curve, moderate)

14. The relationship between the average outgoing quality (AOQ) and the true percent defective is such that
    a. AOQ > true percent defective
    b. AOQ = true percent defective
    c. AOQ < true percent defective
    d. there is no relationship between AOQ and the true percent defective
    e. none of the above
    c (Operating characteristics curves, moderate)

15. The maximum value on the AOQ curve corresponds to the highest average percent defective, and is called the
    a. average quality level (AQL)
    b. average outgoing quality (AOQ)
    c. lot tolerance percent defective (LTPD)
    d. average outgoing quality limit (AOQL)
    e. none of the above
    d (Average outgoing quality, moderate)

FILL-IN-THE-BLANK

16. Two numbers (n, and c) specify a _____ acceptance sampling plan.
    single sample (Sampling plans, easy)

17. _____ is when the units are randomly selected from a lot and tested one by one, with the cumulative number of inspected pieces and defects recorded.
    Sequential sampling (Sampling plans, moderate)

18. An _____ describes how well an acceptance sampling plan discriminates between good and bad lots.
    operating characteristics or OC curve (Operating characteristics curves, moderate)

19. _____ is the risk of rejecting good quality lots.
    Producer's risk (Producer's and consumer's risk, moderate)

20. _____ is the risk of accepting bad quality lots.
    Consumer's risk (Producer's and consumer's risk, moderate)

SHORT ANSWER

21. What is the difference between single, double, and sequential sampling plans?
   A single sampling plan takes only one sample. A double sampling plan takes one sample, and either rejects the lot, accepts the lots, or takes a second sample. If a second sample is taken, the lot is either accepted or rejected. A sequential sampling plan is an extension of the double sampling plan. It takes samples one unit at a time until an accept or reject decision is made. (Sampling plans, moderate)

22. Define producer's and consumer's risk.
   Producer's risk is the chance of rejecting a good quality lot. Consumer's risk is the chance of accepting a poor quality lot. (Producer's and consumer's risk, moderate)

23. What does an operating characteristics curve do?
   An OC curve describes how well an acceptance sampling plan discriminates between good and bad quality lots. (Operating characteristics curves, moderate)

PROBLEMS

24. Seventy-five items are drawn from a lot of 1,000. The total lot is accepted if $c \leq 2$. Develop an OC curve for this sampling plan.

	n=	75 N=	1000
	c=	2 (N-n)/N =	0.925

Percent Defective	λ	Pa	AOQ
0	0	1.000	0.000
1	0.75	0.959	0.009
2	1.5	0.809	0.015
3	2.25	0.609	0.017
4	3	0.423	0.016
5	3.75	0.277	0.013
6	4.5	0.174	0.010
7	5.25	0.105	0.007
8	6	0.062	0.005

OC Curve

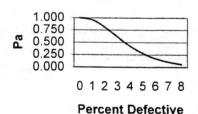

(Operating characteristics curves, moderate)

25. One hundred items are drawn from a lot of 5,000. The total lot is accepted if c ≤ 4. Develop an OC curve for this sampling plan.

	n=		100 N=		5000
	c=		4 (N-n)/N =		0.98
Percent	lamda	Pa	AOQ		
Defective					
0	0	1.000	0.000		
1	1	0.996	0.010		
2	2	0.947	0.019		
3	3	0.815	0.024		
4	4	0.629	0.025		
5	5	0.440	0.022		
6	6	0.285	0.017		
7	7	0.173	0.012		
8	8	0.100	0.008		

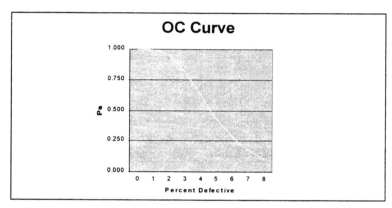

(Operating characteristics curves, moderate)

26. One hundred-fifty items are drawn from a lot of 2,500. The total lot is accepted if $c \leq 5$. Develop an OC curve, and an AOQ curve for this sampling plan.

n=		150	N=		2500	
c=		5	(N-n)/N =		0.94	

Percent Defective	lamda	Pa	AOQ
0	0	1.000	0.000
1	1.5	0.996	0.009
2	3	0.916	0.017
3	4.5	0.703	0.020
4	6	0.446	0.017
5	7.5	0.241	0.011
6	9	0.116	0.007
7	10.5	0.050	0.003
8	12	0.020	0.002

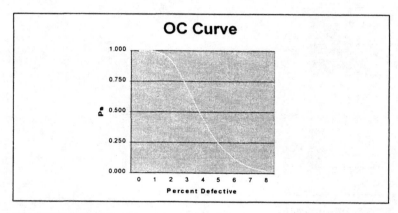

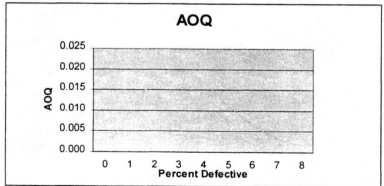

(Operating characteristics curves, and Average outgoing quality, moderate)

CD TUTORIAL 3: THE SIMPLEX METHOD OF LINEAR PROGRAMMING

TRUE/FALSE

1. The simplex method can be used to find the optimal solution to multivariate linear programming problems.
   True (Introduction, easy)

2. Greater-than-or-equal-to constraints can be converted to equations using slack variables.
   False (Converting the constraints to equations, moderate)

3. Variables in the solution mix are called basic variables.
   True (Setting up the first simplex tableau, moderate)

4. The simplex method cannot solve minimization problems.
   False (Solving minimization problems, moderate)

MULTIPLE CHOICE

5. In order to formulate a problem for solution by the Simplex method, we must add slack variables to
   a. all inequality constraints
   b. only equality constraints
   c. only "greater than" constraints
   d. only "less than" constraints
   e. none of the above
   d (Converting the constraints to equations, moderate)

6. In order to formulate a problem for solution by the Simplex method, we must add artificial variables to
   a. all inequality constraints
   b. only equality constraints
   c. only "greater than" constraints
   d. only "less than" constraints
   e. none of the above
   e (Artificial and surplus variables, moderate)

7. The number of variables that can be handled by the simplex method is
   a. virtually unlimited
   b. two
   c. three
   d. unknown
   e. none of the above
   a (Summary, moderate)

8. Basic variables are
    a. variables not in the solution mix
    b. variables in the solution mix
    c. common variables
    d. used to convert less-than-or-equal-to constraints into equations
    e. none of the above
    b (Setting up the first simplex tableau, moderate)

FILL-IN-THE-BLANK

9. The _____ is an algorithm with which we examine corner points in a methodical fashion until we arrive at the best solution in a linear programming model.
    simplex method (Introduction, easy)

10. A _____ is used to convert less-than-or-equal-to constraints into equations.
    slack variable (Converting the constraints to equations, moderate)

11. _____ are variables in the solution mix.
    Basic variables (Setting up the first simplex tableau, moderate)

12. _____ are variables **not** in the solution mix.
    Non-basic variables (Setting up the first simplex tableau, moderate)

13. A(n) _____ variable is added to a greater-than-or-equal-to constraint, while a(n) _____ variable is subtracted.
    artificial, surplus (Artificial and surplus variables, moderate)

SHORT ANSWER

14. What are the five steps in the simplex solution procedure?
    1. Choose the variable with the greatest positive $C_j - Z_j$ to enter the solution.
    2. Determine the row to be replaced by selecting the one with the smallest (non-negative) ratio of quantity to pivot column.
    3. Calculate the new values for the pivot row.
    4. Calculate the new values for the other row(s).
    5. Calculate the C_j and $C_j - Z_j$ values for this tableau. If there are any $C_j - Z_j$ numbers greater than zero, return to step 1.
    (Summary of simplex steps for maximization problems, moderate)

15. What are basic variables? Non-basic variable?
    Basic variables are variables in the solution mix. Non-basic variables are not in the solution mix. (Setting up the first simplex tableau, moderate)

16. How do you convert less-than-or-equal-to constraints into equations? Greater-than-or-equal-to constraints into equations?
    For less-than-or-equal-to constraints, a slack variable is added. For greater-than-or-equal-to constraints, a artificial variable is added, and a surplus variable is subtracted. (Setting up the first simplex tableau, and Artificial and surplus variables, moderate)

17. How do you solve a minimization problem using the simplex method.
Minimization problems are very similar to maximization problems. The one significant difference involves the C_j - Z_j row. The new variable to enter the solution will be the one with the largest negative number in the C_j -Z_j row. An optimal solution is reached when all numbers in the C_j - Z_j row are zero or positive. (Solving minimization problems, moderate)

PROBLEMS

18. Solve the following LP problem using the simplex method.

Max: $4X_1 + 3X_2$

s.t. $4X_1 + 2X_2 \le 40$

       $2X_1 + 2X_2 \le 30$

       $X_1, X_2 \ge 0$

The POM for Window solution follows.

Iterations

Cj	Basic Variables	4 X1	3 X2	0 slack 1	0 slack 2	Quantity
Iteration 1						
	cj-zj	4.	3.	0.	0.	
0	slack 1	4.	2.	1.	0.	40.
0	slack 2	2.	2.	0.	1.	30.
Iteration 2						
	cj-zj	0.	1.	-1.	0.	
4	X1	1.	0.5	0.25	0.	10.
0	slack 2	0.	1.	-0.5	1.	10.
Iteration 3						
	cj-zj	0.	0.	-0.5	-1.	
4	X1	1.	0.	0.5	-0.5	5.
3	X2	0.	1.	-0.5	1.	10.

(Simplex solution procedure, moderate)

19. Solve the following LP problem using the simplex method.

Max: $2X_1 + 3X_2$

s.t. $4X_1 + 2X_2 \le 50$

       $2X_1 + 2X_2 \le 30$

       $1X_1 + 4X_2 \le 40$

       $X_1, X_2 \ge 0$

The POM for Window solution follows.

Iterations

Cj	Basic Variables	2 X1	3 X2	0 slack 1	0 slack 2	0 slack 3	Quantity
Iteration 1							
	cj-zj	2	3.	0.	0	0	
0	slack 1	4.	2	1.	0	0	50
0	slack 2	2	2	0	1	0.	30
0	slack 3	1	4	0.	0	1.	40
Iteration 2							
	cj-zj	1.25	0	0.	0.	-0.75	
0	slack 1	3.5	0	1.	0.	-0.5	30.
0	slack 2	1.5	0	0.	1.	-0.5	10.
3	X2	0.25	1.	0.	0.	0.25	10.
Iteration 3							
	cj-zj	0.	0.	0.	-0.8333	-0.3333	
0	slack 1	0.	0.	1.	-2.3333	0.6667	6.6667
2	X1	1.	0	0.	0.6667	-0.3333	6.6667
3	X2	0.	1.	0.	-0.1667	0.3333	8.3333

(Simplex solution procedure, moderate)

20. Solve the following LP problem using the simplex method.

Max: $4X_1 + 3X_2$

s.t. $4X_1 + 2X_2 \leq 40$

$2X_1 + 2X_2 \leq 30$

$1X_1 \geq 4$

$X_1, X_2 \geq 0$

The POM for Window solution follows.

Cj	Basic Variables	4 X1	3 X2	0 slack 1	0 slack 2	0 artfcl 3	0 surplus 3	Quantity
Iteration 1								
	cj-zj	1.	0.	0.	0.	0.	-1.	
0	slack 1	4.	2.	1.	0.	0.	0.	40.
0	slack 2	2.	2.	0.	1.	0.	0.	30.
0	artfcl 3	1.	0.	0.	0.	1.	-1.	4.
Iteration 2								
	cj-zj	0.	0.	0.	0.	0.	0.	
0	slack 1	0.	2.	1.	0.	0.	4.	24.
0	slack 2	0.	2.	0.	1.	0.	2.	22.
4	X1	1.	0.	0.	0.	1.	-1.	4.
Iteration 3								
	cj-zj	0.	3.	0.	0.	-4.	4.	
0	slack 1	0.	2.	1.	0.	0.	4.	24.
0	slack 2	0.	2.	0.	1.	0.	2.	22.
4	X1	1.	0.	0.	0.	1.	-1.	4.
Iteration 4								
	cj-zj	0.	1.	-1.	0.	-4.	0.	
0	surplus 3	0.	0.5	0.25	0.	0.	1.	6.
0	slack 2	0.	1.	-0.5	1.	0.	0.	10.
4	X1	1.	0.5	0.25	0.	1.	0.	10.
Iteration 5								
	cj-zj	0.	0.	-0.5	-1.	-4.	0.	
0	surplus 3	0.	0.	0.5	-0.5	0.	1.	1.
3	X2	0.	1.	-0.5	1.	0.	0.	10.
4	X1	1.	0.	0.5	-0.5	1.	0.	5.

(Simplex solution procedure, difficult)

21. Solve the following LP problem using the simplex method.
Min: $5X_1 + 3X_2$
s.t. $1X_1 + 1X_2 \geq 20$
$2X_1 + 2X_2 \geq 30$
$X_1, X_2 \geq 0$

Cj	Basic Variables	5 X1	3 X2	0 artfcl 1	0 surplus 1	0 artfcl 2	0 surplus 2	Quantity
\<untitled\> Solution								
Iteration 1								
	cj-zj	3.	2.	0.	-1.	0.	-1.	
0	artfcl 1	1.	1.	1.	-1.	0.	0.	20.
0	artfcl 2	2.	1.	0.	0.	1.	-1.	30.
Iteration 2								
	cj-zj	0.	0.5	0.	-1.	0.	0.5	
0	artfcl 1	0.	0.5	1.	-1.	0.	0.5	5.
5	X1	1.	0.5	0.	0.	0.5	-0.5	15.
Iteration 3								
	cj-zj	0.	0.	0.	0.	0.	0.	
3	X2	0.	1.	2.	-2.	0.	1.	10.
5	X1	1.	0.	0.	1.	0.5	-1.	10.
Iteration 4								
	cj-zj	0.	0.	6.	-1.	2.5	-2.	
3	X2	0.	1.	2.	-2.	0.	1.	10.
5	X1	1.	0.	0.	1.	0.5	-1.	10.

(Solving minimization problems, moderate)

CD TUTORIAL 4: THE MODI AND VAM METHODS OF SOLVING TRANSPORTATION PROBLEMS

TRUE/FALSE

1.   Vogel's approximation method often provides the optimal solution.
      True (Vogel's approximation method: Another way to find an initial solution, moderate)

2.   Vogel's approximation method is easier to calculate than the northwest corner method.
      False (Vogel's approximation method: Another way to find an initial solution, moderate)

3.   The MODI method of solving the transportation problem is more time consuming than other methods.
      False (MODI method, moderate)

4.   The MODI method requires the use of the northwest corner method.
      False (MODI method, moderate)

MULTIPLE CHOICE

5.   Which of the following methods is most likely to produce the best initial solution to a transportation problem?
      a.   the stepping-stone method
      b.   Vogel's approximation method
      c.   the MODI method
      d.   the Northwest corner method
      e.   none of the above
      b (Vogel's approximation method: Another way to find an initial solution, moderate)

SHORT ANSWER

6.   What are the five steps in the MODI method of solving the transportation problem?
      1. Compute the values for each row and column, set $R_i + K_j = C_{ij}$, but only for those squares that are currently used or occupied.
      2. After all equations have been written, set $R_1 = 0$.
      3. Solve the system of equations for all R and K values.
      4. Compute the improvement index for each unused square by the formula improvement index $(I_{ij}) = C_{ij} - R_i - K_j$.
      5. Select the largest negative index and proceed to solve the problem as you did using the stepping-stone method.
      (MODI method, moderate)

7.   What are the six steps of Vogel's approximation method?
      1. For each row and column of the transportation table, find the difference between the two lowest unit shipping costs. These numbers represent the difference between the distribution cost on the best route in the row or column and the second best route in the row or column.
      2. Identify the row or column with the greatest opportunity cost, or difference.
      3. Assign as many units as possible to the lowest-cost square in the row or column selected.
      4. Eliminate any row or column that has just been completely satisfied by the assignment just made.
      5. Recompute the cost differences for the transportation table, omitting rows or columns crossed out in the preceding step.
      6. Return to step 2 and repeat the steps until an initial feasible solution has been obtained.
      (Vogel's approximation method: Another way to find an initial solution, moderate)

PROBLEMS

8.   Develop the initial solution to the following transportation problem (Minimization) using Vogel's approximation method.

	A	B	C	SUPPLY
1	5	4	7	50
2	3	9	4	50
3	8	3	2	50
DEMAND	70	60	20	

The following is the POM for Windows output. Note that Vogel's approximation method produced the optimal solution to the problem.

	Destination 1	Destination 2	Destination 3
Iteration 1			
Source 1	20.	30.	4.
Source 2	50.	7.	3.
Source 3	4.	30.	20.

Optimal cost = 500.00	A	B	C
1	20.	30.	
2	50.		
3		30.	20.

(Vogel's approximation method: Another way to find an initial solution, moderate)

9. Develop the initial solution to the following transportation problem (Minimization) using Vogel's approximation method.

	Destination 1	Destination 2	Destination 3	Destination 4	SUPPLY
Source 1	9	5	4	12	40
Source 2	7	8	4	10	50
Source 3	5	8	6	7	50
Source 4	8	9	7	6	60
DEMAND	80	60	30	30	

The following is the POM for Windows output. Note that Vogel's approximation method produced the optimal solution to the problem.

	Destination 1	Destination 2	Destination 3	Destination 4
Iteration 1				
Source 1	5.	40.	3.	10.
Source 2	20.	0.	30.	5.
Source 3	50.	2.	4.	4.
Source 4	10.	20.	2.	30.

Optimal cost = 1,150.00	Destination 1	Destination 2	Destination 3	Destination 4
Source 1		40.		
Source 2	20.		30.	
Source 3	50.			
Source 4	10.	20.		30.

(Vogel's approximation method: Another way to find an initial solution, moderate)

10. Solve the following transportation problem (Minimization) using the MODI method.

	Destination 1	Destination 2	Destination 3	Destination 4	SUPPLY
Source 1	8	5	4	7	60
Source 2	7	8	5	10	50
Source 3	5	9	6	7	50
Source 4	8	5	7	6	60
DEMAND	80	60	50	30	

The following is the POM for Windows solution obtained using Vogel's approximation method, and MODI.

	Destination 1	Destination 2	Destination 3	Destination 4
Iteration 1				
Source 1	0.	60.	-2.	1.
Source 2	0.	4.	50.	5.
Source 3	50.	7.	3.	4.
Source 4	30.	0.	1.	30.
Iteration 2				
Source 1	2.	30.	30.	1.
Source 2	30.	2.	20.	3.
Source 3	50.	5.	3.	2.
Source 4	2.	30.	3.	30.

Optimal cost = 1,160.00	Destination 1	Destination 2	Destination 3	Destination 4
Source 1		30.	30.	
Source 2	30.		20.	
Source 3	50.			
Source 4		30.		30.

(MODI method, moderate)

11. Solve the following transportation problem (Minimization) using the MODI method.

	Destination 1	Destination 2	Destination 3	Destination 4	SUPPLY
Source 1	5	9	10	8	30
Source 2	9	6	4	3	30
Source 3	6	5	6	11	40
Source 4	7	8	9	12	60
DEMAND	40	30	50	40	

The following is the POM for Windows solution obtained using Vogel's approximation method, and MODI.

	Destination 1	Destination 2	Destination 3	Destination 4
Iteration 1				
Source 1	30.	3.	3.	-2.
Source 2	11.	7.	4.	30.
Source 3	2.	30.	10.	2.
Source 4	10.	0.	40.	10.
Iteration 2				
Source 1	20.	3.	3.	10.
Source 2	9.	5.	2.	30.
Source 3	2.	30.	10.	4.
Source 4	20.	0.	40.	2.

Optimal cost = 980.00	Destination 1	Destination 2	Destination 3	Destination 4
Source 1	20.			10.
Source 2				30.
Source 3		30.	10.	
Source 4	20.		40.	

(MODI method, moderate)